Racism in Mind

Racism

in Mind

EDITED BY MICHAEL P. LEVINE / TAMAS PATAKI

Cornell University Press ITHACA AND LONDON

First published 2004 by Cornell University Press
First printing, Cornell Paperbacks, 2004

Printed in the United States of America

Library of Congress Cataloging-in-Publication Data

Racism in mind / edited by Michael P. Levine, Tamas Pataki.
    p. cm.
Includes bibliographical references and index.
    ISBN 0-8014-4231-1 (cloth : alk. paper) — ISBN 0-8014-8878-8
(pbk. : alk. paper)
    1. Racism.   I. Levine, Michael P., 1950– II. Pataki, Tamas.
HT1521.R3418   2004
305.8—dc22   2003022174

Cornell University Press strives to use environmentally
responsible suppliers and materials to the fullest extent possible
in the publishing of its books. Such materials include vegetable-
based, low-VOC inks and acid-free papers that are recycled, totally
chlorine-free, or partly composed of nonwood fibers. For further
information, visit our website at www.cornellpress.cornell.edu.

Cloth printing   10 9 8 7 6 5 4 3 2 1
Paperback printing 10 9 8 7 6 5 4 3 2 1

A portion of chapter 2 is reprinted by permission of Sage
Publications Ltd. from J. L. A. Garcia, "Philosophical Analysis and
the Moral Concept of Racism," *Philosophy and Social Criticism* 25,
no. 5: 1–32. Copyright © 1999 by Sage Publications. Another portion
is reprinted from J. L. A. Garcia, "Racism and Racial Discourse,"
Philosophical Forum 32, no. 2 (2001): 125–45.

Chapter 7 previously appeared as "The Characters of Violence"
copyright © 2003 Elisabeth Young-Bruehl, reprinted with permission
of Other Press, LLC.

Human thought is by no means as private as it seems, and all you need
in order to read somebody else's mind is the willingness to read your own. . . .

There are certain scenes that (far more than artifacts dug up out of the
ground or prehistoric cave paintings, which have a confusing freshness
and newness) serve to remind us of how old the human race is, and of the
beautiful, touching sameness of most human occasions. Anything that is
not anonymous is all a dream. And who we are, and whether our parents
embraced life or were disappointed by it, and what will become of our
children couldn't be less important. Nobody asks the name of the athlete
tying his sandal on the curved side of the Greek vase or whether the lonely
traveler on the Chinese scroll arrived at the inn before dark.

—William Maxwell, *The Château*

CONTENTS

PREFACE

We would like to tell you how and when the idea for this book originated, but neither of us can remember exactly. We do know that we began discussing racism and ethnic and religious prejudices three or four years ago in relation to the seemingly intractable and bloody conflicts in Africa, Europe, and the Middle East. Successive Australian governments' policies toward Aborigines and refugees—policies that reflect the views of many Australian citizens—placed our discussions in a more local and pressing context. As we read the literature on racism, examined the newspapers, and listened to the news, we sought a more specifically philosophical clarification and explanation of the issues than the current literature provided. It was at that point that the idea of an edited volume emerged.

The book appears at a time when the international order is experiencing turmoil not seen since the Second World War, the outcome of which it is impossible to foresee. We can hope that the motives of those who have sought to violently recast the world order will not endure or vitiate future developments. Students of racism and group conflict who have observed the malign dehumanization of "the enemy" and the shocking indifference to life displayed by the agents of terror and of war—and by the many, on *all* sides, who whoop and rejoice in their actions—may well see reason for darkest pessimism.

Several of the essays in this volume underwent five or six major revisions, and nearly all underwent at least two or three. Our thanks go first and foremost to the contributors to this volume for engaging with each other's work and constructively reviewing each other's essays. We would also like to thank Amy Barrett-Lennard, Judy Berman, Damian Cox, Raimond Gaita, James Hopkins, Graeme Marshall, Howard McGary, Maureen Perkins, and Tommie Shelby. Finally, we are indebted to our copyeditor, John LeRoy, and to Catherine Rice, Louise E. Robbins, and other staff at Cornell University Press for the enthusiasm and efficiency that turned our manuscript into the present book.

Racism in Mind

INTRODUCTION

I

In many parts of the world, including the most developed, societies are torn by enmities that originate in racial, ethnic, tribal, national, class, and religious differences. Some of these enmities—we use the word in its broadest sense—have reached the highest pitch of barbarity. Others, less extreme, manifest as social exclusion and oppression, segregation, adverse discrimination, derogatory personal attitudes and conduct, and the promulgation of doctrines and legislation designed to promote or justify the other manifestations of enmity.

These are *group* enmities, and it is one part of their strange nature that they subsist between human groups that identify themselves and their targets as substantially discrete collectivities, although the concepts under which they do so are patently vague: neither *race* nor *ethnicity*, nor most other kindred concepts of human groups, admit of the rigid demarcation on which the enmities often claim to be founded. Of course, one can be a racist or a religious bigot in isolation: one can hate or contemn or act alone. But in general, in setting oneself against a group or groups, one acquires an identity as a member of another group: as someone who, for example, hates some group, is superior to some group, or belongs to the best group. Usually, one acts in unison or imagines oneself acting in unison with like-minded others; and for some people the achievement of this group identity is a more potent motive than the enmity that is its instrument.

Our times are witness to numerous violent and cruel expressions of these group enmities. Ethnic collectivities in Africa and Europe, some with historical, cultural, or territorial claims to definition, others with claims largely imaginary, have been violently fragmenting the states that had earlier accommodated them. In Southeast Asia and the Pacific Islands, ethnic, religious, and tribal affiliations are subverting earlier aspirations toward inclusive pluralist societies. Waves of desperately poor, deracinated, and dispossessed migrants from Asia, the Middle East, Eastern Europe, and Central America are reaching the shores of Europe, Australia, and North America. These "outsiders" are received by governments and by many citizens with vilification, remorseless hostility, and repulsion. Even

Simon Burgess, Raimond Gaita, and Michael Levine saved me from many errors. In some errors, I fear, I have willfully persisted, and many others remain unknown to me.

within the more settled states there seems to be a recrudescence of group antipathies and oppressive social and political discriminations that have been dormant over many decades. As this is being written, responsible commentators speak darkly of a clash of civilizations founded, supposedly, on separate religious identities, and a few powerful Western nations are overwhelming a Middle Eastern state with massively lethal force. In all these cases the terrifying unconcern for the lives and livelihood of the victims would seem inexplicable without reference to an underlying racist (and race-related) contempt.

Today, racist and related enmities and the prejudices and doctrines that stoke them are rarely expressed overtly. In the West, at least, the people for whom racism, religious intolerance, or sexism are still points of honor are relegated to the fringe (though such relegation does not apply to exclusionary nationalism and so-called homophobia). Instead, the enmities frequently take on disguises and try to pass as economic or social wisdom, environmental concern, patriotism, or enthusiasm for cultural diversity. But their assertion of fundamental differences between human groups, and their demands for partition and exclusion to prevent racial, cultural, or religious contamination, remain of a piece with their more overt and cruder cousins.

II

Racism and its kin—ethnic or cultural contempt, religious intolerance, class hatred, and so on—are complex and problematic phenomena. It is not surprising that their understanding remains partial and controversial despite the considerable attention that social scientists, psychologists, historians, and, to a lesser extent, philosophers have given it in the decades since the Second World War. Clearly these phenomena share fundamental commonalities. At the individual or personal level they are all—it is mostly agreed today—prejudices, though disagreement over the precise nature of the prejudices is so extensive that it qualifies the notional agreement considerably. It does seem likely that similar psychological configurations are involved in their attitudinal expressions. From the sociological perspective such prejudices appear to be conditioned and precipitated by historical, social and economic configurations that can be systematically and informatively related. The prejudices sometimes appear to be interchangeable, or to reinforce each other, and these observations have led to conjectures about a prototypal prejudiced (or authoritarian) personality. Some other commonalities will be noticed presently, but we need to mention some of the many important differences as well.

Group concepts that determine the targets of enmities impose certain formal constraints on their character. If, for example, a person is prejudiced against and hates or disparages the members of a group because of their race, then that person is committed to enmity against children of that group, is likely to believe that all members of that group share some hateful essential characteristics—avarice, laziness, lasciviousness, and so on—and is also likely to believe that these characteristics cannot be divested or altered. People who hate or disparage the members of a group because of their culture, religion, class, or sexual preference are not so committed—unless they have racialized their enmities and have come to treat the target groups as if they were race-like, insofar as that is possible. One can perhaps hate all bankers, Bulgars, or Baptists, but one cannot hate them racially, except by grossly misunderstanding how these classes of people are constituted.

In contemporary discourse race concepts and the formal constraints on racism imposed by those concepts are vague and equivocal. It is common in the public domain today to find almost any group enmity that involves notions of ethnic, national, religious or linguistic identity described as racial and, often, as racist. Hence it is commonplace to hear or read of racist hatred of Asians, Moslems, Jews, blacks, Koreans, Mexicans, Hispanics, and so on. The conflation of these group concepts occurs partly because of popular indifference to distinctions; partly, perhaps, because of an obscure apprehension that there are underlying similarities between the various group enmities falling under the different group concepts; and partly because the conceptions of race dominant in the West from roughly the mid-eighteenth to the mid-twentieth century, now discredited and eschewed by the disciplines that once fostered them, have become vague and promiscuous ideas in the popular mind.

But it is of real importance to mark these distinctions of group (or kind). The evolution of race concepts (and, to a degree, of the racism that supervenes on them) took place largely in deliberate contraposition to other group-defining concepts such as *culture, linguistic community,* and *nation.* They evolved in scientific (some may prefer to say "quasi-scientific"), historical, and philological thinking, and in popular consciousness, in a search for what were considered to be the most fundamental ways of classifying and describing humankind. (The motives for that search were, of course, complex and often egregious.) The racial conceptions that emerged, though they varied in important respects, invariably divided humankind into something like natural kinds or species distinguished by unalterable and essential physical, psychological, or spiritual characteristics. They were sharply contrasted with what were considered to be the more superficial categories defined by culture, language, or nationality. An understanding of these conceptions is essential for understanding some of the most significant characteristics of racism.

III

What, then, are these racial conceptions? Some light can be thrown on them and the racism they inform by looking briefly at the history of their development and isolating a few of their conspicuous features. About 2,500 years ago Herodotus wrote: "For if anyone, no matter who, were given the opportunity of choosing from amongst all the nations of the world the set of beliefs which he thought best, he would inevitably, after careful consideration of the relative merits, choose those of his own country" (Herodotus 1992: 309–10). Herodotus goes on to tell the story of the debate between Greeks and Indians arranged by the Persian Darius. The Indians were disgusted to hear that the Greeks burned the corpses of their dead parents; the Greeks were appalled that the Indians ate theirs: "One can see from this what custom can do, and Pindar, in my opinion, was right when he called it 'king of all'" (1992: 309–10). Herodotus's judgment was framed in the context of a philosophical converse on the relationship between custom (law) and nature, *nomos* and *physis*. The Greeks generally considered themselves superior to those they called barbarians. But the sense of their superiority seems not to have subtended from any conception of innate or *natural* moral or intellectual differences between peoples.[1] What mattered most was *ethnos*—language, custom, belief—and, in particular, the achievement of good rules or laws—*eunomics*—for the right conduct of life expressed in politics. The trouble with the barbarians, in Greek eyes, was not a natural deficiency but the absence of politics, and therefore a deficiency in freedom and the capacity for the exercise of cardinal virtues. The worst Thucydides would say of barbarians was of the savage Scythians whom he knew well: "In fact if the Scythians were united there is not even in Asia a race that could stand up to them by itself, though of course in governing themselves wisely and in making intelligent use of their resources they are below the average level" (Thucydides 1972: 188–89).

The idea that whole peoples could be morally or intellectually inferior by nature, or *physis,* and thereby necessarily restricted to lower levels of cultural achievement seems, as Toynbee said, to have been "alien from the Hellenic genius" (Rankin 1964: 74).[2] That is not to say that all notions of innate worth were lacking. Plato in *The Republic* made much of differences in individual innate ability, and aristocratic notions of being highborn or of noble lineage were prominent in the ancient world. But, crucially, the ancients appear to have been largely indifferent to group phenotypic differences, and they never mixed them with variations in innate endowment and capacity for cultural achievement to

1. The discussion here and in the following paragraphs owes most to Hannaford 1996 (a superb study), Arendt 1979, Banton 1998, Jahoda 1999, Rankin 1964, and Voegelin 1997; also Blum 2002, Appiah 1999, and Mosley 1999.

2. Aristotle's view that "the barbarian and slave are one in nature" is often cited as an exception and adumbration of a racial conception. An alternative reading seems viable, however. "By nature a slave" seems to have meant, for Aristotle, "lacking 'the deliberative faculty,'" a faculty, he believed, that women and barbarians lacked and whose absence rendered them servile. But the basic thought may be: *given* the despotic political dispensation into which barbarians are born and under which they live, it is entirely *natural* that they should be lacking in the self-regulative principle and so be by nature slaves. In *Laws* Plato emphasizes that slaves are often better men than their masters.

concoct a poisonous brew like the one that fed modern racism. It is important to see that a social dispensation in which racial distinctions play no significant part is possible: there was such a dispensation.

Modern racism in most of its varied expressions holds, near enough, that *nature* is king of all. The conceptions of race that underlie it are fused from many sources. They include ancient and medieval elaborations on the biblical story of Ham's transgression; the notion of polygenesis, traceable perhaps to Paracelsus in a work of 1520; ideas about blood purity that arose during the medieval Inquisitions; fanciful travelers' tales about monstrous peoples and imaginative discursions on monstrous births; aristocratic conceptions of inborn superiority; Romantic conceptions of innate personality and genius; the eighteenth- and nineteenth-century historians and philologists who sought to identify the "original peoples" of Europe and replaced the history of civilizations and politics with that of races or a *Volk*. But the decisive contribution stemmed from the scientific and cultural achievements that allowed for the comprehension of humankind as a part of nature to be studied by natural means. Modern conceptions of race could be articulated only after Galileo, Harvey, Descartes, and others had advanced the study of the human being as a *natural object*. This applies to folk or popular—as much as to scientific—conceptions of race. Ivan Hannaford writes:

> It is unhistorical to perceive the concept of race before the appearance of physical anthropology proper, because the human body, as portrayed up to the time of the Renaissance and Reformation, could not be detached from the idea of the *polis* and *ecclesia*. . . . In both instances a people (*populus*) was bound together and assumed an identity through law (*nomos*) and faith, and not through biology, secular history, and an autonomous physical or moral order. . . . [N]ot until the early years of the seventeenth century did the idea of race begin to take its familiar modern form. (Hannaford 1996: 147–48, 149)

Hannaford accords to François Bernier the distinction of making, in 1684, "the significant methodological departure from the old ways of seeing humankind in terms of the age-old distinctions between Christian and heathen, man and brute, political virtu and religious faith by classifying human beings mainly in terms of differences in their observable characteristics" (1996: 191). From such beginnings proceeded the unembarrassed investigation through subsequent centuries of the *natural* characteristics—as it were the *primary qualities*, to borrow Galileo's abstraction—of humankind. But what Europeans soon claimed to find were natural *distinctions*.

By 1766 David Hume could write:

> I am apt to suspect the negroes and in general all the other species of men (for their are four or five different kinds) to be naturally inferior to the whites. There never was a civilised nation of any other complexion than white, nor

even an individual eminent either in action or speculation. No ingenious manufacturers amongst them, no arts, no sciences. . . . Such a uniform and constant difference could not happen in so many countries and ages, *if nature had not made an original distinction betwixt these breeds of men.* (1985: 72–73; italics added)

Thomas Jefferson (1782), reflecting on the supposed inferiority of his black slaves concluded: "It is not their condition then, but nature, which has produced the distinction" (Banton 1998: 29). This "original" or "natural" distinction was intended to have the force of marking a deep, fundamental division between human types independent of the contingencies of culture, political form, and language. As one influential race thinker, William Ripley, expressed the contrast in 1899, "Race denotes what man is; all these other things denote what he does" (Hannaford 1996: 328). With the first intimations of evolutionary and genetic thought the specious ideas inherent in this notion of natural distinction came to be elaborated in ways that can be summarized roughly as follows: the characteristics assigned as definitive of each race are (i) essential (every member of any race necessarily has certain defining characteristics); (ii) inherited (the defining characteristics of each race are transmitted through passage of genes, blood, soul, germ plasm); (iii) exclusive (if one is a member of a particular race one cannot also be a member of another race); (iv) immutable (the essential characteristics cannot be removed or altered); and (v) consistent with "the doctrine of the countenance" (there is a correlation between specific physical characteristics of each race and its intellectual and moral capabilities).[3]

Thus the race theorist Madison Grant in his *Passing of the Great Race* (1916) sums up much of this in a typical way: "The great lesson of the science of race is the immutability of somatological or bodily characters, with which is closely associated the immutability of psychical predispositions and impulses" (Hannaford 1996: 358). Similarly, Henry Osborn, professor of biology at Columbia, states in 1916: "Race implies heredity, and heredity implies all the moral, social and intellectual characteristics and traits which are the springs of politics and government" (357). Biological classification was important in this understanding of race, though not exclusively. In the messianic racism of the pan-German and pan-Slavic movements of the last two centuries there was little attempt to link "the soul characteristics of races" (Voegelin 1997), supposedly hereditary psychical or spiritual traits, to biological constitution.[4] But even in these popu-

3. The idea that there are correspondences between physical and intellectual and moral characteristics is of ancient provenance. The Cabala developed an elaborate and influential variation on the idea and gave it this name (Hannaford 1996: 36).

4. The innateness of "psychical characteristics" was taken to bizarre lengths. Fritz Lenz assigned to the Nordic person innate "intelligence, creative mental powers, outstanding character traits, steadiness of will and caring foresight, self-control, talent for technology

lar expressions of race thinking and racism the central idea remained: the most fundamental way of classifying humankind is through the inherited, essential, immutable, and exclusive moral and intellectual characteristics correlated with salient phenotypical markers.

IV

The classical conceptions of race are incoherent, and the ideologies that incorporate them are false; both are generally repudiated in considered discussion today.[5] But their shadows remain, and preserve some of their menace. Even where racism is conceived broadly to include enmity against cultural, national, and kindred groups, these categories may in certain circumstances be treated *as if* they were classical racial ones: the enmities directed against these groups take on the conformations projected by the racial conceptions. This is the process of racialization referred to earlier. It may in some cases have complex historical and social dimensions, but in other cases it seems to stem largely from various psychological needs that exploit (and to some degree fashion) the racial conceptions; such, for example, are the common needs to divide the human world into the good and the bad, to keep things simple and steady, to keep oneself and one's kind pure, to feel superior to some others, and so on. These and the related needs discussed below rest at the core of much popular racist and related enmity. The conceptual discipline of distinguishing between *race* and other group concepts, and between the constraints each imposes on its associated enmity, allows for a more perspicuous view of racism. It also provides a coign of vantage for observing the other enmities in their unalloyed expression and their transformation, if and when they become racialized.

Now, it is clear that the concept of racism is not necessary for racism to exist: there was racism before it was articulated as such. But it would seem to follow from the considerations above that conceptions of race *are* necessary: being a racist necessarily implies being in possession of racial conceptions. And to many people this may seem an excessive, perhaps an excessively intellectualist, constraint. After all, would we not say of a white person who has an aversion or a repugnance to blacks—people with black skin—or to people of Middle Eastern appearance, or just to "those people," that she was a racist, even if she appears to have nothing like a concept or organized set of beliefs about racial types? Instructively, the answer seems to be in the negative. Interrogation makes this

and mastering nature, love of the sea, a gift for the fine arts, architecture and profound research, 'northern boldness,' the 'pathos of distance,' aristocratic reserve, honesty, sincerity, cleanliness and the love of nature" (Voegelin 1997: 85).

5. It does not follow, of course, that *all* race concepts are incoherent. For the possibility of reasoned applications in biology see Kitcher 1999; in paleoanthropology see Wolpoff and Caspari 1997. See Boxill's discussion of race in chapter 10.

plain. Does she also have an aversion to white people—people in her family, say—who have very dark tans or look unusually Middle Eastern? Will her aversion be suspended for the light-colored child of a black couple? If so, then she is afflicted by something more like a phobia than racism, for there is nothing in her classifications, or in her affective organization, that employs discriminatory concepts even remotely related to race. The grounds for classifying her as a racist fall away.

But if she does so discriminate—that is, if her enmity extends to the light-colored child of a black couple—then the appearance that she employs no racial conceptions is false. She operates at the least with a fairly well organized set of beliefs, perhaps with a tract of rudimentary racial ideology, that allows her to classify people in certain ways not geared to immediate appearances. For, of course, "black person" really means so much more than "person with black skin," and "person of Middle Eastern appearance" so much more than the stereotyped visual portrait. The phenotypical features are rarely the objects that underlie racial classifications and enmity. In general, they are merely the markers for other real or imagined characteristics, frequently moral and intellectual ones, that provide the grounds for racist discriminations. Color (hue) is not the issue for the racist; it is the set of racial concepts and beliefs that the racist has about the person of color that create the issue.

These observations return us to where we began this discussion. For when we enter into the more or less rudimentary apparatus of classification employed by contemporary racists, we find once again many of the elements—muddled or inarticulate, it is true—of the principles of classical race thinking. "Those people can't change," you hear. "They're all the same." "It's in their blood." "It's their genes." "*Those* people . . ." These slack references organize their victims under the concepts of inheritance, immutability, essentiality, and so on. Certainly, racists make exceptions among their targets that strain the conditions imposed by the classical conceptions, and in complex hybrid cases it is difficult to decide whether "(indirect or unintended) racial *discrimination*" or "racist enmity" is the appropriate description of the phenomenon. These borderline cases are always illuminating in conceptual investigation, and several are elucidated in the following chapters. But the core of race thinking and of racism has, despite the inflation and accretion of its diverse expressions, remained remarkably durable. Racism in its individual expressions, if not also in its social and institutional ones, seems deeply embedded in mind.

The classical conceptions retain their significance for one other baleful reason. Hereditarian, innatist thinking has returned to the foreground of several academic disciplines and, fortified by (rash) sociobiological speculation, is reviving racial (and racist) conceptions. Once again, following the pattern that typified so-called scientific racism since the eighteenth century, alleged racial differences in intelligence and temperament are being used to justify social inequalities and inaction in rectifying them.[6]

V

Because we are ignorant creatures, and obstinate in error and wishful belief, it doesn't matter much in the consideration of racism whether there "really" are races, whether any race concepts identify objects in the "furniture of the world," or whether science is in need of them. Race has, as many philosophers express it, a "social reality." Many people *think* that there are races, divide and scale the human world according to their racial conceptions and beliefs, and persist in doing so even in the face of contrary evidence. But racism clearly entails more than classification by racial conceptions and related beliefs, popular or scientific. It presupposes racial conceptions, though merely being a proponent of them—being a race thinker or racialist—is not in itself sufficient to consign one to a racist camp, although, of course, the world according to the racialist is very congenial to the racist. Being a racialist (as the term is used here) is consistent with admiration of, or benevolence toward, all races. However, commitment to some such racial concepts and related beliefs, even if only at an unconscious or unarticulated level, is, as we have seen, necessary to being a racist. So what needs to be added to racialism to get racism?

It is easy to list the categories of things racism has been said to be. Racism has been said to be an ideology of biological difference and value in human groups; derogatory or inferiorizing beliefs (believings) or value judgments about racially designated groups; hostile or oppressive actions or conduct of individuals or groups; a form of aversion or disgust; an incapacity or inability to make certain kinds of discrimination; certain affective, volitional, or orectic states of mind or dispositions, such as ill will or hatred; certain *unconscious* affective and orectic states; institutional processes of adverse discrimination; and social and political structures of disadvantage.

Listing the basic categories of things that racism may be does not take us very far, however. For, of course, racism is not just *any* inferiorizing belief, enmity, or instance of adverse discrimination directed against racially designated groups. Enmity, disparagement, and adverse discrimination are sometimes appropriate responses and justified; and in the philosopher's laboratory of thought experiments it is easy to fashion cases in which, in principle, enmity toward an entire racially designated group is justified and appropriate. And here, to distinguish racism *within* the categorial plurality of its manifestations, philosophers and social scientists have been drawn in two main directions. Some have emphasized

6. Herrnstein and Murray 1994 and Levin 1997 are typical of this kind of work. Gould 1996 is a brilliant critical discussion of it.

that racism is primarily a prejudice or conduct motivated by prejudice, and these are usually conceived as irrational states of mind or modes of action. Those philosophers and social scientists whose main interests lie in the causal-psychological conditions of racism tend to understand racism in this way, as something largely irrational, although they may disagree significantly about the causes and nature of irrationality. In this volume that broad approach is represented in the chapters by Neil Altman and Johanna Tiemann, Michael Dummett, Michael Levine, Elisabeth Young-Bruehl, and myself. Others have emphasized that racism is a vicious state of mind or mode of action: it instantiates some vice, or it offends one or more virtues or consequentialist principles of moral appraisal. In this volume Lawrence Blum and J. L. A. Garcia explicitly explore this second approach, and several other contributors in their different ways presuppose it. (Most people probably think that racism is both a prejudice and a vice; but the conditions and consequences of that compelling thought appear not to have been explicitly probed in the literature.)

There are, of course, links between categorial manifestations of racism: racist intent, belief, action, and so on. Given the philosophical propensity to identify central or fundamental instances of things and to educe the other instances from them, it is unsurprising that much attention has been directed toward locating the core or "heart" of racism and showing how it relates to the more peripheral instances. Thus it has been argued that acts are racist only when they are caused by racist states of mind, that institutional adverse discriminations are racist only if there is racist agential intent, that racist intent exists only if causally related to certain kinds of deep psychological substructures, and so on. It is tempting to suppose that a thread passes through and unites all the phenomena of racism. A unified account would certainly be helpful in sorting out the troublesome borderline cases where racism melts into the amorphous domain of race relations. Whether it is in fact possible to bring all the phenomena of racism under one intension, or to show how each can be derived from one or more central instances, is a key issue underlying several of the essays in this volume. Garcia and, in his quite different way, Levine are most sanguine about this prospect; Blum, Haslanger, and I are more skeptical. It may well be that although we have but one tired word to designate a plurality of racist phenomena, they in fact exhibit a family resemblance: a result that would not be entirely surprising in light of the way the concept of racism has grown historically through adaptation and accretion.

VI

According to one of the earliest definitions of racism, dating back to the 1930s but still prominent in the dictionaries, racism is principally an ideology, doctrine, or set of beliefs that divides, classifies, and scales humankind along the lines outlined above. A racist, then, is a person who embraces such an ideology. Racism on these accounts is principally doxastic. *Belief* is a complex notion and the line between conviction and passion—as between cognitive, affective, and volitional notions generally—is often fuzzy. But clearly the doxastic view captures something important, at least about some forms of racism. Lawrence Lengbeyer considers and adopts a view on which racist belief is central. He argues here that a person who possesses racist beliefs—beliefs that are inferiorizing or derogatory of a race—is ipso facto a racist. The chief tendency in his essay is reformative; he is concerned to identify the requisites for the eradication of racist beliefs. He provides a novel and sophisticated cognitive account of the persistence of such beliefs and stresses the difficulty of the purifying project. His conclusion, however, is optimistic: the processes of cognitive management he describes are accessible and they can be effective.

Near the end of the first half of the twentieth century a different perspective on racism began to be articulated. J.-P. Sartre (1972) argued powerfully that racism was not principally a matter of opinion or belief but of passion. The anti-Semite does not hate because he believes, Sartre insisted; he believes because he hates. Racist opinion or belief becomes a kind of rationalization or epiphenomenon concealing mental conditions less rationally vulnerable. The title of a book on the "Nazi hallucination" by Maurice Samuel, *The Great Hatred* (1940), leaves little doubt that European anti-Semitism, at least, was now understood not just as an opportunistic political doctrine or opinion but as a deep and savage enmity. Also at this time psychoanalytically influenced scholars were beginning to articulate the views that racism was an expression of irrational unconscious wishes, phantasies, and defensive character structures.[7] Racism came to be seen as a problem not of ideological commitment but of disordered personality. The racist personality was prejudiced, and prejudice was the result of distortions in belief and attitude caused by impingements of unconscious or other irrational desires and emotions. In the study of racism the inner life of affective and orectic dispositions moved center stage.

It did not stay there, however. Two significant developments edged it out. In academic social science the dominant social learning theories applied to the psychology of racism came to focus on the cognitive assimilation of prejudicial attitudes and beliefs and largely neglected the role of emotional and orectic aspects of personality. And, second, interest within the wide, amorphous field of race relations shifted from individual prejudice to the more or less systematic forms of racial discrimination exercised institutionally and in social and political structures. The publication of Stokeley Carmichael and Charles Hamilton's *Black Power: The Politics of Liberation in America* provided a decisive impetus in this direction.

These developments are still very much with us but there has also been a re-

7. An outstanding account of these views is given in Young-Bruehl 1996.

vival of interest in the broadly psychological-characterological approach to individual racism. Psychodynamic theorists continue to emphasize the inner life and character structure, and within philosophy renewed interest in virtue ethics, motivation, and agency has converged on the same result. In the last decade J. L. A. Garcia, more perhaps than most philosophers, has insisted on the primacy of vicious volitional and affective dispositions in defining racism. Garcia characterizes his view of racism as "focally a matter of volitions, desires, and hopes"; and since these can offend the virtues at the heart of the moral appraisal of character and action, he is able persuasively to explain why racism is a vice. But these motivational dispositions are also linked systematically to our actions and projects and to some of their consequences, and that fact gives promise of showing how the plurality of racist phenomena can be unified and traced back to what is in the hearts of individuals. As Garcia observes in chapter 2,

> Racism, at its core . . . consists in racial disregard, including disrespect, or most gravely, in ill will. Racially based or racially informed disregard (or ill will) is an indifference (or opposition) to another's welfare on account of the racial group to which she is assigned. . . . Such a view helps explain the range of potentially racist phenomena. Actions, beliefs, projects, hopes, wishes, institutions, and institutional practices are all racist insofar as they are informed by racial hostility or disregard. This account also makes manifest why the term *racism* is properly pejorative. The ill will or disregard that constitutes racism is inherently contrary to the moral virtues of benevolence and justice, and often to others as well.

It is a particular strength of Garcia's approach that he is able to rebut so many competing views, in some cases decisively, and to argue for the order and moral unity of manifestations of racism.

In his book *I'm Not a Racist, But . . .*, Lawrence Blum argues that in ordinary use the terms "racism" and "racist" have become so inflated or overextended as to obscure both the variety of race-related phenomena and the variety of race-related evils and wrongfulness. Today, just about anything that goes wrong in the arena of race is described as racism. We lose the capacity for fine discrimination among manifestations of racism and other race-related evils. In his contribution to this volume Blum extends his argument, departing in an important respect from the earlier work. In his book Blum urged recognition of the categorial plurality of racist expressions and variety among racial moral ills but still considered that there were two things that could be said to be at the core of racism: antipathy and inferiorization. He is no longer confident that there is a certain thing (or two) that racism is, or that the major philosophical task is to give an account of this thing. Instead, we should take our "task to be an account of the diversity of racial phenomena that constitute moral ills, and a careful delineation of the moral character of each."

One main line of his argument proceeds by way of a detailed critique of several contentions central to Garcia's account. Blum is in sympathy with much of the general trend of Garcia's work, particularly the insistence on the irreducibly (im)moral character of racism, his recognition of the categorial plurality of racist manifestations, and the detailed attempt to articulate what is wrong with them. But Garcia holds that there *is* a heart of racism: instances of racism manifest or are causally related to the racial ill will or disregard in some human heart. If an institution is racist, for example, that is because of the intrusion at some point of individual racist ill will or disregard. So although at one level Garcia recognizes categorial plurality—the manifestation of racism in acts, beliefs, institutions, and so on—he fails to recognize the plurality of distinct racial ills. Blum also raises searching questions about the relationships between the vices that do much of the work in Garcia's account, and he questions whether that account has actually identified the *distinctive* features of race-related wrongs (that is, the features distinguishing such wrongs from those normally attending hatred, disrespect, adverse discrimination, etc.). Blum contends that Garcia's account does not, and he provides his own answer, which, he notices, is partly consequentialist.

VII

The social science literature on racism and race relations more generally is vast. As we should now expect, "racism" is the term of choice to describe a host of conflict-laden economic, social, and political configurations where the groups involved are susceptible to racial (or kindred) classification. In these discussions, as in so many areas of social science, conceptual confusion is endemic. For example, it is common to find racism undistinguished from other aspects of race relations, as when conflicts between racially identified groups that are motivated largely by competition for employment or territory are misdescribed as racial conflicts. Racial antipathy is certainly common enough, but it cannot be the only motive that sets racially designated groups against each other. And, of course, instances from that mixed bag called "race relations" can sometimes be good or benign. The sociological study of race relations has, however, uncovered two important conceptions: the notion of unintended, indirect racial discrimination and the notion of institutional or structural racism or racial discrimination.

By the 1960s it was recognized that institutions, administrative practices, and social and political structures can operate in adverse, racially discriminatory, or exclusionary ways. It was also recognized that in some cases the discriminatory processes have a life of their own, causally independent of the agency of individual bigots or racists. The concept of racism has been extended to cover these forms of institutional or structural discrimination by affinity. Whatever else a racist is, she is a person who has an adverse attitude toward members of a racially assigned group and, given the opportunity, would probably try to harm or discriminate against them. Practices, institutions, and political structures do not have attitudes, but they can certainly discriminate against and harm the interests of members of a group *because of their race*. Thus there is significant affinity between individual racism, prejudice, and bigotry, on the one hand, and institutional or structural adverse discrimination and harm, on the other.

The exact relations between individual racism, structural racism, and adverse racial discrimination are, however, problematic, as are their distinctive harms and vices. It is far from clear that the model of individual racism constructed around (say) vicious orectic and affective dispositions can be expanded to explain the racially discriminatory processes and operations of institutional and social structures and their particular viciousness. When Carmichael and Hamilton introduced their distinction between individual and institutional racism, it was evident that they conceived of the latter as parasitic on the former: "institutional racism relies on the active and pervasive operation of antiblack attitudes and practices" (1968: 19). But the character of that dependency—whether for example it is causal as well as conceptual and, if so, precisely how—is far from transparent.

In her contribution here Sally Haslanger argues that the individualistic approach fails causally to account for all the operations of the social structures of racial oppression: for one thing, in structural oppression there may not be an (individual) agent responsible for the oppression, and "social structures are often beyond the control of individual agents." She argues that the distinctive wrongs of structural oppression cannot be derived from, or explicated in terms of, the wrongs inflicted by individual agents. Whether or not structural racial oppression in the absence of individual racist agency, either in a proximate or historical sense, is appropriately classified as racism, Haslanger is certainly correct in insisting on the moral, social, and political importance of such structural oppression: "for many of those who suffer injustice, 'private' attitudes are not the worst problem; systematic institutional subordination is." Both individual agent and structural racial oppression must be accommodated. Her argument leads to the construction of an exceptionally careful and elegant theory of structural racial oppression—or racism.

VIII

Racialist conceptions have been essential to shaping modern racism and, contrariwise, racism has contributed to shaping some of the racialist conceptions. Conceptions of race and race ideology have, as we saw, a long history and were subject to numerous formative influences. The story of the evolution of racialist conceptions does not provide an explanation of their appeal, however. The strong appeal of race thinking and its often savage exploitation cannot be explained adequately as the suasion of biology or physical anthropology or on any other probative scientific, historical grounds. Many thinkers from various disciplines (Arendt 1979, Banton 1998, Hobsbawm 1987) have argued cogently that racism did not spring primarily from racialism. Hannah Arendt, in particular, has emphasized the gulf between the enormities of modern racism and the racial conceptions of the seminal Enlightenment thinkers. The latter were never "seriously concerned with discrimination against other peoples as lower races." "There is a world of difference" she averred, "between the men of brilliant and facile conceptions and men of brutal deeds and active bestiality" (Arendt 1979: 182, 183).

The historical, economic, and social conditions for the emergence of racism in different parts of the world at different times are, it goes without saying, immensely complex. For the historical causes of Western racism some theorists have turned to the upheavals and strivings for new identities following the Reformation. Others have emphasized the breakdown of European class structures during the nineteenth century and the unstable status consciousness that sought satisfaction in the humiliation of subject peoples. Also noted is the link with the ascendancy of capitalism: racism is an instrument of labor exploitation and, with the commodification of human value, it becomes fashionable to dispel the guilt of wronging other human beings—inferior races, lower classes, women, the poor—by despising and devaluing them. Many writers have linked the development of racist ideologies and emotional postures to the insistent need (especially in aspirant egalitarian societies) to rationalize or palliate imperialism, economic self-interest, and, in particular, the exploitation of slavery.

There is no doubt much to be said for the explanatory force and scope of these high-level causal constructions. It is evident, however, that they must be supplemented with accounts of lower-level processes, the quotidian stuff of home economics, small ideas, aims, fears, and ambitions. In particular, the high-level constructions are neither inconsistent with nor independent of psychological causal explanation. Racism satisfies a host of important psychological needs. Though it is not often highlighted, this fact is implicit in the recurrent explanations that hinge on the "rationalizing function" of racism, as in the "rationalization of domination, exploitation and slavery" (Blum 2002: 145). For, of course, such rationalization is not other than the palliation of guilt, the expedient settling of consciences and successful self-deception. The processes falling under the head of rationalization are important, but they are only special cases of the diverse range of orectic and emotional needs to which psychodynamically orientated thinkers have drawn attention: the sustainment of self-esteem and identity, the suppression of fear and anxiety, the displacement of aggression, the projection of unwanted aspects of the self, the fulfillment of wishes for specialness, superiority, and belonging, and the pleasures of contempt and subordination.

These processes, which are often unconscious, deform the normative relations between the racist and her victims. Perhaps the two most conspicuous features of racism are that racists' beliefs about their victims rarely correspond to the facts and that their emotions and desires are frequently inappropriate to their putative objects. As noted earlier, racism (or at least most racism) is often regarded as the expression of prejudice, where prejudice is understood to involve irrational attitudes and emotions, or beliefs arrived at irrationally. Some social scientists, however, have argued that racial prejudice is not, or is not necessarily, irrational; it is, instead, the acceptance of false beliefs and attitudes acquired innocently during acculturation or through faulty but untendentious generalization. Prejudice is error sustained in ignorance. Some significant philosophical work has also questioned the case for irrationality (e.g., Goldberg 1999) and some, as we saw earlier, simply skirts it; preferring to distinguish racism always as a moral vice rather than as an intellectual one, forgetting, perhaps, that it could be both. Evidently quite normal processes of learning and related influences do play a part in some cases. But psychological, including clinical, investigation, together with considerations from other disciplines, suggests that the role of irrational, often unconscious, mental processes in the genesis of racism are important factors that cannot be ignored.

Michael Dummett argues in chapter 1 that racism is prejudice manifesting itself in a variety of hostile attitudes directed against racial groups. Racism, he contends, is always irrational. Though irrational, racism as such does not go deep, and Dummett contends that racism can be suppressed or eliminated by suitable legislative and political sanctions. The human needs or propensities that engender racism may go deep, but specifically racist expressions of them do not, and the cover of race is fungible.

> Racist feelings, being quite irrational, are difficult to dislodge by argument or persuasion. They are also often very passionate. These characteristics lead commentators to describe them as very deep. There may be rare individuals among the perpetrators of the most terrible racial crimes in whose psyches racist feelings go very deep. But among the great majority of racists these feelings, though irrational, dangerous, and often passionate, are very superficial. The psychological need to have some group to despise and push around may go deep; the identification of some racial group as the target of the contempt or hostility does not.

Against the backdrop of the general neglect of racist motivation in the philosophical literature, one can discern here some affinity of perspective with psychodynamically minded authors. The emphasis on the irrationality of racist manifestations and their source in deep human needs is important common ground. But there are also differences. One significant difference is that in psychoanalytically influenced work the perceived racial characteristics of the victims—real, imagined, projected—are not matters of indifference but reflect or mobilize particular unconscious mental structures that determine the forms racism takes. And, more generally, as may be expected after a century of clinically oriented thinking, psychoanalytic accounts are able to offer detailed causal stories relating racist orectic, emotional, doxastic, and defensive dispositions to individual developmental factors and the relevant formative and precipitating social conditions. These causal accounts are simultaneously historical (developmental) and proximate; a consequence—to condense a mass of theory into a Freudian phrase—of the "timelessness" of the unconscious.

Perhaps the most impressive and comprehensive of recent psychoanalytic treatments of racism is Elisabeth Young-Bruehl's *The Anatomy of Prejudices* (1996). A brief exposition of some key themes in this book may help locate her contribution here and also provide a useful backdrop for several of the other chapters in this volume.

Young-Bruehl begins the constructive section of the book by distinguishing ethnocentric prejudices from orectic prejudices. The ethnocentric prejudices are (more or less) cultural givens acquired through learning. The orecticisms are generated and shaped by individual unconscious desires and projects, but when sufficient numbers of people share them they may sum to something that *looks* like ethnocentrism. The orecticisms are a kind of (nonpathological) "social defense." They utilize other people for the purpose of psychological defense, much like some character disorders, in contrast to neuroses that are largely played out in one's own person. Young-Bruehl considers racism in its modern form—which she distinguishes from anti-Semitism, sexism, and homophobia in terms of distinct psychological substructures—to be entirely orectic.

The preponderating psychological defenses used by an individual largely determine character structure. Young-Bruehl develops a detailed theory of character types based on Freud's attempt in "Libidinal Types" (1961b). The main types are obsessional, narcissistic, and hysterical (Freud's "erotic"). The character types are then coordinated with the different types of prejudice. Thus anti-Semitism is generally associated with the obsessional types, antiblack racism with the hysterical, and sexism and homophobia with the narcissistic types. The different character types can also target the same groups, so that there are obsessional, hysterical, and narcissistic modalities applied to Jews, blacks, Asian "middleman" types, and so on. Here are some examples with the focus on the modality of defensive splitting. Obsessionals may see in the black something feculent or contaminating that has to be segregated or eliminated; and the prejudice—which is essentially a defensive operation—has the unconscious significance of being purged. Hysterics may focus on the black's supposed sexual power and imagined bodily gratifications. They may project their forbidden desires and projectively identify with them, so they are bound to their black objects and dependent on them. At the same time the function of the prejudice is to maintain a split within the racist's self, to keep the higher (moral) and lower (sexual) natures separate, and this is achieved by subordination of the objects who bear part of the self—

"keeping them in their place"—but in a way that keeps them available. The hysterical propensity to segregation, hierarchy and ranking mirrors the dissociation that stems from the intense need for the object and, simultaneously, aversion to it. Similarly, white narcissists may be preoccupied with enforcing subordination and deference or, in the common male case, with appropriating the black's imagined phallic power in the service of maintaining self-esteem or denying envy.

Young-Bruehl discusses how different kinds of society promote the different character types and how particular social and political circumstances will trigger the activation of the maneuvers typical of each type. For example, the perceived loss of status that follows upon social deracination or deprivation is likely to provoke, in the obsessionally inclined, segregating or eliminative defenses against a suitable target group that is experienced as contaminating, insidious, or persecuting. The narcissistically inclined will be sensitive to envy, humiliation, and narcissistic hurt and, typically, defend themselves by projection, denial, and self-idealization. Following Arendt (1979), Young-Bruehl also attends carefully to the characteristics of the target groups. So, for example, Arendt had noticed how perceptions of the Rothschilds as "powers behind the throne," as identified with the state, as a conspiratorial family, contributed significantly to anti-Semitism. Young-Bruehl is able to show how *the unconscious significance* of these and similar perceptions (which are already phantastically distorted perceptions) interact with specific social circumstances to forge anti-Semitic sentiments. The attention to details of the victims, real and perceived, and to social circumstances is a considerable advance both on the earlier projective and scapegoat theories and on accounts like Michael Rustin's (1991) that sever the associative links between the racist's state of mind and the characteristics of their target group.

In her contribution to this volume Young-Bruehl outlines some of the conclusions of her earlier work on prejudice and extends them to provide a psychoanalytic account of violence: "Prejudice is the idea for which violence is a mode of action. Prejudice says what violence does." Just as character provides the template for modes of prejudice and other object-relational behavior, so it provides the template for modes of aggressing. One important permissive cause of violence is that the victims be seen not as individuals "in their personhood" but as members of groups defined by certain preconceived images or categories—as rivals, deprivers, the sexually satisfied, for example. These are categories, as we saw, that also loom large in the racist mind.

Neil Altman and Johanna Tiemann develop a considerably different but not incompatible psychoanalytic account of some forms of racism. They build, not as Young-Bruehl does on the strand of ego psychology associated closely with Anna Freud, but on the object-relational views stemming from Melanie Klein. The authors begin by succinctly exposing some aspects of Melanie Klein's views on early infant development, including the chief defensive processes which influence that development. They recognize the significance of social dynamics in the formation of racism and emphasize the interaction between these and psychological processes. They then develop a complex and detailed account of racism as an expression of the manic defense (Klein 1975). The defense is characterized by foreclosure of psychic space, fantasies of omnipotence, and projective identification. It is activated by the painful experiences associated with the depressive position: feelings of guilt, dependence, and vulnerability. In infancy, excessive use of such defenses block the development of a "theory of mind," of the capacity to interpret others as subjects of Intentional attitudes. This malign process excludes others as objects of empathy or humane consideration. The sad result is a precondition of some virulent expressions of racism. Racism can thus function to ward off "the sense of human vulnerability, dependence, and limitation." Altman and Tiemann's chapter illustrates these processes with a highly illuminating study of William Pierce and the supremacist National Alliance.

Now if depth-psychological causal accounts of the sort we have been examining are correct, they may have the same radical consequences for the understanding of the nature of racism that scientific analysis has had for the understanding of many other phenomena of interest to philosophers. Familiar space for conceptual revision (or discovery?) opens up, in this instance either for the contingent identification of racism with the depth-psychological structures or for the establishment of the latter as necessary causal conditions of racism. More precisely, different sets of such structures can be conjectured to be identical to, or to be necessary causal conditions of, different kinds of racism or prejudice. Michael Levine draws out some of these radical consequences. He argues vigorously that nothing less than psychodynamic causal theories can provide an adequate account of the nature of racism. Because these have been largely neglected and unutilized in philosophy, philosophers have failed to explain the nature of racism. Commonly, for example, it has been contended that racism involves hatred of racial groups, or some kindred attitude. But, Levine argues, "Until one understands what it is that motivates such hatreds and attitudes, why they come about and in what circumstances, where the circumstances are part of the explanation—it is impossible to understand what racism *is*."

Levine seems sometimes to suggest that the underlying structures are identical to (the various forms of) racism, as when he writes, "For what one terms 'racist behavior' will in fact *be* racist behavior in the relevant sense if it stems from racism, and this cannot be ascertained from the behavior alone." At other times he seems to hold that the underlying structures are necessary conditions of racism, as when he emphasizes that behavior that *looks* racist will not be so in the absence of the appropriate structures: when symptoms are mistaken for the disease. The causal story is (in one way or another) part of the story of the nature of racism. In either case, if the arguments are sound, his conclusions are highly significant. For, as Levine proceeds to argue, if philosophers have failed to explain the nature of racism they will as surely fail to explain its distinctive wrongs as fail to prescribe the appropriate remedies.

Bernard Boxill's chapter is largely concerned with the dangerousness of the idea of race, and that aspect will be discussed below. In its course, however, he develops a causal account of an arresting expression of racism: the racism that springs from the barriers to compassion that a governing "race idea" or racial identity imposes on those who are (excessively) dependent on it for their identity and self-esteem. Racial identity in such cases impedes the capacity for empathy or imaginative identification with those who are perceived to be racially other, either because they are so different physically or culturally or because our own racial identities are so important to us that we "cannot or will not exchange them, even in imagination." Why can racial identity assume such importance for us? Boxill considers a number of grounds, but the chief motive he suggests is "a desire to have an unconditional ground for self-esteem" which membership in a supposedly superior race provides.

My chapter explores three related themes in the psychology of racism: its motivation, the rationality of racism, and the ways in which cultural lore (for example, racialist doctrine or popular beliefs about race) interlocks with individual motives to satisfy some of the needs of the racist mind. The chapter is psychoanalytic in spirit, but I give special emphasis to the complexity of the causal relations between certain object-related psychological needs and the racialist and racist lore embedded in cultures. I think that racism is a family resemblance concept: there is no single intensional thread that binds the plurality of manifestations that fall under it. So no simple, univocal story is to be expected about racism, and certainly not about the character of its motivation. Much racism, I claim, is motivated by unconscious intentions directed at satisfying object-related needs, but some racism is unmotivated: it may be caused subrationally or the result of ignorance, acquired prejudice, or other misfortunes. Racism (it follows) may, though rarely, be rational. But most racism is irrational, and the source of the irrationality is frequently—not always—due to the operation of unconscious orectic, affective, and doxastic structures. The role of unconscious destructive envy in the genesis of some forms of racism demonstrates the influence of unconscious dispositions on racist belief and behavior.

IX

One does not have to believe that racism is an irreducibly moral notion to recognize its diverse and far-reaching moral, social, and political consequences. Few scourges have been responsible for so much atrocity, enmity, and injustice as racial ideas combined with malevolent passions and common frailty. Ideas can be dangerous artifacts. Bernard Boxill argues that the idea of race is so dangerous that it should be eschewed even if it is not a false idea. Running against the grain of most recent philosophical work that contends or assumes that there are no races, Boxill argues that there may well be: at any rate, whether there are is a question best left to biologists. But even if there *are* races the idea of race remains calamitous. It provides specious grounds for self-esteem, builds barriers to compassion for our fellows, disposes us to cruelty and immorality, and is associated with some of the great crimes of recent centuries. Philosophers, Boxill concludes, should "spend less time arguing that there are no races, and more time exploring the dangerousness of the race idea."

Cynthia Willett's wide-ranging chapter has several aims. She asks why, after the demise of the influence of racist ideology, blacks in the United States continue to choose to segregate themselves and experience alienation and the malaise of not belonging. These are cruel facts, unexplained even after all the usual suspects are considered. For Willett, the explanatory failure points to still deeper failures in liberal and leftist political theory. "Neither the traditional liberal view of the individual as an autonomous agent nor the contemporary model of social space as a set of institutional practices provides us sufficient tools for explaining the malaise." Teasing out Merleau-Ponty's undeveloped political views from his poetics of space in an extended and detailed discussion, she develops a critique of liberal theory that penetrates to its implicit Cartesianism. The individual consciousness cannot be abstracted from its experience of social and spatial reality. Spatial reality is an integral part of social reality. Space is replete with meaning, including the meanings of color and race. Willett combines Merleau-Ponty's exploration of the prediscursive meanings of space and sociological investigations in U.S. schools that reveal how whites mark out exclusionary spaces, through gesture and other means, which leads blacks to feel as though they are intruders. "Space as an experience of depth and color, or of an interconnecting 'tissue' of sensitivities, offers a way of understanding the persistence of racial segregation." Social space is essentially tinctured by color, and the liberal goes wrong in thinking "that we can construct formal principles of fairness in abstraction of social realities. We do not live and work in a void but in a space that establishes our status and power, in part, through color."

Kant's moral thought has often been assailed for failing to give experience its due. Laurence Thomas develops a complex and novel argument of this broad stripe, recusant to brief summary, which throws light on conditions for racial equality. Although Kantian thought provides for equality of moral worth, Thomas argues, it does not provide for the kind of equality where race and ethnicity are morally irrelevant. To experience another as fully one's equal requires not only a recognition of their equal moral worth but recognition also of what Thomas dubs equality of personal social index (PSI): roughly, that the other is worthy of a quality of life higher or as high as one's own. The notion is intended to capture many aspects of human worth not implied by the notion of moral worth. Thomas employs the condition of upside-down equality—a political dispensation that is governed by blacks—to show up the difficulty for Kantian thought. It would, of course, be desirable for Kantian thought to entail commitment to upside-down equality, but in the unideal world it does not. It does not because commitment to upside-down equality entails a commitment to PSI-equality whereas the Kantian notion of equal moral worth does not. PSI is contingent in a number of ways on deep visceral emotional responses (VERs). The overcoming of deep VERs, those differentiating ethnic groups for example, can hardly be done by acts of ratiocination. To recognize each other as PSI equals, to be able to judge another ethnic or racial group worthy of governing, we do need the transformation that can come only from experience of one another. But this precondition of thoroughgoing equality is one that Kantian thought does not meet.

Our kind has not been uncreative in manufacturing varieties of enmity, prejudice, and oppression. It is natural to wonder whether these spring from a single source and whether there are any significant relations between them. There is now a large feminist literature that explores the relations between sexism and racism. In her chapter Marguerite La Caze undertakes a critical survey of the high points. She shows that reflection on sexism and racism do indeed generate insights into both: although "the two forms of oppression are distinctive, they share a general structure which emerges in personal experiences of oppression, in institutionalized racism and sexism, and in approaches to overcoming oppression." La Caze discusses a large range of analogies and disanalogies proposed in the recent literature. In many cases these are overly simple, sweeping, or extreme and fail properly to appreciate the experience and needs of the oppressed. Most notably, she argues that "we need the concepts of race, sex, and gender for the foreseeable future . . . because they are central to people's identity and will remain so even if they are not oppressed. . . . We continue to need the concept of race because there has been so much cultural loss for some groups that 'ethnicity' does not suggest their exceptional historical situation." La Caze expresses affinity with Beauvoir's insights into oppression and the strategies for dealing with it, and she exposes and develops these views at length and dialectically contrasts them with the more recent contributions.

X

The chapters in this volume are grouped into sections dealing with three questions: What is racism? What are some of the causes of racism? What are some of the moral and political implications of racism? Of course, the answers to these questions do not fall into neat sections, and even a brief immersion in the subject will soon disclose why.

The study of racism draws upon many largely empirical disciplines: biology, anthropology, psychology, ethnology, sociology, history. Racism is also of very great philosophical interest. Many unresolved conceptual matters lie at the roots of disagreement about racism, not only in philosophy but in the empirical disciplines as well. Indeed, no one can stand apart from this subject. Our collective attitudes to racism have profound social and political consequences. Individually, our convictions place us in the inescapable circle of moral attitudes to other people and to ourselves. For these reasons philosophers are in an unusually responsible position in relation to the study of racism. Philosophy is the discipline most adept at clarifying conceptual confusions, integrating multidisciplinary endeavors, and drawing out the philosophical and social implications of the relevant empirical issues. It is the discipline that studies the life of the mind in action. It is, or should be, the discipline in which one strives to know oneself.

An unstated premise of the essays collected here is that understanding racism and its consequences can assist in eradicating it. This is a special instance of an unstated hope in much scholarly work, and history has shown, and our consciences prescribe, that such work is valuable even in the bleakest times.

I

WHAT IS RACISM?

1 : THE NATURE OF RACISM

If we have a definition of racism, it is surely easy to explain what antiracism is: it must simply be opposition to whatever we have defined racism to be. But there are both narrower and wider conceptions of antiracism than that. Many years ago my wife, who has devoted her whole career—once our children were old enough for her to have a career—to fighting racism, was invited to be one of several speakers at a meeting of left-wing activists about the 1971 Immigration Act. After she had spoken, one of the other speakers spoke at length in favor of abortion. My wife felt impelled to dissociate herself from this. "I thought this meeting was about the Immigration Act," she said, "but I do not wish, by being on the same platform, to be taken as agreeing with the last speaker about abortion, which I think is a very wicked thing." The entire audience joined in vociferous hissing and booing. These political activists subscribed to a very narrow conception of antiracism. They shared a number of objectives, all bundled together into a single package: political success for the Labour Party, suppression of racial discrimination, abortion, gay rights, full employment, and, no doubt, nationalization of the means of production. An antiracist was for them anyone who accepted the entire package; anyone who rejected any item in it was an enemy, and, if not actually a racist, certainly not a bona fide antiracist. I have read in print a reference to "the Society for the Protection of Unborn Children and other Fascist organisations." In the United States acceptance of a similar package is required in order to qualify as a liberal.

My own reaction is to think that those attending this meeting did not understand what being an antiracist involves. It is not just that working for any aim demands cooperation with all who support that aim, however much you disagree with them on other matters. It is that the eradication of racism demands a respect for others whatever their differences from oneself. It cannot be achieved simply by not treating racial differences as a ground for denying such respect, though perhaps denying it on other grounds, such as differences of religion, of moral views, or even of culture. Unless you cultivate a respect for other people despite any of the ways in which they differ from you, you have not grasped the spirit that ought to animate the desire to overcome racial prejudice and its manifestations. This, of course, is a wide definition of antiracism; more exactly, a generalization of it. Wide, that is, in its conception of what antiracism should involve: it would rule out from deserving the name of antiracist (as many would not) the narrow conception held by the audience at the meeting my wife addressed.

Racism, in the strict sense of the word, consists of prejudice against one or more racial groups that manifests itself in hostile behavior toward all members of those groups (or, sometimes, toward all but a very few rich or powerful ones). The term "racial group" is defined by social attitudes, not by biology or even by appearance: by the attitudes of those belonging to the group as well as of those not belonging to it. What makes it a racial group is that descent is a criterion for belonging to it. You will be regarded as a member of that group if, and only if, at least one of your parents belonged to it; usually only one parent is sufficient. As a definition—an inductive definition—this is obviously deficient: its application will depend on identification of some people as members of the group by some criterion other than descent. For present purposes, it does not matter how this is done. It may be by geographical origin or by religion or by appearance. It does not matter whether members of the group thus identified really share some common descent or not, although they will be believed to do so: what is essential is that membership of the group is taken to be transmissible by descent, usually through a single parent. A film called *Sapphire* helped to propagate racist attitudes in Britain in the early days of immigration from the Caribbean. A police inspector stalked through the film, asking witnesses, concerning a murder victim, "Did you know she was colored?" They might well not have done, seeing that her skin color was indistinguishable from theirs. Hers was a color not visible to the eye; "colored" here was a purely racial epithet.

The word "prejudice," as used in defining racism, can cover almost any hostile attitude felt toward the members of a racial group. It may be a reluctance to meet or converse with any member of the group, or the desire that no member of it should enter one's house, or live in one's street, or join the same club, trade union, or work force, or even enter the country: perhaps no more than a disgust at the thought of any member of the group marrying one's sister or daughter. "Members of the group" is too cumbersome an expression to keep repeating: let us substitute for it "the Others." The prejudice may take the form of a more virulent hatred that may manifest itself in one or another attempt to do harm to the Others, by burning their houses, or by physical attack, even murder. It may be based on a belief in the inferiority of the Others, intellectual or moral, or simply on the attitude that they do not count as human beings toward whom ordinary virtues need be exercised.

Is it right to define racism as a "prejudice" against some racial group? Is it not part of the meaning of the word that a prejudice is irrational? Must hostility toward or contempt for a racial group be irrational? Or can it be based on rational grounds, such as the astonishingly ill-informed David Hume believed himself to have, in regard to all nonwhite groups, for thinking those groups to be inferior? The answer depends on two things. What does it mean to think of one group of people as inferior to another? And what sort of behavior is such a belief held to justify? No one can rationally think that the great majority of members of any racial group are intellectually or artistically inferior to the great majority of members of some other group. It is obvious that within any racial group there is a great range of intelligence and of artistic talents. A belief in the inferiority of a whole racial group in either respect can be sustained with some show of rationality only if it is held that the group will never produce anyone of the highest achievements: that, say, there will never be a great orator, writer, artist, musician, or scientist from that group—say, from Africa and the black population of the New World, or, again, from the Indian subcontinent. It would need a remarkable ignorance to put forward such a proposition; but then, some people, though rational, are remarkably ignorant. Can a rational belief be based on ignorance? Not if the ignorant individual palpably knows too little to form a judgment on the matter. An ignorant but rational person can be no more than agnostic about questions that require a moderate degree of knowledge to answer.

In any case, to what behavior toward members of a racial group might a belief in its intellectual inferiority rationally lead? Not to behavior of the kind that usually characterizes racists. It would be a poor reason for not wanting someone of a certain racial group to enter one's house or buy the house next door that one did not expect any great scientist or artist to stem from that group. No great amount of either intelligence or artistic talent is needed for ordinary day-to-day dealings between human beings. One could not justify withholding common courtesy, just treatment, or compassion from someone by a plea that that person lacked high intelligence and great talent, even if one was oneself a genius or prodigy. Still less could it be justified by his belonging to a racial group among whose members one expected no high degree of intellectual or artistic achievement. Plainly, no belief detrimental to any racial group as a whole, even if it could be rationally, if misguidedly, arrived at, could rationally lead to racist behavior toward all members of that group; if it did not, it would not qualify as racism under the foregoing definition. Rather, any rational person holding such a belief, if he were not a racist, and knew how irrational others often are, takes care to avoid propagating his belief. It is true that racist actions might be a rational consequence of paranoid beliefs such as that most members of some racial group carry infectious diseases or, as Enoch Powell said, are planning to get the whip hand over others; but this is no defense of the rationality of racism. We may safely characterize racism as something irrational.

It is characteristic of racism that it very readily fuses with other kinds of hostility and can often disguise itself as such another form. Since difference of race (in the social sense) frequently accompanies difference of culture, racial prejudice easily coalesces with cultural prejudice. In the early days of Britain's adaptation to the result of immigration from the Indian subcontinent, it was frequent to hear complaints against the wearing of saris or shalwars: "Once they're here, they ought to dress like us," English people would declare. If you said, "If you and your husband went to India, you would not wear a sari and your husband would not wear a dhoti," they could not see the point. Racism also combines with religious antagonism. Germans of the present day explain their greater antipathy toward Turkish "guest workers" than to those from other European countries by saying that they have a different religion; and obviously a similar thought contributed to the prewar anti-Semitism that blossomed into the most stupendous crime of the crime-bespattered century.

Racial prejudice also forms an amalgam with economic anxieties. It is of great importance not to dismiss such an amalgam as "merely economic." In the introduction to this book, Tamas Pataki writes: "In these discussions, as in so many areas of social science, conceptual confusion is endemic. For example, it is common to find racism undistinguished from other aspects of race relations, as when conflicts between racially identified groups that are motivated largely by competition for employment or territory are misdescribed as racial conflicts."

I am afraid that it is the author of these remarks who has manifested conceptual confusion. Indirect discrimination may occur when some rule unintentionally disadvantages members of some racial group; plainly, when this has happened by accident, it is due to thoughtlessness rather than racism. But this is not an example of *conflict* or of competition between groups. There is no aspect of race relations—as the term is normally and properly used—that does not have racism at its root: "race relations" is not normally applied to relations between groups between which there is no friction or competition, such as French speakers and German speakers in Switzerland. In a similar way, competition for employment between men, as a group, and women, as a group, must have sexism at its root, if "sexism" is taken to cover any belief that one or other of the two sexes ought to be favored in some particular type of employment: if no such belief is present, how can anyone conceive of competition between the sexes? A celebrated strike by bus drivers and conductors in Bristol in the 1960s took place in opposition to the employment of "colored" conductors by the bus company. "This is not a color bar," the strikers proclaimed. What on earth did they mean by saying that their demand was not for a color bar, when just that was what it obviously was? They were evidently free from the supposed conceptual confusion between racial conflicts and those conflicts between racially identified groups that are motivated by competition for employment. The strikers did not object to the proximity of "colored" people: they wanted to deny them the opportunity to compete for scarce jobs.

A distinction of principle cannot be maintained. The desire that jobs of any kind should be reserved for people of one's own racial group, or even that those people should have the priority in obtaining them, must obviously rest on the idea that the Others deserve less, and have less right, to be employed than people of Our Own Kind. Without this racist idea, there is competition for jobs only between individuals, not between racial groups. The same goes for complaints that They are obtaining housing or beds in hospitals that should be going to Us. There is no conceptual confusion in labeling such complaints, and all drives toward racial discrimination, as products of racism. Whether or not some action is racist is not affected by what it is intended to deprive the Others of—a house in some area, a job in some firm, entry to the country, or even their lives. What makes it racist is that it is directed against members of some racial group in virtue of their being members of that group.

A counterexample has been suggested to me by Tamas Pataki, concerning an episode of which I have no other knowledge. It seems that in the mid-nineteenth century Australian workers objected to an influx of Chinese laborers to the newly discovered goldfields because they were willing to work for lower wages; they were resented because they accepted lower wages, the argument runs, not because they were Chinese. What, if so, makes the affair an "aspect of race relations" rather than simply a labor dispute? If we suppose that the race of the newcomers was really quite irrelevant, so that they would not have been resented if they had been willing to work only for the same wages as the Australian miners, it would not, at least at the outset, have had anything to do with race relations. It would not ever have had anything to do with race relations if it had never affected the attitudes of white Australians toward Chinese or of Chinese toward white Australians. If it had nothing to do with race relations, it would not be a counterexample to my assertion that there is no aspect of race relations that does not have racism at its root. But is that likely? Is it not far more likely that the Australian miners would have stigmatized the newcomers as Chinese as well as workers undercutting their wages? Would not other white Australians have used the dispute as bolstering the case for keeping Chinese out of the country? If so, the affair would merely illustrate how readily racism combines with other grounds of hostility between different groups of people.

Racism, strictly so called, is evidently more irrational, and hence morally viler, than hostilities toward groups identified in some other ways, such as religion, political belief, or even language. It is frequently entangled with hostility that has some other base; but even less can be said in its defense. One may rationally disagree with particular political beliefs and think that to act on them would be disastrous. One may rationally dislike a particular religion and think it socially divisive or individually corrupting. One may even have a rational distaste for a particular language, or rationally believe that linguistic unity is needful for the cohesiveness of society. But race is sometimes a pure social construct, and at most is a matter of physical characteristics that can have no bearing on anyone's abilities or moral character. Racist attitudes are almost always backed by wildly erroneous beliefs about the Others as a group. Above all, the hostility is cruelly based on something the Others have no power to change. Insofar as the Others are brought to suspect that it may have some foundation, which, tragically, they sometimes are, it goes to the heart of their identity: they, and all those from whom they come, are irreparably inferior.

One cannot change what is taken to be one's race. One can change one's religion or political beliefs; one can learn to speak another language. To that degree, racial prejudice, hostility, or contempt is more unjust than any other kind. But these other forms are closely akin to it: they deny to others the respect that is their due. One may indeed rationally disapprove of some particular religion: only arrogance and lack of charity will cause one to ignore how precious it is to its believers and how integral it is to their identity. For that reason, while temperate criticism of a particular religious belief, or even of an entire religion, is always legitimate, no one ought ever to insult, ridicule, or caricature any religion; to do so manifests a cruel disrespect for the most intimate feelings of others. Equally, only arrogance and lack of charity can cause anyone to be oblivious to the injustice of demanding, under threat of punishment, that anyone should do what his conscience forbids him to do. This latter injustice is manifested by the persecution of people for their political as well as for their religious beliefs. People may believe it their duty to propagate opinions of either kind. The obligation not to force people to violate their consciences is one ground for maintaining freedom of expression—a freedom which must always be limited by a prohibition of what provokes hatred of or contempt for people of particular ethnic, religious, or linguistic groups. A person's language is also integral to his identity, even if it does not possess so strong an emotional charge as his religion: attempts to deny people the right to use their own language are assaults on their individuality very similar to racial discrimination or displays of racial prejudice.

Why are people racially prejudiced? Obviously in great part because they have been so indoctrinated by parents or the society around them; but what makes them receptive to such indoctrination? Human beings tend to have a strong desire to have some group toward which they can feel and show contempt and whose members they can subject to mistreatment, so far as these are socially acceptable. Before the civil rights movement changed what white Americans regarded as legitimate, even proper, to say and do, racist attitudes toward those now known as African Americans were usual among the great majority of white people in the United States, though indeed more virulent among some than others. Now, the open expression of such attitudes is extremely rare, although it is apparent that they are still held by very many; the general culture is no longer racist, but many subcultures still are. Where has the hostility gone? In some part into prejudice toward the use of the Spanish language; but the group that is most widely derided and pushed around is that of smokers of tobacco. Opposition to tobacco smoking is in itself perfectly rational; but the vehemence, among middle-class Americans, of their hatred of smokers, and the manner in which smokers are treated, illustrate the strength of the psychological need to be able to despise another group and treat its members with disregard and contempt. Of course, the transference of such attitudes from black people to smokers is a great improvement. Still, the irrational emotional violence most white middle-class Americans manifest toward tobacco smokers—far more now than toward users of cocaine or heroin—helps us to understand the attraction of racism within a society unashamed of it.

It could be argued that the psychological need to despise some group of people and treat its members with contempt is deep, even if the specific choice of a racial group as the target is not: such a need, it might be said, unconsciously motivates many, and its satisfaction will come from directing hatred or contempt against any group that is a socially acceptable target for such emotions. I do not think we have enough evidence to say whether this contention is true or false; it certainly does not always happen that, when some variety of racism fades, the antipathy of the former racists is switched to some new sector of the population. No doubt we should beware that this will occur; we cannot be sure that it will. But even if the need that underlies the expression of hostility is deep, the choice of a *racial* group as its object is not.

All hostilities toward other groups, however based, lead frequently to horrendous cruelties; racial hostility inspires greater cruelties than any other variety. All hatred of or contempt for other groups, religious, linguistic, or cultural, is therefore dangerous; racial hatred and contempt are the most dangerous of all. Recent events in Bosnia and Rwanda, the Nazi massacres of the Jews and of the Gypsies, and the earlier Turkish massacre of the Armenians, teach us that subterranean enmities may erupt into savageries and murders which the greater part of a whole people participate in or applaud. We need to understand what triggers outbreaks of such barbarity; more urgently, we need an international rapid reaction force to intervene as soon as they occur. Racist feelings, being quite irrational, are difficult to dislodge by argument or persuasion. They are also often very passionate. These characteristics lead commentators to describe them as very deep. There may be rare individuals among the perpetrators of the most terrible racial crimes in whose psyches racist feelings go very deep. But among the great majority of racists these feelings, though irrational, dangerous, and often passionate, are very superficial. The psychological need to have some group to despise and push around may go deep; the identification of some racial group as the target of the contempt or hostility does not. People adopt racist attitudes when they find themselves in a social milieu in which it is acceptable or encouraged to display such attitudes, and in which maintaining them is advantageous. Notoriously, white immigrants to South Africa under apartheid, for example, Irish people, quite rapidly developed rampantly racist attitudes and beliefs. They may have had no such attitudes or beliefs before they left their native lands; and they certainly did not acquire them as the result of learning any genuine facts they had not known before. They simply imbibed them from the white people among whom they had come to live. Conversely, white expatriates working in

West African countries with no substantial settler population, especially after independence, exhibit no trace of racial prejudice. They will repudiate as despicable and preposterous any suggestion that they harbor any such feelings, and will deny that they have ever done so. Their reactions are genuine and sincere. It is not at all that even the faintest racist feelings lurk within them, unconfessed because it would be catastrophically unwise to voice them: they really have no such feelings, and honestly believe that they have never had any. That belief may be false; it is quite possible that before they left their own countries they shared some low level of racial prejudice which now they have wiped from their memories. The reason for their quite truthful lack of even the mildest racist ideas is that they live in an environment in which it would be utterly unacceptable and unprofitable to manifest them. Human beings have a great propensity to believe what it will be favorable to them to believe.

If racism has taken hold of a section of a national population, or of all of it, leaders of the nation who want to eradicate it will make little progress by moral exhortation or rational argument. They will gain little by seeking deep psychological causes of racial prejudice; we already know as much about that as we need to know for practical purposes. What the leaders need to do is to create a society in which there is only disadvantage to be had by expressing or acting on racist views or feelings. That, of course, is not an easy recommendation to follow. But, if it can be accomplished, racism will melt away like morning mist, save perhaps from the minds of a handful of dangerous psychopaths.

2 : THREE SITES FOR RACISM
SOCIAL STRUCTURES, VALUINGS,
AND VICE

This essay philosophically examines some recent and important understandings of racism. The distinguished historian George Frederickson (2002) conceives of racism as constituted by certain forms of conduct between social groups. Recent treatments within cultural studies, represented here by critical and creative surveys that Mike Cole (1997) and Peter Sedgwick (1999) offer of that literature, see it as consisting in social structures of hierarchy or disadvantage. The social theorist Albert Memmi (2000) maintains that racism resides in various value judgments unfavorable to a group. I present reasons to reject each of these views, reasons which, I maintain, lend support to an understanding of racism as essentially affective, desiderative, and volitional in its core. I briefly explicate this view and defend it against two objections. I conclude by revisiting Frederickson's account to discuss the progression implicit in the sequence of accounts I treat and the lessons it teaches about what matters morally, and I offer a suggestion about ways to reform social inquiry.

I. RACISM AS INTERGROUP BEHAVIOR

Near the end of his definitive review of racism's varied history, Frederickson (2002: 170) offers the understanding of racism to which, he thinks, his study has led: "Racism exists when one ethnic group or historical collectivity dominates,

I am grateful to many. Lawrence Blum generously shared with me his thinking and writing. He and Lani Guinier, Sally Haslanger, Jeffrey Jones, Glenn Loury, Lionel McPherson, Ifeanyi Menkiti, Martha Minow, Tommie Shelby, David Wilkins, Ajume Wingo, and David Wong provided continuing discussion of related topics. Errors and misinterpretations in this chapter are not theirs, of course. An invitation from this volume's editors, Michael Levine and Tamas Pataki, stimulated my renewed reflection, and they showed patience with my revisions. Boston College generously enabled ample research assistance, particularly that of Michael Formichelli and Jason Taylor.

excludes, or seeks to eliminate another on the basis of differences that it [the first group] believes are hereditary and unalterable." Despite the authority his career of expert scholarship properly commands, I think this account flawed in ways that make it untenable.

We can distinguish several problems. The first is that of reification. Frederickson's account talks of the conditions in which racism "exists," but he does not tell where—that is, in what—it then exists. *What* is racist when racism exists? Is the whole society then racist? Is it only the group that dominates or excludes or seeks to eliminate that is racist? Does Frederickson think that only groups, and not individuals, are and can be racist? If so, his account is plainly implausible and inadequate, for giving us too limited an account. Indeed, we rightly think that we must understand talk of racism's existence in terms of people and things being racist. If not, then does Frederickson think someone S can be racist only if S's group (or some other group) is racist? That too is implausible. Suppose S1 simply wants (what she thinks of as her racial) group G1 to dominate some other group G2. Suppose she even takes steps toward this end, but her efforts are unsuccessful and her preference is never realized. Is what Frederickson's account entails—namely, that S1 wants and attempts racism, but no racism "exists" and therefore she is not herself a racist—really correct? In fact, because there is then no racism—again, none "exists"—it cannot even be true on Frederickson's account that S1 has a racist desire! We want to know when, and in virtue of what, people, actions, preferences, statements, beliefs, and much else are racist, not just when it exists. Frederickson's conception of racism does not do this explicitly, and the answers it suggests are not credible.

Second, if Frederickson is correct in holding that group G1's simply "seek[ing] to eliminate" group G2 suffices for racism, then should not G1's seeking to dominate or exclude G2, rather than G1's actually *succeeding* in dominating or excluding G2, also suffice? If not, why not? What does Frederickson think makes such a crucial difference between eliminating, on the one hand, and dominating or excluding, on the other? He provides no answer and I cannot see any plausible one. That suggests that success is required for racism in either all three projects or in none. There are good grounds to think the latter alternative is true. Actual domination or exclusion by one group over another (normally, that is, successful domination or exclusion) seems not to be necessary for racism. We would count a group's pursuing, longing for, and rejoicing in the prospect of dominating or excluding another group as racism—better, as racist—irrespective of whether their preferences and projects bore fruit. It may not even be sufficient. It is not entirely clear whether accidental or otherwise unintended domination or exclusion by one group of another is even possible. Remember that Frederickson requires that the dominant or excluding group engage in its conduct on a certain (racial) basis. That indicates that they do it for a certain kind of reason, and therefore on purpose, with intent. However, even if unintentional racial domination or exclusion is somehow possible, it should not suffice for racism. It is not enough that exclusions happen to trace a racial divide. As Frederickson's own account indicates, we think it must be more deeply informed by race.

The same goes a fortiori for racism in individuals, for they cannot normally dominate or eliminate whole groups. Moreover, their racism will more commonly be targeted against individuals they think belong to the racial group, not against the group itself. That fact exposes another lacuna in Frederickson's overly socialized conception.

Third, we should remember a fact that Frederickson's account, centered as it is on how racism tends to dominate and exclude, tends to obscure. What matters for racism is not so much what is done, or even what is desired or sought for the targeted group (or some of its members), but *why*, on *what basis*, and *for what ends* it is sought for them. The distinguishing feature of racist persons, societies, projects, actions, institutions, and the like is their viciousness—the malicious, or contemptuous, or callous frame of mind from which they spring.

Fourth, these last considerations should lead us to notice how unjustifiably narrow is the list of what we might call "racist projects" that are internal to Frederickson's account. Why should wanting only domination, exclusion, or elimination be necessary for racism? Ought not group G1's seeking (or just wanting, or wishing for, or delighting in) *other* harms for G2 similarly suffice for racism? And remembering what we said above, ought not *individual* members of G1 (or other groups) wanting ills (as such) for G2 or (various of) its members also suffice? If not, Frederickson owes us some explanation why. All these reflections on Frederickson's account of racism, and the corrections those reflections motivate, urge us toward thinking of racism as consisting chiefly in such vicious mental stances as ill will, disrespect, and unconcern for others on account of their believed race or shaped by it. I return to develop this line of thought below and indicate some of its implications.

II. RACISM AND RECENT CRITICAL THEORY OF CULTURE

In an article in a reference work in so-called cultural studies, summarizing the history and current state of the discussion and proceeding to draw out what he sees as its implications, theorist Michael Cole (1997: 450–51) conceives racism

as entailing a process of racialization whereby social relations between people are structured by the signification of human biological and or cultural characteristics in such a way as to define and construct differentiated social collectivities. Such groups are assumed to have a natural unchanging origin and status. They are seen as inherently different and causing negative consequences for other groups and/or as possessing certain evaluated characteristics [perhaps evaluated positively as well as, or instead of, negatively]. Since these evaluated characteristics are stereotypes they are likely to be distorted and misleading. . . . [T]here is no logical correlation between cognition and action. However, the distinction [between cognition and action] is of limited use . . . because it is only when ideologies are expressed and or actioned [*sic*] that there is any need to attend to them or indeed to worry about them. In order to understand the phenomenon [of racism] it needs to be situated economically, ideologically, historically, and geographically. It takes different forms at different historical conjunctures and is justified in different ways according to different circumstances. Notwithstanding the fact that there are common features to all forms of racism, there is in fact a variety of racisms. . . . Thus the above definition needs to be context-specific.

In a similar reference work, the influential social thinker Peter Sedgwick (1999: 325) states his view, based on his understanding of the direction the discussion has taken in the field.

Racism draws a hierarchical distinction between races, opening a gulf between them and setting one racially designated group over and above another on a scale of worth, intelligence, or importance. A racist ideology, therefore, is constructed on the basis of hierarchical distinctions drawn between different groups. . . . Racism thus embodies the attitude of a rigid and naturalized conception concerning the nature of individuals and groups. Whether or not racism should therefore be defined solely in terms of ideologically constructed attitudes or additionally in terms of the norms and practices of a given society is a matter of some debate.

Similar problems afflict both these accounts. First, both are murky and boil down to claims that racism consists in beliefs or in some complex of beliefs and actions ("practices" in Sedgwick), opening them to the literature's objections to doxastic and behavioral accounts of racism. As for doxastic accounts of racism, we need only note that there is little reason to call someone's believing something racist (save in a counterfactual sense) when she believes it from an innocent epistemic error, independent of any contempt or insensitivity. However, people and their attitudes and actions can be racist if they are so dependent. I point out some problems in behavioral accounts in other writings.[1] There are issues to sort out here, but it is plain that these cultural theoretic accounts introduce little genuinely novel, little that is not subject to the problems identified in

---

1. For more on belief-centered and action-centered conceptions of racism, see the critical discussions of Appiah, Ture and Hamilton, Goldberg, and others in, *inter alia,* Garcia 1997a, 1997b, and 2001b.

other accounts.[2] Second, claims, such as that explicit in Cole, that ideologies matter only when acted on, are ugly and obtuse. Beliefs can matter morally and socially because of the affective, conative (desiderative), and volitional stances they express (and come from) as well as for their results. In fact, the moral significance of actions is plainly derivative, for we condemn them for being ill-intended, malicious, thoughtless, and so on, and praise them for being connected to the opposed mental states. Third, it is unclear whether the racial hierarchy explicitly invoked as essential to racism in Sedgwick's account, and, I think, implicit in Cole's, needs actually to be socially instantiated or may be merely desired or believed in. The latter position is more intuitively appealing, but it approximates and anticipates core claims of an attitudinal account of racism.

Making racism depend on social structures and historical context can have grotesque consequences. Shaylee Ledbetter, a foul-mouthed, thieving, perverted, and incestuous White junkie prostitute in a theatrical fiction, affirms, "I'm not a racist. I just don't like niggers."[3] This is in protest to her brother's charge of racism after she has delivered herself of various contemptuous remarks. Permit me to speculate a bit on the character's psychology. To her, it appears, racism is a complicated matter, a business of widespread ideologies, theories, systems of thought, social meanings, and perhaps of complex social and institutional ar-

2. This may not be true of all those who emphasize the social in their understandings of racism's nature. Haslanger, in chapter 5, deliberately contrasts her social approach to oppression with another approach that is individualistic and emphasizes what she calls "agent oppression." This is not the place for a detailed rebuttal of her position. Suffice it to observe, first, that I see no future for an account of oppression in which there are no agents of the oppression, for oppression is not something that merely exists or happens, but is done and therefore done by some agents. (Haslanger is not consistent on this point, sometimes contrasting "structural oppression" with "agent oppression," but sometimes talking of all oppression as having agents.) The same goes for several other related phenomena whose essentially agentive nature Haslanger only poorly obscures by her use of the passive in talk of being disadvantaged, etc. (Who is doing the mistreating?) Second, Haslanger's position hinges on structural oppression of a race involving "nonaccidental" correlation between disadvantage and race without the oppressive behavior being targeted at harming the race's members, nor grounded in contempt or insensitivity toward them. This strategy, I think, is likewise hopeless. My little desk dictionary defines the accidental as involving lack of intent or foresight and characterized by carelessness. Without pursuing the matter here, we should note that this suggests that the nonaccidental disadvantaging Haslanger emphasizes will involve disadvantage that the agents intend or foresee and that they take care to insure. Contrary to Haslanger's project of rebutting views that, like mine, require vicious malice or contempt or insensitivity for racism, this resort to the nonaccidental will on examination lead right to those mental states.

3. Adam Rabb, *Stone Cold Dead Serious,* act 1; produced at the American Repertory Theater, Cambridge, Mass., February 2002. Ms. Ledbetter seems to mean that she does dislike, even detests, those she so designates.

rangements. In contrast, she seems to see herself merely as voicing her own personal likes and dislikes, loves and hates, independent of any such highfalutin theories or high-level conspiracies, to which she, a figure at the margins of society, may plausibly see herself as in no position to make a contribution even if she were so disposed. An account of racism should show why her presuppositions are incorrect and why it is precisely in the depths of our individual minds, in our fears and choices, our disdain and hatreds, that racism dwells, with the other moral vices there lodged. It is a shame that nowadays many accounts of racism, focusing as they do on ideologies and theories and grand social structures, side with Shaylee when they should be helping to educate her and us about where her assumptions are in error.

III. RACISM AS VALUE JUDGMENT

"Racism is a generalizing definition and valuation of differences, whether real or imaginary, to the advantage of the one defining and employing them, and to the detriment of the one subjected to the act of definition, whose purpose is to justify (social or psychological) hostility or assault." Thus writes the contemporary European social theorist Albert Memmi (2000: 100). He continues, "Heterophobia would designate the many configurations of fear, hate, and aggressiveness that, directed against an other, attempt to justify themselves through different psychological, cultural, social, or metaphysical means, of which racism, in the biological sense is only one instance" (118).

This view is appealing and insightful in viewing Blum's "inferiorizing" beliefs (that is, beliefs that a group is inferior in important ways) as racist in that they rationalize (actual, believed, or desired) victimization (see Blum 2002: 8, 181–82). Still more promising, the second quoted passage suggests that Memmi may conceive racism more as an emotional (and volitional?) matter. Elsewhere, and again below, I suggest we conceive racism as focally a matter of volitions, desires, and hopes. However, Memmi's account is different from, and less appealing than, my own in several ways. (i) It concentrates on the evaluative and doxastic rather than on the volitional, understanding racism as consisting in doxastic, judgmental states and processes (evaluating differences); (ii) it requires racism differentially to distribute beneficial and detrimental effects; and (iii) it assumes that racism is always directed against an other. As I indicated, each of these commitments is problematic. The first serves to exclude from the class of racists such people as the Black-hater who does not bother to rationalize her hatred with beliefs about the supposed inferiority of Black people. (Indeed, some racists may think the targets of their hatred superior to themselves, and hate them precisely from resentment.) The second excludes from it racism that is passive, for one reason or another never issuing in action. Indeed, it excludes even racist action that is merely *unsuccessful* in its aim of harming. The third leaves no room within racism for the type that consists in internalizing as self-hatred an ambient loathing for one's own group.

There is a lesson. We all generalize about people, and need not do anything immoral thereby. The distinguishing marks of racism do not lie in these illative details. Nor ought we reflexively classify as racist someone who loves all people of all races but has a personal favorite among what she thinks to be the human races. She is foolish and dangerous, but not necessarily a racist simply because of her evaluative generalizations. Rather, racism's central forms lie in what a person wants for those assigned to a racial group, and in how she feels about them, what she hopes for them or aims to do to them, and so on.

It is worth remarking at this point that some work in virtue epistemology indicates that beliefs are made epistemically unjustified by being intellectually vicious, infected by some intellectual vice, in their formation (or maintenance). However, the intellectual vices as a class cannot be easily, persuasively, or sharply differentiated from the moral vices. Many intellectual vices share the same name as moral vices—cowardice, pride, diffidence, laziness—and perhaps the same nature as well (see Zagzebski 1996: 137–211). This properly suggests that, if we follow the trail of racist value judgment, we will find ourselves looking for racism's heart in moral vice, that is, in deformations of character, in our dispositions to want, desire, choose, ignore, or neglect what we ought not.

IV. MOTIVATIONAL AND VOLITIONAL CONCEPTIONS OF RACISM

The upshot of our critical discussions of the accounts of racism found in Frederickson, in the cultural theorists Cole and Sedgwick, and in Memmi is that an adequate account of racism needs to attend more to the quality of the racist's motives, aims, decisions, preferences, and so on. In short, to matters of moral virtue and vice. Let me say a bit more about this, sketching an account of racism that moves these matters front and center.

Tzvetan Todorov (1986: 370) claims that racism is "a type of behavior which consists in the display of contempt or aggressiveness toward other people on account of physical differences (other than those of sex) between them and oneself." Thomas Schmid (1996) has similarly proposed what he calls a "motivational approach," which identifies racism in its central, "morally most objectionable" sense as "the infliction of unequal consideration, motivated by the desire to dominate, based on race alone." Both views highlight the morally objectionable factors feeding into someone's behavior. They capture the deep truth in Emmanuel Eze's observation that "racism . . . manifests itself in a refusal to love others . . . .

[R]acism [is] already a sign of our incapacity to love enough" (2001: 179, 180).[4] Indeed, if a view like the ones Todorov and Schmid (and I, below) offer is correct, departure from love, that is, from goodwill, is not just what racism "manifests" or signifies but is.

I have elsewhere (Garcia 1999, 2001b) registered my reservations about details of Schmid's and Todorov's positions.[5] For my purposes here, it will have to suf-

---

4. Counseling that we need to "practic[e] to live in service to a particular future . . . a future where there could be love and care enough for everyone," Eze (2001: 179, 180) asks rhetorically, "Isn't love the cure for hatred?" In my virtues-based view, love is justified not instrumentally, as Eze's language suggests, for its effect on hatred. Rather hatred, malevolence, is morally bad (vicious) in that by its nature it stands in opposition to the virtue of benevolent love. Eze ties his hope for an end to racism to his ideal of a "postracial future," by which he seems to mean a time when people no longer credit racial distinctions. While I agree that race-centered thinking and the recent vogue of racial "identity" are confused both intellectually and morally, I do not hold that racism can end only when racial beliefs are eliminated. Rather what is needed is an end to racial hostility and disregard (and their de-institutionalization).

5. Todorov's position misses other crucial features of racism. The racist's hostility, contempt, or indifference need not be directed to those she deems different from herself. Sometimes, *pace* Todorov, the racist is a person who internalizes the vicious attitudes others feel for her and those classed with her, coming to despise herself and those assigned to the *same* race as she is. Moreover, despite what Todorov says, not just any nonsexual physical difference is such that responding contemptuously to those thought to have it can constitute racism. That would make immoral discrimination on the basis of height, physical disability, and perhaps even age into forms of racism. Rather, the racist must do the thinking that shapes her responses in roughly racial terms—that is, especially, in terms of what are deemed heritable characteristics of skin and hair, etc. as differentiated in ways tied to the major continental land masses. (This holds whether or not, in her more theoretical moments, she denies the reality of race as a biological or cultural category.)

Likewise, Schmid's implicit concession that a less controlled race hater would be a racist seems not to jibe with his view that racism demands a desire to "dominate" (indeed, a desire put into practice in the form of unequal treatment); for even if hatred always involves some desire to harm, it need not be anything so extreme. More important, Schmid does not adequately or consistently explain why racism is immoral. He locates racism's immorality in its "opposition to the principle of human equality," among whose "elements" are both a "perception of all humans as essentially equal" and a "willingness to extend to all humans and human groups the same basic rights." However, it is unclear that one can properly talk, as Schmid does, of principles demanding that we perceive this or that. Belief is not so fully under our immediate control as that seems to require, although a person may be vicious—not just epistemically but morally—in allowing herself to develop certain cognitive habits. Besides, Schmid wants to distinguish the real, immoral racist from someone who innocently comes to hold ugly racial beliefs. However, contrary to what Schmid's distinction needs, even the "merely cognitive racist" will violate his principle of equality simply by perceiving some as unequal. (For more on these thinkers, see Garcia 1999 and 2001b.)

fice to point out two. First, contrary to a central features in both views, it seems counterintuitive to maintain that racism need find expression in behavior. We ordinarily think the person who feels racial hostility, contempt, or indifference is already marked with racism whether or not she "display[s]" it behaviorially. Second, any such account needs to tell us more about how they explain the wider range of racist phenomena, how not just individual actions but also feelings, beliefs, persons, social practices, and institutions are related.

In a series of papers over the last decade, I have urged an account of racism as vicious ways of falling short in regard to the moral virtue of benevolence. This account retains factors of the sort that are motivational in Schmid's and Todorov's positions, but without their presupposition, which we saw to be problematic, that racism requires that racial contempt, desire to dominate, and the like actually motivate action. What matters for racism is that someone's preferences, dislikes, and choices be of a certain sort, whether or not they lead to action, let alone successful action. Here I wish to stress, as I have not before, the character of the benevolence to which the chief forms of racism stand in opposition. The interpersonal moral virtue is a distinctively *human* benevolence, one grounded in recognition and appreciation of any human person's status and dignity as a person. Thus, a person who genuinely is benevolently disposed toward people, in the ways in which benevolence constitutes moral virtue, is someone who wishes them well. She wishes every one of them each of a variety of central and distinctive human goods, goods whose possession enhances and helps them realize the fuller humanity of their lives. Turning against any of these goods, or treating someone's possession of any of them as a light matter, beneath pursuit, is to respond to the relevant person and the good so inadequately as to constitute moral vice. This is an important fact to keep in mind, as it will play a significant role below in our effort to understand certain kinds of racial paternalism, both in their relation to racism and in their immorality.

Racism, at its core, then, consists in racial disregard, including disrespect, or most gravely, in ill will. Racially based or racially informed disregard (or ill will) is an indifference (or opposition) to another's welfare on account of the racial group to which she is assigned.[6] Since, so conceived, racism is primarily a mat-

---

6. An intriguing related question, raised for me by Blum, is whether racists have to believe in races. It seems to me that, just as someone could make a racial classification without realizing (and even while denying) that she is doing so, someone could make a racial classification while sincerely denying that there really are races. So perhaps someone who is what we might call an "antiracialist" (a disbeliever in races) could still be a racist. I return to this briefly below.

Eze agrees that racism can involve either ill will or insufficient goodwill. He holds that the opposition to moral care that constitutes racism may take the form of either commission or omission—it is commissive when someone "actively seeks to exclude" and omissive when she restricts her care to those she views as her own kind (Eze 2001: 179). I here call this

ter of what a person does or does not wish, will, and want for others in light of their race—the contents of her will, broadly conceived—I call it a volitional conception of racism.

Such a view helps explain the range of potentially racist phenomena. Actions, beliefs, projects, hopes, wishes, institutions, and institutional practices are all racist insofar as they are informed by racial hostility or disregard. This account also makes manifest why the term "racism" is properly pejorative. The ill will or disregard that constitutes racism is inherently contrary to the moral virtues of benevolence and justice, and often to others as well. The vice may be conscious or unconscious. Perhaps I do not realize that what motivates me, when I let the elevator you are riding pass and wait for the next, is the fact that riding with someone of (what I take to be) your race troubles me. Still less may I see that this troubles me because of stereotypes I have internalized to soothe my conscience as I benefit from the exploitation of your group. Racism is thus always and inherently wrong, and wrong for the same basic reason in every instance.

The sort of view I have proposed locates racism, like other forms of moral viciousness, in the hearts of individuals—in their likes and dislikes, their hopes and wants, their preferences and choices. Racists are *against* those assigned to a certain race. Notice I do not say simply those *of* a certain race: I leave open the vexed question of whether race is real. What matters is that racial assignments are real. These classifications may be conscious or unconscious, and they may be made by the racist herself or by others to whose classification she defers, reluctantly or not, with or without awareness. That someone declares, and even believes, that there are no races does not exempt her from racism. Whether she is a racist depends on how she, in fact, classifies and responds internally to those classifications, her theoretical convictions notwithstanding.

What makes someone a racist is her disregard for, or even hostility to, those assigned to the targeted race, disregard for their needs and well-being. She is racist when and insofar as she is hostile to or cares nothing (or too little) about some people because of their racial classification. So conceiving racism thus allows for the possibility, implicitly denied by some accounts of racism, that someone may be racist against her own group.[7] The phenomenon of racism internalized as self-hatred is too tragic a one to pretend it is impossible. Similarly, this conception of racism allows that the weak, the powerless, even the oppressed, can be racists, unlike some accounts, which treat personal or group power as a precondition for racism. Poor, marginalized White skinheads who hate Black people in order to feel good about themselves can be racists, as can poor, marginalized Black people

---

omissive type of racism "disregard" and understand this sort of viciously insufficient goodwill to include modes of disrespect, which offend against the virtue of justice. Disrespect can also figure in acts of ill will by removing or weakening appropriate side constraints.

7. See Todorov 1986 and the discussion below of the position taken therein.

filled with rage against Asians because of perceived slights by a local storekeeper, as can poor, marginalized Asians or American Indians embittered against those at, above, or below their own social or economic level. Neither high income nor social power is a precondition for racism.

It is important to remember that hate and callous indifference (like love) are principally matters of *will* and desire: what does one want, what would one choose, for those assigned to this or that race? Those who fail to act—because of lack of power, opportunity, or for other reasons—can nevertheless be racists. The view taken here has this advantage over accounts that see racism exclusively in personal or institutional *conduct,* or as dependent on such behavior and its success. As we saw, such views give a pass, for example, to the isolated race hater, alone in her room, longing for the oppression of the Black people she sees outside her window, who are beginning to prosper. It is absurd to think that if and when, contrary to her wishes, such a system of oppression ceases to exist, then she *eo ipso* ceases to be a racist. It is no less absurd to think she cannot be racist because, in her isolation, she cannot take effective action against Black people and her longing to do so is frustrated. We thus avoid some conceptual confusions that plague attempts to understand racism as a social system or as a form of behavior. Similarly, our old woman can be a racist even if she never rationalizes her hostility by coming to believe that Black people are her moral or intellectual inferiors. Thus, our account avoids the error of the large number of theorists (not just Memmi, but also thinkers from Ruth Benedict to Dinesh D'Souza) who identify racism with a belief, ideology, theory, or doctrine.[8] On the contrary, racism is chiefly what a recent religious intervention called it: "a *sin.*"[9] It is a form of moral viciousness. It is correct to insist, as some have, that racism need not involve immoral intentions.[10] However, it must involve immoral mental (that is, intentional) states, and often it involves, more specifically, states of intending someone some evil or of failing to intend someone a good. It is, thus, an offense against the moral virtues of benevolence and justice.

8. See Garcia 1997a for examples and further criticism of those espousing views of each of these kinds.

9. "Racism is a sin. It is fundamentally a lie, a concept deliberately invented to create division in humanity" (Holy See 2001: 1). The claim that racism is a lie may be a crude statement of the view that it consists in false beliefs. I think this misstates the way in which racism is a sin, what sort of immorality it chiefly involves. Later, the document talks more promisingly of "racist attitudes and racist practices" (4). I am in full agreement with the statement that racism's elimination awaits "a fruitful interaction of peoples founded on equitable, just, and fraternal relations in solidarity" (2).

10. "Racism may be intentional or unintentional. . . . [R]acism may involve a complex array of mental states some of which are intentional and some of which are unintentional" (Corlett 1998: 31) Similar claims are common; see, for example, Haslanger's essay in this volume.

Racism, we have said, is not, and need not involve, action. However, many actions—both individual and institutional, discursive and nondiscursive—are racist. Action and beliefs are racist on the basis of their input, not their output: they must come to exist or be sustained in the right ways by racist desiderative, volitional, or affective attitudes. Despite what many say, nothing is made to be racist simply by its effects.[11] (Indeed, I should make the same claim if we replaced the term "racist" by any other basic term of moral approbation or disapprobation.) The bigot who rationalizes her racial disregard or contempt by accepting doctrines of racial inferiority holds racist beliefs. So, too, does someone whose antipathy stems from her antecedent belief in one race's inferiority. She is racist in holding them; it is racist of her to think like that. Similarly, her behavior is racist when it emerges from those racist feelings, desires, and choices *directly,* as when she tries to harm someone because the latter is deemed Black (or Red or White or Yellow). It is also racist when it emerges *indirectly,* as when she discriminates on the basis of beliefs she holds to rationalize her racial hostility. This is also true of speech acts. Like other actions, they are racist when they stem directly or indirectly from racial antipathy or disregard.[12]

As racism may seep outward from an individual's heart to pollute her behavior, so it may go on to infect the conduct of an institution as well. Racist attitudes and beliefs and behavior may become *institutionalized.* While racism is chiefly a sin, it may come to inhabit what Pope John Paul II calls "structures of sin."[13] This relationship can become reciprocal as racist structures strengthen and perpetuate the (noncognitive) racist attitudes that gave rise to them. Thus, the volitional/desiderative/emotive conception of racism advanced here—in contrast to views of racism as social practices or as discriminatory deeds or as types of judgment—can explain how each of these phenomena came to be racist.

My view largely fits that of a joint statement on racism, issued by a group of interreligious leaders: (i) "*Racism is a problem of the heart* and *an evil* that must

11. See my critique of Goldberg's claims in Garcia 2001b and of Ezorsky's in Garcia 1999.

12. We should acknowledge a general problem that input-sensitive accounts like mine face. We might say that an act is racist when it is "prompted by a racist motive" (Blum 2002: 14; see also 2, 8–10, 14–16). Unfortunately, problems arise from some nonstandard motivational chains. What if my racism prompts me to do things to become more racially sensitive and benevolent? Those acts are motivated by my racism, but not in such a way as to be themselves racist. (Similar problems arise for other virtue and vice terms, of course.) Perhaps we do better to use such verbs as "express," "epitomize," or "embody," instead of such causal ones as "prompt" to note this point and help avoid absurd implications. Not just *any* motivational or causal relationship will do for our purposes, but only those that proceed along certain paths, which paths we can often recognize but are difficult clearly to demarcate, delineate. The problem is a familiar one in philosophy, similar to that of the "wayward causal paths" that bedevil some accounts of intentional action.

13. See Pope John Paul II's 1987 encyclical letter "Solicitudo Rei Socialis."

be eradicated from . . . *institutional structures.*"[14] This view of racism as chiefly a moral deformation—located in the heart's desires, choices, and hopes, but also infecting social institutions—closely matches my own. However, the statement's authors also say: (ii) "Racism is *learned behavior* that is rooted in ignorance and fear," and they condemn (iii) "denigrating, disrespecting, or oppressing people based on the color of their skin or their ethnicity or their culture." This second passage may suggest that racism is not a matter of feelings and choice but of (presumably external) behavior, which I deny. However, the authors probably mean that racism leads to such behavior, not that it consists in conduct, since the third quotation appears to include "denigration" and "disrespect" within racism, and they are certainly mental states in their origin, not forms of external behavior.[15]

14. National Conference for Community and Justice, statement for the year 2000, available from the NCCJ Washington office; italics added here and below.

15. Though I make no detailed response in this essay to Blum's critique of my volitional view of racism (see chapter 3), perhaps I should point out here that I do not make the sharp distinction between justice and benevolence he seems to presuppose. I should state my view that the gap between justice and benevolence is greatly exaggerated nowadays, fueled perhaps by Kant's misleading image of love bringing people closer together and justice driving them apart. For our purposes, it is important just to point out the interrelation between racism's offenses against benevolence and its offenses against justice, and the connection between acting with viciously insufficient benevolence (even with malevolence) and acting unjustly. Plainly, the forms of action to which racism most characteristically leads are not only contrary to benevolence but also to justice. Discrimination, even lynching, offends not just benevolence but also justice, for the goods that the racist tries to strip from her victim are ones the victim is entitled to have anyone seek to protect. The sort of goodwill toward a human being that constitutes moral virtue is willing her the human goods, the things that enhance human life; and respect and limited autonomy certainly belong within their number. There can be no fully virtuous benevolence toward a human person that is not also characterized by the deference and respect for her dignity that is properly seen as foundational to justice. Likewise, racist acts against justice are acts of disrespect for the victim's moral status and human dignity. Respect, however, is neither a mere feeling nor a matter simply of believing that the other has that status. It crucially involves a characteristic disposition of the will, a willingness to defer to the other. This amounts to the just agent's willing the other person the good of some limited autonomy, i.e., self-management; it requires benevolence. More important, injustice, *qua* disrespect, involves a vicious departure from the virtue of benevolence. I cannot see how someone could respect another precisely in virtue of her dignity as a human being without also wishing to see her well-being advanced. More can be said about the general connection between justice and goodwill, of course. Whatever conceptual differences may distinguish benevolence for justice, I should think that what violates justice will normally therein offend against benevolence, and vice versa. So, I make less than Blum over my failure sometimes to say explicitly that disrespect, and thus injustice, counts as the kind of insufficiency of regard that is vicious, and sometimes racist. In sum, for our purposes here, we will not go far wrong, I think, if we say that racism is a

V. PROBLEMS FOR VOLITIONAL ACCOUNTS

Broadly volitional understandings of racism have drawn criticism. I will not here dwell on criticisms directed specifically against my own account.[16] Rather, I will discuss the implications of claims otherwise directed within the literature.

The legal scholar Harlon Dalton (1996: 92–93) entertains a view like mine but rejects it. After asking, "What does racism mean?" he suggests, "One view—perhaps the most common—centers on race-based animosity and disdain. Racism [thus viewed] equals disliking others (or regarding them as inferior) because of their race." He repudiates this "most common" understanding on the grounds, first, of its purported "indifference to hierarchy and social structure," which he thinks requires one to say that an imaginary White-hating Rodney King "would be just as guilty of racism as the white officers who beat him." Dalton explains that his complaint is that such a view "ignores material consequences," which, he thinks, morally differentiates "fox and hound, that is, relevantly distinguishes hatred in those below for those on top from hatred in those on top for those on the bottom." Moreover, he worries that such an account identifying racism as "race-based animosity or disdain" cannot capture the racism of people "who have no malice in their hearts but nevertheless act in ways that create and reproduce racist hierarchies." For Dalton, "racism consists in culturally acceptable ideas, beliefs, and attitudes that serve to sustain the racial pecking order."

It is not hard to see where both Dalton's criticism and his advocacy go wrong. That Black and White racists are both racists does not mean that their racism is equally bad, nor does it imply that there is no moral difference between the conduct of one who performs racist actions and the conduct of one who does nothing. Suppose you steal Mary's nail file and I steal her purse. You are just as guilty of theft as I am, but not guilty of as bad a theft. The moral difference, to be sure,

---

kind of ill will or disregard that constitutes an offense against the virtues of both benevolence and justice.

Perhaps I may also add at this point that, contrary to what Blum suggests, I have always held and affirmed that any human, any person, has such dignity and is so linked to us that benevolence toward her is moral virtue and its lack or insufficiency is therefore moral vice. Tying virtues to roles, as I do, need not exclude any from the circle of human caring. Everyone ought to feel and show benevolence to everyone, in my view, as I think my writings in general moral theory make clear.

16. See the essays by Blum, Haslanger, Levine, and Pataki in this volume, as well as by Shelby (2002). Charles Mills (2002) extends some criticisms of what he sees as my positive view of racism, though his main project is rebutting my criticisms of his book. (The thrust of his response is to explain how the racial contract, while "real," "historical," and "explanatory," nevertheless is "nonexistent" and "hypothetical." Needless to say, this doesn't succeed, though Mills does show that he is not alone among devotees of contract in wanting thus to have things both ways.)

is not that of "material consequences." However, if I could reasonably foresee that my theft would cause Mary substantial inconvenience, loss, and distress, and did it anyway, that shows a more vicious indifference to her welfare, added on to the offense against the virtues of justice and goodwill involved in both your and my intentionally taking something whose taking violated her rights. Contrary to what Dalton suggests, it is not merely what happens to ensue that aggravates my offense, but my vicious callousness to the likely effect. These considerations also allow us to see some of the problems in Dalton's preferred account of racism. Mere causation is without moral import, and there is no reason to impute racism to agents or acts that merely happen to worsen things racially. What is crucial is whether these contributions are intended (stem from "malice in the heart") and, if not, whether they nevertheless manifest some other morally vicious attitude— indifference to likely suffering, disrespect or contempt for those affected, and so forth. Dalton's view threatens (indeed, seems designed) entirely to absolve from racism race haters, White or Black, who are inactive, ineffective, socially in the minority, culturally marginal, or loners. In fact, it implies that if enough of you stop being racists so that my racism stops being "culturally acceptable," then my racism automatically disappears along with yours, though I and my attitudes remain exactly the same. Finally, it seems that someone who seeks, or merely hopes for, a "racial pecking order" is a racist independently of Dalton's require- ment that she enjoy success in efforts she may direct to that end. (That is, she is racist at times *prior* to her success, *after the end* of the racial hierarchy she de- sires, and in situations where success *never* comes to her, perhaps because, for one reason or another, she never moves from wanting such hierarchy to pursu- ing it actively.)

Certain queries can also help highlight certain difficulties besetting Dalton's critique in ways that draw us back to an account more focused, like mine, on in- tentions formed or spurned. With respect to the first of his complaints against volitional accounts, we can ask why we ought think that it is *actual* hierarchy that crucially matters, rather than a person's *attitude toward* hierarchy. Concerning his second criticism, we can ask: If material consequences are unsought, unfore- seen, unforeseeable, why ought we to think them pertinent? And what of inef- fectual or counterproductive acts of racial hatred or disregard? Regarding his third objection to volitional views, we can ask: Why should we deem acts racist simply on the basis of their effects, when these effects are not just unintended but precisely counterproductive to those aimed at? Should we blithely follow Dalton to the implicit conclusion that to determine who and what is racist, we must always wait (how long? one wonders) to see how things turn out? I decline that invitation.

Henry Louis Gates Jr. raises an important objection to Todorov's under- standing of racism, according to which it consists in "a type of behavior . . . dis- play[ing] contempt or aggressiveness" (1986: 370). Gates (1986: 403) dismisses such views as Todorov's (and, by implication, mine) because he thinks history provides plentiful "examples of 'racist' benevolence, paternalism, and sexual attraction which are not always, or only, dependent upon contempt or aggressiveness."

Here the conspicuous array of qualifiers is what matters. Notice, for example, that Gates himself feels the need to put the term "racist" in scare quotes, as if aware that his talk of "racist benevolence" is paradoxical. Likewise, J. Corlett is careful twice to put scare quotes around the term "benevolence" when he talks of "'benevolence'-based racism."[17] Observe, also, that Gates realizes that he needs to show not merely that there has been racist paternalism and lust, but that there have been instances of it that were not derivative from the vicious sentiments on which Todorov's account of racism and mine focus.[18] This last, however, cannot be so easily read off from the historical record and is doubtful on its face. After all, paternalism implies treating another like a child, and regarding a responsible, mature adult as one would a child bespeaks forms of disdain and disrespect that are plainly contrary to the virtue of goodwill.[19] Anyone who rejects the extreme consequentialist doctrine that the end can always justify the means will recognize that some actions that are good in their ultimate intentions are nonetheless wrong in their means. Thus, an input- and intention-centered account of racism, such as the virtues-based one offered here, can allow that the paternalist may be racist precisely in her adopting infantilizing, disrespectful means to her (putatively) protective, benevolent goal.

The paradox we alluded to in Gates is thus clarified. Benevolence, which is virtue, can never simply be racism, which is vicious. Even allowing that our paternalist is benevolent in her ultimate goal, however, underdetermines the relevant question of whether she acts with some disregard that offends against the virtues of goodwill. When, on account of race, she adopts arrogant, haughty, self-important, supercilious, and manipulative treatment toward another, even in

17. "Racism can be motivated, jointly or separately, by hatred, perceived inferiority, 'benevolence,' perceived superiority, fear, and power. . . . Yet another basis for racism is ideological dogmatism" (Corlett 1998: 28; see also 29). It is interesting that in this list of purported bases for racism, Corlett qualifies only one, "benevolence," with scare quotes, therein implicitly acknowledging that there is something problematic in something's being both racist and benevolent, and thus that racism is incompatible with benevolence in the unqualified, literal sense.

18. Gates also insists that racist benevolence is not "only" dependent on vicious attitudes, but this is just a distraction. Obviously, it may have many sources. The issue is whether such benevolence is always in part informed by vicious attitudes, for, if it is, a sophisticated version of a position like Todorov's or mine is vindicated, since internal moral vice would remain the core of racism.

19. The morality of paternalism is a difficult matter, but I attempt a treatment of racist paternalism also in Garcia 1996.

pursuit of what she perceives as the latter's good, she manifests the kind of moral vice that brands her actions racist.[20]

VI. CONCLUSION: WHY CARE?

I have discussed understanding racism as forms of social structure, as certain value judgments, and as vices of preference, affection, and will. I also delineated problems in each such account. I suggested that this volitional account of racism, according to which racism in its heart consists in race-based disregard or contempt (in which an action is racist in the principal sense of that term when it expresses such a stance), can explain how both individuals and institutions, and both attitudes and conduct, can be racist. Recognition of this fact could, I think, change and improve our thinking about racial matters. Some, especially on the political Left, pride themselves nowadays on deeming personal racist sentiments insufficient for racism and even insignificant.[21]

People who think that the real problem of racism resides in comparative holdings or representation among socioeconomic elites similarly delude themselves with the comforting illusion that racism lies out there, somewhere in externalities. That is not to say that there is no institutionalized racism.[22] What it does is de-center institutions in favor of people, their minds, and their interpersonal relationships. Frederickson, with whom we began, looks to the causes of historical effects. This approach, though understandable, especially in a historian, tempts the social thinker to identify racism with whatever causes the salient effects that interest her and only with what causes them. It is a short step from this to Frederickson's conception of racism: "My theory or conception of racism . . . has two components: difference [more precisely, differentiation] and power. It [racism] originates from a mind-set that regards 'them' as different from 'us' in ways that are permanent and unbridgeable. This sense of difference provides a motive or rationale for using our power advantage for treating the ethnoracial Other in ways that we would regard as cruel or unjust if applied to members of our own group" (2002: 9).[23]

The difficulties that, I hope to have shown, afflict any account of this sort, not

20. My discussion here follows that in Garcia 2001b.

21. For a summary and discussion of one such position, Benjamin DeMott's, see Garcia 1999.

22. Haslanger suggests that I discredit institutional racism (see chapter 5). In fact, I have never denied that racism is sometimes institutionalized; I have repeatedly affirmed it and have criticized thinkers who pretend institutional racism does not exist. Among many places, see especially my criticism of D'Souza's position in Garcia 1999.

23. This preliminary account eventually issues in the final, summary understanding of when "racism exists," the one stressing social structures, that Frederickson offers in his book's appendix and that I analyzed in section I above.

only Frederickson's but also those of the cultural theorists, seems to me to arise from at least two sources. The first is a failure to think conceptually. In chapter 5 of this volume Haslanger insists that social philosophy needs to be informed by empirical study of history and society. Maybe she is correct. It is, however, no less true, and in fact more important, that sociohistorical studies need careful conceptual reflection if they are to keep the contingent actualities that are found empirically from being mistaken for defining and essential features. Frederickson is aware of this temptation besetting the empiricist and tries to correct for it by broadening the range of his most recent book's inquiry to include forms of racism that characterized different times and places.[24]

Unfortunately, as we saw, Frederickson and others continue to defend accounts of racism that are too narrow in some ways and too broad in others, because the examples on which they are based remain limited to those that are historically salient.[25] These theorists do not consider the broader possibilities that are conceptually and logically open. We cannot adequately grasp what racism is, in what it consists, until we consider not only what it has been and how it has been experienced, but also what it might have been and could be in situations and experiences quite different from those familiar to us. I have sometimes deployed fanciful scenarios in arguing my case. Far from being embarrassed by this, I wish to insist such reflection is indispensable to achieve the much-needed liberation of social inquiry from its distorting and enervating thralldom to the empirical.

A second source of error may lie in the tendency in today's social inquiry to depreciate or misunderstand moral features. In fact, in the sequence of analyses treated here—which emphasize and focus on, first, social structures, then on value judgments, and finally on vice—I think we can discern a movement from the outside to the inside and also a progression from the shallower to the deeper, from what is morally peripheral to what is central. Appiah, discussing Frederickson's recent book, is driven to pose the crucial question *why* racism is "wrong" (immoral). Is it, he asks, because of (i) the racists' hatred and contempt, (ii) their epistemic irrationality, (iii) the bad treatment to which these lead, (iv) the anti-individualistic way in which racists take account of their race in regarding peo-

24. Frederickson (2002: 157) chastises himself, for example, for earlier identifying racism with efforts to maintain hierarchy. This claim, formed under the influence of his close studies of the recent American past, he now sees as too narrow, in that it excluded forms of racism, found in other times and places, that sought not merely to subordinate but utterly to destroy targeted races and their members. "When I myself [in earlier works] defined the essence of racism as the ideas, practices, and institutions associated with a rigid form of hierarchy, I was unwittingly privileging the white supremacist variant [of racism] over the antisemitic form [which seeks to exile and even exterminate]."

25. More surprisingly, these accounts, undone by their empiricism, are also sometimes too abstract, as when Frederickson (2002) purports to tell us when "racism exists" but never specifies in what it exists (that is, *what* is racist when racism "exists").

ple, or (v) the fact that racism operates through "law and social life" to some people's disadvantage? (Appiah 2002: 11). Two explanations, (ii) and (iv), concentrate on what is central to epistemology but not to ethics. It is difficult to justify a moral theory stressing such epistemic matters as how someone reasons or thinks about others, except insofar as the ways involve treating them disrespectfully.

In contrast, (iii) and (v) stress external results, not internal cognitive states and processes. Any such approach goes astray because it cannot avoid misconstruing racism as whatever it is that has certain undesirable effects. It is easy to show that this construction cannot be adequate. First, the undesirable effects of an action, policy, or structure may be merely aleatory. Yet nothing is racist simply by chance. It follows that its bad effects are not sufficient for something to be racist.[26] Second, undesirable effects that an agent expects or prefers or intends in a course of action can be blocked, not just by chance but sometimes also in ways that an expert familiar with the situation could predict. Yet it remains vicious, and racist, of anyone to expect, prefer, or intend certain bad effects. So, bad effects that actually occur are not necessary for some people and their and mental phenomena to be racist. Third, by their nature as contingent concomitants, undesirable effects of individual or social actions cannot explain why racism has to be immoral (at least, *prima facie*).[27] Nor can they well explain even why racism is always (in fact, in this world) immoral.

26. Aware of this problem, Haslanger resorts to insisting that the bad effects she thinks sufficient to render some social practices racist must be "nonaccidental" (see chapter 5). Whether or not this move is desperate, it is doomed. We can see this in two ways. Dictionaries say that what is accidental is either unintended or unexpected. If Haslanger, in saying that the undesirable effects must be "nonaccidental," means they cannot be unintended then she is committed to holding that they must be intended, and thus joins my side in rooting racism in volitional phenomena, though I would not say racist actions are always viciously intended. To avoid that, she must hold that the requisite effects are unexpected. However, Haslanger would still need to offer adequate explanation of why this epistemic phenomenon has such moral significance. Suffice it to say that she cannot do this save by noting how undertaking a course of action expecting such harmful results for others manifests a disregard or lack of respect for them. Likewise, we can note that the chief charges we should raise against someone who acts expecting bad results are that she and her action are either negligent or reckless. In an important discussion, White (1985, chap. 7) argues that both notions derive from, and need explication in terms of, the concept of care. Reckless actions, we can say, adapting his position, show insufficient care, and negligent ones indicate insufficient taking care. He distinguishes these but, I think, exaggerates the difference. He himself observes that "sometimes we take care because we do care" (1985: 93). More important, failure to take care matters morally when and because it reveals a failure adequately to care. What is important is that, again contra Haslanger, the epistemic state takes on its moral significance from the affective/volitional ones behind it.

27. Shelby (2002) denies that racism need be even presumptively immoral, but any such denial is implausible.

Only (i), a view that, like the one advanced here, focuses on individual states of will, preference, and affection is one that highlights what is morally central. That is because caring, respect, regard, and the like are definitive of human personhood and of the modes of personal response due it. Of course, those mental states and events are also the engines of human agency. We cannot pursue the fuller moral theory here, but this approach can help provide us an answer to one of the things we might mean in asking, Why care? We morally ought to care for others in that such attitudes are the ground of the modes of personal and interpersonal relationship that constitute and configure our moral lives. If so, then racism is primarily of moral import not because of what it causes but because of what it originally is: a deformation in someone's affective and volitional stance toward others.

Appiah concludes, against Frederickson, that we need such an account of racism, one focused more on matters of heart than on beliefs.[28] Here and elsewhere I have tried to show how the volitional view is comprehensive, explaining how and why supporting or participating in certain practices, deciding on or engaging in certain actions, and holding certain beliefs (including making some value judgments) can all be racist, and therein immoral, insofar as they are infected by racist, and therein vicious, attitudes toward other people.

Even if there is reason to regret hatred, ought we nevertheless focus our social effort on changing social practices rather than on changing attitudes? Modifying the effects of social practices may be comparatively easy to effectuate.[29]

28. "There is a deeper difficulty here, that the attitudes Frederickson stresses are, as he says, 'sets of beliefs' about the immutable awfulness of other races, rather than hostile feelings toward them. But . . . at least as important in the everyday life of racism are the deep feelings of revulsion, hostility, contempt, or just plain hatred that many racists feel. As . . . Garcia has put it, racism lives more in the heart than in the head" (Appiah 2002: 12). This is an especially gracious remark of Appiah's, in light of the fact that I explicitly develop my volitional approach as an improvement over the doxastic one that he himself had earlier offered. See Garcia 1996.

In fairness to Frederickson, we should note that whatever the problems in his account of what racism is, he does find it salient that the racist treats certain people in ways she would find it "cruel or unjust" to have her own people treated (Frederickson 2002: 9). That closely approximates my claim that racism entails some vicious disregard or disrespect. As for Appiah's reading of my own position, more broadly than he suggests, my account focuses as much on volitional states as on "feelings" (or on preferences) and, more narrowly than he suggests, I think the will of *anyone* who is a racist in the word's central senses must be in a vicious state, not just that "many" are.

29. Note that altering the *effects* of social practices need not even involve changing the practices themselves. We can sometimes alter effects of a certain type simply by *adding* some forces to block the efficacy of what remains inclined to cause them, whether on a case-by-case or practice-by-practice basis, or more systemically.

However, it will be difficult to *motivate* such social change, let alone sustain it, without also achieving more difficult, deeper changes within persons. The social change is thus *unstable,* and it is also morally and politically *inadequate.* Justice requires more than mere nonviolation of rights to receive various material goods. We can see justice is itself founded in the recognition and appreciation of human dignity, status, personhood. The right to respect is often and rightly regarded as foundational even within liberal individualism. In traditions that conceive justice as community and social comity, the inadequacy of changing mere effects is still more obvious.

The volitional, vice-and-virtue-driven account of racism can stand on its merits. It and the sort of methodology that I have employed in its support can, however, hold larger promise. Social inquiry, particularly into race, in addition to being mired in the empirical in the ways I have suggested, has, when it reached the theoretical, usually had recourse to airy discourse about genders, classes and their supposed struggles, social identities, "materialism," and similar theoretical flights. My hope is that focus on mental and moral realities can offer a more sober counterpoint to these speculations. The current moral campaign against terrorist hate groups has resurrected the language of evil, unfashionable till quite recent days, the battle against which pits not just some people and regimes against others, but every society and every heart against itself. There is, then, some basis for hope that the new century's serious political thought, in intrasocial inquiry as well as international affairs, will outgrow the specters of nineteenth- and twentieth-century social thought and return to these ancient and deep realities: the struggle against evil (even if not simply *by* the good), the primacy of the internal over the external, and the need to cultivate love and respect for persons, to understand and appreciate their value. It can be tempting to hate or depreciate others, a nice shortcut to utilize them merely as means to our ends, as if they were not people but things. Things would be simpler, easier, if racism and our racial problem lay only in social structures and their operation, in faulty generalization, and inaccurate assessments of value. The hard fact and the real problem is that they reside within the states of will, desire, and affection that ground our personhood and hold the power also to deform it.

3 : WHAT DO ACCOUNTS
OF "RACISM" DO?

Quite extraordinary confusion continues to surround the notion of racism.
K. A. Appiah rightly noted in his influential "Racisms" that "we see it everywhere,
but rarely does anyone stop to say what it is, or to explain what is wrong with it"
(1990: 3). Philosophers and social theorists have subsequently risen to Appiah's
challenge, producing several accounts. However, the first part of Appiah's statement does not seem correct. Many people do not see "racism everywhere." In
much popular consciousness, racism is something that mostly ended with the
civil rights legislation of the 1960s, and with the well-documented decline in
whites' belief in the biological inferiority of blacks since the 1950s (Schuman et
al. 1997: 156–57). Dinesh D'Souza's 1995 best seller, *The End of Racism,* captures
the spirit of this view, and Stephan and Abigail Thernstrom's 1997 *America in
Black and White* attempts to document in great detail a decline in racism.

Yet this development renders Appiah's challenge even more acute. Is there in
fact such extreme empirical disagreement between those who see racism everywhere and those who think it has largely disappeared? Or do the two sides mean
something different by "racism," and so do not really disagree?

The need to gain some clarity about the meaning of "racism" is further reinforced by the generally severe opprobrium attached to it. Outside the avowedly
racist right-wing fringe, almost everyone agrees that racism is a very bad thing,
and "a racist" an extremely bad thing to be.

At the same time, the terms "racist" and "racism" have come to be our primary, and often the sole, means of naming race-related evils or wrongfulness.
This was not always so. It is useful to remember that before the 1920s and 1930s
the word "racism" was never used.[1] Outrages perpetrated against blacks and Native populations in the United States, in colonies in Africa, in Latin America, and
elsewhere were not called racist. They were condemned in other terms. For example, in 1830 the black abolitionist David Walker drew on an array of moral ter-

I am grateful to Sally Haslanger and the editors of this volume for insightful comments on
an earlier draft.

1. George Frederickson (2002: 156) dates the first uses of the term "racism" to the 1920s.
Scholars have agreed in crediting Magnus Hirschfeld's 1933 book *Rassismus* (published in
English in 1938 as *Racism*) as the first book to use the term in its title.

minology to express his outrage at slavery. Colored people under slavery were "wretched, degraded, abject"; white perpetrators of slavery were "ten times more cruel, avaricious, and unmerciful" than the "heathens" they professed to condemn (Walker 2000: 134–35). Lynching and segregation were severely denounced as race-based murder, violation of human dignity, oppression, subordination, the maintenance of unjust and undeserved privilege based on race, and the like. But the word "racism" was not part of that arsenal of moral condemnation.

Indeed, the term "racism" was coined by European social scientists in response to the rise of Nazism, and it was not until the 1960s that it came into general use in the United States in relation to the treatment of blacks. Why is this important? After all, racism could have existed before the term "racism" was coined, just as gravity existed before Sir Isaac Newton named it.

But racism is not analogous to gravity. It was not just that Newton invented the word for gravity; he invented the idea that there was a natural force drawing bodies (entities with mass) toward one another. By contrast, Walker did not lack a full understanding of the moral wrongfulness of slavery as a racial institution. He just did not name that wrongfulness "racism." It is not clear what calling it "racism" adds to the moral understanding that Walker already possessed.

It is useful to recall the prehistory of the term "racism" in order to recognize that we have historically possessed the linguistic resources to condemn many forms of wrongfulness related to race without using the word "racism" and without thereby incurring any diminution of understanding. This is useful because we have become so wedded to the terms "racist" and "racism" that, to many people, it is virtually unintelligible to speak meaningfully of something going wrong in the arena of race without calling it "racism." It seems to many people that this is the *only* way we can condemn racial wrongfulness.

We should, I think, be struck by the irony that a term that was scarcely used before the 1960s and not at all before the 1930s should have come so to dominate the moral vocabulary we use in the domain of race. I will suggest that common contemporary usage of these terms and, to some extent, philosophical accounts of them, have had two deleterious effects on the challenges of moral understanding in the area of race.

First, they have obscured the wide range of different types of moral wrong or ill. That is, these accounts have made it seem that what goes wrong in the area of race is something like one type of thing ("racism") that is morally wrong in its several manifestations always for the same reason. When a plurality of manifestations of racism is explicitly acknowledged (as Garcia, discussed below, does more explicitly than most), the plurality is seen as either directly derivative from or secondary to a core form of racism; the assumption is retained that all significant forms are wrong or bad for the same reason.

Related to this, contemporary understandings of racism also render difficult an adequate understanding of forms of racial ill or wrongfulness—such as failing, out of thoughtlessness or cultural insensitivity, to take steps to make a workplace culturally comfortable for members of a racial-cultural group (such as Mexican Americans)—that are of relatively lesser moral weight than core forms of (what is generally understood as) racism. These understandings tend to be pushed in either of two unsatisfactory directions. One is to inflate their moral significance by implying that the opprobrium generally attached to un-questioned instances of "racism" applies equally to these lesser racial ills. The second, contrary, effect of contemporary accounts of racism on lesser racial ills is to block them from sight entirely—to imply that, insofar as they do not meet the standard of moral opprobrium appropriate to phenomena rightly called racist, they are unworthy of moral concern at all. No one that I have read ever explicitly draws this conclusion. But insofar as "racism" is taken to encompass the whole of racial forms of moral wrongfulness, if someone regards a lesser wrong as falling outside what she understands "racism" to be, this frequently carries the implication that the lesser wrong is not immoral at all, or is only triv-ially so. So, for example, one often hears people say, "She wasn't being racist, just ignorant" or (discussed in more detail below) "That may be prejudice, but not racism." In context, such remarks generally imply that ignorance and prejudice cannot be very serious ills; they are not accorded a status as distinct, morally significant, race-related wrongs (even if of somewhat lesser significance than "racism").

We would do well to draw from the historical perspective the lesson that a broader and more varied and nuanced vocabulary for racial ills may well be still available today. We might even go a step further and adopt the guideline that when inclined to condemn something in the racial arena, we attempt first to do so in other terms. This stricture would help to bring this wider vocabulary to the fore and into greater usage.

I. "RACISM": THREE COMPETING MEANINGS

Let us proceed, then, to some accounts of racism to see what exactly they are offering us. Jorge Garcia has pressed the point that some accounts of racism fail to say what precisely racism consists in, proceeding instead to various alleged truths about the forms or manifestations of racism. An important strand of con-temporary writing about racism, for example, emphasizes that many people op-erate with a narrow vision of racism and that contemporary developments show that racism can take many forms not contemplated by earlier accounts. David Goldberg, for example, in the preface to his important collection *Anatomy of Racism*, says, "The prevailing critical presupposition of the social scientific at-tack on racism from its emergence in the 1930s is that racism is unvarying in its nature. . . . There is a growing recognition now . . . that racist discourse is more chameleonic in its nature" (1990: ix).[2]

Goldberg is pointing to at least two developments. One is that although adherence to the sort of distinctly biologistic ideologies of racial superiority and inferiority prominent in nineteenth- and early-twentieth-century American racial thought, and reaching a particularly hideous pinnacle in Nazism, has definitely waned throughout the world, new ways of talking about the very groups previously alleged to be biologically inferior have been used to exclude these groups or to sustain them in inferior positions. For example, these groups have been claimed to have inferior cultures, or to be wedded to ways of life allegedly inconsistent with some vision of a particular national culture.

This pluralizing discourse regarding conventionally understood "racial" groups is indeed an important feature of the racial scene in Western societies. Garcia is, however, also correct to point out that merely pointing to it does not clinch the issue of whether racism is involved, until one has been provided with an account of what racism actually consists in. Perhaps once a group is viewed primarily as a *cultural* group, even one largely coextensive with what was formerly viewed as a racial group, then insults to its culture are no longer helpfully called "racism." Perhaps such insults are still wrong and ill founded—but not racist.

We must, therefore, distinguish between an account of what racism consists in and an account that claims that racism thus defined possesses other social, psychological, and institutional features.[3] I am less confident than Garcia that these two forms of account can always be kept separate. But we should at least attempt to do so.

On the broadest level, we can distinguish three distinct uses of "racism" on the contemporary scene. (I will leave "racist" aside for the moment.) The first is the original 1930s definition, in which racism is an ideology of biologically grounded superiority and inferiority. This is the definition that Goldberg (rightly in my opinion) thinks fails to capture what most people who use the word "racism" nowadays mean by it. Nevertheless, it, or something like it, not infrequently turns up in official definitions of racism, and I have the impression that many people regard this as somehow its "true" definition.[4] For example,

2. Another example: "Multiple 'racisms' . . . have been articulated and rearticulated, embraced and employed, not only by various parts of the state, but also by other actors such as the working class and intellectuals" (Small 1994: 13).

3. For an example of the sort of quasi-empirical claim I have in mind, consider the following: "The duality of fear and aggression is integral to the structure of all racist practices" (Memmi 2000: 103).

4. Authoritative sources still support this view, though sometimes with slight modifica-

Charles Taylor (1989: 7) says, "Racists have to claim that certain of the crucial moral properties of human beings are genetically determined: that some races are less intelligent, less capable of high moral consciousness, and the like."

The next two usages of "racism" depart radically from the first in encompassing symbols, actions, practices, attitudes, societies, and so on, without requiring an ideology of biological racial superiority to be present or even lurking in the background. The second use connotes anything bad in the racial domain, without regard to the severity of moral wrong involved—for example, looking to a black student in one's class for participation when discussing racial issues, or making an unwarranted but not unflattering generalization about a racial group, such as "All Hispanics have close families." The third use refers to a subspecies of the second, encompassing only particularly egregious forms of racial badness or wrongfulness.

Some of the confusion and miscommunication rife in the racial arena stems from conflating the second and third definitions. If Jane uses "racism" to refer to anything that can go wrong, racially speaking, while Lourdes uses it more narrowly for egregious wrongs, Lourdes will feel that Jane is morally overloading behavior, attitudes, and so on that are lesser faults, while Jane will feel that Lourdes is failing to acknowledge racism.[5]

I suggest that many accounts of racism—both in Garcia's strict definitional sense and in the vaguer sense of offering important general truths about racism—should, on the one hand, be regarded as attempts at accounts of the third, narrower sense: however, they fail to distinguish this project from a comprehensive account of all race-related wrongdoing. The result is a failure to appreciate various dimensions of moral and racial plurality among racial ills.

II. THE SOCIAL ACCOUNT OF "RACISM"

Let me consider two prominent examples of accounts of racism to illustrate this failure—racism as a structure of inequality between racially defined groups, and Garcia's view of racism as a form of racial ill will. The first is expressed in

tion. Blackwell's 1993 *Dictionary of Twentieth Century Social Thought* begins its entry on "Racism" thus: "Any set of beliefs which classifies humanity into distinct collectivities, defined in terms of natural *and/or cultural* attributes, and ranks these attributes in a hierarchy of superiority and inferiority, can be described as 'racist'" (emphasis added). See also Michele Moody-Adams's entry on "Racism" in Blackwell's *Companion to Applied Ethics:* "Racism is essentially a distinctive conception of the nature of reality"—a somewhat more sophisticated version of the view stated above.

5. The broader, second usage might be acceptable among persons who recognize that this is how they are using the term. It may not always be necessary to mark out the minimally bad from the appallingly bad.

definitions of racism as "an institutionalized system of power" or "a system of advantage based on race" (Derman-Sparks and Phillips 1997: 10). The purpose of such definitions has frequently been to shift focus from individual manifestations of prejudice and bigotry to larger structures of inequality between racial groups, especially where a history of mistreatment of the disadvantaged groups has provided the foundation for current significantly unequal life prospects. Proponents of these definitions generally wish to claim that these inequalities (for example, that black students lag substantially behind whites and Asians in school achievement) are of greater moral concern than the individual prejudices (for example, the degree of antiblack racial prejudice among the white population). Such definitions are generally also responsive to the widely though not universally accepted notion that the inequalities in question are no longer primarily caused by current prejudicial attitudes.[6]

This account of racism is undoubtedly onto something important. Where deficiencies in the life prospects of a racial group is clearly, at least in part, a product of a history of racial depredations, and where the gap is substantial, it seems perverse to focus all our attention on individual prejudices and stereotyping, neglecting these larger structures and patterns. And yet identifying the relevant race-based inequalities that are to count as racism has not always been given sufficient attention. Bare inequality between racial groups is not, purely in its own right, a source of concern. This is obvious, though perhaps instructive, with regard to *ethnic* groups. Suppose, for example, that, nationally, Japanese Americans have substantially higher incomes than Lithuanian Americans. This is not a cause for concern, as long as (1) there is no suggestion of injustice in the processes that have produced this result, and (2) Lithuanian Americans are not doing badly. The same point holds for racial groups, although here injustice is more likely to be present. The reason that, for example, the school achievement levels and the wealth levels of African Americans are (or should be) a matter of concern is not simply that they are lower than those of white Americans. It is that the levels are, in their own right, unsatisfactory, *and* that they are, at least in part, a product of past discrimination and oppression as well as current discrimination.[7]

6. Glenn Loury (2002: 95–99) has developed in convincing detail the argument that current black disadvantage, constituting a form of racial injustice, is primarily a product of past discrimination and oppression and of current unobjectionable practices such as racial preference in the choice of intimates.

7. Garcia, whose other views I will discuss below, argues that social structures, practices, and processes cannot themselves be regarded as racially unjust unless they are animated by racial antipathy of some sort. Let me concede briefly at this juncture that it is unlikely that any large-scale racial injustice operates without some historical (or present) antipathy or inferiorizing to animate it. Nevertheless, it seems wholly implausible to think that the inequalities in life chances with regard to education, housing, schooling, and occupational

While the social account of racism is, then, surely correct to point to unjust inequities between racially defined groups with regard to life prospects as of moral concern in their own right, defining "racism" in terms of such structures of inequality has some troubling implications with regard to the moral status of *individual* wrongs in the racial domain. Taken literally, and if combined with the view that what is not "racism" is of little moral concern, the social account implies that individual bigotry, hatred, and antipathy are matters are of little moral concern. Some proponents of the social position might be willing to embrace this result, holding to the view that only systemic racial inequities are of real concern. This implication is brought out explicitly in those who contrast "racism" with (mere) "prejudice," often implicitly belittling the latter as of minor consequence. But most of us will wish our theory of racial ills to provide the resources for criticizing individuals as morally abhorrent for their racial attitudes and behavior.

The social definition can, it is true, be modified or extended in a fairly natural way to encompass individual behavior, belief, and attitude, by saying that individuals are racist to the extent that they engage in behavior that helps to sustain systems of unjust racial inequity (or possess attitudes that would have a similar effect were they to be put into practice). For example, out of distaste for blacks and in opposition to their presence in her neighborhood, a white homeowner planning to sell her house tells a black prospective buyer that the house has already been sold when it has not, thus contributing to the segregation and inequality in housing accommodations from which blacks notoriously suffer in the United States.

However, this tack has some troubling and counterintuitive moral implications. Consider a white homeowner in a largely white neighborhood into which some blacks have recently moved. This homeowner, let us stipulate, has no animosity toward blacks as neighbors, but believes, with some warrant, that property values in her neighborhood are likely to take a significant slide were the neighborhood to become majority blacks. To avoid a greater financial loss to herself in the future, she sells her house to a black prospective buyer, though her action contributes to a sense of "white flight" in the neighborhood that hastens the very result (lower property values) she wishes to avoid in her own case, while also potentially contributing to the creation of a black segregated neighborhood with lower property values for its residents.

---

success between whites and blacks or Mexican Americans are due *entirely* to those historical or current forms of individual prejudice or discrimination. Other economic, social, political, and cultural factors must be taken account of as well. The social definition of racism seems to me correct in presuming that the wrongness of the inequities to which it points is not exhausted by the racial prejudices and forms of individual discrimination that may have played a role in the processes leading to these inequities.

The homeowners in both examples contribute to larger structures of unjust racial inequality. But their actions seem morally quite distinct. The first directly discriminates against blacks in her actions, and does so from racial animus. The second homeowner engages in no racial discrimination and does not act from racial animus. Yet the approach being considered will label them both "racist," thereby implying a kind of moral equivalence between the two. Indeed, it would even be plausible on that definition to regard as "racist" a neighbor of the second homeowner who, knowing of her intentions and of their effect, fails to attempt to discourage her from selling her house. All three individuals contribute to housing segregation and its attendant injustices.

Advocates of the social definition might wish to modify the proposed definition of individual racism by saying that individuals are more or less racist to the extent that their actions more or less contribute to structures of racial inequity. But our intuitions about what is more or less morally wrong in the racial area does not, in general, correspond to degrees of causal impact on such structures. For example, the first individual's refusal to sell to a black prospective home buyer might actually contribute to sustaining a racially mixed neighborhood. So despite her discriminating racially against individual black home buyers, her action's impact on the larger structures might be positive, or at least not negative— in contrast to the second homeowner. Yet the racially discriminatory nature of her action, and her racial antipathy, render her more morally blameworthy than the second homeowner.

As this example suggests, we do not normally treat "contribution to structures of racial injustice" as the sole yardstick of individual fault in the racial area, contrary to the implication of the social definition of racism. Though we may think that, in general, racially discriminatory acts are wrong because they *characteristically* do contribute to larger structures of injustice, we also think them wrong *in themselves*, as the example of the first white homeowner illustrates. We especially think them wrong when they are motivated by racial animus, and Jorge Garcia is surely correct when he emphasizes that a powerless, pathetic white bigot possesses a deficiency of character even though she is unable to harm members of the groups who are the target of her bigotry (Garcia 1997a: 13). Her bigotry may, from a societal point of view, not matter very much; it may be of less general concern than a powerful person's racial bigotry. But it is bigotry nonetheless, and it matters in an assessment of her character.

"Individual prejudice or discrimination" and "unjust racial inequality" cannot be ranged on a single scale of moral concern with the latter at the high end and the former at the low end, nor can the moral fault of the former be exhaustively accounted for in terms of its relation to the latter. Individual racial prejudice and hatred is certainly of moral concern, with regard to the character of the persons manifesting those attitudes. Just as it is an important fact about, and (at least ideally) to, Jim that he is a dishonest or callous person, so it is similarly important whether Jim is racially prejudiced. The importance of individual moral character regarding racial matters stands in its own right; it is not something that needs to be vindicated by reference to its impact on the relation between racially defined groups.

A second way to bring individual racism in to the social definition of racism is familiar in the literature, and that is to define racism as "prejudice plus power" (Barndt 1991: 28).[8] That is, an individual is racist if she is prejudiced and has the power to give effect to these prejudices. This move differs from the previous in requiring racially problematic intentionality on the agent's part. But, like that definition, it falls afoul of the purely individual dimension of what is plausibly called "racism." The powerless can be racially bigoted; indeed entirely socially powerless white people can be found among the ranks of virulently bigoted persons.[9] It does indeed matter morally whether one realizes one's racial prejudices in harmful action; but individual members of socially powerless groups can do so (e.g., in personal violence).[10] Further, whether one's racial attitudes issue in harmful action is not the only thing that matters morally about individual prejudice and bigotry.

In sum, then, proponents of the "social" definition of racism are onto something morally important; (unjust) social, economic, and political inequalities among racial groups are of moral importance. The social definition of racism is meant to call attention to these inequalities. Given current understandings of "racism," this definition accomplishes this shift of attention because, to the extent that racism is understood as a grave racial wrong, what comes to be understood as racism will be seen as a grave racial wrong. But this worthy moral accomplishment comes at a high price. It provides no plausible way of talking about racial wrongs committed by individuals, nor of faults of individual moral character related to race.

We do best to recognize the plural nature of wrongfulness in the moral domain. There can be societal forms of wrongfulness as well as individual forms, without either of these being derivable from the other. Were the social definition to confine its aspirations to articulating *one form* of racial wrongfulness—al-

8. See also Derman-Sparks and Phillips 1997: 10 (recounting the views of "many antiracist educators"). This definition is generally allied with the further claim that only white persons can be racist. I argue elsewhere (Blum 2002: 33–42) that the proffered definition does not have this implication, and also that, independent of this argument, it is not plausible to claim that only white people can be racist.

9. I argue (Blum 2002: 42–52) that the power someone has to give effect to her prejudices, as well as the power relations among racial groups, can be pertinent to the degree of moral concern appropriate to an instance of racial hatred or prejudice—but not to its existence.

10. See Blum 2002, chap. 2, for an extended discussion of the role of personal and social power in the moral assessment of instances of racism.

lowing for the existence of other forms not captured thereby—it would be on stronger grounds, subject to the qualifications mentioned above concerning the specific forms of inequality that are the appropriate targets of moral criticism.

Yet a different shortcoming of the social definition is that it can be read as implying that all racial disparities (especially with regard to the groups mentioned above) are themselves *caused by* manifestations of individual racial prejudice or animus, contempt, or other individual attitudes. This may seem to contradict the very point of the social definition, which is to shift attention away from such individual attitudes to larger systemic or structural inequities. However, an argument can be made that the common understanding of "racism" contains an ineradicable implication of individual wrongfulness; if so, then in practice the social definition will tend to drag this understanding along with it, in the form of an implication that the social wrongfulness arises from individual wrongfulness. In this case, the social definition will, in practice, be quite misleading about the character of racial wrongs, even independent of any of the arguments above.

III. GARCIA'S ACCOUNT

Let us turn then to Garcia's very different approach to an account of racism,[11] although, like the social definition just considered, the point of Garcia's account seems to be to elucidate what is morally of greatest concern in the racial domain (Garcia 1997a: 6). Garcia says that the label "racist" "is today thoroughly moralized. To call a person, institution, policy, action, project, or wish racist is to present it as vicious and abhorrent" (7). An account of racism, Garcia says, should make it clear why it is always immoral, without making this true by definition. By contrast, advocates of the social definition do not generally tend to make explicit the moral import of their definition, notwithstanding that their definition is indeed "thoroughly moralized"; it concerns what is (regarded as) the worst thing that happens in the racial domain (i.e., inequalities of power or life chances).

Garcia is particularly convincing in arguing that many contemporary manifestations of what most thoughtful persons are inclined to call racism have tenuous, if any, links to the beliefs in biological inferiority central to the earliest definitions of racism (and, as we have seen, retained in some contemporary definitions as well). Raul need not have any beliefs about Xavier's racial inferiority in order to hate Xavier because of his race; yet to do so is a vice, and has a strong

---

11. I will be discussing four of Garcia's articles: Garcia 1996, 1997a, 1999, and 2001b. I understand that the point of view of Garcia's essay in this volume generally follows that of these earlier pieces, especially the last one.

claim to be called racism under contemporary understandings.[12] Garcia is surely also correct to argue, as I have above, that a failure to possess social, economic, or political power does not prevent racial hatred from being a blot on someone's moral character (1997a: 11, 13).

Garcia sees racism as manifesting two distinct but related forms—race-based ill will or hatred, and "racially based or racially informed disregard" (1997a: 13; 1996: 6). Racism is morally bad because it is a type of vice, a vice that Garcia often describes in terms of its being the opposite of, or offending against, certain virtues (especially benevolence and justice) (1999: 13), but also describes as malevolence.

Garcia's account possesses many strengths. No other account with which I am familiar is as careful to clarify the grounds on which the account is offered; to relate its definition to such a wide range of alternative accounts of racism;[13] to attempt to show what is valuable in those alternative accounts but also what falls short; to recognize that an account of racism must show how a plurality of distinct categories—practices, societies, actions, motives, fears, desires, beliefs—can instantiate racism; to have so clearly brought out a dimension of racial wrongfulness (racial ill will) that many contemporary accounts fail adequately to articulate; and, finally, to have recognized so clearly that the contemporary understanding of racism is, at its core, moral and so must be analyzed as a moral notion.

I wish, however, to note several shortcomings of Garcia's account. All of these, I will suggest, stem from a failure adequately to recognize, or to elucidate, the *plurality* of forms of race-related disvalue, or adequately to account for what is in fact wrong with or bad about some of the forms that his own account encompasses. I will suggest that, though Garcia does well to turn to the virtue tradition to elucidate racism, he does not cast his virtuist net wide enough to encompass the full range of value and disvalue in the domain of race.

RELATION BETWEEN RACIAL ILL WILL AND RACE-BASED DISREGARD

First, the relation between Garcia's two different forms of racism—ill will and race-based insufficient regard for others' well-being—is not clear. Garcia describes it differently in different places. Sometimes he implies that the two forms are not so different, and that they are both morally bad for the *same* reason—that they involve vicious attitudes toward persons because of their race (1996: 11).

12. Garcia's argument that racial ill will is more fundamental than racial ideology in some central forms of what most persons think of as racism is particularly effective against K. A. Appiah's belief-centered account in "Racisms" (Appiah 1990). See Garcia 1997a: 14–20

13. Garcia discusses alternative accounts offered by Manning Marable, Thomas Schmid, Lewis Gordon, Michael Omi and Howard Winant, Robert Miles, Dinesh D'Souza, Judith Lichtenberg, David Goldberg, Michael Philips, K. Anthony Appiah, and others.

But the category "vicious" when it means "manifesting a vice" does not possess that kind of moral unity. In contrast, a more colloquial meaning implies something like a particular degree of moral opprobrium. "Teresa isn't just insensitive or even mean; she's really vicious." For example, laziness and cruelty are both vices; but it is much worse to be cruel than lazy. (If it is replied that "laziness" is not a moral vice, "inconsiderate" will serve the same purpose; it is worse to be cruel than inconsiderate. "Joan might be inconsiderate; but she isn't cruel.")

At other points Garcia appears to recognize that different unsatisfactory race-based attitudes have quite distinct moral valences. It is worse to *hate* someone because of her race than to *fail to have adequate regard for her welfare* on this basis. Thus, Garcia says that racial ill will manifests the vice of malevolence while racially differential regard instantiates the vice of disregard (1997a: 29).

At another point, Garcia speaks of the ill will form of racism as primary, and the disregard form as "derivative" (1996: 6). It is not clear whether Garcia means this primacy in a historical, psychological, or conceptual sense. That is, was racial malevolence historically or psychologically primary, with racial indifference flowing from it? Or is racial ill will a more paradigmatic sense of "racism," with racial disregard less so, although still falling within the concept? Yet in his most recent piece (of the ones I am considering), Garcia appears to reverse the earlier claim of the "core" form of racism: "My own view is that racism, in its core, consists in racial disregard, or, more gravely, in ill will" (2001b: 134).[14]

I suggest that Garcia may be unclear on this point because, on the one hand, he thinks of "racism" as naming a single distinct vice, like cowardice or dishonesty, and as having a single, distinct moral valence; and because, on the other hand, he recognizes that there are quite distinctive forms of racially bad attitudes or sentiments with quite *different* moral valences. It may be less elegant and theoretically less satisfying to countenance multiple (or even just two) irreducibly distinct forms of what one thinks of as "racism," yet doing so may be more in line with the moral phenomenological strand in Garcia's thinking. Malevolence is not the same as a mere absence of benevolence; they are two distinct vices, even if they can usefully be seen as ranged along a single spectrum. Other vices with distinct moral valences cannot be so ranged.

THE ROLE OF RACE

Even if Garcia were to embrace this moral plurality within the concept of racism, he would still not have given an adequate account of the moral valence of what he himself encompasses within that concept. Garcia generally implies that the reason race-based malevolence is bad is simply that it instantiates the vice of malevolence. Malevolence is a vice in its own right, independent of

14. In another essay (Garcia 1999: 13) racial disregard is said to be the "root" of racism, while hate and ill will is its "core."

whether race is involved as the basis for the malevolence. Garcia's implication is that if I hate Andres and wish him ill out of jealousy, this is as bad—because equally a form of malevolence—as if I hate him because he is black.

Unwarranted hatred and malevolence is indeed a vice, and is so whether it is based on race or not. Nevertheless, I do not think we ordinarily regard all forms of ill will as of *equal* moral import. In particular, we tend to think that race-based ill will is a *worse* form of ill will than many others. The concept of a "hate crime" is a legal analogue to this moral intuition. The idea behind a hate crime is that a crime, such as assault, committed out of hatred of someone grounded in certain group-based characteristics—such as race, ethnicity, religion, gender, sexual orientation, and the like—is worse, and deserving of more severe punishment, than the same crime committed for a different reason. (Indeed, the term "hate crime" is somewhat misleading, since it is not hatred as such that warrants the more severe punishment, but only hatred targeting certain group-based characteristics of the victim.)

Why might it be worse to hate someone because of her race than to hate her for purely personal reasons, such as envy or jealousy? One reason is purely consequentialist. When someone is targeted for hatred because of her race, other members of the same race may feel anxious or fearful, or suffer some other form of psychic harm, either because they think that they could have been the victim (or could be in the future), since all that mattered was membership in the racial group in question, or because they personally identify with the victim.

I do not think this consequentialist reason is the whole story, and want to suggest that the full opprobrium attached to race-related manifestations of hatred or ill will derives from the severe forms of discrimination, oppression, degradation, dehumanization, and violence perpetrated historically in the name of race—derives, that is, from the embeddedness of individual forms of racial wrongfulness in wider patterns, historical and sometimes contemporary, of comparable racial wrongfulness.[15] I am not taking a stand here on whether there are group characteristics *other than* race that ground a moral valence comparable to race and that are distinct from the same forms of wrong or evil lacking such characteristics.

My argument has not, to this point, been that Garcia's view that racism is a type of race-based malevolence is false. It is that Garcia's understanding of how this constitutes a virtuist account is incomplete or insufficient. For he implies that what is distinctively vicious about racism is simply that it involves ill will. But I have argued that "ill will" comes in some morally distinct subvarieties, one form of which depends on the different targets of the ill will. (There might be other crosscutting subdivisions of ill will.) Race-based ill will is bad not only because it involves ill will, but because the ill will is based on race. One might put

15. This view is defended, though not entirely adequately, in Blum 2002, chap. 1.

this point by saying that "racism" understood in the way Garcia does involves a *different vice* from, say, ill will based on personal jealousy. Or at least one might regard it as a morally distinct subvariety of the vice "malevolence," where subvarieties are distinguishable at least by the forms of and degree of moral opprobrium attached to them.

ANTIPATHY AND INFERIORIZATION

I have argued that one problem with Garcia's account of racism is his failure to provide an adequate account of how the two vices with which he associates racism—ill will and disregard—are related to one another as forms of racism. I suggested that one source of this difficulty is an attempt, which Garcia often resists but sometimes capitulates to, to see "racism" as naming a single type of racial viciousness, one with a particular, seriously negative valence. A different, but related, problem with his account is his imposing an artificial unity on the items that he sees as *either* ill will *or* disregard. Garcia recognizes in several of his articles that two apparently distinct families of phenomena have been encompassed in contemporary meanings of racism. One is racial ill will. The other is a viewing of the racial other[16] as inferior in some humanly important respect, or attitudes that manifest such a view (such as disrespect, disdain, and contempt). I will refer to this as the "inferiorizing" form of race-related wrong.

Garcia often recognizes that ill will and inferiorizing are distinct forms of racial ill, in that he says that malevolence can exist without a belief in the inferiority of the racial other. That is certainly correct; it can be directed toward those thought of as superior or those thought of as neither inferior or superior. Some anti-Asian and anti-Jewish racist malevolence views its targets not as inferior to the racist but as in important respects superior.[17] Asians may be seen as "too smart," perhaps, by the Asian hater, but this vague handwaving at a deficiency is not the same as viewing the other as fundamentally inferior.

Garcia, however, in claims that belief in inferiority is generally a rationalization of ill will (1996: 9). Historically this is certainly false. During the slavery and segregation eras in the United States, for example, most whites believed blacks to be inferior, even barely human, but many did not harbor ill will toward them. The inferiorizing of blacks was clearly more fundamental than whatever ill will

---

16. I agree with Garcia that not all racism is directed toward a racial other; it can be directed toward members of one's own group, or even oneself as a member of that group. This qualification does not affect the argument in the text, which is concerned with different types of racial ill, no matter who its target.

17. Nazi anti-Semitism is distinct from this form (although there are some similarities or continuities) in that the Nazis saw Jews as morally and humanly inferior (or even as not human beings) while still seeing them (inaccurately) as exercising overwhelming power in German society.

might have accompanied it, as this inferiorizing provided the primary rationalization of slavery and segregation. Consider the following words of Jefferson Davis, the president of the Confederacy, from a debate in the Senate in 1860 about slavery: "The condition of slavery with us is, in a word[,] Mr. President, nothing but the form of civil government instituted for a class of people not fit to govern themselves. . . . In their subject and dependent state, they are not the objects of cruelty" (Davis 1860).

Racial hatred was certainly often a part of the mix of attitudes that whites held toward blacks during the slavery and segregation eras (not to speak of the present); yet even then, that hatred was often directed more specifically at blacks who too visibly flouted the rules of behavior that signaled (in the mind of whites) that they regarded themselves as inferior (failing to show "proper deference" to whites, for example) rather than at blacks in general. If there has been a sea change in white attitudes such that, nowadays, inferiorization is *always* driven by and is a rationalization for racial ill will, Garcia has given no reason to think this is so.

Garcia also argues, independently, that belief in the racial others' inferiority *is not itself racist* unless it does in fact stem from racial ill will (1996: 9). This seems mere stipulation—working out a consequence of a definition to which Garcia is already committed. He provides no reason for us to abandon the intuition that treating or regarding someone as a racial inferior is, by itself, racist. In any case, Garcia's more frequent argument concerning the relation between inferiorizing attitudes and racial ill will is yet a third view—quite different, and contrary to this one, and distinct from the rationalization view. It is that the two forms are not really distinct—that inferiorizing is a *form* of ill will or disregard. Garcia imagines a racial paternalist who regards blacks as inferior but, far from harboring ill will or indifference toward them, takes himself to be furthering their interests when he treats them as something like children, as Davis expresses in the passage just mentioned.

Garcia rightly points out that the paternalist is not *in fact* furthering the blacks' interests, all things considered (for example, their interest in autonomy). In an obvious sense, he does not have their real interests at heart. But this does not make the paternalist a type of race hater. The race hater may not regard the racial other as inferior; and the paternalist need not (and generally does not) hate the racial other. Even though in some sense neither one has the interests of the racial other at heart, their ways of being "racist" are morally distinct. Hating someone is wrong for a different reason than regarding her as humanly inferior is wrong.

If one shifts from race hatred to racial indifference or disregard, Garcia's other characterization of racism, the paternalist is not indifferent to the welfare of the racial other. He misconstrues that interest, but he is still concerned about it. Both the racial inferiorizer and the racial disregarder, perhaps, fail to be concerned about the actual interests of a group; but there is an important moral difference between failing to do so because one views the group as inferior and failing to do so because of race-based indifference (or, a third possibility, because one is simply mistaken in what one takes those interests to be because of false empirical beliefs).

Garcia (1996: 17) sometimes puts his point by saying that the racist is someone who "stand[s] against the advancement of Black people." But one can stand against the interests of black people for a variety of morally distinct reasons— hatred being one, lack of respect for autonomy being another. Indeed, other reasons suggest themselves. Garcia himself mentions persons who engage in racially discriminatory practices, not out of racist motivations but simply to hold on to their jobs, as, for example, employees of the Denny's restaurant chain were compelled to do in a case that came to national attention in the early 1990s.[18] One could do so on a dare, or (another of Garcia's examples) in order to hurt someone toward whom one has animosity but not racial animosity. These are all quite distinct reasons, with distinct moral valences. Of course they are all forms of racial vice or wrong. They involve doing something wrong or vicious in the area of race. But, contrary to Garcia's implication, they do not all instantiate the selfsame vice (or only two vices, disregard and ill will).

One of the criteria of adequacy for an account of "racism" that Garcia lists is that it should "have a structure similar to, and be immoral for some of the same reasons as are central forms of anti-Semitism, xenophobia, misogyny, the hostility against homosexuals that is nowadays called 'homophobia,' and other kinds of ethnic, cultural, or religious enmity familiar from history" (1997a: 6). Garcia is right to see his list as all involving a kind of group-based enmity similar to racial ill will; and I agree that some of what is commonly called "racism" takes this form. However, it seems to me to beg the question to restrict "racism" to such forms of enmity. Why not say that racism must have a structure similar to a belief in women's inferiority, or in the inferiority of some cultural groups to others? Laurence Thomas and others have written of the differences between antiblack racism and anti-Semitism, the latter involving hatred of a group seen as in some ways superior and the former disdain or disrespect for a group seen as inferior (Thomas 1992: 94–108, esp. 107–8). Perhaps Thomas understates antiblack antipathy; but it seems arbitrary for Garcia to set enmity as a paradigm for racism, and circular to conclude that racism always takes the form of enmity.

Ironically, despite his attempt to reduce racial inferiorizing to racial enmity, disaffection, or ill will, Garcia more than once speaks of racism as involving "insufficient concern *or respect*" (1996: 9; italics added), as offending against benevolence *and* justice. He says, "Racism can offend against justice, not only benevolence, in the withholding of proper respect and deference" (10). Such

18. On the Denny's case, see Feagin, Vera, and Batur 2001: 76–83.

statements seem to concede that there are indeed distinct forms of racial ill that are not reducible to one another. Justice is not the same as benevolence, and, though Garcia does not quite say this here, one can offend against justice without offending against benevolence, just as one can be benevolent while failing in a form of respect related to justice. These are morally distinct virtues (and corresponding vices).

CATEGORIAL PLURALITY

Garcia's partial but inadequate recognition of the plural nature of racial ills within what he wants to call "racism" is mirrored in a failure to give due recognition to another dimension of plurality within racial ills—what one might call "categorial plurality." On one level Garcia does recognize—more so than the social account of racism and other accounts as well (for example, Appiah's cognitive account)—that beliefs, practices, institutions, utterances, propositions, actions, feelings, attitudes, societies, and more can all be racist. An account of racism should explain the sense in which each of these is, or can be, racist. But Garcia's recognition of this plurality at the level of categorial distinctness is abandoned in his account of how each of these categorially distinct items can instantiate racism. On his view, they can be racist only insofar as they manifest racial ill will (or disregard). So Rose's belief in proposition P is racist only if Rose is led to her belief by racial disregard.

But what about the proposition P itself? Is not the proposition "blacks are subhuman" a morally repulsive proposition, independent of what leads anyone to believe it? That is, isn't there something about the content of propositions itself that can make them racially objectionable—that they declare a racial group to be humanly deficient, or inferior in some fundamental way, or, closer to the spirit of Garcia's account, that they portray a racial group as worthy of hate ("Arabs are all terrorists who are attempting to destroy our way of life")?

Isn't the swastika a racist *symbol,* independent of what leads someone to display that symbol? (The displayer may not recognize that it is a racist symbol, be attempting to recover an earlier—pre-Nazi—nonracist meaning of the swastika, or might just be attempting to do what he thinks, for whatever reason, is "cool.") And what about *practices*? Cannot a practice be racist in the sense of perpetuating or constituting a racial injustice, even if the practice is not driven by racial animus or racial inferiorization? Consider, for example, the educational practice of tracking, by which children are assessed according to some alleged measure of ability, then placed in ability-grouped classes that are provided with widely varying levels of stimulating and demanding curricula. In racially integrated schools, this practice is recognized to lead to wide disparities in the education provided for white as opposed to black and Latino children. The ability grouping may in part be driven by racist or racially problematic assumptions about the latter students. But it need not be, certainly not by everyone who participates in it, who might hold no general beliefs about the abilities of black children, but who simply buy into a range of nonracial assumptions about the character of "intelligence," about the best teaching practices, and other such assumptions. This tracking could exacerbate previous inequalities in performance (not capacity) at an earlier stage of schooling.

Yet it is at least plausible to argue that the practice of ability grouping deprives black and Latino children of equal educational opportunity;[19] and the practice can be condemned on that basis alone, not because of the racial attitudes of those who implement it or who created it. Practices can be racially unjust, and so constitute racial wrongs for a different reason, or in a different way, than attitudes are "racist" and propositions are "racist." What makes a category of item racist, or racially problematic, need not be the same for every category.

I think that Garcia wants to see a single source for everything that he wants to call racism because, although we have seen that he is not consistent in this regard, he wants all racism to be morally bad for the same reason—that it violates a single virtue. Related to this explanation is that he does not want to allow something to count as racist for reasons that smack of consequentialism.[20] He might well resist condemning tracking for this reason, unless he is able to find racial animus in its operation.

RACE-RELATED WRONGS OTHER THAN "RACISM"

My final criticism of Garcia draws in a somewhat different way on the moral diversity within the domain of racial ills. The criticism is that Garcia's account of racism is not clearly situated within a broader category of racial ills, of morally problematic racial phenomena. Garcia does not make it clear that things can go wrong or badly in the area of race without being "racist." This criticism actually applies less to Garcia than to those accounts of racism that appear to be aspiring to a general account of everything that goes wrong (or goes nontrivially wrong)

---

19. On tracking and equality of opportunity see Oakes 1985.

20. In one passage, Garcia does appear to allow that there can be "racist beliefs" in the sense of racist propositions, the racist character of which is not explained by the racist sentiments that explain adherence to them. He speaks of another philosopher as having provided convincing examples (e.g., the character of Huckleberry Finn) of people who innocently come to hold "racist beliefs," such that doing so does not make them racists (Garcia 1999: 14). This example suggests a possible further reason why Garcia generally strives to see racial disaffection across the wide variety of categories of possible "racism." It is because he generally does not want to count something as a manifestation of racism unless doing so is grounds for regarding some agent in the situation as herself a racist. I think Garcia is correct to think that people are too quick to say that someone is a racist on the basis of having made a certain objectionable remark or engaged in racially problematic behavior on one occasion. However, as Garcia acknowledges in this example, it is possible for a proposition to be unequivocally and fully racist, without the person who holds the proposition being racist.

in the domain of race. As mentioned earlier, the idea that racism is a structure of unjust racial domination is often treated in this fashion; anything not en-compassable within this definition (e.g., a powerless racial bigot) is seen both as not racism and as morally trivial.

By contrast, Garcia mentions some racial phenomena that seem clearly prob-lematic but that, in his view, lie outside the range of his definition of racism—stereotyping, or seeing persons too much in terms of groups rather than as individuals (1997a: 21). On the other hand, Garcia's discussions of these phe-nomena never fully and unequivocally acknowledge that they can be morally bad, not be instances of racism, and be morally bad for reasons other than those that make (what he calls) racism bad. Let me take two examples, both of which are discussed in more than one of Garcia's articles. One is the issue of "black dis-advantage." In one of his essays (1996) Garcia takes up the oft cited example of employers hiring through word-of-mouth recruiting. This practice privileges the networks of current employees, who in most workplaces are generally dis-proportionately white. Taken together with the fact that most people's networks are in large part monoracial, this practice has the effect of making jobs less avail-able to nonwhites, and to blacks in particular.

Although at one point Garcia mentions that this practice is "possibly unde-sirable and perhaps even unjust" (1996: 25), his main purpose and emphasis is that such practices are not necessarily racist. He rightly notes that factors that disadvantage blacks or "impede black progress" are diverse (1997a: 12). Direct racial discrimination is one, but others may have little relation to race in their intrinsic character (developments in the economy, class-based advantage and disadvantage, seniority protections), or might concern race but not be prob-lematic in their own right. (Garcia cites Glenn Loury's example of endogamous friendship and marriage among racial groups.) Against those who want to say that the causes of black disadvantage do not matter, that only the result—that is, the fact of disadvantage itself—does, Garcia wants to press the point that it is important to disaggregate the different factors, partly (he implies) just to help us understand what is going on, and partly because we ought to make moral dis-tinctions among these factors. Some may have unfortunate results, but not be morally wrong for that. In particular, Garcia wants to say that it is only factors that stem from racial animus or disregard that should count as racist. "Racism is not only presumptively immoral but conclusively immoral, while not everything that disadvantages blacks is conclusively immoral" (1997a: 12).

Garcia is correct to note the different moral weight of distinct factors that lead to black disadvantage. But his argument has the effect of not making it clear whether he sees the inequality constituted by black disadvantage as *itself* morally problematic. Although not all disadvantages are unjust or otherwise of moral concern, Garcia provides no theory of social injustice, for example, that would allow us to see the disproportionate unemployment rate of blacks as a form of injustice. Doing so would allow one to acknowledge that a practice (seniority, for example) may not be morally and racially problematic in its own right, but might nevertheless contribute to a racial injustice and therefore be morally problematic in that respect.[21]

This failure to give a distinct moral standing to a phenomenon that is other than (what Garcia defines as) "racism"—to recognize that something might be morally bad for reasons other than that racial hatred is morally bad—is reinforced by an example Garcia uses to illustrate that not all factors that disadvantage black people should count as "racism." The example is of an alien force that is hostile to Earthlings and that engages in offensive action against the continent of Africa because of its mineral deposits (1996: 26) This action has a disproportionately negative impact on the well-being of black people but clearly is not an instance of racism, nor, Garcia rightly implies, is it any form of race-related wrong on the part of the aliens.

Garcia uses this example to support his view that only the presence of racial disaffection renders a practice racist; but by analogizing this fanciful example to ones in which nonracial factors contribute to black disadvantage in the context of a history of racial wrongs perpetrated against blacks, the example has the effect of pulling him even further from exploring the ways that a practice can involve, constitute, or contribute to racial injustice, even though no racism (in his sense) is involved.[22]

In summary, I have argued that Garcia fails to recognize an existing plurality within what he himself wishes to call racism, a further plurality within what can plausibly regarded as racism outside of Garcia's definition, and a yet further plurality of racial ills beyond what can be regarded as racism.

21. As mentioned, Garcia does suggest that word-of-mouth recruiting might be unjust. But he appears to regard the injustice in question as a *nonracial* injustice—perhaps an unfairness based on a failure to use consistent, qualification-based criteria for hiring, or to provide equal access to all for information about available positions. What his account lacks is a clear recognition of a distinct and diverse range of *race-related wrongs*, with different explanations as to their moral faultiness.

22. I want to mention briefly a further shortcoming of Garcia's moral monism about racism that I am not able to explore in depth. Garcia implies that the identity of the racial group (or members thereof) that is the target of racial animus has no bearing on the moral status of the animus, or the acts flowing from it. But it is at least arguable—and is certainly a belief held by many—that racial animus against racially vulnerable groups such as blacks, Native Americans, and Arabs is of greater moral concern than such animus against whites. I argue for such racial asymmetry in Blum 2002, chap. 2.

IV. SECOND THOUGHTS ON *"I'M NOT A RACIST, BUT . . ."*

In *"I'm Not a Racist, But . . ."* I argued more directly for many of the bases on which I have criticized Garcia's virtuist and the social accounts of racism. On the most general level, I attempted to show that to take adequate account of the range of distinct race-related wrongs and ills, we require a more variegated and nuanced moral vocabulary than we generally operate with. I suggested that racial ignorance, racial insensitivity, racial injustice, unwarranted racial privilege, failure to recognize the importance of someone's racial identity to her, failure to see a member of a different racial group as both an individual and a member of the group, and attributing too much importance to race in one's understanding of what is important to persons constitute examples of this range of nonracist racial ills. I argued that what goes morally wrong in these different cases is by no means one thing, such as racial domination, or racial ill will. Rather, the phenomena embody diverse sources of moral wrongfulness.

I contended in the book that the historical trajectory of the words "racism" and "racist" is part of what has blinded us to this moral and racial diversity. There has been a tendency in ordinary discourse to use these terms so broadly as to encompass virtually everything that goes wrong in the area of race, while at the same time retaining the idea (inconsistent with that usage) that "racism" is a term of severe opprobrium and should be used to refer only to very serious moral ills or forms of wrongfulness in the racial domain. I advocated that we rein in the scope of what we call racism, while simultaneously attempting to avail ourselves of the wider moral resources our language provides for referring to the broader range of racial ills beyond racism. I advocated also that we try to be careful about the category of items to which we apply condemnation in the racial domain— not tacitly assuming, for example, that everyone who makes a racist remark or tells a racist joke is "a racist."

In the book, I offer a reined-in definition of racism. I recognized that this definition would be to some extent stipulative, that the word "racism" has not acquired a sufficiently stable, long-standing, and unified use for one to capture its ordinary-language meaning in a single definition. However, I called the chapter in which I offered this definition "'Racism': Its Core Meaning." I now consider this a misleading way to describe what I offered in that chapter, as if there could be one thing (or, as I argued in the book, two things) that constitute a core of what racism actually is. I have become a good deal less confident than Garcia that one can set as a helpful condition on an account of "racism" that it "conform to everyday discourse about racism, insofar as this is free of confusion," or that his criterion of "accommodating clear cases from history and imagination and exclude cases where racism is clearly absent" (1997a: 6) can be applied without at least some presupposing of an already existing account of racism. I do not think one can with confidence say, as Garcia does, that "there is some one thing in which racism *now* consists, some single thing that the term means as *we* use it *today*" (9; italics in original).

Perhaps more important, I am now less confident that the major task of those working in the area of philosophy, race, and morality should be to attempt to proffer an account of "racism." While I think that there is a good deal that philosophers can contribute in the way of clearing up confused thinking about race, I am less confident that focusing so exclusively on "racism" is the most constructive way to make that contribution. I would urge, more strongly than I did in my book, that we take our task to be an account of the diversity of racial phenomena that constitute moral ills, and a careful delineation of the moral character of each. Perhaps we might even attempt temporarily to put the words "racism" and "racist" on hold; or, at least, whenever we are tempted to use them, we might try to use different words to express what we mean. Perhaps doing so will lead us to a more comprehensive, yet more nuanced, understanding of what we thought we were trying to do in offering accounts of "racism."

4 : PHILOSOPHY AND RACISM

The future which the dream shows us is not the one which will occur but the one which we should like to occur. The popular mind is behaving here as it usually does: what it wishes, it believes.—Freud, On Dreams

I

I shall argue that a causal account of racism, in particular one that involves a psychological or psychoanalytic underpinning, is necessary to understanding what racism is and what is morally wrong with it. It is also necessary to formulating strategies for addressing racism. An adequate analysis of racism—there are actually many varieties of racism—will also show why, along with other long-standing prejudices like sexism and homophobia, it has proven so intractable. I also discuss the bizarre character of racism. It seems odd after all—inexplicable—that someone should be hated merely because of his race or color. It turns out that race and color have little to do with racism.

While there is undoubtedly a plethora of issues concerning racism that should be addressed by philosophers, including various relationships between philosophy and racism, two interrelated questions are primary. First, what is racism? And second, what are the causes of racism? "Causes" should be taken broadly as referring to the nature of racism—those conditions without which racism in its various forms would not exist.[1] Thus, it is something of a surprise that in the collection of essays edited by Susan Babbitt and Sue Campbell, *Racism and Philosophy,* neither of these questions is regarded as a focus for the volume as a whole or for any of the essays individually. What then is the focus? The editors write:

> The contributors to this volume attempt to identify and clarify important structures of meaning through which Western philosophy has both evaded acknowledgement of racism, and has at the same time, offered influential conceptual schemes that have helped produce the destructive rationalizations of contemporary society. . . . [T]his volume suggests that acknowledging the importance of racism can effectively inform development in all areas of philosophy. . . . [T]he authors draw on empirical, historical, and sociological in-

My thanks to Damian Cox, Susan Datz, Marguerite La Caze, and Tamas Pataki.

1. Elisabeth Young-Bruehl (1996) convincingly argues that prejudices come in a multitude of forms and that racism itself has many different forms. It is an obfuscating oversimplification to talk about prejudice rather than prejudices, racism rather than racisms.

vestigation, and on the work of both activists and theorists, while undertaking the task of identifying and explicating the central philosophical issues involved in or emerging from these investigations. . . . The first part of this volume . . . addresses questions about the implications of racism for the practice of philosophy. . . . Part 2 . . . addresses questions about the nature of both U.S. and colonial systemic racism and about what is involved in understanding and taking responsibility for it. . . . [T]he last part . . . involve[s] consideration of how we relate to each other through structures of ethnicized and racialized difference in ways that keeps racism intact . . . [and] focus[es] on the development of identities adequate to antiracist commitments. (Babbitt and Campbell 1999: 1–5)

All well and good, and yet it is impossible to imagine any of these tasks undertaken apart from prior assumptions, explicitly or implicitly argued or presupposed, about the nature and causes of racism. In fact, some of the essays in Babbitt and Campbell 1999 do obliquely address these questions. They would have to.

Moral, social, and political philosophers have contributed remarkably little to understanding the causes of racism or the nature of various other prejudices. Some even claim that causal, especially psychological, accounts of racism are peripheral to understanding it. Despite their ability to draw fine distinctions and attend to moral principles, philosophers have been beating around the bush. For example, questions are raised, not only by philosophers, about whether, scientifically speaking, there really are races and what the implications of such a question are for racism, whether people of color can themselves be racist, who is a racist, and whether racism is institutionalized. These are neither very interesting nor illuminating questions, but any adequate answer to them must be given in terms of an analysis of the nature of racism. Rooted in philosophers' inability to explain racism is the related fact that moral philosophers have been unable to adequately explain what is morally wrong with racism in its various guises or with other prejudices. A more interesting but nevertheless secondary set of questions relates to what policies are racist.

One would expect that moral philosophy would have something distinctive and significant to say about how to understand racism and why it is morally reprehensible. Instead, what one often gets is an account of racism's immorality in terms of a general moral theory or principle. For example, we are told racism is bad because such discrimination fails to treat people as ends in themselves or because it denies basic human rights. If it is the case that racial prejudice always involves these or other pat moral failings, then it does constitute a reason for supposing racism, in thought or action, to be immoral. But such an account goes little or no distance toward explaining the nature of the various prejudices or in giving any distinctive set of reasons as to why they are immoral. It gives the same reasons for the immorality of prejudice in general as it does for murder, theft, or assault.

J. L. A. Garcia (1996: 9), for instance, says that the immorality in racism "stems from its being opposed to the virtues of benevolence and justice" and that "racism is a form of morally insufficient . . . concern or respect for some others." Both assertions are true, and yet it may be false that the immorality of racism resides in them in any distinctive way. For one thing, it is possible to oppose benevolence and injustice, and to have insufficient concern for others in ways and for reasons that have nothing to do with racism. Racism may be immoral for reasons that make other things immoral as well. But when people talk about the immorality of racism, I take it that they mean something more. They want to tie its immorality to something specific about the nature of racism. To say, for example, as Garcia does (1996: 9), that it "tries to injure people assigned to a racial group because of their racial identity" does not explain the specific nature of its immorality or how it is connected to perceptions of racial identity. To explain these things racism must first be understood in a (deeper) way that keeps it, at least temporarily, separate from moral issues. What needs to be understood is *why* people hate and try to injure others *on the basis of* racial or other perceived differences.

A cognitive approach to racism—one that sees racism as rooted in false beliefs or other cognitive defects is, for example, going to suggest a different account of the immorality of racism than an affectively based one like Garcia's. But dividing accounts of racism along cognitive and affective lines lacks the requisite nuances and is too superficial to capture any intrinsic connection between racism and its immorality. Psychoanalytic accounts of racism, as we will see, reject the split as mistaken and misleading. But even aside from psychoanalysis, the split must be rejected. On philosophical grounds alone contemporary analyses of emotion have shown affect to be connected to cognition and belief in ways that undermine any approach to racism along the lines of such an archaic and artificial dichotomy.[2]

Thus, for moral philosophy to engage with prejudice, explain its immorality, and offer correctives, it must take into account the nature of prejudice. That this should include an understanding of its causes may seem uncontroversial (it does to me), and yet some philosophers, remarkably, deny this. This is part of what Ruth Benedict means when she says "in order to understand race persecution, we do not need to investigate race; we need to investigate *persecution*" (1999: 38). But there is not much reason to suppose that Benedict understood the nature of persecution or its cure. She saw democracy as the antidote to racism even though it is apparent that racism, along with a multitude of other injustices, can thrive

2. See, for example, Oakley 1993.

in a democracy. She appears to conceive of genuine democracy as incompatible with or at least inhospitable to racism. Although this is not necessarily the case, it is at least arguable that democracy, as opposed to certain other forms of government, does not lend itself to the kind of social, political, and cultural milieu in which gross injustices, perhaps even prejudices such as racism, can easily thrive over (very) long periods of time. Yet given Young-Bruehl's (1996) account of racism even this seems rather optimistic. Let me illustrate the contentions above.

II

Rhetorically, Lawrence Blum (1999: 81) asks, "Well, what then *is* racism?" His answer is instructive. "I do not want to give a general definition but to indicate two distinct forms that individual racism takes. . . . the first is *racial hatred, animosity, or bigotry*—hating blacks or Jews, or Croats or Hutus[3] because they *are* blacks, Jews, Croats, and Hutus. The second form . . . involves seeing another group as *humanly inferior* . . . the ways Westerners have seen blacks." Despite his reluctance to attempt a general definition of racism, it seems that Blum means to give an ostensive definition. But his examples do not tell us, ostensibly or otherwise, what racism is, and they are misleading if they are meant to illustrate what it is.

Is his account meant to be a causal one? Does one hate blacks *because* they are blacks? Is the hatred *caused* by their blackness? This seems to be what he is suggesting, and if so it is an unintelligible account. To understand what racism *is* you have to understand *why* racism takes the forms Blum cites as examples. What is the explanation for it? Why would one hate blacks as blacks—unless perhaps one had some color phobia? Racism cannot be explained merely as racial hatred or seeing another group as humanly inferior. These are just examples. Until one understands what it is that motivates such hatreds and attitudes, why they come about and in what circumstances, where the circumstances are part of the explanation—it is impossible to understand what racism *is*.

To put the matter contentiously, if I am right, and if we can generalize somewhat from the case of Blum and Garcia, then contemporary analytic moral philosophers often address the problem of racism without understanding what racism is—or at least what it is apart from or in addition to its immorality. Thus, in discussing various aspects of what is morally wrong with racism, and in addressing related questions such as who is racist and what counts as racism, moral philosophers may not really be talking about racism or what is wrong with it; or they may be doing so without an adequate account of racist prejudices. They are talking instead about what is wrong with the ways in which some people act to-

3. Blum has this wrong. It was the Hutus that committed genocide against the Tutsis.

ward others. This is within the purview of what moral philosophers do and should do, but it is not distinctively about racism or intrinsically tied to racism in any particular way. The mistake is not just a kind of intentional fallacy or failure of recognition—talking about something under a different name. They are not talking about racism *at all*—confusing the symptoms or signs of racism with racism itself. My claim is not that they have an account of racism that others may disagree with, but rather that they have no account of racism: or less contentiously, they mistake superficial surface phenomenological characteristics or symptoms of racism for racism itself.

To some extent one may be able to recognize racism though its signs ("racist behavior") just as one recognizes measles through spots. But to say that one recognizes racism through racist behavior is circular in a way that recognizing measles via measles spots is not. For what one terms "racist behavior" will in fact *be* racist behavior in the relevant sense if it stems from racism, and this cannot be ascertained from the behavior alone. Measles spots are, however, a sure sign of measles. Of course one can be racist and not outwardly behave in racist ways (generally). But the relevant point here is that someone can behave in racist ways and still not be racist even though they will likely taken for one.

The above points can better be illustrated if a genuine account of racism, of what it is, is given. Elisabeth Young-Bruehl says, "We can define prejudices by saying that they are the reflections in attitudes towards groups (and individuals as members of groups) of characteristic modes (usually complex modes) of defense" (1996: 209).[4] She goes on to give a detailed account of those defenses in which she relies on psychological and especially psychoanalytic concepts, theories, and data. If one accepts her account of what prejudices are or something like it, then it will not be possible to explain the immorality of racism or its broader moral significance on personal, social, or political levels alone. How, for example, can one endeavor to answer the question as to whether the subjects of racisms (e.g., people of color and Jews) can themselves be racist (of course they can) if one does not know what racism is or the forms that it can take? In Young-Bruehl's account, the nature of racism is not to be explained in terms of (some inexplicable) hatred toward some race, but rather in terms of the nature and sources of the various prejudices—an account of hatred itself. Whether or not her particular accounts are correct, or to what extent they are correct, is not really the issue here.[5] The point is that this is what an account of racism must do.

Psychological or psychoanalytic accounts of racism do not split theories of

4. See also the chapters in this volume by Young-Bruehl and Pataki.
5. I have chosen Young-Bruehl's account because it is monumental in its depth and scope. It is a classic work on understanding the nature of prejudices, and I know of no work on the prejudices, including racism, that is more significant.

racism along cognitive and affective lines. They recognize that racism involves both cognitive and affective aspects, and that these are integrally related. In distinguishing the approach of the essays in his edited volume, *The Psychoanalysis of Race*, Christopher Lane says,

> Since most studies of prejudice derive from ego psychology and the social sciences, they tend to reproduce the limitations of behavioral theory. Much of this work assumes that racism derives largely from ignorance and false consciousness. If teachers and social scientists could influence a person's views, the argument goes, that person would realize that his or her assumptions about different racial and ethnic groups are shallow and false. Correspondingly, the person's racial fantasies and hostility would diminish and ideally would cease to exist. (1998: 4)

It is questionable whether "most studies of prejudice derive from ego psychology and the social sciences." Many historical studies appear to derive from neither. And even if true, the alleged connection between this derivation and "the limitations of behavioral theory" are questionable. However, it is true that many studies of prejudice, including historical, social scientific, and philosophical/ moral studies, assume that racism "derives largely from ignorance and false consciousness." Racism, the story goes, stems from a cognitive defect of sorts. It is a matter of false beliefs personally and socially engendered for various reasons.

Lane contrasts this "ignorance and false consciousness" view of racism with one that he presumably endorses and claims is at least complementary. Referring to his edited volume, Lane says, "What this collection of essays argues, additionally, is that psychic issues complicate our chances of achieving and sustaining egalitarianism" (1998: 32 n. 3). However, a harsher and more accurate contrast than Lane's can be drawn between the "ignorance" and "psychic issues" views. This harsher contrast claims that the "ignorance" view is fundamentally false and utterly different from psychological, mainly psychoanalytic, theories that seek to explain racism and racist *beliefs* themselves on psychological rather than cognitive grounds. Psychological, and specifically psychoanalytic, accounts of racism see themselves as subsuming cognitive accounts partly by explaining the origin of racist beliefs in desire and wish fulfillment. Furthermore, Lane's typology is skewed. The "ignorance view" should not be linked to a false-consciousness view but differentiated from it. The latter is clearly within the purview of "psychic issues" views. False consciousness is a matter of a special kind of ignorance that "psychic issue" views, such as psychoanalytic accounts, seek to explain.

Lane nevertheless illustrates the significance of a psychoanalytic view for understanding why people are racist and for attempting to contain racism. He says that the "ignorance and false consciousness" approaches to racism share ... an assumption that knowledge enhances cultural understanding while diminishing inter- and intragroup hostility. This emphasis often betrays a foundational hope that humankind, freed from alienation and political strife, would be wholly communitarian.... these approaches argue that a person's beliefs and assumptions, though determined by his or her class and racial background, can be altered simply by raised consciousness. Studies that aim to resolve urban strife and ethnic warfare often reproduce these assumptions: They anticipate that people locked in conflict want an end to struggle in order to secure the material gains they can achieve only in times of peace. To this perspective, psychoanalysis adds a difficult truth: When people and groups are locked in conflict, they are—beyond their immediate interest in securing sovereignty over another land or people—*already* experiencing intangible gains ... a group's "gain" might consist in depleting another's freedom.... if we ignore these psychic issues, we promulgate fables about human nature, maintaining idealist assumptions while unexamined psychic factors fuel acrimony, resentment, and hatred.[6] (1998: 5)

Trying to understand racism and other prejudices, along with certain kinds of seemingly inexplicable violence (September 11, 2001), independently of a psychoanalytic approach is like trying to understand motion without physics or how a car runs with no mention of its engine. Trying to morally assess the horrific attacks of September 11 with recourse merely to just war theory, or any consequentialist or deontological normative theory—focusing on that horror out of context (historical, political, psychological, personal) and by itself—is hopelessly narrow. There is no vacuum quite like a philosophical vacuum.

Lane makes two specific criticisms of Young-Bruehl's approach. He claims (1998: 10) there is an "irony that Young-Bruehl, using the psychic categories of hysteria, narcissism, and obsessional neuroses, makes prejudice more monolithic and universal than [Gordon] Allport."[7] Young-Bruehl does see prejudices as more universal than Allport, partly because she recognizes that there are a variety of kinds of prejudices related to an array of causes. But it is hard to understand Lane's claim that her account is more monolithic since her primary thesis, argued for in various ways throughout her book of over six hundred pages, is

6. See Lane's discussion (1998: 5–7) of a major source of these ideas in Freud's *Civilization and Its Discontents*. People experience their neighbors, says Freud (1961a: 111), not only as a "potential helper or sexual object, but also someone who tempts them to satisfy their aggressiveness on him, to exploit his capacity for work without compensation, to use him sexually without his consent, to seize his possessions, to humiliate him, to cause him pain, to torture and to kill him."

7. Young-Bruehl critiques Allport (1954) for failing to see that there are a variety of prejudices.

that prejudice is not a monolithic phenomenon in its causes or manifestations. It is Allport's account that sees racism as stemming from a single type of authoritarian personality, not Young-Bruehl's.

Lane's second criticism of Young-Bruehl is similarly unfounded but more peculiar. He says, "While I appreciate Young-Bruehl's frustration with 'universal' statements about how prejudice functions, it seems to me not only conceptually mistaken but profoundly antipsychoanalytic to assume that valuable diagnoses can be made of the prejudices affecting specific groups" (1998: 10). It is no small part of Young-Bruehl's thesis that such diagnoses can be properly made and that the specific characteristics of certain political systems, national characteristics, and cultural milieus are conducive to specific forms of prejudice. Lane does not explain why he thinks it is antipsychoanalytic. Why is this any more antipsychoanalytic than generalizing (usefully) about certain groups of children in certain kinds of situations, or indeed certain character types on the basis of clinical data? Why is any such generalizing antipsychoanalytic? Freud certainly extrapolated from individuals to types and groups. Indeed, apart from the kinds of diagnoses about prejudices affecting specific groups that Young-Bruehl makes, there are only individual accounts of prejudice that cannot be used to explain anything at all about the prejudicial nature of larger social and cultural networks. It is unclear how Lane can, on the one hand, claim that social science is virtually stymied in its effort to understand racism apart from psychoanalysis, and yet, on the other hand, see Young-Bruehl as antipsychoanalytic in her assumption that "valuable diagnoses can be made of the prejudices affecting specific groups." I take it that she would deny it is an assumption rather than a well-established fact supported by clinical data, social and historical facts, and psychoanalytic and other theory.[8]

III

Some think that a cursory definition or account of racism is all one needs for an analysis of what makes it morally wrong. They assume that it is obvious what racism is. It is unlikely that what is morally wrong with racism pertains to racism alone—that there is something morally wrong with racism that pertains to it alone. Nevertheless, suppose, for example, one wants to move away from a generalization such as "racism is morally wrong because racists fail to treat humans as ends in themselves" (an irony coming from Kant, who arguably was a racist) to something more specific. If one seeks to find the immorality as more specifi-

---

8. Lane's view might be that the psychoanalytic account that one needs must necessarily be general. But even if this is the case, a psychoanalytic account of racism can be, as Marguerite La Caze has pointed out (in correspondence), general in one sense and specific in another.

cally or intrinsically connected to racism, then it must be located in the nature of racism itself. It could be that even when one does understand the nature and causes of racism, the racist's moral reprehensibility may be no different than the kind stemming from less invidious and better-understood sources. This, however, is not the case. The immorality of racism and other prejudices is intrinsically and extrinsically tied to the specifics of an account like Young-Bruehl's in important ways.

How might the immorality of racism differ from the immorality of theft or murder? From a Kantian perspective, one thing that is wrong with theft and murder is that they involve a failure to treat human beings as ends in themselves. As such, the immorality of such practices is something they share with other kinds of actions or institutions—including racism. Perhaps then it is a mistake to look for something intrinsic to racism that makes it immoral. What makes it immoral is the same kind(s) of things that make many other things immoral. But if this is the case, then perhaps philosophy's contribution in regard to racism is not so much analyzing its moral aspects, indicating how and why it is immoral, as it is understanding its nature and causes, along with its social, political, and personal implications. The philosophical task in regard to racism would then be (surprisingly?) not fundamentally moral but rather explanatory—or epistemological.

However, if understanding racism involves, as it must, understanding racism's personal, social, and political manifestations and implications, then moral philosophy's task in regard to racism should be seen as a central part of any philosophical effort to understand racism. Thus, a moral philosopher's account of the immorality of racism will, or should be, intrinsically connected to a particular account of racism. Most moral analyses are not so connected because they lack the requisite understanding. Given a fundamentally flawed account of racism, you can no more explain what is morally wrong with it than you can explain the significance of love given a wildly aberrant view of human nature.

Having discussed racism and its immorality in general terms let us return to Garcia's account. Garcia conceives of racism as

> fundamentally a vicious kind of racially based disregard for the welfare of certain people. In its central and most vicious form, it is a hatred, ill-will, directed against a person or persons on account of their assigned race. In a derivative form, one is a racist when one either does not care at all or does not care enough (i.e., as much as morality requires) or does not care in the right ways about people assigned to a certain racial group, where this regard is based on racial classification.

He continues,

> Racism, then, is something that essentially involves not our beliefs and their rationality or irrationality, but our wants, intentions, likes and dislikes and

their distance from the moral virtues. Such a view helps explain racism's conceptual ties to various forms of *hatred* and contempt. (1996: 6–7)

The confusing aspect of Garcia's account is how he gets from the first conception to the second, and the false dichotomy he sets up between them. What is the connection between racism as being "fundamentally a vicious kind of racially based disregard for the welfare of certain people" and its involving "not our beliefs and their rationality or irrationality, but our wants, intentions, likes and dislikes"? Racially based disregard obviously involves beliefs as well as likes and dislikes. Elsewhere Garcia recognizes this and correctly emphasizes the primacy of affective over doxastic accounts.[9]

This, however, is not the main problem with the account. Despite its seeming to capture what, at first glance, many would agree racism is, it conflates what he alleges to be the nature of racism with what he sees as immoral about it.

Garcia's account is first and foremost an account of what is morally wrong with racism—not, as he claims, an account of what racism is. But except for the fact that he explicitly invokes the notion of race, his account of the moral wrongness of racism relies solely on what is morally wrong in treating or regarding people in a certain (immoral) manner. There is nothing distinctive about race in his account except that race is what evokes the moral wrongness. He says that his conception of racism "helps explain racism's conceptual ties to various forms of *hatred* and contempt," but it does not. Where is the explanation? Instead, it defines racially based hatred and contempt as essential to racism. What we have is a viciously circular definition rather than an explanation—not an account of racism but a redescription of it. Garcia believes he has captured both the heart of racism and the essence of what is morally wrong with it. But in failing to distinguish between the two he misses crucial aspects of both.

Although Garcia and Blum give very little account of how and why racial hatred comes about, some such account is crucial to understanding racial hatred and its immorality. It is insufficient to note that it is a "vicious kind of racially based disregard for the welfare of certain people." A discussion of the immorality of racism must take into account racism's causes, what a person is responsible for, a person's character, the extent to which persons can control their desires, and other fundamental issues in moral philosophy. And it must do this in relation to a specific theory of racism—of what it is.

There is a tendency for moral philosophers to give a psychologically superficial causal account of racism and to claim, in varying degrees, that such causal accounts are either otiose or relatively neutral with regard to an explanation of the immorality of racism or the nature of racism. This approach is mistaken. In-depth causal accounts of racism are essential for both tasks. It is also necessary,

9. But see Garcia 1996: 40 n. 17.

and this seems obvious, for any strategy to curtail racism. It is perhaps less clear, but nonetheless the case, that any historical causal account of racism that gestures toward completeness must likewise include a complex psychological account as the key ingredient.

Garcia misunderstands the significance of causal accounts of prejudices. He says (1996: 39 n. 15), "We should label haters of Jews or black people anti-Semites and racists even if we know their hatred had different causes"—that is, causes other than the ones the prejudices are allegedly causally rooted in. That may be. But the point of giving a causal account is to explain the nature and source of the prejudice as it in fact is. It is not about labeling. If, in fact, antiblack racism does require a particular causal story (or closely related stories), then, in the absence of such a story, there may be good grounds, in certain circumstances—like those in which we are trying to understand the nature of racism—for claiming that an individual is mislabeled, that is, misunderstood, as an antiblack racist.

Garcia's argument for the irrelevancy of the psychological causes of racism to an adequate account of racism, including its irrelevancy to his account, is unsound.[10] He argues as follows (1996: 29):

> Suppose that [Cornel] West and Young-Bruehl are right to think that most of the white racists around today (or in history) were driven to their racism through fear of black male sexuality. Even if this claim about the psychological causes of racism is true, it leaves unaffected our claim about what white racism consists in. It is implausible to think such insecurity essential to (a necessary condition for) racism, even for white racism, because if we came across someone who hated black people, thought us inherently inferior, worked to maintain structures of white domination over us, and so on, but came to all this for reasons other than sexual insecurity, we would and should still classify her attitude as racism. Nor is this hypothesis a near impossibility; we may come across such people quite often, especially, when we consider other forms of racism—hostility against Asians for example. "Psychocultural explana-

10. Garcia says, "Elisabeth Young-Bruehl and Cornel West have recently articulated the common view that white male sexual insecurity is at the heart of white racism. 'White fear of black sexuality is a basic ingredient of white racism.'" To say that "white fear of black sexuality is a basic ingredient of white racism" is quite different from saying, as Garcia does (1996: 29), that such fear "is at the heart of white racism." Young-Bruehl (1996) argues that various prejudices have different and varied sources. There is not just one cause of racism and not one form racism takes. White fear of black sexuality is one among many causes, albeit a principal one, of antiblack racism. It may not even be part of the story in some cases. It depends upon the psyche of individual racists. Her *principal thesis* is that the whole story of racism as one among many prejudices is vastly more complicated both causally and in terms of prejudicial outcomes.

tion" is unlikely to reveal (logically) necessary truths about the nature of racism.

Young-Bruehl does not deny that racism against Asians, although having quite a different causal history than antiblack racism, is racism nevertheless. She affirms and explains this.[11] Racism in its various forms has various sources according to Young-Bruehl—not just one.

Garcia relies too heavily on intuition in claiming that "even if this claim about the psychological causes of racism is true, it leaves unaffected our claim about what white racism consists in." Suppose one discovers a substance that is just like water in every way except that its chemical makeup is other than H_2O. Is it water nevertheless? Well, that depends upon one's views of the semantics of various kind terms. It is one of the preeminent metaphysical and modal questions in recent years.[12]

Young-Bruehl intends her account of the actual causal conditions of racism to refer to this world. Hypothetically, she need not deny that in some other possible world we may wish to say that racism or racist behavior may occur for causal reasons other than the ones she cites. Martians no doubt would have their own set of psychological problems to deal with. Supposing that Martians lacked envy would be insufficient reason for thinking they could not be racist. I think, however, that the case of racism is clearer than that of H_2O. Once one understands the causal history of, for example, antiblack racism, where that story is rooted in some perceived inadequacy of the racist herself, as Cornel West and Young-Bruehl suggest it is; then it is not at all clear that, as Garcia claims, "we would and should still classify her attitude [that is, the attitude of someone who hated black people] as racism" in the absence of its associated causal conditions. We might still *call* it racism, but we would understand it as importantly different from the real thing. Except in cases where the specific causal history of a prejudice is more or less intact, it will not be clear when we are dealing with "racism" rather than with something similar in behavioral terms—perhaps a historical descendent of real racism. The reason that the racism case is clearer than that of H_2O is that in the latter case the concept is itself tied to the periodic table and a certain chemical understanding. One is, as it were, pulled both ways between the scientific and commonsense understanding of H_2O. Nothing similar occurs in

11. See Young-Bruehl 1996, chap. 4, "The Prejudice That Is Not One."

12. Hilary Putnam (1975) claimed that natural kind terms pick out kinds that we typically interact with rather than things that fit stereotypical descriptions. This is usually described as a form of semantic externalism. Putnam would probably not agree that racism is a natural kind term in his sense. Nevertheless, whether or not racism is a natural kind, I am claiming an externalist semantics for "racism" and its cognates. My thanks to Damian Cox.

the case of racism. If one understands racism to be rooted in some underlying psychological structure, then while what is ordinarily called racist behavior may well be indicative of such an underlying structure, it need not be.

Garcia is able to draw the conclusion that he does—that the causal history of racist behavior is irrelevant to regarding it as racist—only because he has peremptorily divorced the conceptual content of the term "racism" from any causal history, choosing to define it solely in behavioral terms. Garcia may be right in claiming that "'psychocultural explanation' is unlikely to reveal (logically) necessary truths about the nature of racism." But Young-Bruehl would not wish to press any such claim. Her claim, and presumably West's, is that there is an intrinsic connection between certain forms of racism and what causes it. Although they would not put it in these terms, perhaps the connection might be seen as an empirically necessary one.[13] The claim that the connection is intrinsic means that behavior that appears racist but has no racist etiology is not—could not be—a form of racism.[14]

Coercion can suppress the manifestations of racism, but no amount of external coercion is going to change the racist mind very much. On my view, coercion will not suppress racism because I equate racism proper with the racist mind and not with its manifestations. It may be convenient to call "racist behavior" that is not intrinsically connected to the racist mind "racist." However, on my account, which regards the etiology of the behavior as essential, it will not actually be racist unless rooted casually in the racist mind. Tamas Pataki sees racism, at an abstract level, as a relation—or a set of relations (e.g., hatred, derogation), or a complex with a relation—linking racist minds, and other things, to their targets. I see racism as psychological structures or mental states—as identical to such structures—where such structures will, sooner or later, lead to racist

13. Following Kripke (1980), an empirical necessity is not a different order of necessity from logical necessity. If it is necessarily the case that water is H_2O, then there is no possible world in which water is something other than H_2O. XYZ just never is water; in any possible world—period. As Kripkeans put it, the term "water" rigidly designates the stuff H_2O. My thanks to Damian Cox for this.

14. Damian Cox succinctly sums up my position (in correspondence): "So we might say that any instance of racism is one or another member of a cluster of psycho/cultural causes; or that racist behavior/attitudes/etc. is behavior/attitudes/etc. with a racist etiology. Necessarily, if some apparently racist set of behaviors does not have such an etiology, then it is not an instance of racism. And this is a claim about certain necessary features of racism. (Say a previously nonracist person suffers a brain injury that causes them to react with great fear and hostility toward any person with dark skin; necessarily, they are not racist.) It might clarify things to call this an empirical necessity rather than a logical necessity (so that this is not a 'logical truth' in the way that modus ponens might be a logical truth), but these two kind of necessity are distinct only in how they are arrived at, not in what they amount to."

behavior. To treat racism as a natural kind, or at least to argue that it has the semantics of natural kind terms, this is how I must regard racism. Pataki disagrees with the equation I make. He says (in correspondence) that equating racism with psychological structures or mental states "could maybe be done for the racist mind, but racism is categorically different. For me [Pataki], racism—most of what is called racism, but excluding learned ethnocentric beliefs—necessarily involves, as essential constituents, such psychological structures, but racism is not identical with them. I draw this distinction between the racist mind and racism to mark this kind of distinction." This distinction is misleading insofar as it suggests that "racism"—genuinely "racist" behavior—can occur apart from being grounded in the racist mind.

IV

Some ailments can be treated successfully by addressing symptoms.[15] However, given the truth of a deep psychological account, such as Young-Bruehl's (1996), of prejudices, it is clear that attempting to seriously curtail racism by addressing symptoms such as racist behavior—whether legally, socially, or otherwise—is hopeless. Certain social and economic structures at specific historical periods do exacerbate and are conducive to certain forms of racism. But racism cannot be curtailed by simply seeking to alter those structures, since the structures are themselves the result of racism. The well-meaning moral exhortations one finds in so much of the philosophical and historical literature on racism is even more insubstantial as a basis for change in this (and most other) areas. This leaves one with the quite pressing and complex question as to just what is the basis of change. (It is a million-dollar question.)

Policies and practices can be unjustly discriminatory without being racist in the primary sense of being rooted in one or more of the psychological ways Young-Bruehl describes. They can, of course, also be unjust or unsatisfactory in ways having little or nothing to do with prejudice. Nevertheless, where such discriminatory practices and policies persist there is bound to be a significant connection at some level—not as far down as some would like to believe—between such policies and genuine first-order racial hatred. Prejudicial and racially discriminatory policies, for example anti–affirmative action policies, are almost always grounded by racial hatred or antipathy. They are not just policy mistakes rooted in ignorance. Policy makers and citizens who extol the virtues of equality and claim affirmative action to be unfair are often either "in denial," mistaken, or both. Their belief in such pseudo-equality, like their being in denial in rela-

15. Arguably, psychiatrists nearly always focus treatment on symptoms. Many would argue that insofar as the causes of mental illness are in fact chemical and biological, then by treating symptoms chemically they are actually treating causes.

tion to their own racism, is itself a function of racial antipathy. As in so many cases, one believes what one wants and needs to believe.

Garcia (1996: 33–34) does not discuss affirmative action in detail, but he links it to his broader discussion of institutional racism and his account of the heart of racism. He points out that not all instances of institutional racism are viciously or fundamentally racist—connected to the heart of racism, even if they have the kinds of results that practices closer to the "heart of racism" also have. That may be, but it misses the more important point. I would emphasize, instead, just how much institutional racism—and it is everywhere—is tied to racism proper and how much "fair play" arguments against affirmative action and "reverse discrimination" are more closely grounded in racial antipathy (not always conscious) than perhaps Garcia, and those with radically different perspectives like George W. Bush, are willing to grant.

Similarly, "right-wing" policies that tend to favor the very well off as opposed to, or arguably at the expense of, less affluent racial minorities, while conceivably grounded in moral, social, and economic policy theory or greed, are likely to have elements of racist bias in them as well. Policy theory and beliefs may result from rationalization.[16] The quarrels that racial minorities have with right-wing and not-so-right-wing political parties (in the United States the Republican *and* Democratic Parties) are not just about economic and social policy; they are often rightfully seen as engendered by underlying racist tendencies and practices. The immigration policy and various policies directed at Australian Aboriginals of the current and past Australian governments are racist.

An account of racism should be able to guide one in answering practical questions in a way that indicates the connection between theory and practice. The kind of fundamentally psychological or psychoanalytic account discussed above can do this. Consider, for example, the person who wants to know if he or she is a racist. This is a question that many people ask themselves from time to time. The account that Young-Bruehl gives suggests that since few are utterly free from the psychologically motivating sources that result in various prejudices, including racism, most people will be prejudicial or racist in varying degrees over different periods of their lives. It turns out that racism, or being prejudicial in some other manner, is not an all-or-nothing thing and is not something one rids oneself of once and for all.

Furthermore, such a theory suggests that victims of racial and other preju-

16. If one doubts the strength of self-deception and ensuing rationalization where antiblack racism is involved, or if one wishes to talk of the partial or misguided "truth" of the so-called white-man's burden, then a walk through South Africa's black townships graphically belies any such psychologically comforting strategies. One wants to ask: "What could the proponents of apartheid have possibly been thinking?"

dice will likewise be perpetrators of it as well. Indeed, there is no reason to suppose that victims will be any less inclined to harbor prejudice or racism. There may even be grounds to suppose that they will be more prone to do so. They are, after all, subject over time to the same kinds of prejudicially motivating psychological features as others. Can Jews and people of color be racist (or sexist)? Can homosexuals and lesbians be sexist (or racist)? *Of course.* Why are some inclined to think they could not be, or be less so? Wishful thinking grounded in a need to believe in moral order and at least rough justice is part of the answer. Straightforward prejudice informing one's beliefs is another.

Consider one further practical question. When walking down a quiet street a person may sometimes feel afraid or uncomfortable when in the presence of, for example, black teenagers. And this is a feeling one might not have if the individuals were white. Does this make one a racist? The account of racism outlined is perhaps less clear on this point but helpful nevertheless. The person may well be a racist or have racist tendencies, but if so, crossing the street to avoid the figures perceived as threatening is not necessarily indicative of racism. It can also be indicative of justifiable fear—though the two (fear and racism) are not incompatible. The fear might be generated by racism, but it might not be and, in fact, it seems unlikely that it would be. Racism is generated by fear and also generates it, but not in a way that makes one want to cross the street. A racist's crossing the street will likely have nothing to do with racism.

While it is true that one must more or less understand the causes of racism in order to curtail it, such an understanding indicates why even then the prospects for quashing racism are not good. Why they are not good and why we have reason to be pessimistic, albeit not despairing, about it is evident once the causal factors constitutive of the *many hearts* of the many prejudices and varieties of racism are understood. Racism is not caused by racial hatred. It *is* racial hatred. Furthermore, such hatred or antipathy, in all its guises, has sources and explanations of both a general and specific nature. In general terms racism is a defensive reaction, related to denial, repression, guilt, self-hatred, narcissism, and sexual frustration and rooted further still in problematic aspects associated with specific character types. As Young-Bruehl (1996: 200–252) argues, all character types have some predominant form of prejudice associated with them. This explains why paternalism and other attitudes and behavior that may not appear overtly racist, or that may even appear beneficial, may be racist nevertheless. Paternalism, for instance, may be a reaction to guilt—like the guilt that white Australians, for example, may feel toward Aboriginals.

There is thus a sense in which racism is not fundamentally about race at all but about psychic defense. Race is, as it were, an excuse for racism. This accounts for the bizarre nature of racism. If you think that it is odd that one would hate other people because of their skin color, you are right. And as it turns out one is not really hating others because of their skin color, sexual preference, or the like but instead because of how those others are being psychically portrayed. All of the causal factors of prejudice may be exacerbated or quelled to a degree by the particularities of one's own personal, social, political, cultural, and historical circumstances. Thus, James Baldwin (1967: 19) hits the nail on the head when he says, "White people in this country [the United States] will have quite enough to do in learning how to accept and love themselves and each other, and when they have achieved this . . . the Negro problem will no longer exist, for it will no longer be needed."

There are two questions that follow on from these considerations. The first has already been touched upon: Given this way of understanding racism, is a different kind of explanation of racism's immorality in order? It seems that a different kind of explanation is in order from that offered by, say, Garcia, Blum, or Dummett in this volume. It is an explanation that is rooted specifically in the nature of racism rather than with what racism or racist behavior has in common with other immoral behavior. Racism, like other prejudices, is grounded in character defects and a variety of psychological disorders and problems. Thus, an explanation of the immorality of racism would at least include reference to the moral reprehensibility of having such a character, to and one's responsibility for that character along with associated traits. This is undoubtedly true of other forms of immorality as well. This explanation would also, as previously noted, discuss the extent to which such features were under one's control and how the issue of control related to moral responsibility.[17] Even if it is hard to change, this does not necessarily give the racist an excuse. But it does help us understand the entire phenomena of racism, morally and otherwise, better.

These considerations considerably complicate the role or significance of a person's motivation when assessing moral culpability because motivation itself becomes a complex and problematic category. One is motivated on various levels, conscious and unconscious, and in many, often conflicting ways. Extensive self-deception involves considerable effort on the part of the self-deceiver, and such deception is always motivated and intentional. It is also far more prevalent than most realize. These are complex moral issues, yet they must be addressed if one is to explain just what it is that is morally wrong and problematic with racism.

Garcia says, "Output-driven concepts [such as being dangerous or harmful] cannot suffice to ground assigning any moral status, because vice and virtue are by nature tied to the action's motivation" (1996: 33). But morally assessing an action in relation to an agent's vice and virtue involves more than merely tying it

17. These perennial issues have been widely discussed in recent literature in moral psychology especially in relation to the emotions. For an introduction see Schlossberger 1992 and Fischer and Ravizza 1993.

to its motivation; and tying it to its motivation is a complex matter. There are often deep psychological motives and conflicting motives and issues of character to consider when one is assessing moral responsibility and a person's vice and virtue. The reason output-driven concepts are, as Garcia says, often useful for moral judgment is because they "can help us to decide whether the action is negligent or malicious or otherwise vicious" (33). Racisms and prejudices are grounded in our natures insofar as we are psychologically constituted as we are: beings who routinely and unavoidably make use of various defense mechanisms, who repress, project, maintain conflicting attitudes and beliefs, and so on.

This leads us to the second question. What are the prospects for white people sorting themselves out in the (unelaborated upon) ways James Baldwin suggests are necessary to overcome antiblack racism in the United States—that is, for whites to rid themselves of those defensive, repressive, projective, narcissistic features that are the sources of racial hatreds? Or to generalize, what are the prospects of altering those features of our psychological selves that are the sources of the plethora of potent prejudices and racisms that continue to have such devastating consequences?

The prospects cannot be good since what appears to be called for is a reconstitution of our psychological selves. This in turn may depend on reconstituting ourselves in various other ways, some known and some not—for example, economically and politically. That getting rid of racism calls for such fundamental, far-reaching, and wide-ranging changes is no surprise and nothing new. After all, some feminists have noted that misogyny and other anti-women prejudices likewise call for vast and fundamental alterations in our psychological, social, and political selves.

Given that certain historical, social, and political, conditions help various prejudices thrive while others help thwart them, it may be possible to curtail if not eliminate prejudices like racism by legislating in ways that inhibit their growth. But this is problematic, given that legislation and various forms of institutionalized racism are themselves products of such prejudices. In other words, it is difficult although not impossible to see how meaningful, far-reaching legislation designed to curtail racisms and other prejudices can come from societies that are fundamentally and broadly racist.

Perhaps the prospects are dismal because substantial change requires too much in too many ways—ways that seem to mutually entail one another. It requires that we change fundamental psychological features of ourselves that seem damned near impossible to alter, like envy or jealousy. Indeed, in some cases eliminating racism requires eliminating envy and jealousy. Nevertheless, for one who has achieved a certain level of consciousness and self-awareness, such change appears possible—*just* possible. Of all the difficulties one may have with oneself—with one's character, personality, sexuality, and psychological makeup, it seems that being a racist need not necessarily be one of them. Given a certain level of awareness, and some luck, one's desires, repressions, projections, and denials need not take specifically racist forms. It is not just charity that begins at home, but also the kinds of self-knowledge required to extirpate racism.[18] I think about Martin Luther King's "I have a dream." It has all the qualities of a dream.[19]

18. Although it was not always so, the current Israeli-Palestinian conflict is primarily about "racial" and deep-seated prejudice on both sides. A disturbing feature of it is the way the present Israeli government's leaders and propagandists hide behind charges of anti-Semitism to masque their own spiraling racist and murderous prejudices. This is odious in part for historical reasons, relying as it does on connections to anti-Semitism for insidious reasons. The past to which Israel refers is one on which they have no moral purchase. Given that they claim to have learned much from anti-Semitism, one wants to ask how they could do such things to a virtually helpless, humiliated, desperate, and oppressed minority. This barbarism is occurring despite the activity of citizens in the peace movements. It is these people who are pro-Israel, rather than those Jews and non-Jews, Israelis, and U.S. citizens, who support Israel's brutal and politically unwise subjugation of the Palestinians. If the thesis of this essay is right, then Israeli barbarism can be explained, in part, by self-hatred—that is, it is itself a manifestation of anti-Semitism (i.e., anti-Jewish anti-Semitism not anti-Arab). The claim that the conflict is about Israeli security obfuscates and exacerbates the problems—making them seem politically manageable. It is a ploy by the Israeli and U.S. governments and many of their citizens. Silence regarding the actions of Israel is, as they say, deafening. It is a potent reminder that the psychic distance many would draw between themselves and those who stood by while other atrocities were committed is not as great as they feign to believe. Karl Jaspers said in 1946, "We see the feelings of moral superiority and we are frightened: he who feels absolutely safe from danger is already on the way to fall victim to it. The German fate could provide all others with experience, if only they would understand this experience! We are no inferior race. Everywhere people have similar qualities. We may well worry over the victors' self-certainty" (Jaspers 2000). See also Arendt 1994.

19. Malcolm Bowie (1993: 20) remarks,

Dreams are not prophecies but wish-fulfilments. They provide not advance glimpses of future time, but hallucinatory annulments of such time. Prophets and fortune-tellers talk about future events in naively chronometrical and desire free terms, and imagine the charm of dreams to lie simply in their allowing us earlier access to a later point in a single untroubled temporal succession. Psychoanalysts, on the other hand, know better than to remove the perturbations of desire from the study of human temporality: while wishfully propelled towards the future, the unconscious nevertheless constantly retrieves that future into the present of its representations.

5 : OPPRESSIONS
RACIAL AND OTHER

The term "racism" is used in many different ways and, at least in the contemporary United States, many things count as racist: racial hatred and racial contempt (whether overt or covert), explicit discrimination, subtle exclusion, unintentional evasion, cultural bias in favor of Eurocentric norms of behavior and beauty, negative racial stereotypes portrayed in the media, arts, and public discourse. The list could go on. My focus in this chapter will be on racial oppression. The phenomena of racial oppression in general and White supremacy in particular are ones that anyone concerned with racial justice has reason to attend to, regardless of disagreements about how to use the term "racism."[1] I believe that racial oppression is counted as a form of racism both in popular discourse and in some academic contexts. So an inquiry into what racism is and how we should combat it reasonably includes attention to racial oppression.

What is racial oppression? Group domination is caused and perpetuated in many different ways. Presumably, in order to understand racial oppression, we should consider oppression in general, as well as historically specific instances

Thanks to Jorge Garcia, Michael Glanzberg, Elizabeth Hackett, Lionel McPherson, Ifaenyi Menkiti, Tommie Shelby, Ajume Wingo, and Stephen Yablo for helpful conversations related to this essay. For this and for comments on earlier drafts, thanks to Elizabeth Anderson, Lawrence Blum, Tracy Edwards, Roxanne Fay, Eva Kittay, Michael Levine, Ishani Maitra, Mary Kate McGowan, Tamas Pataki, Lisa Rivera, Anna Stubblefield, Ásta Sveinsdóttir, and Charlotte Witt. An earlier version was presented at the University of Glasgow, August 2002, and to the New York Society for Women in Philosophy, November 2002. Thanks to the participants in these discussion, especially Anna Stubblefield (my commentator at NY-SWIP) and Jimmy Lenman, for helpful questions and suggestions.

1. I prefer to capitalize the names of races ("White," "Black," "Latina/o," "Asian"). Doing so is warranted, I believe, in order to be consistent between races that are referred to using color terms and those referred to using names of continents, to highlight the difference between ordinary color words and the homonymous use of such words as names for some races, and highlight the artificiality of race in contrast to the apparent naturalness of color (or geography). Moreover, in other work I use the lowercase terms "black," "white," "latina/o," and "asian" to refer to body schemas associated with races and reserve the uppercase terms for racialized groups; making this distinction between "color" and race explicit is, I believe, theoretically important.

where racial injustice is at issue. I believe that an adequate understanding of racism cannot be achieved a priori, but depends on a close analysis of historical examples where race is a factor in the explanation of injustice. Philosophical tools are important, especially at points where the analysis becomes normative, but work done by historians, social scientists, legal theorists, and literary theorists is invaluable in revealing the sometimes subtle ways that injustice is woven through our social life.

This chapter is an attempt to explicate how racism and other forms of social injustice can be seen as structural, and as crucially concerned with power. Work on race and racism in philosophy often focuses on the individual (Piper 1990, Piper 1993, Appiah 1990; cf. Ezorsky 1991); there has even been a move to discredit the idea of structural or institutional racism (Garcia 1996, 1997a, 1999). In the first part of the chapter I develop a contrast between what I will call "structural" oppression and "agent" oppression and discuss briefly the normative basis for the wrong of each. In the second part I consider the *group* component of group oppression. In particular, I ask what link between the group—the race, sex, class, etc.—and the injustice should define group oppression. I will argue that group oppression does not require that the group be explicitly targeted by the unjust institution, but more than just an accidental correlation between the members of the group and those unjustly treated is necessary. My goal is to articulate a middle ground between these two options.

I. OPPRESSION: AGENTS AND STRUCTURES

What is oppression? The notion of oppression has been used to point to the ways in which groups of individuals are systematically and unfairly disadvantaged within a particular social structure.[2] This said, the notion of oppression remains elusive. Let's start with a brief overview of some circumstances that might reasonably be considered oppressive in order to explore the basic grammar of oppression.

The most familiar notion of oppression is one that implies an agent or agents misusing their power to harm another.[3] Drawing on this, we might begin with the idea that *x* oppresses *y* just in case *x* is an agent with some power or authority and

2. It would be interesting to look at the history of the term "oppression" and its uses in the context of political debate. I have chosen this term as the subject of the chapter mainly in order to situate our discussion within a certain tradition of political interpretation central to feminist and antiracist work, and with the hope that by explicating the notion further, those suspicious of this tradition will find it more accessible and valuable.

3. I'm leaving out cases such as "oppressive heat," or "oppressive headache," or "oppressive sadness."

that y is suffering unjustly or wrongfully under x or as a result of x's unjust exercise of power. This leaves open what sort of power is exercised, and whether x and y are individuals or groups. Consider, first, oppression's agents and patients. There are four possible combinations: individual oppresses individual, individual oppresses group, group oppresses individual, and group oppresses group.

Are there plausible examples of each type? The fourth definition of oppression listed in the *Oxford English Dictionary* (2d ed.), although marked as obsolete, appears to provide an example in which an individual oppresses another individual: "forcible violation of a woman, rape." Although the use of "oppression" as a synonym of rape is obsolete, people do classify individual relationships as oppressive—for instance, a particular parent-child or husband-wife relationship. An example of the second type (individual oppresses group) is perhaps the most common use of the term historically, as it captures a relationship gone wrong between a sovereign and his subjects: the tyrant is one who oppresses the people. The simplest examples of cases in which groups are oppressors would simply extend the previous ones: if rape is oppression, gang rape would be the oppression of an individual by a group; also lynching, and the torture of an individual by a group. Similarly, if an individual tyrant can oppress the people, presumably so can an oligarchy (or even a democracy!).

We will look shortly at senses of oppression that do not imply an oppressing agent (group or individual), but before doing so let's start by disentangling two distinct sources of power in the definitions and examples we've considered thus far. Often examples of oppression concern an unjust exercise of power where the source of power or authority is social or institutional; such examples presuppose a background social hierarchy (possibly just, possibly unjust) already in place. Consider the example of rape. In a contemporary context, where rape is often acknowledged to be about social power and not just about sex, it is easy to read cases of rape in these terms: men who rape are exercising their social power over women unjustly through coerced sex. (Plausibly in rape they are exercising their *unjust* social power unjustly!)

However, it is arguable that some rapes aren't exercises of social power: it isn't inconceivable for a rapist to have equal or even less social power than the rape victim (recall the possibility of same-sex rape). If we continue to think of rape as a paradigm of individual/individual oppression, then perhaps we should conclude that oppression's wrong lies in the use of power—not just social power but power of any kind, including physical power—to harm another unjustly. In short: x oppresses y iff x unjustly causes harm to y. On this view oppression is more than simply causing harm (allowing that causing harm is sometimes just or warranted, for example, in self-defense);[4] but oppression is not necessarily

4. If one maintains that the notion of "harm" is of *wrongful* injury, then of course the point should be restated so to allow that causing injury is sometimes warranted.

about the exercise of social power: a terrorist may oppress a hostage through brute force (capture, torture, or the like). The hostage-taking may even be motivated by the fact that the hostage has greater social power and authority than the terrorist himself.

So is this notion—causing unjust harm—the core notion of oppression? It may seem promising insofar as it defines oppression in terms of something that is clearly morally wrong;[5] and as we've seen, the term is sometimes used to capture the harm that one individual, the oppressor, inflicts on another, the oppressed. And yet, unless more can be said about *unjust* action as distinct from *immoral* action, oppression would just collapse into wrongful harm. This suggests that there is something missing from the account.

Undoubtedly there is more than one way of thinking about oppression and its wrongs. However, it is helpful, I believe, to begin by contrasting two sorts of cases. In one sort of case, oppression is an act of wrongdoing by an agent: if oppression of this kind occurs then a person or persons (the oppressor(s)) inflicts harm upon another (the oppressed) wrongfully or unjustly. Let's call these, unsurprisingly, cases of *agent oppression*. It is not clear that *all* cases of an agent wrongfully causing harm should count as oppression; the quote we started with suggests that the harshness of the action and the abuse of power are factors that may distinguish oppression from other sorts of wrongful harm.

In the other sort of cases, the oppression is not an individual wrong but a social/political wrong; that is, it is a problem lying in our collective arrangements, an injustice in our practices or institutions. Consider tyranny. Tyranny is wrong not because (or not just because) tyrants are immoral people intentionally causing harm to others, but because a tyrannical governmental structure is unjust. Theorists will vary on what exactly constitutes its injustice, but key considerations include such matters as the fact that tyranny is not a structure in which individuals count as moral equals. (On a broadly liberal account one could argue that such a structure could not be justified in terms that a community of reasonable equals would accept, and the distribution of power and resources under tyranny depends on invidious and morally problematic distinctions between individuals and groups.) The oppressiveness of a tyranny may be compounded by the evil designs of the tyrant, but even a benign tyrant rules in an oppressive regime. Let's call this second kind of case *structural oppression*.[6]

In cases of agent oppression, the focus is on individuals or groups and their actions; it is the job of our best moral theory to tell us when the action in question is wrong. In cases of structural oppression, the focus is on our collective

---

5. This criterion for an acceptable analysis of racism is suggested by Garcia 1997a: 6.

6. This form of oppression, sometimes more narrowly construed, has also been called "institutional oppression" ("institutional racism"). See, for example, Ture and Hamilton 1992, Ezorsky 1991, Blum 2002: 22–26.

arrangements—our institutions, policies, and practices—and a theory of justice should provide the normative evaluation of the wrong. Of course there are contexts where we need to consider both the individuals *and* the structures, the moral *and* political wrongs.[7]

The idea of an agent oppressing another is relatively familiar; it may be less familiar to think of laws, institutions, and practices as oppressive. So it will be helpful to consider some plausible cases of structural oppression:[8]

- Cases of explicit formal discrimination appear to be straightforward cases of structural oppression: for example, "Jim Crow" legislation enforcing racial segregation in the United States; the disenfranchisement and broad disempowerment of women in Taliban-ruled Afghanistan.

- Under "Jim Crow," poll taxes and (often rigged) literacy tests prevented nearly all African Americans from voting; although such practices did not explicitly target Blacks, they were oppressive. In 1971, the U.S. Supreme Court considered a case in which Blacks were systematically disqualified for certain jobs due to mandated tests that could not be shown to correlate with successful job performance. The Court found that "practices, procedures, or tests neutral on their face, and even neutral in terms of intent, cannot be maintained if they operate to freeze the status quo of prior discriminatory practices" (*Griggs v. Duke Power Co.* 401 US 424).

- U.S. civil rights legislation of the 1960s has been interpreted so that policies and practices that have an unjustified disproportionate adverse impact on minorities can be challenged. In 1985, the Supreme Court recognized that injustice toward the disabled can occur when, for example, architects construct buildings with no access ramps (*Alexander v. Choate* 469 US 287). In the opinion, the Court emphasized that unjust discrimination can occur not just as a result of animus but simply due to thoughtlessness and indifference.

- Cultural norms and informal practices that impose unfair burdens on or create disproportionate opportunities for members of one group as opposed to another are oppressive. Gender norms concerning child care, elder care, housework, appearance, dress, education, careers, and so forth oppress women.

- Cultural practices and products that foster negative stereotypes of particular groups are oppressive, not simply because they are insulting to

7. The boundaries of moral theory and political theory are by no means clear. I will tend to speak of moral theory as a theory of human conduct, so concerned primarily with individuals (and by extension, groups); the focus of political theory is our collective arrangements, i.e., our practices, institutions, policies, etc. Of course it is consistent with this that individual wrongdoing and structural injustice are both morally wrong.

8. Thanks to Elizabeth Anderson for suggesting some of these examples.

members of those groups or foster contempt or hatred toward them, but also because they can have a distorting effect on the judgment of those who are asked to apply discretionary policies. We'll consider some cases of this below (Roberts 2002, 47–74).

I suggested above that oppression is importantly linked to the abuse of power. This fits well with a paradigm of power being abused by an individual who wields power without due regard for moral constraints. But how do we make sense of this in the structural cases? Focusing entirely on individuals and their wrongdoings can prevent one from noticing that social power—the power typically abused in oppressive settings—is relational: it depends on the institutions and practices that structure our relationships to one another (Foucault 1978, Fraser 1989a). When the structures distribute power unjustly, the *illegitimate imbalance* of power becomes the issue rather than an individual abuse of power per se.

For example, in certain contexts (though not all) professors have greater power than their students by virtue of the rules, practices, and expectations in force in academic contexts. Individuals can gain power by developing skills in navigating the practices; they can also lose power by failing to understand or conform to them. If the professor/student relationship in question is structured justly, then we should plausibly look for individual moral failings to account for any wrongs that might occur under its auspices. For example, consider a case in which the practices and institutions constituting the role of professor are just, but an individual in that role, let's call him Stanley, gives low grades to all women of color who take his class, regardless of their performance. In such a case, the injustice arises through the abuse by the particular individual of what would otherwise be a legitimate relationship of unequal power. In cases where the practices constituting a social relationship are just, if someone is wrongly harmed, it is plausibly due to one party or the other acting immorally.

In other cases, however, the problem lies in the structure of relationships and the distribution of power. Contrast the case of the benighted professor, Stanley, who abuses the power granted him within a just social framework, with a case of institutional injustice in which, for example, only males and White women are allowed to serve as professor and to enroll as students. The women of color treated unfairly in the former case are not structurally oppressed, although they are the victims of Stanley's moral wrongdoing. In the latter case they are structurally oppressed, even if the educational resources were made available by professors attempting to undermine the unjust framework: perhaps another professor, Larry, opens his classrooms to unmatriculated women of color.

If we consider only agent oppression, then if some are oppressed we should look for the oppressor. But in cases of structural oppression, there may not be an oppressor, in the sense of an agent responsible for the oppression. Practices and institutions oppress, and some individuals or groups are privileged within those practices and institutions. But it would be wrong to count all those who are privileged as oppressors.[9] Members of the privileged group, for example, Larry in the case above, may in fact be working to undermine the unjust practices and institutions. Nevertheless, in the context of structural oppression, there may be some who are more blameworthy than others for perpetuating the injustice; they may be more responsible for creating, maintaining, expanding, and exploiting the unjust social relationships. In such cases an individual counts as an oppressor if their moral wrongdoing compounds the structural injustice, that is, if they are agents of oppression within an oppressive structure.[10] But not all those who are privileged by an oppressive structure are oppressive agents.

These considerations suggest that both agent oppression and structural oppression can sometimes be intentional and sometimes not, and sometimes there are individuals to blame for the harm and sometimes not. In the case of agent oppression, the question is whether the agent has wrongfully harmed another through an abuse of power.[11] Malicious or hostile intentions are not required: one can abuse one's power to wrongfully harm another by being insensitive and indifferent. Whether the agent is blameworthy is a further matter still; in some cases blameworthiness will depend on the agent's intentions, yet in other cases what matters is the agent's negligence with respect to determining the full impact of his or her actions.

In the case of structural oppression, the question is whether the structure (the policy, practice, institution, discursive framing, cultural norm) is unjust and creates or perpetuates illegitimate power relations. Again, the oppressive structures in question may be intentionally created or not. A structure may cause unjustified harm to a group without this having been anticipated in advance or even recognized after the fact; those responsible for the structure may even be acting benevolently and with the best information available. Whether an individual or a group is blameworthy for the injustice will depend on what role they play in causing or maintaining the unjust structure.

9. For a useful discussion of attributions of blame in contexts of oppression, see Calhoun 1989.

10. The precise conditions for being an oppressor will depend on one's background moral theory; the question is: when does someone's moral wrongdoing compound the structural injustice. On some accounts one's actions may be morally wrong if one is simply a passive participant in an unjust structure; on other accounts not.

11. I am suggesting here that oppression involves an abuse of power or an imbalance of power, though I have not argued specifically for this claim, nor will I resolve here whether we should ultimately endorse it. It is a promising way, however, to distinguish oppression from other forms of moral and political wrong.

II. INDIVIDUALIST AND INSTITUTIONALIST APPROACHES

An important factor motivating the distinction between agent oppression and structural oppression is that although sometimes structural oppression is intentionally caused, say, by policy makers, it is possible for a group to be oppressed by a structure without there being an agent responsible for its existence or the form it takes. Admittedly, individuals play a role in creating and maintaining the social world, but most of the practices and institutions that structure our lives, although made up of individuals and influenced by individuals, are not designed and controlled by anyone individually. The government, the economy, the legal system, the educational system, the transportation system, religion, family, etiquette, the media, the arts, our language, are all collective enterprises that are maintained through complex social conventions and cooperative strategies. And they all distribute power among individuals—for example, a public transportation system that is inaccessible to the disabled disempowers them relative to the able-bodied. Rules of etiquette that preclude women from asking a man on a date, or that require a man to pay for all expenses incurred on the date, are not neutral with respect to the distribution of power.

In some cases social institutions have relatively costless exit options. But even what might seem to be the most malleable practices depend on background expectations and communicative cues that are not within the control of a single individual; so it would be wrong to think of them, except in the rare instance, as created or directed by an individual (or collective) agent.[12] If power resides in the relationships created by practices, and no individual agent is responsible for a particular practice, then there is an important sense in which the distribution of power may be unjust and yet the injustice not be properly explicated in terms of an agent's wrongdoing.

This point, that social structures are often beyond the control of individual agents, counts against what we might call an *individualistic approach* to oppression. On an individualistic approach, agent oppression is the primary form of oppression and the agent's wrongdoing is its normative core: oppression is primarily a moral wrong that occurs when an agent (the oppressor) inflicts wrongful harm upon another (the oppressed); if something other than an agent (such as a law) is oppressive, it is so in a derivative sense, and its wrong must be expli-

---

12. Moreover, although it may be possible to determine in the case of an individual's action what the "meaning" of the action is, for example, by considering the intention behind it, social practices and institutions are embedded in a complex web of meanings with multiple consequences that might be relevant to evaluating their point or purpose. Although in some contexts we are offered legal opinions or transcripts of legislative debate that help sort out the intention behind a law or policy, most institutions are governed by informal norms based in conflicting traditions.

cated in terms of an agent's wrongdoing. For example, one might claim that laws and such are oppressive only insofar as they are the instruments of an agent (intentionally) inflicting harm. The individualistic approach rejects the idea that structural oppression is a distinct kind of wrong.[13]

As I mentioned, a theoretical reason to reject the individualistic approach is that it cannot account for some forms of injustice for which no individual is responsible. Although I've suggested some examples to support this, a fuller discussion would consider specific individualist proposals that attempt to accommodate such cases.

However, there are also more pragmatic reasons for thinking that the individualistic approach is inadequate, viz., what counts as evidence for oppression and what counts as an appropriate remedy. For example, to show that a group suffers from agent oppression, we must establish that there is an agent(s) morally responsible for causing them unjust harm; but tracing the wrong back to an agent (perhaps also determining the agent's intentions) may not be possible. In contrast, to say that a group suffers from structural oppression, we must establish that power is misallocated in such a way that members of the group are unjustly disadvantaged. Likewise, the remedy in the first case will plausibly focus on the individual agent(s) responsible for the harm, whereas in the second it will plausibly focus on restructuring society to make it more just.

Of course both kinds of situation certainly obtain and are of concern: our societies are unjustly structured, and immoral people with power can and do harm others. Moreover, individual and structural issues are interdependent insofar as individuals are responsive to their social context and social structures are created, maintained, and transformed by individuals. Nonetheless, there will be situations that are clearly unjust even when it is unclear whether there is an agent responsible for the oppression; we don't need a smoking gun to tell that a system of practices and policies that result in women being denied adequate health care is unjust. I also submit that we should have more hope in the prospects of social and political change bringing about a significant improvement in people's lives than in the prospects of anything like the moral improvement of individuals. As Liam Murphy (1999: 252) suggests: "it is obviously true that, as a practical matter, it is overwhelmingly preferable that justice be promoted through institutional reform rather than through the uncoordinated efforts of individuals— a point worth emphasizing in an era characterized by the state's abandonment of its responsibility to secure even minimal economic justice and by politicians' embrace of 'volunteerism' as a supposed substitute." I will not attempt to justify

13. Although Garcia does not frame his discussion of racism in terms of oppression, his view of racism seems to fall under what I describe here as an individualistic approach to oppression (Garcia 1996, Garcia 1997a, Garcia 1999). See also the debate between Garcia and Mills (Mills 1997, Garcia 2001a, Mills 2002).

this hope in structural as opposed to moral reform here. But in my experience, not only is structural reform usually more sweeping and reliable, but it also allows ordinary individuals who unwittingly contribute to injustice to recognize this and change their ways, without the kind of defensiveness that emerges when they find themselves the subject of moral reproach.

However, those who emphasize the force of social structures in our lives, and reject an individualistic approach to oppression, sometimes err in the opposite direction. A structuralist or—what may be a better term to avoid other connotations—an *institutionalist approach* to oppression takes structural oppression as the primary form and either denies that individuals can be oppressors or maintains that acts are oppressive insofar as they contribute to maintaining an oppressive structure (Frye 1983, chaps. 1–2, esp. p. 38). Although it is important to capture the sense in which all of us perpetuate unjust structures by unthinkingly participating in them, it is also important to distinguish between those who abuse their power to harm others and those who are attempting to navigate as best they can the moral rapids of everyday life.

On the view I've sketched here, oppression is something that both agents and structures "do," but in different ways. Structures cause injustice through the *misallocation* of power; agents cause wrongful harm through the *abuse* of power (sometimes the abuse of misallocated power). Allowing space in our account for both kinds of oppression provides greater resources for understanding the ways in which social life is constrained by the institutional and cultural resources available, and the ways in which we have agency within, and sometimes in opposition to, these constraints.

For example, one theme in discussions of oppression is the systematic, and one is sometimes tempted to say inescapable, constraint imposed upon the oppressed (Frye 1983, chap. 1). The idea that oppression is a structural phenomenon helps capture this insight. Return once again to the contrast between the benighted professor (Stanley) in a just system and the morally responsible professor (Larry) in the unjust system. The relevant contrast between the two cases and those like them is not simply the degree to which the constraint is avoidable (Stanley may be very powerful, the institution of segregation quite weak), nor is it the systematic nature of the harm (the benighted professor can be quite systematic). Nor is it the multiplicity of the barriers (presumably just the illegality of marriage alone would be enough to oppress gays and lesbians), or the macroscopic aspects of social phenomena (it may be that one has to look at the minute details of a practice to see its injustice) (cf. Frye 1983, chap. 1). The contrast lies in the extent to which the injustice resides in the structure of the institutions and practices—for example, the ways they distribute power—and the extent to which the wrong is located in the particular acts and attitudes of individuals within them. Structural oppression occurs where the structures are unjust, not where the wrong lies simply in the moral failings—the acts and attitudes—of an agent.

At this stage I have not provided an argument for the conclusion that the notion of oppression should be "analyzed" in terms of agent and structural oppression; nor have I argued that such an analysis should be framed as the misuse or misallocation of power to cause harm. I have simply suggested that a concept of oppression developed along these lines is useful for those concerned with group domination. I believe that an individualistic approach to group domination is inadequate because sometimes structures themselves, not individuals, are the problem. Likewise, an institutionalist approach is inadequate because it fails to distinguish those who abuse their power to do wrong and those who are privileged but do not exploit their power. I recommend a "mixed" approach that does not attempt to reduce either agent or structural oppression to the other. I've opted to use the term "oppression" to cover both kinds of case.

III. GROUP OPPRESSION

So far I have suggested an outline for a theory of oppression that provides placeholders for accounts of justice and of individual moral wrongdoing. At this point it might seem that further progress in understanding oppression depends on providing substantive normative theories. As an example of a structural account of justice I have pointed toward a broadly liberal sentiment that requires of a social structure that it be one that reasonable equals could accept. To this (and related) liberal sentiments I am sympathetic, though one can endorse the kind of approach to oppression I've outlined without endorsing liberalism. Obviously I cannot develop and defend full accounts of justice and moral wrong in the context of this chapter. So what further can be accomplished?

As indicated at the outset, a crucial task for a theory of oppression is to explicate the link between groups and wrongs that make for group-based oppression. In what follows I will focus on this link in structural as opposed to agent oppression in order to understand structural racism, sexism, and the like. Of course my discussion will not be normatively "neutral" between competing conceptions of justice. In the background will lie a broadly democratic, egalitarian, and materialist sensibility, but this will not be articulated or made the focus of discussion.[14] No doubt there are particular conceptions of justice which, if

14. It may be helpful to make explicit some background assumptions that will continue to guide the discussion. First, injustice occurs not just in courts and state houses, but in churches, families, and other cultural practices. Second, although an understanding of justice and oppression must employ a meaningful notion of "group," we must avoid overgeneralizing about the attitudes, experiences, or social position of members of the groups. Third, those in subordinate positions are not passive victims of oppression, nor are those in dominant positions full agents of oppression. Society "imposes" dominant and subordinate

plugged into my account, would yield unacceptable results by any standards. However, my goal at this stage is simply to make progress in understanding how an account of structural oppression can be sensitive to multiple group memberships without falling back on an individualist model that specifies who suffers oppression in terms of an agent's (or agents') intentions. I will be happy if I can describe a framework within which further discussion of the different factors and their interplay will be fruitful.[15]

So, what makes a particular instance of structural oppression "group-based oppression," such as racist, sexist, or class oppression? As I see it, there are two parts to the question. One part is to determine whether there is oppression: whether there is a misallocation of power causing wrongful harm. This is a part where one must rely on a substantive theory of justice. Another part is to determine how or whether the wrong is linked to membership in a group. In many cases one can at least analytically distinguish between the fact that something is unjust and the fact that the injustice is specifically "racial" and/or "sexual."[16] It is this latter question to which we turn now.

On its face, the issue seems simple enough: sex oppression is injustice that targets women; racial oppression targets members of racial minorities. But how should we understand this idea of "targeting"?

Several ideas come to mind: perhaps whether something counts as a "racial injustice" depends simply on whom the injustice affects; does it affect almost all and almost only members of a particular race in a particular context? This, at least stated this simply, can't be right. There are racially homogeneous contexts in which an injustice affects virtually everyone, but we wouldn't want to say that the injustice was racial. For example, a Japanese company with all Japanese

---

identities on members of both groups, and groups negotiate and transform them. However, some identities are more empowering and more empowered than others. Fourth, oppression cannot be explained by reference only (or primarily) to any single factor, such as the attitudes or psychologies of social groups, economic forces, the political structure of society, culture. Fifth, injustice, and so the wrongs of structural oppression consist not simply in unjust distributions of goods, opportunities, and such, but in inegalitarian social relationships, that is, in relational obligations and expectations that distribute power hierarchically (Anderson 1999b: 312; Young 1990a, chap. 1).

15. Methodologically, I see the search for counterexamples to a proposed account useful in understanding the phenomenon, even if they show that the proposal as it stands fails. Presumably, an account of justice that cannot capture the broad range of phenomena that are plausibly structurally oppressive would be, for that reason, inadequate. Some have argued that Rawls's account of justice is inadequate for this reason (e.g., Cohen 1997).

16. I leave open whether there are some inherently racial or sexual wrongs, where the wrongness of the act or the injustice of the structure is not separable from its racial or sexual meaning. Hate crimes could be an example.

workers might exploit those workers, but this would not make the exploitation a racial injustice.[17]

Moreover, given that individuals are always members of multiple overlapping groups, even when a group is adversely affected, it is not always clear under what guise they are being subjected to injustice. For example, since the 1970s socialist feminists have argued that class exploitation and sex oppression should not be seen as two autonomous systems each with their own distinctive causal/explanatory principles and their own (overlapping) target groups (Young 1980). Instead, class exploitation and sex oppression are intertwined, not just in the sense that there are some who suffer both, or that one system affects the other, but in the sense that the relationships that distribute power along the lines of class also distribute power along the lines of sex. Broadly speaking, this is the phenomenon of *intersectionality* (Crenshaw 1995). So to analyze the situation of Mexican-American domestic workers by looking only at class, or only at nationality/ethnicity, or only at race, or only at gender, would be inadequate. An account that correctly determines whether a particular situation is just or not must include multiple categories of critical analysis; it must also attend to the different ways, in different kinds of relationships, that the demands of justice may be violated. The particular form injustice takes may depend on the mix of group memberships in the target population.[18]

Alternatively, one might insist that the injustice must be motivated by racial animus or intended to disadvantage members of a racial group. But as we've seen, this requirement is too strong, for not only are there cases of racial injustice where racial animus is not the cause, but there may not even be an individual or group of individuals in any clear sense perpetrating the injustice. So effects alone and motivations alone are not the key. Where should we look next?

In *Justice and the Politics of Difference*, Iris Young suggests that oppression occurs when a social group suffers any of (at least) five different forms of subordination: exploitation, marginalization, powerlessness, cultural imperialism, and systematic violence (1990a: 48–63). Although tremendously valuable for its insight into the variety of forms oppression can take, for the most part Young's discussion assumes preexisting social groups and examines the variety of structural injustices they might suffer. As a result, she avoids some of the questions that arise in understanding the relationship between the group membership and injustice.

17. Although this is true in general, it isn't guaranteed, for if the company relied on particular Japanese cultural norms or practices to exploit the workers, it might count as a kind of ethnic oppression. Thanks to Roxanne Fay for pointing this out.

18. Given that there are laws against some forms of discrimination and not others, it can matter tremendously how to characterize the group basis for the injustice. See, for example, *DeGraffenreid v. General Motors* (413 F. Supp. 142 [ED Mo. 1976]).

Let's pause to reflect a bit on the idea of a group. Some groups are well-defined social entities whose members recognize themselves as such and take their membership in the group to be important to their identity (Young 1990a: 44–45). However, some social groups have little or no sense of themselves as a group, and may in fact come to understand themselves as such only as a result of policies imposed on them. Consider two cases: suppose at a particular company, call it BigCo, wage employees are required to submit to drug testing as a condition of continued employment. One might argue that the policy is unjust, and the injustice extends to all wage employees even if some have no objection to being drug tested.[19] (If you are unhappy with the suggestion that mandatory drug testing is unjust, then substitute your own example of an unjust burden placed on the employees in question.) In many work contexts, the distinction between wage employees and salaried employees is a meaningful division that organizes the individual interactions within and between the two groups. The imposition of a policy that relies on this distinction may reinforce the division and affect the groups' interactions, but the division was meaningful prior to the policy.

However, policies can also make divisions meaningful that were not before. Suppose that BigCo distinguishes types of job by numbering them from 1 to 100. The salaried positions are coded from 80 to 100 and the wage positions 1 to 79. If the company institutes the drug testing policy for employees in positions coded 25–50, this might well make salient a distinction among the wage employees that was not significant before. The employees in these categories may come to identify with each other, may organize against the policy, and may come to interact quite differently with employees in other categories. If the policy is unjust, however, it would be wrong, I think, to claim that oppression only occurs once the employees see themselves as a group and identify *as* members of the group. So to say that someone is oppressed *as an F* is not to imply that they *identify* as an F. Rather, the point can be that one is oppressed by virtue of being a member of the Fs; that is, being an F is a condition that subjects them to an unjust policy or practice (regardless of whether being an F is meaningful to them or not).

Social groups are dynamic entities whose membership and sense of identity change in response to sociopolitical circumstances. Their origin, shape, and development is crucially bound up with the institutions within which they are embedded and the history and future of those institutions (Lieberman 1995: 438–40). So the question before us can't simply be: Is this preexisting (racial, sexual, socioeconomic) group being exploited, marginalized, or the like (cf. Young 1990a, chap. 2)? But rather: How does a particular policy or practice construct or affect the identity of the group, as well as its position within the broader sociopolitical system? To answer this question we will need to ask such questions as: Do different institutions define the group in the same way? Does the policy

19. For insight into the effects of such policies on employees, see Ehrenreich 2001.

divide a social group into new groups, granting benefits to some members and not others?

However, there are disadvantages in focusing too much on policies and practices that name or specify the oppressed groups *as such*. First, as we've seen, given a history of group domination, the effects of earlier injustice position subordinate groups socially and economically so that their members have much more in common than their group membership. Policies framed to pick up on these other commonalities can reinforce the unjust social divisions (Lieberman 1998: 11). This is sometimes called "secondary discrimination" (Warren 1977: 241–43; Rosati 1994: 152–59).

Second, although for convenience we've been considering explicitly stated policies, we want the account to apply to both formal policies and informal practices.

Third, sometimes policies and practices that are articulated in a way that is "blind" with respect to a social group may nonetheless be motivated by animus toward the group and may have serious consequences for its members. In fact, as oppression is identified and condemned, it is a familiar tactic of the dominant group to reframe discriminatory structures to have the same effects without the discrimination being explicit.

Fourth, if oppression requires that the policy or practice make membership in a group an *explicit* condition for the policy's application, then there is a temptation to think that the basis for the wrong is in the intentions of the policy's framers. But this is to return to a more individualistic approach to oppression. We want to allow that a structure motivated by good intentions may be unjust in its distribution of goods and power and in the social meaning of the relationships it creates.

Thus it appears that in some cases the institution in question targets a social group explicitly; in some cases it does not explicitly target such a group but has clear ramifications for it; and in other cases its target is a group that has not previously had an established sense of itself. Is there some useful way to organize these different sorts of cases?

IV. STRUCTURAL OPPRESSION OF GROUPS: AN ATTEMPT AT A DEFINITION

RACE-LADENNESS
In analyzing the Social Security Act of 1935 and its legacy for contemporary race relations, Robert Lieberman offers the term "race-laden" to describe institutions that perpetuate racial injustice without doing so explicitly:[20]

20. This characterization of "race-laden" does not quite capture what Lieberman is after

By "race-laden," I refer to the tendency of some policies *to divide the population* along racial lines without saying so in so many words. . . . But race-laden policies are *not simply programs whose tendency to exclude by race is merely incidental or accidental*. . . . Moreover, they can be expected *to affect Blacks and Whites differently in the normal course* of their everyday operations, whether or not their framers or administrators intended that result. (Lieberman 1998: 7, italics mine)

The notion of "race-laden" policies is suggestive. Some institutions may accidentally map onto unjust power relations without being oppressive; but some institutions that appear to map only accidentally onto unjust power relations are not only rooted in a history of such injustice but also perpetuate it.

Drawing on these insights, here's a first proposal for understanding structural oppression of groups:

> (SO_1)*F*s are oppressed (as *F*s) by an institution *I* in context *C* iff$_{df}$ in *C* ($\exists R$)((being an *F* nonaccidentally correlates with being disadvantaged by standing in an unjust relation *R* to others) and *I* creates, perpetuates, or reinforces *R*.)

Consider a couple of examples:

- Nonfluent English speakers are oppressed (as such) by English-only ballots in California in 2002, iff in California in 2002 being a nonfluent English speaker nonaccidentally correlates with being disadvantaged by being disenfranchised, and English-only ballots create, perpetuate, or reinforce the disenfranchisement.
- Women are oppressed as women by cultural representations of women as sex objects in the United States in the late twentieth century iff being a woman in the United States in the late twentieth century nonaccidentally correlates with being subjected to systematic violence, and cultural representations of women as sex objects creates, perpetuates, or reinforces the systematic violence.

As mentioned before, I leave open for present purposes the large and important issue of how to understand the specific requirements of justice. However, there are several elements of this proposal that deserve further discussion:

---

because it does not distinguish between just and unjust institutions. Although in the context it appears that he intends the term "race-laden" to refer to unjust policies, it is possible for an institution to "reflect" racially structured power arrangements and to have differential racial effects, but also function to lessen injustice. One might argue that certain affirmative action plans designed to aid socioeconomically disadvantaged groups reflect racially structured power arrangements, and have racially differential effects, but are nonetheless just.

1. How does this analysis of *group* oppression apply to individuals: under what condition is an *individual* oppressed by a structure?
2. Why am I supposing that the injustice involves being disadvantaged by a standing in an unjust *relation*?
3. What is meant by a *nonaccidental correlation* between the group membership and the injustice?
4. What sort of relation between the institution and the injustice counts as *creating, perpetuating, or reinforcing*?

I will speak to each of these in turn.

First, the proposal thus far is ambiguous in its mention of "*F*s being oppressed" for it is unclear whether the claim is that (in the context in question) *all Fs* are oppressed or only *some Fs* are oppressed. Is the claim in the second example that *all* women in late-twentieth-century America are oppressed by the cultural representation of women as sex objects, or that *some* women are?

My view is that the practices in question are oppressive to all members of the group, but of course to different degrees and in different ways, depending on what other social positions they occupy. For example, a wealthy woman who can afford to take a taxi whenever she is anxious about her security on the street is not oppressed by the prevalence of violence against women to the same extent as a poor woman who must use public transportation and walk several blocks home from the bus stop after her shift is over at midnight. But that women are at greater risk of rape, domestic violence, and sexual harassment than men is an injustice that affects all women, whether or not they are ever the direct victim of such acts, and whether or not they are typically in a position, by virtue of their wealth or their location, to protect themselves. As a result, I would endorse the general claim for any individual x:

> x is oppressed as an F by an institution I in context C iff$_{df}$ x is an F in C and in C $(\exists R)$((being an F nonaccidentally correlates with being disadvantaged by standing in an unjust relation R to others) and I creates, perpetuates, or reinforces R.)

Further examples would include:

- Tyrone is oppressed as a Black man by race/gender-profiling in the United States in the early twenty-first century iff Tyrone is a Black man in the United States in the early twenty-first century and in that context being a Black man nonaccidentally correlates with being subjected to police harassment and brutality, and race/gender-profiling creates, perpetuates, or reinforces the police harassment and brutality.
- William is oppressed as a gay man by the health insurance policies at BigCo in 1990 iff William is a gay man employed at BigCo in 1990 and in

that context being a gay man nonaccidentally correlates with an inequitable distribution of benefits based on sexual orientation, and the health insurance policies create, perpetuate, or reinforce the inequitable distribution.

Some may prefer to limit oppression to those who suffer directly from the specified disadvantage (the victims of violence, those denied benefits, and the like). However, plausibly the imposition of certain risks on groups is itself oppressive, so I endorse the wider account; I will not defend it here, however, and it is open to one who prefers the narrower account to qualify the proposal as indicated.

Second, on relations: I've indicated several ways that injustice is relational: it concerns relative distributions of goods and power, and relationships that define the expectations, entitlements, and obligations of the different parties. In oppressive circumstances there will be, then, a background framework of relationships that disadvantages some and privileges others. Consider Young's example of powerlessness (Young 1990a: 30–33). Although it may be possible to define, say, powerlessness in nonrelational terms (e.g., lacking autonomy in crucial areas of life), powerlessness occurs within a system of social relations that defines the spheres of freedom and control within which we are entitled to act. My proposal, as it stands, is articulated to encourage a recognition of such background relational structures.

Third, on "nonaccidental correlations" between group membership (F) and injustice (R): Let me first note two points: First, in order for there to be a correlation between *being an F* and *being a G*, it is not necessary that all Fs are G, or that only Fs are G. There might be a nonaccidental correlation between smoking and lung cancer even if not all smokers get lung cancer and some nonsmokers do. Similarly women in the United States might be oppressed by wage discrimination even if a subset of women earn fair wages and some men don't. Second, in requiring that the correlations must be "nonaccidental," the point is to find a middle ground between requiring that the unjust policy or practice *explicitly target* a group, and requiring only that there be *some adverse effect* of the policy on the group. In some circumstances unjust policies will affect a group "merely accidentally" without there being any evidence that the group identity is relevant to the injustice. For example, suppose NASA implements an unjust policy applying to all astronauts; in fact, there will be a correlation between those affected by the policy and White men. But in most such scenarios it would be wrong to maintain that those White men affected by the policy are thereby being oppressed *as White men*.

What might count, then, as a nonaccidental correlation? In general, a correlation counts as nonaccidental because it supports certain kinds of counterfactuals; the idea is that the group's being a group *of F*s is causally relevant to the injustice. A full account should specify exactly what counterfactuals are necessary and sufficient for the kind of nonaccidental correlation in question. I will not be able to provide that here; instead I will offer a series of examples that suggest a set of relevant counterfactuals to consider.

EXAMPLE: RACISM AND CHILD WELFARE

Let's turn to a more sustained analysis of a real life case. In her work *Shattered Bonds*, Dorothy Roberts argues that current child welfare policy is racist. She uncovers ways in which state intrusion into Black families in the name of child welfare systematically (i) reinforces negative stereotypes about Black families, (ii) undermines Black family autonomy, and (iii) weakens the Black community's ability to challenge discrimination and injustice (Roberts 2002: ix). But as Roberts acknowledges, we must be careful in charging that the system is racist, for there are other variables that might explain why the Black community is disproportionately affected: "Because race and socioeconomic status are so intimately entwined, it is hard to tell how much of what happens to Black children is related to their color as opposed to their poverty" (47).

There is evidence that Black children are more likely to be separated from their parents than children of other races, that Black children spend more time in foster care and are more likely to remain in foster care until they "age out," and that Black children receive inferior services. This, of course, is disturbing, but by itself it doesn't show that the system is racially biased; it could also be that there are other features of the cases in question—level of poverty, degree of substance abuse, incarceration of parents and other family members—that better explain the rate of removal, time in foster care, quality of service, and so forth. Is there further evidence that race is the relevant variable that explains the disparity in the numbers? The evidence is mixed.

Roberts points to considerations supporting the conclusion that the system is racially biased. First, there is a huge racial imbalance in child welfare involvement between Black and non-Black families, even though studies show that children in Black families are no more likely to be mistreated than children in non-Black families (Roberts 2002: 47–52). Yet both popular opinion and expert studies are ridden with racial stereotypes and misunderstandings of cultural differences that sustain the belief that Black families are dysfunctional and dangerous. Because decisions about removal and reunification are "discretionary," the result is that removal of children from Black families often appears warranted when it isn't.

Such a random process for identifying maltreated children could not so effectively target one group of families without some racial input. I am not charging that [caseworkers and judges] deliberately set out to break up Black families because they dislike their race. To the contrary, they may believe that they are helping Black children by extricating them from a dangerous environment. But race negatively affects their evaluation of child maltreatment and what to do about it, whether they realize it or not. (Roberts 2002: 55)

Second, looking at the history of child welfare policy, Roberts notes that there has been a major shift in its goals and policies. Whereas once the idea was to provide programs to help families in need, currently "The system is activated only after children have experienced harm and puts all the blame on parents for their children's problems. This protective function falls heaviest on African-American parents because they are the most likely to suffer from poverty and institutional discrimination and be blamed for the effects on their children" (Roberts 2002: 74). Over the past thirty years, the changes in the system have correlated with the racial makeup of the population it serves: "child protective services have become even more segregated and more destructive. As the child welfare rolls have darkened, family preserving services have dried up, and child removal has stepped up" (Roberts 2002: 99). And yet, the harsh policies do not address the deeper social problems: "At the same time that [the child welfare system] brutally intrudes upon too many Black families, it also ignores the devastating impact of poverty and racism on even more children. . . . The child welfare system reinforces the inferior status of poor Blacks in American both by destroying the families who come within its reach and by failing the families who don't" (91).

Third, Roberts considers the claim that the child welfare system is not racially biased because—*all things being equal*—Black families are no more likely to be disrupted than White families. Roberts argues that even if this were true, "all things are not equal" (Roberts 2002: 94) for there is, of course, a history of racial oppression that has systematically disadvantaged Black families. If Black families make up a disproportionate number of those in extreme poverty—due in part to a history of racial oppression—and if those in extreme poverty suffer unfair disadvantages (which research clearly shows), then the unfair treatment of the poor in fact perpetuates the injustice Black families have suffered.

This point is important for several reasons. Our focus at the moment remains on nonaccidental correlations. In the case we're considering a history of unjust institutions has explicitly targeted African Americans, and these institutions are largely responsible for the current disproportionate number of Blacks in poverty. Recent child welfare policies, however, unjustly disadvantage those in poverty. It would be plausible to claim that Black families suffer the current injustices in child welfare because of the history of racist policies: if Blacks as a group hadn't suffered historical injustices, they wouldn't be suffering the current ones in the child welfare system. I maintain that this is sufficient to count as a nonaccidental correlation between being Black and being subject to demeaning and disempowering child welfare policies. The point is that the racial correlation occurs, not because those designing and implementing the policies have intended to harm Blacks as such, but because an adequate explanation of the current disadvantage must rely on the history of unjust policies that have targeted Blacks.

Clearly the Roberts analysis is highly controversial, and I have not attempted to summarize the research supporting her view. But for our purposes, whether her analysis is ultimately correct is not the issue. The point is to illuminate some of the ways that there *could be* a nonaccidental correlation between group membership and injustice. Drawing on the form of Roberts's arguments, we can articulate several factors that are relevant in determining whether there is a nonaccidental correlation of the type required by the proposed definition of oppression (this list is not intended to be exhaustive):

1. Does the unjust institution *I* in question explicitly target (or was it designed to target, but not explicitly target) those who are *F*?
2. Does the unjust institution *I* allow discretion in its application, in a context where there is widespread misperception of and bias against *F*s?
3. Does the history of the institution *I* reveal a correlation between an increase in the harshness/injustice of its policies and practices and the *F*ness of the target population?
4. Is there a history of injustice toward the group *F*s which explains how members of that group are now affected by the injustice resulting from *I*?

THE SLOGS

Even with these considerations in mind, however, a problem remains.[21] Consider a fictional society in which there is a group, call them the Slogs, who are truly lazy. They don't like to work, and when they are given work they are irresponsible about getting it done and do it badly. Let's suppose too that this laziness of the Slogs is not the result of a previous injustice. Further, in this society the Slogs and only the Slogs are lazy, and the Slogs and only the Slogs are poor; although the Slogs are provided at least the minimum that justice requires, everyone else earns a more generous income and has a significantly better standard of living. Suppose now that the society imposes a harsh policy affecting the

21. Thanks to Jimmy Lenman for this example. A similar one was brought to my attention by Roxanne Fay and Ishani Maitra: If it isn't an accident that astronauts are predominantly White men, then an unjust policy that targets astronauts may be sufficient for a "nonaccidental correlation" between being a White man and being subject to the injustice. But intuitively this would not be a case of "White male oppression." The revised formulation below would avoid this because the privileges granted White men don't count as a primary oppression of them.

poor—for example, the denial of medical care to those who can't afford to pay for it. Note that in this society there is a nonaccidental correlation between being lazy and being denied medical treatment. Should we say then that the Slogs are oppressed *as lazy*? Is this a case of secondary discrimination against the lazy, or only primary discrimination against the poor? On the proposal as articulated, because of the nonaccidental correlation between laziness and poverty, and between poverty and denial of medical care, the case would satisfy the conditions for "laziness-oppression"—that is, if we substitute "lazy" for *F* in the condition, then we seem to have a case of group oppression of the Slogs (and individual Slogs) *as lazy*.

Let me be clear: the issue is not whether there is primary oppression against the poor. This can be granted. The question we are addressing is not just who is oppressed, but what groups are oppressed *as such*. In our fictional society the Slogs are oppressed because they are poor and the poor are being unjustly denied medical care. But are they oppressed *as lazy*? Could the Slogs claim that an injustice has targeted them as lazy? Or only as poor?[22]

If, as seems plausible, we don't want to allow this to be a case of "laziness oppression," then the example highlights that "secondary discrimination" does not occur in every case in which one is subject to injustice due to the effects of a prior condition, but occurs only when there is a primary injustice on which the current injustice piggybacks. In keeping with this, one might argue that it is not an injustice that the Slogs are poor, given their laziness (recall that they were initially provided the minimum that justice requires). It is an injustice, however, that they are now denied medical care, given their poverty. The proposal I've offered does not capture this distinction. Drawing on the Roberts example, here is the kind of secondary discrimination we want to capture, in contrast to the Slogs case:

> Blacks are oppressed *as Blacks* by child welfare policies in Chicago in the 1990s because in that context being poor results in having one's family unjustly disrupted, and being poor nonaccidentally correlates with being Black *due to a prior injustice,* and the child welfare policies cause or perpetuate unjust disruption of families.

Hopefully, this captures what we're after in a more general way:

> (SO_2) *F*s are oppressed (as *F*s) by an institution *I* in context *C* iff$_{df}$ in *C* ($\exists$R)(((being an *F* nonaccidentally correlates with being unjustly disadvantaged either primarily, because *being F* is unjustly disadvantaging in C, or secondarily, because ($\exists$G) (*being F* nonaccidentally

22. Although this question may seem to be splitting hairs (see note 18 above), it is often a matter of serious political and legal concern whether a form of injustice or a crime is group based or not, and if so, what the relevant group is.

correlates with *being G* due to a prior injustice and *being G* is unjustly disadvantaging in C)) and *I* creates, perpetuates, or reinforces *R*.)

On this account, Blacks are oppressed both *as poor* (primarily) and *as Black* (secondarily), in the context in question. The Slogs, however, are only oppressed primarily, viz., as poor.

Fourth and finally, let us address the question: What is involved in saying that an institution *creates, perpetuates, or reinforces* injustice? In considering oppression it is important to ask three separate questions:

1. Does the institution *cause* or *create* unjust disadvantage to a group?
2. Does the institution *perpetuate* unjust disadvantage to a group?
3. Does the institution *amplify* or *exacerbate* unjust disadvantage to a group?

There is a tendency to focus on (1) when asking whether an institution is oppressive. But (2) and (3) are no less important to promote justice.

We considered above how the child welfare system perpetuates racial injustice. Consider also the situation of women in a context where women were not educated and so, for the most part, were not literate. If one then argued that women should not have the vote because they were not literate, the policy would perpetuate sexism, even if sex were not a basis for discriminating between those eligible to vote and those not. This suggests that in order for a system or a structure to be nonracist it must not remain "neutral" with respect to the impact of past racial harms. Institutions conveniently becoming "race" or "gender" blind after great harm has been done are not just; systems that remain "neutral" in such contexts actually perpetuate injustice (see MacKinnon 1989, esp. chap. 12).

In some cases institutional "blindness" to groups keeps groups in an unjust status quo; in other cases it actually exacerbates the problem. Returning to Roberts, she argues that recent child welfare policies not only perpetuate racism, but exacerbate it by, for example, disrupting the Black community. What's at issue is the effects of the policy, not just on individuals or particular families, but on the Black community more broadly. So *even if* a policy doesn't discriminate between similarly situated Black and White families, it still may be the case that it affects Black and White communities differently. If the Black community starts out in a bad position due to past racism and the policy makes things worse, then it doesn't just perpetuate the unfairness but amplifies it. Poor White communities are also unfairly disadvantaged, for the policies augment their class oppression, but there is a racial dimension to the disadvantage that affects Blacks as *a racial group:* by systematically perpetuating racist stereotypes and preventing the Black community from becoming more powerful in having its needs addressed, Blacks suffer a racial injustice.

V. RACIAL OPPRESSION

Given the definition of structural oppression offered in the previous section, we can now explicitly apply it to races or ethnoracial groups. Let the *F*s be the ethnoracial group in question. Earlier examples of oppression and the Roberts case study have, I hope, given sufficient examples of what could be plausible substituends for *I* and *R*.

I have not attempted to explicate what it means to be oppressed *simpliciter*. Some may want to reserve the claim that someone *is oppressed* for only those cases in which they suffer from substantial and interconnected oppressive structures, on the grounds that to show that a single policy oppresses someone is not to show that they are oppressed. Nothing I say here counts against such a view. Of course, not all oppressive structures are equally harmful, and they should not all be regarded with the same degree of concern. My goal has not been to analyze ordinary uses of the term "oppression" or to legislate how the term should be used, but to highlight how we might better understand structural group domination.

That said, it is worth considering whether the proposal for understanding structural oppression is also useful in thinking about agent oppression. We saw before that an agent may oppress another without intending to. Unconscious racism and sexism are common. So just as we needed to ask what "links" an unjust structure with a group to constitute *structural* oppression, we should ask what "links" an agent's action with a group to constitute *agent* oppression, that is, a racial or sexual wrong. Here's a straightforward application of the first proposal to agent oppression (O = oppressor, V = victim):

> O oppresses V *as an F* by act A in context C iff$_{df}$ in C (V is an F (or O believes that V is an F) and (being an F (or believed to be so) nonaccidentally correlates with being morally wronged by O) and A creates, perpetuates, or reinforces the moral wrong.)

For example, Oscar oppresses Velma as a woman by paying her less than her male counterpart at BigCo iff, at BigCo, Velma is a woman (or Oscar believes that she is) and being a woman (or being believed to be so) nonaccidentally correlates with being wrongly exploited by Oscar (i.e., Velma's being exploited is at least partly explained by Oscar's belief that she is a woman), and Oscar's paying Velma less than her male counterpart contributes to her exploitation. The point again is that membership in the group (or groups) in question is a factor in the best explanation of the wrong. As before, we'll need to complicate the proposal to take into account the issue of secondary discrimination in the agent case. (I leave this to the reader.)

One might object, however, that the account I've offered is not helpful, for whether group membership is relevant in explaining an injustice will always be a matter of controversy. In short, the account does not help us resolve the very disagreements that gave us reason to develop an account of group oppression in the first place.

Admittedly, in depending on the notion of "nonaccidental correlation," I inherit many of the philosophical concerns about such connections—for example, by what method should we distinguish between accidental and non-accidental correlations? Empirically, they will look the same. If the difference between them rests on counterfactuals, don't we need a clear method for evaluating the relevant counterfactuals? Such a method is not readily available.

Note, however, that the point of this discussion has not been to offer an *epistemic* method or criterion for distinguishing oppression (or group oppression) from other rights and wrongs. In many cases the judgment that an action or policy is oppressive is convincing on its face, and the question is how to understand the content of our judgment and its implications. Of course there are controversial cases for which it would be helpful to have a clear criterion for resolving our disagreements: Does affirmative action oppress White males? Does pornography oppress women? Does abortion oppress fetuses? However, in a majority of the controversial cases, the real disagreements are moral/political—they concern one's background theory of right and wrong, good and bad—rather than epistemic. Even if the parties to the controversy agreed on relevant counterfactuals (e.g., if no one in the United States produced or consumed pornography, then women in the United States would not be coerced to perform sex acts on film), they would still disagree on the moral conclusion. Because I have bracketed substantive moral and political questions, my discussion cannot render verdicts in such controversies. Instead, my hope is that I have clarified the content of some claims being made and identified where the agreements and disagreements lie.

Finally, one might complain that I am helping myself to racial categories that are illegitimate. If, as many argue, there is no such thing as race, then by what rights am I invoking races as groups that suffer oppression? I have argued elsewhere that we can legitimately employ the term "race" for racialized social groups (Haslanger 2000). If one is unhappy with this terminology, then one may speak instead of "racialized group" rather than "race"; the issue then becomes "racialized group–based oppression" rather than "race-based oppression" (Blum 2002, chap. 8).

How does all this help us understand racism? Bigotry, hatred, intolerance, are surely bad. Agreement on this is easy, even if it is not clear what to do about them. But if people are prevented from acting on their bigotry, hatred, and intolerance—at least prevented from harming others for these motives—then we can still live together peacefully. Living together in peace and justice does not require that we love each other, or that we even fully respect each other, but rather that we conform our actions to principles of justice. Should we be concerned if some members of the community are hypocrites in acting respectfully toward others without having the "right" attitude? Of course, this could be a problem if hypocrites can't be trusted to sustain their respectful behavior; and plausibly hatred and bigotry are emotions that involve dispositions to wrongful action. Nonetheless, for many of those who suffer injustice, "private" attitudes are not the worst problem; systematic institutional subordination is.

Moreover, love, certain kinds of respect, and tolerance are no guarantee of justice. A moment's reflection on sexism can reveal that. For women, love and respect have often been offered as a substitute for justice; and yet unjust loving relationships are the norm, not the exception.

Persistent institutional injustice is a major source of harm to people of color. Of course, moral vice—bigotry and the like—is also a problem. But if we want the term "racism" to capture all the barriers to racial justice, I submit that it is reasonable to count as "racist" not only the attitudes and actions of individuals but the full range of practices, institutions, policies, and suchlike that, I've argued, count as racially oppressive. Cognitive and emotional racial bias do not emerge out of nothing; both are products of the complex interplay between the individual and the social that has been a theme throughout this chapter. Our attitudes are shaped by what we see, and what we see, in turn, depends on the institutional structures that shape our lives and the lives of those around us. For example,

> Is it hard to imagine that young White people who look around and see police locking up people of color at disproportionate rates, might conclude there is something wrong with these folks? Something to be feared, and if feared then perhaps despised? . . . Is it that difficult to believe that someone taught from birth that America is a place where "anyone can make it if they try hard enough," but who looks around and see that in fact, not only have some "not made it," but that these unlucky souls happen to be disproportionately people of color, might conclude that those on the bottom deserve to be there because they didn't try hard enough, or didn't have the genetic endowment for success? (Wise 2000)

Of course, individuals are not merely passive observers; attitudes are not inert. We stand in complicated relationships to the collectively formed and managed structures that shape our lives. Structures take on specific historical forms because of the individuals within them; individual action is conditioned in multiple and varying ways by social context. Theory, then, must be sensitive to this complexity; focusing simply on individuals or simply on structures will not be adequate in an analysis or a normative evaluation of how societies work.

In this chapter I have been especially keen to highlight the role of structures in oppression to offset what I find to be an undue emphasis on racist *individu-*

als and racist *attitudes* in recent philosophical work. Unjust societies full of well-meaning people can exist and even flourish. Working for social justice while ignoring structural injustice is, I believe, a sure recipe for failure. The battle to end racism and other forms of oppression must take place on many fronts, but without due regard for the power of structures to deform us—our attitudes, our relationships, our selves—we cannot hope to end racial oppression in particular, or group domination in general.

II

THE PSYCHOLOGY OF RACISM

6 : RACISM AS MANIC DEFENSE

In this chapter we will argue that some forms of racism are a manifestation of what Melanie Klein originally called the manic defense. Before speaking about racism in particular, we will take up the nature of the manic defense and the theory of mind in which the concept is embedded.

Building on Freud's (1955) dual instinct theory, Klein saw the human mind as fundamentally constituted and organized by the life instinct and the death instinct. The life instinct shows up as sexuality and love, the death instinct as aggression and hate. In the context of the life instinct, the outside world is experienced as good; in the context of the death instinct, the outside world is experienced as bad. From very early on in the life of the infant, Klein believed, psychic defensive operations were at work. Specifically, overwhelming states of aggression and rage led to projection, or the expulsion of the feelings and mental states, in fantasy, onto others. Thus were constituted, in Klein's theory, the "good breast" and "bad breast." The reference to "breast," rather than to persons, reflects Klein's (and Freud's) idea that the infant at the earliest stage experiences the world in terms of oral processes or the processes of feeding. Persons as persons do not yet show up for the infant, on this account.[1] The young infant's world, then, might be imagined as consisting of a good breast, experienced as the source of life-giving nurturance and love, and a bad breast, experienced as frightening and dangerous on account of the infant's own aggression that has been projected into it. In cases where, for constitutional or environmental reasons, there was a surplus of hate and aggression, the infant would feel himself to be in an intolerable situation, living in an overwhelmingly dangerous world. This situation would lead to reinforcement and rigidifying of the splitting of the good breast from the bad breast, in the interest of preserving some sense of good in the world. Klein (1976) referred to this basic situation as the "paranoid-schizoid" position. "Paranoid" here refers to the sense of a malevolent world; "schizoid" refers to the splitting of the ego and the object world into "good" and "bad." This

1. Infancy research (Stern 1985) demonstrating that the infant discriminates among persons from birth might lead one to conclude that Klein was simply wrong on this point. But one might read Klein as referring to an infantile way of experiencing the world, reflecting the overwhelming salience of feeding processes, not as referring to the infant's capacities.

splitting has its origin in the primal split inherent in the hypothesized dual instincts, which then is reinforced for purposes of psychic defense.

As the infant develops, a second position develops that Klein called the "depressive position." This position entails the recognition of whole persons, in the sense that the infant is thought to realize that the parenting person or persons are good *and* bad. In other words, the process of realizing that the good breast and the bad breast are the same breast coincides with the recognition that there is a person out there who is sometimes experienced as good and sometimes as bad. Thus, destructive impulses may be directed at a loved object. This position is called "depressive" because of the potential for feelings of loss attendant to fears of destroying the loved object. There is also the potential for guilt at this point as the infant realizes that he hates the same person whom he loves. In the Kleinian view of development, the depressive position comes later than the paranoid-schizoid position but does not supplant it. In normal development, both positions, or states of mind, are available to the child. In abnormal development, due to a surplus of aggression and the need to protect a sense of "goodness" in oneself and in the world, splitting is not transcended and the depressive position is not reached.

Thomas Ogden (1986: 67–99) has elaborated on Klein's concepts, pointing out that in the depressive position is the "birth of the historical subject." That is, in the depressive position, a sense of history emerges as the child realizes that the same person who is good today was bad yesterday. In the paranoid-schizoid position, there is no history, or history is continually rewritten; yesterday's bad person and today's good person are experienced as different people. The person may realize, cognitively, that these are the same person, but the cognitive knowledge does not alter the radically different emotional constellations. In the depressive position, subjectivity emerges as the child realizes that, if yesterday's mother was good and today's mother is bad, then it is the experience that is different, not the person. A space opens up between subject and object—psychic space, one might say. In the paranoid-schizoid position, things are what they are, in the sense that for the paranoid person people *are* malevolent. In the depressive position, *I* am frightened or angry, and so I experience people as frightening or malevolent.

The manic defense, in Klein's theory, is a defense against painful psychic states associated with the depressive position, including guilt and the vulnerability and dependence consequent on giving up the omnipotence associated with the paranoid-schizoid position. The manic defense takes the form of a reinforcement of the paranoid-schizoid position with three major features: foreclosure of psychic space (as we have just described), fantasies of omnipotence, and projective identification. Omnipotence operates in the service of denial, in the sense that fantasies develop that (omnipotently) remake reality; projective identification operates to rid the self, magically, of unwanted psychic states by projecting them onto other people.[2] It is important to note here that if subjectivity is a function of the depressive position, as Ogden explains, then the effort to avoid psychic pain necessarily entails the closing down of psychic space.

To summarize, in the Kleinian perspective the mind, or subjectivity, evolves as problems involving the management of love and hate are negotiated by the developing child. Complications involving this management crucially affect the form taken by the person's subjective experience. The manic defense is one such form, which, we will now seek to demonstrate, predisposes toward racism as a way of warding off intolerable psychic states.

I. THE MANIC DEFENSE

Racism involves the attribution of negatively valued characteristics to people based on their assignment to pseudo-genetically-based racial groups.[3] Racism can be more or less conscious, and more or less rigid and unmodifiable by experience. The intractable racist is certain that "blacks" or "whites" or "Asians" are this way or that; his belief is conscious, not a matter of psychic conflict, and is consistent with his general worldview. In other cases, racism is more a matter of conscious or unconscious preconceptions about people based on racial categories that may be subject to modification when made conscious or through experience that does not fit the preconception. Racism can be a group or societal phenomenon, when whole social groups or societies share common stereotypes, prejudices, or preconceptions about people based on "race."[4] There is an inter-

2. The concept of projective identification has evolved considerably in contemporary Kleinian thought. Whereas Melanie Klein thought of projective identification as entailing a *fantasy* of ridding the self of some psychic quality—for example, aggression—by placing it in another person, more recent theorists (Bion 1961, Racker 1968) have emphasized that the projector can induce the projected quality in the other person, so as to actualize the projection. For example, the person who has a preconception of another person as malevolent can act in such a hostile way as to induce hostility in the other person. Further, the second person can identify with the projection, so that he comes to experience himself as the source of the malevolence, for example. In short, what was originally thought of as an intrapsychic phenomenon has attained an interpersonal dimension in recent elaborations. This updated concept of projective identification will become a key concept below as we seek a psychological basis for racism in the way the races are socially and psychically constructed.

3. Racial groups, of course, do attain sociocultural-historical reality as people identify themselves and others with them, building cultures and communities with distinct traditions.

4. We put "race" in quotes here because it is well established that race is entirely a social construction, with no valid genetic basis. We will use quotation marks when referring to the

action between socially produced and transmitted racial stereotypes that are internalized by individuals as part of the socialization process, and psychological dynamics that produce these stereotypes and reinforce their adoption in a rigid and pervasive way. In this chapter we will be focusing on these psychological dynamics, while acknowledging that there are distinct social dynamics that produce and reinforce racism as well. For example, Joel Kovel (2000) considers that capitalist economic systems produce and reinforce racism as a way of ensuring that there will always be a pool of poorly paid workers. If one adopts this point of view exclusively, individual racists are produced by their society; the psychological dynamics of their racism are merely programmed in by the socialization process. In an equally one-sided account, one might postulate that racist stereotypes are solely a function of psychological dynamics, such as the defensive need to project onto others noxious psychological characteristics. From our perspective we need to make room for both social and individual factors in interaction; further, however, we will propose that psychological processes, such as the manic defense, can be operative in parallel on both the individual *and* group level. Thus, we are conceiving here of mental processes on both the individual and group level, *group* minds, as it were, as well as individual minds with dynamics that can be characterized in similar terms.

In the American context in which we live and with which we are most familiar, racism begins with European settlers engaging in "ethnic cleansing" of Native Americans from the European settlement in the New World. On one level, what occurred was invasion and conquest, as has occurred innumerable times throughout human history; in this case, however, the native inhabitants of the New World were not merely conquered but removed from the land and segregated in reservations. The justification for doing so was racist. That is, European settlers, considering themselves to be more advanced culturally and economically, felt entitled to get rid of the "primitive" natives. The doctrine of "manifest destiny" reflected this belief that Euro-Americans, by virtue of their superior culture, were destined to expand their dominion.

The enslavement of Africans obviously had an economic function, to provide free labor for the agricultural economy of the American South. Stereotypes then formed about people of African origin that persisted beyond the freeing of the slaves, remaining a powerful force in the American psyche to this day: that African Americans are less intelligent than Euro-Americans, more highly sexed, more lazy, more criminally inclined, and so on. Racism often resulted in white preoccupation with male African-American sexuality, leading to thousands of lynchings of black men who were accused of raping white women. While there were, until 1967 when the Supreme Court ruled them unconstitutional, laws that

---

racist's construction of "race" as genetically based. We will not use quotation marks when referring to race, more properly, as a social construction.

forbade marriage between blacks and whites in sixteen states, the primary goal seems not to have been to prevent miscegenation, since white men routinely raped and impregnated black women with impunity. Rather, the goal seems to have been to prevent black males from mating with white women. There have been legal advances in recent years in the United States, in terms of voting rights and an end to legal segregation in schooling, employment, and housing. As the 2000 election in the United States demonstrated, however, blacks may still be prevented from exercising their right to vote, neighborhoods remain segregated de facto, major economic disparities endure between blacks and whites, "racial profiling" and the selective imprisonment of blacks persist in law enforcement.[5] As more African Americans have attained middle-class and upper-middle-class status, some of the prejudicial stereotypes have come to be applied selectively to blacks of lower socioeconomic status, as in the characterization of welfare recipients as simply lazy. Such stereotyping has led to welfare "reform," that is, the setting of absolute time limits on how long people can stay on welfare during a lifetime, regardless of their personal situation. Some of the attacks on affirmative action in the United States rest on a denial that racism persists in this country.

II. PSYCHOLOGICAL DYNAMICS OF AMERICAN RACISM

With the historical and socioeconomic context for American racism in mind, we can now proceed to consider some of the psychological dynamics of this phenomenon. We will postulate three basic processes: *projective identification, intolerance of guilt* with an associated foreclosure of psychic space, and *denial of human vulnerability,* or omnipotence. The reader will recognize these as also the basic features of the manic defense, as just outlined above.

As noted above, the concept of projective identification has undergone an evolution in Kleinian thought. Melanie Klein herself thought of the process as occurring at the level of fantasy, a fantasy of expelling unwanted parts of the self into another person, or, more properly, into an internal image of another person, while the unconscious identification with the disowned aspect of the self remained. Later theorists, especially Thomas Ogden (1986), Heinrich Racker (1968), and Wilfred Bion (1961), have expanded or "interpersonalized" the concept so as to allow for the fact that the fantasy of projective identification gives rise to behaviors that have a real impact on people in the world, inducing them

5. According to Kupers (1999: 94) over 30 percent of African-American males between the ages of twenty and twenty-nine were under criminal justice supervision in 1994, and these figures rise to 42 percent of eighteen- to thirty-five-year-old males in Washington, D.C., and 56 percent in Baltimore.

to behave in ways that the projector had already expected. The recipient of the projection in turn may identify with that which has been projected onto or, now, into them. If you wish to disavow aggression in yourself, and insist on seeing it in me, you will behave toward me with fear and preemptive aggression, as if I were aggressive and dangerous.[6] I, in turn, seeing myself as aggressive and dangerous in your eyes, may identify with that image, given my own propensity to experience myself as aggressive or to fear aggression in myself. I experience your aggression toward me, which you experience as preemptive, as unprovoked by me, and I may react with my own hostile response, which you will experience as confirmation of your original preconception about me, while I experience it as having been induced by you. This dynamic pervasively characterizes racist interaction and stereotypes, especially around the projection of sex, aggression, exploitativeness, and sloth by white people onto black people. The stereotypical image of the violent, criminal, sexually predatory black man is the final outcome of this process. Consider how the violence entailed in forcibly wrenching people from their homes, their families, and their cultures and enslaving them got transformed into an image of the violent black man. Or consider how the routine sexual use of black women for the sexual education or pleasure of white men got transformed into an image of the sexually predatory black man. These processes, of course, are ongoing. They can be found, for example, in the stereotype of the violently criminal, ghetto-dwelling black male that results in "racial profiling" and the disproportionate imprisonment of black men, while white society turns a blind eye to white police brutality in the ghetto. They can be found in the focus, in the U.S. Congress, on the exploitative black "welfare queen" who needs to be disciplined by being cut off welfare, while corporate welfare—the subsidy, via tax cuts, of the richest Americans—proceeds apace. There is, of course, all too much violence, exploitativeness, and so on in American ghettos. The point is not to deny that these phenomena exist, but rather to observe that racist white Americans experience them as inherent in black people, while disavowing that they are also found in whites, and that, in any case, they may be induced by discriminatory housing and employment practices, for example. Black people may also identify with the negative images of themselves they see in the media and, more generally, in the eyes of white people, further perpetuating the vicious circle.

For people with some development of the "depressive position," as described above, awareness of how black people have been, and are, mistreated by white people and white society might provoke guilt. Indeed, white liberals are famously

6. It is typical of projective identification that the very quality disavowed (e.g., aggression) is ultimately manifested by the projector, but now experienced as reactive to the *other* person's aggression. Thus, the sense of the aggression as originating in the self is lost, and the aggression can be expressed without conflict.

described as "guilty." The dismissive implication of "white liberal guilt," however, reflects the way in which this form of guilt actually is seen as functioning as a facile form of guilt *avoidance*. Guilty white liberals, on this account, too easily portray themselves as racially enlightened. In the Kleinian view, guilt is an extremely painful recognition of destructiveness that is very deeply rooted and predominantly unconscious. Conscious well-meaning attitudes barely scratch the surface from this point of view. In the Kleinian view, depressive guilt, when it can be borne, leads to truly reparative action, as opposed to lip service. The nature of truly reparative action when it comes to American racism is an all-important question, but beyond the scope of this particular chapter.

The white liberal, then, manifests a form of avoidance that reflects a sense of guilt, which must quickly be counteracted by a sense of moral superiority that denies ongoing destructiveness. In some cases, the experience of guilt is selective, so that one experiences guilt only in relation to people with whom one identifies. Interaction with "not me" group members is associated with a state of mind in which guilt is foreclosed or precluded. For those with less development of depressive-position tolerance for guilt, guilt avoidance may take the form of rigid clinging to the projection of destructiveness onto the other, so as to foreclose any possibility of awareness of the damage that one has done or is doing. Blaming others serves to exonerate the self; the constant threat that the self could be implicated creates the need continually to renew the indictment of the other. Here is one powerful source of the intractability of racism in the United States and elsewhere. This need to foreclose the potential for guilt via continual demonstration of the badness of the other should be distinguished from sadism, which is characterized by the gleeful, excited, destructiveness seen in some photos of lynchings in the United States and elsewhere.

It is important to recognize that in the Kleinian perspective, space in which to experience guilt is nearly tantamount to mental space per se. Since the emergence of personal subjectivity is so closely tied to the process by which people are recognized as simultaneously good and bad, a rigid splitting off of the good and bad undermines the development of a sense of actively creating one's own experience. Put in other terms, the realization that the same person is experienced in different ways (sometimes good, sometimes bad) is associated with the recognition that one is implicated in the nature of one's experience. Guilt, which in some people must be warded off at all cost, is associated with the sense of producing one's own experience to some degree. In the paranoid-schizoid position, things are what they are without the mediation of an experiencing subject; good people are just good, bad people are just bad. If one has a destructive impulse toward a bad person, that impulse is fully justified by the other person's badness. One does not feel implicated in the "badness" associated with the reciprocal destructive attacks that ensue.

Associated with the foreclosure of psychic space and excessive use of projective identification is the failure to develop an adequate theory of mind. As we noted above, a sense of having a mind of one's own, or subjectivity, depends on attainment of the depressive position. The recognition that others have minds of *their* own depends on recognition of their separateness from oneself. Heavy reliance on projective identification as a defense means that when one looks at another person, one sees one's own disavowed self, the "not me," to use Harry Stack Sullivan's (1953) term. The manic defense, then, blocks the development of a "theory of mind" (Baron-Cohen 1995) in the sense that a theory of mind depends on having a sense of the other person as having an *independently generated* mind. Without an adequate theory of mind, other people are seen as objects, without thoughts, feelings, and a sense of self like one's own. Along these lines, Donald Moss (2001) points out that in the racist mind, people are treated as "transparent," as "objects of perception"—not as separate people having minds of their own, recognition of which would make them to some degree "opaque" and knowable only by an act of imagination and identification. Failure to identify with other people makes it possible to exploit and do violence to them (Fonagy and Target 1998) without the guilty inhibitions that would arise were one to reflect with empathy on their feelings.

Finally, racism serves the effort to ward off the sense of human vulnerability, dependence, and limitation. Consider in this connection Toni Morrison's point that slavery served to help white Americans feel free. Morrison (1993) points out that the early European immigrants came to North America seeking freedom: freedom from religious oppression, freedom from rigid class structures, freedom to make a new life. Once here, however, these immigrants discovered a whole new set of constraints on their freedom: the presence of Native Americans who had a claim to the land, the need to clear forested land before it could be farmed, and so on. Faced with the inherent constraints of human life, these immigrants could seek a sense of freedom, illusory in a fundamental respect, by contrast with the enslaved blacks. Racism entails both creating a concrete difference between "free" people and enslaved people and imaginatively exploiting that difference to enhance the privileged group's sense of freedom as nonenslavement.

Or, along similar lines, consider James Baldwin's point that white privilege reflects a wish to avoid a sense of deprivation and risk that, again, is inherent in human living (Baldwin 1967). Deprivation, sickness, and death, of course, are part of the human condition. By creating conditions in which one group is subject to *surplus* deprivation, sickness, and death, the privileged group produces for itself an illusory sense of invulnerability. Baldwin argues that by seeking an illusion of invulnerability via socially structured privilege, the European-American psyche is impoverished, for the sense of being truly alive entails an embracing of risk and vulnerability.

In contemporary America, the effort to ward off a sense of vulnerability and limitation is perhaps best reflected in the social segregation of poor people, typically people "of color," but including poor whites as well. Following the reasoning of Toni Morrison, it is as if non-ghetto dwellers imagined that, by contrast with the extreme vulnerability and deprivation of ghetto dwellers, their lives were privileged and unconstrained. The American dream as reflected in advertising images, for example, indeed holds out the hope of beauty, youth, comfort, and freedom through possession and consumption of things. Consumer culture thrives on the impossibility of these hopes; the more people find that the good life eludes them, the more things they feel driven to buy. The American dream is like a carrot to a horse, a carrot that keeps moving away. The presence of a clearly miserable and underprivileged group of people in our society makes it possible for the rest of us to avoid being aware that the American dream is fundamentally illusory for all of us. One might say that these processes reflect another form of projective identification: in this case, the disavowal and projection of vulnerability and of limitation onto the suffering poor. Once again, the psychic space of the white racist is impoverished as an effort is made, unconsciously, to foreclose, rather than reflect on, the experience of the human condition with all its pain and suffering as well as joy and transcendence. Meanwhile, people in the ghettos of the United States suffer, while the larger society looks away.

To sum up, from a Kleinian perspective, as developed by Ogden, the management of destructiveness and guilt is at the very heart of the development of mind itself. To be sure, self-reflectiveness, or what Peter Fonagy and Mary Target (1998) call the processes of "mentalization," depends on cognitive maturation; but cognitive capacity is a necessary tool that may or may not be put to use. In the Kleinian view, the discovery that the same person, self or other, can be good *and* bad is a critical moment in the emergence of mind and creativity— that is, in the awareness that one's perspective or mental state is a crucial element in how people are perceived and experienced, that one participates in creating the world one lives in. Put another way, having a mind, being an active agent in the creation and construction of one's world, makes one a *responsible* being, thus subject to guilt. Intolerance of guilt, and the associated manic defense, forestall the moment of self-reflection and responsibility and block the emergence of mind. Racism, along with sexism, anti-Semitism, and homophobia, is prototypical of the defensive processes that simultaneously constrain mental development and sustain violence and injustice at the social level.

III. WILLIAM PIERCE AND THE NATIONAL ALLIANCE

One of the most extreme doctrines of racism is held by the National Alliance, the white supremacist group most notorious for its association with the bombing of the Oklahoma City federal building in 1995. Timothy McVeigh, who was executed for perpetrating the bombing, was thought to have modeled his plan of attack on a segment of *The Turner Diaries,* a novel about white revolution written by William Pierce,[7] the intellectual force behind the National Alliance. *The Turner Diaries* is a fantasized account of the fictional Earl Turner's participation in the violent overthrow of a Jewish-dominated U.S. government, the worldwide annihilation of Jews and nonwhites, and the founding of an all-white planet.

While the National Alliance, speaking through *The Turner Diaries,* advocates extermination of all who are excluded from its membership—including whites who do not share its ideology—the Jewish people are identified as its ultimate nemesis. In the minds of the National Alliance members, Jews seek world domination, and to that end, conspire to cripple the white spirit by imposing materialist values and liberal ideas that deter the white man from his natural destiny. In *The Turner Diaries,* Jews have been successful in their ruthless subjugation of gentiles; as Pierce writes, "We have allowed a diabolically clever, alien minority to put chains on our souls and our minds" (Macdonald 1996: 33) The "Jewish-run" government and the media serve as the vehicles for seduction and brainwashing, instilling decadent, liberal "TV values" advocating "an essentially feminine, submissive world view" (42). In the novel, the quintessential act of emasculation of the white man is the passing of the Cohen Act, which has forbidden ownership of guns. Left defenseless, whites are then subject to constant attack by the savage minorities.[8]

The "General Principles" of the National Alliance describe its founders as "objectivists" who base their recognition of white superiority on hard scientific fact. In so doing, the authors fashion their own version of evolutionary theory to fit their beliefs, reasoning that whites are the most highly evolved of the human species because the race developed in the temperate zones, where climactic extremes necessitated strong planning and problem solving skills and the ability to delay gratification. In contrast, those races that developed in warmer, more consistent climates were not required to develop higher mental functions or the capacity for self-restraint, and are therefore less capable of building and sustaining a civilized society. The National Alliance enjoins all non-Jewish white people to rally to their own cause, to acknowledge the danger that submission to nonwhite values entails, and to "lend a conscious hand to Nature in the task of evolution."

7. Pierce wrote *The Turner Diaries* using the alias Andrew Macdonald. He used the pseudonym to create the illusion that there were more authors involved in writing for National Alliance–related publications. "I didn't want readers to think I was a one-man band," he said (Blythe 2000).

8. One can see here the way in which disowned psychic qualities can have meaning, simultaneously in stereotypical gender terms, as well as in stereotypical racial terms. In other cases, that which is disavowed by the racist mind can have meaning in terms of stereotypical social classes as well as race.

Bearing the plot of *The Turner Diaries* in mind, we can safely infer that this evolution entails violent revolt and genocide, ostensibly to protect the white race from eradication by its enemies and thereby ensure the furthering of the human species. Pierce's call to arms in *The Turner Diaries* is passionate: "If we fail, God's great Experiment will come to an end, and this planet will once again, as it did millions of years ago, move through the ether devoid of higher man" (Macdonald 1996: 35). There could hardly be a more dramatic example of the polarized thinking characterizing the paranoid-schizoid position and the manic defense, of the way in which integration of psychic qualities can be experienced as intolerable. In this case, activity and passivity, dominance and submission, are seen as totally can not be integrated. To the degree that the "races" are identified with these polarities, they too must be kept totally separate, or one pole must be violently extirpated.

Moss (2001) writes of the standardized hatreds that both construct and target the objects of our racism. These hatreds exist as if part of the collective unconscious of our society, like so much common knowledge, to be summoned as needed to relieve unbearable intrapsychic conflict. Given this resource, we might wonder why the philosophers of the National Alliance would bother to invoke— however weakly—the name of science to justify their cause. This use of evolutionary theory seems to have several aims. Having developed a taxonomy of the human species that places whites at the end of evolutionary development, the authors of the "General Principles" articulate a rigid hierarchy that facilitates disidentification. Science proves the inferiority and hatefulness of nonwhites; it turns a belief into an indisputable truth. Furthermore, the denigration of subjectivity and the glorification of objectivity feigns commitment to rational thinking and intellectual prowess, which is consistent with the authors' exposition of white superiority. Most important, science gives the National Alliance members a sense that they are identified with a group that is not only courageous and tough but intelligent and refined.

In actuality, this pseudoscientific stance thwarts the use of the most complex mental faculties, trading on the illusion that only what is within the realm of perception can be true. In Moss's language, this foreclosure of the full dimensionality of thought allows us to see people as transparent, that is, instantly knowable by virtue of preformulated prejudice. When others are regarded as transparent, thought is supplanted by the relatively crude operations of perception; perceived characteristics dictate knowing. In the case of *The Turner Diaries*, black represents stupidity, violence, rape, and cannibalism; white represents intelligence, cunning, victimization, and the potential for greatness. These characteristics, constructed solely from mental processes, take on the aura of solid, objective, truth grounded in physical reality. White Jews are perhaps hated all the more because their whiteness interferes with coding by skin tone. Mental faculties beyond perception must be employed in order to determine what lies beneath the skin, threatening involvement of a more subjective kind. In the white supremacist's experience, the doubt that is introduced by skin color makes Jews all the more deceptive, cunning, and seductive.

The fodder for the mechanism of disidentification appears to be a sense of victimization on the part of the National Alliance members. We can only speculate about how individual members came to view the world as persecutory; what is clear is that racism has organized their thinking and clarified the lines of battle. Several National Alliance members who were interviewed spoke as if they felt like casualties of a pro-integration society, explaining their choice to join the National Alliance with statements such as "I got tired of just watching what was being done to our people and to America" and "I want to be a hammer instead of an anvil." Before his execution, McVeigh dieted in an attempt to appear "thin and gaunt—like a Holocaust victim—when they strapped him down to die" (Bragg 2001), apparently to capitalize on this image of victimization. Scenes from *The Turner Diaries,* in which brainwashed whites are portrayed as seeing racism as an evil rather than a necessity, dramatize their experience of persecution. Minorities revert to their feral nature, and the whites who are subjected to their violent impulses are not allowed by law or by conscience to strike back for fear of being perceived as racist. Pierce writes: "Nowadays gangs of Black thugs hang around parking lots . . . looking for any attractive, unescorted White girl and knowing that punishment . . . is extremely unlikely. . . . Gang rapes in school classrooms have become an especially popular new sport. Some particularly liberal women may find that this situation provides a certain amount of satisfaction for their masochism, a way of atoning for their feelings of racial 'guilt'" (Macdonald 1996: 58). And then, when the revolution begins, Earl Turner writes, "I'm exhilarated. We have finally acted!" (1). In his exuberant renunciation of his passive stance, he has traded up; he now defines himself as a soldier in the army of the powerful and righteous rather than a "soft, self-indulgent, careless, and befuddled" feminized man who deserves violation and enslavement. He and his comrades have exchanged the helplessness and pain of victimization for the powerful clarity of a well-defined hatred.

And what of guilt? Is there any evidence of remorse about Pierce's role in the denigration and slaughter of human life? As we read *The Turner Diaries,* we are struck by the eerie absence of these feelings and by the branding of "liberal guilt" as a symptom of the corruption of the white spirit. Whites are repeatedly warned against buying into antiracist propaganda and enjoined to renounce compassion for those who must be destroyed in order to ensure the survival and proliferation of the white race. We might expect that disidentification, as Moss has said, would allow for suppression of guilt, but this mechanism alone would not account for its complete absence.

As the earlier discussion of the Kleinian perspective explained, this inability to relate to the suffering of those you hurt and to condemn without remorse is a manifestation of the paranoid-schizoid position. Absence of compassion arises from the conviction that the object world is sharply and eternally divided between good allies and bad enemies. Movement into the depressive position, which invites an integrated view of the object world, poses an annihilative threat when the bad is believed to be so powerful as to override the good. Transposed to the macrocosmic level, this kind of thinking makes integration of the races seem tantamount to the annihilation of the good (white) race. The only alternative then seems to be annihilation of the bad (black/Jewish) race. At the same time, an unwavering belief that others are inherently good or bad obviates subjective involvement with them. In fact, subjective involvement, which implies a theory of mind, is incongruous with this psychic organization. Others are seen only as embodiments of stereotypes who lack a personal dimension; they are only quasi-existent, and in a sense already dead.

Within the context of his racism, the clearest evidence of Pierce's dependence on this organization of experience is his response to the threat of racial integration and miscegenation. His fantasy in *The Turner Diaries* is that all children of interracial couples be brutally destroyed, and that all whites who engaged in intimate relationships with nonwhites or Jews be publicly executed. In the days after the success of the revolution, Earl Turner writes:

> Today has been the Day of the Rope—a grim and bloody day . . . from tens of thousands of lampposts, power poles, and trees throughout this vast metropolitan area the grisly forms hang. . . .
>
> . . . at practically every street corner I passed this evening on my way to HQ there was a dangling corpse . . . each with an identical placard around its neck bearing the printed legend "I betrayed my race." There are many thousands of hanging female corpses like that in this city tonight, all wearing identical placards around their necks. They are the White women who were married to or living with Blacks, with Jews, or with other non-White males. (Macdonald 1996: 160–61)

In Pierce's mind, these whites who have "defiled" the white race deserve the harshest punishment of all because they have personified the union of the two affective poles, good (white) and bad (black), that Pierce must, for the sake of his own psychic stability, keep forever apart.

The evening before Earl Turner's attack on the FBI building—and this is the attack that McVeigh imitated—Turner ruminates about the nonwhites and Jewish people:

> Why didn't we rebel 35 years ago, when they took our schools away from us and began converting them into racially mixed jungles? Why didn't we throw them all out of the country 50 years ago, instead of letting them use us as cannon fodder in their war to subjugate Europe? Why didn't we rise up in righ-

teous fury and drag those arrogant aliens into the streets and cut their throats then? Why didn't we roast them over bonfires at every streetcorner in America? Why didn't we make a final end to this obnoxious and eternally pushy clan, this pestilence from the sewers of the East, instead of meekly allowing ourselves to be disarmed?

. . . If the Organization fails at its task now, everything will be lost—our history, our heritage, all the blood and sacrifices and upward striving of countless of thousands of years. The Enemy we are fighting fully intends to destroy the racial basis of our existence. No excuse for our failure will have any meaning, for there will be only a swarming horde of indifferent, mulatto zombies to hear it. (Macdonald 1996: 34)

When the attack is finished, Turner writes:

All day yesterday and most of today we watched the TV coverage of rescue crews bringing the dead and injured out of the building. It is a heavy burden of responsibility for us to bear, since most of the victims of our bomb were no more committed to the sick philosophy or the racially destructive goals of the System than we are. But there is no way we can destroy the System without hurting many thousands of innocent people—no way . . . we are all completely convinced that what we did is justified. (42)

In this passage, the author tempts us by offering us a softer Earl Turner, one who appears to be capable of remorse. We are, perhaps, eager to see his humanity, if even for a brief moment. We might be seduced by the possibility that this man is not so ruthless as his actions might suggest; that he, in fact, has dimension. The suggestion that even a man who is capable of good might murder out of principle is more palatable than the idea of cold-blooded killing. However, after reading through endless scenes of gleeful murder, these few shallow words of regret fall short. We have to view them not as indicative of introspection or guilt, but only as an attempt to make Earl Turner, the paradigmatic soldier of the National Alliance, someone who feels more like us. In fact, this passage makes plain Pierce's justification for murder, a justification that had the power to encourage McVeigh's actual destruction of the lives 168 men, women, and children. Turner's victims—who might be any of us—are again portrayed as oblivious dupes who lack a strong, subjective stand. They are the embodiments of Pierce's own experience of mindlessness, and are hated to death.

The Turner Diaries manifests many of the characteristics of the manic defense as outlined above. We have noted the splitting and projective identification around dependency and aggression, the foreclosure of psychic space and guilt manifest in the objectification of African Americans, and the treatment of African Americans solely as "objects of perception" (in Moss's words) who lack an inner life of feelings and thoughts, In the case of William Pierce and his followers in the National Alliance, we have noted the omnipotence displayed in the fantasy of taking over the world and exterminating nonwhite people and their collaborators. It would seem that the manic defense operates principally to ward off dependence and vulnerability rather than guilt. Given that black people and Jews are seen in such one-dimensional terms, as objects of perception as opposed to objects of identification, the potential for guilt seems remote. Reading Pierce, one feels his strong hatred of dependence, his loathing for the way white people have allowed themselves to be manipulated by Jews. White people, in Pierce's mind, are meant to be strong and independent—invulnerable. Black people, the white person's Other, are meant to be dependent and vulnerable. If white people find themselves, nonetheless, in a vulnerable position in the world, the natural order has been perverted and someone must be to blame—Jews, or whites perversely willing to be led away from their true nature. The fantasy of revolution, of world domination, of elimination of blacks and Jews to create a whole world of strong, self-sufficient people, restores the manic dream of invulnerability.

7 : THE CHARACTERS OF VIOLENCE AND PREJUDICE

As the turn of the millennium approached, Americans were asking all the questions about violence that had been urgent since the 1960s, when our streets overflowed with antiwar protests and race war, when the daily coverage from Vietnam was punctuated with assassination footage. Social scientific literatures on violence had exploded along with the violence, and the frame of reference was so shared that when Hannah Arendt published a book called *On Violence* in 1969, no subtitle was needed to explain what violence she was addressing. For the next two decades, questions about why we are such a violent people arose repeatedly. Yet, our attention was focused not so much on war and revolution—political violence—as on our homicide rate (so much higher than that of any European nation), our frightening spouse-battering and child-abuse statistics, our film industry's anything-goes attitude, our incivility. A new question became pressing as well, to which experts and op-ed pundits flocked starting in the early 1990s: Why are children going to school with knives, guns, even bombs to assault their classmates, their teachers? Why do we have so many juvenile criminals? Columbine High School galvanized us. Even the usually unpolitical American Psychoanalytic Association made a "position statement" on violence in May 2000 that referred to the "crisis of violence in our country." And, as is characteristic of our reactive social science industry, government funding for violence research was on the rise—we needed solutions, interventions, quickly!

I. VIOLENCE NOW

Since September 11, 2001, it has hardly been possible in America to speak of any violence other than the terrorist assaults perpetrated in New York City and Washington, D.C., on that horrifying day. But I think it is important, nonetheless, not to lose the thread of attention to our own violence that the "Attack on America" so overshadowed, not least because that momentous event holds many clues to the way that the American government has responded, with a "war on terror," and to the way that most Americans have supported that response.

In the millennial year, when George W. Bush was running for president, both he and his Democratic Party opponents made a major theme out of juvenile violence in America. At that moment, juvenile homicide and most other juvenile crimes had actually decreased nationally, and deaths in schools were less than half what they were in 1993. Young people were, overall, "at less risk of participating in violence than any time in a generation," as *The Nation*, 9 October 2000, noted editorially. But nonetheless, the election campaign whipped up fear about "the culture of carnage surrounding our children" that is "turning some of them into killers," as Joseph Lieberman, the Democratic Party vice-presidential candidate said, evoking a common image of a pollution of violence that is seeping into people. This image was meant to justify putting constraints on the pollution that comes from the entertainment industry, in order to protect our children—and to protect us from our children.

In this pre–September 11 antiviolence rhetoric, which, as I will note again in a moment, had a very obsessional quality to it, were present all of the many ways in which Americans have typically misstated their questions about violence and reached for simple answers to them. We have long felt compelled to talk about a single thing: "violence." The American Psychoanalytic Association statement, for example, contained the sentence "Violence is a major public health issue." And we have felt compelled to find a single reason, a single cause for this single thing, a cause that will be either located in our nature or supplied by our nurture—an either-or of amazing persistence. The single cause is always referred to as "the root of violence," because, of course, if there is a root that can be named and located, it can also be torn out, extirpated. The hope is clearest in the recurrent search for a genetic root to violence, a quest which, like the quest for a "homosexuality gene," ignores all that is known about how complex human behavior is. The metaphor means we must find a tangible root for which a procedure of uprooting can be designed.

Along with the "violence gene" research, three other major types of "root of violence" research were being funded and widely reported before September 11.[1] As Robin Karr-Morse and Meredith Wiley (1997) have shown in *Ghosts from the Nursery: Tracing the Roots of Violence,* neuroscientific research has shown that many kinds of childhood traumas—head injuries, including those from child abuse, environmental toxins, and so forth—impair children's brains in a way that makes affect regulation nearly impossible for them. Meanwhile various sociological projects concentrate on the ways in which violence breeds violence, or in which violence is intergenerationally transmitted. "Risk factors" are weighed. One criminologist, for example, has very intricately mapped a process he calls "violentization," a developmental line along which a child becomes violently molded and shaped for violent behavior.[2] Finally, evolutionary psychologists

---

1. See the summary of research in *Science* 289 (28 July 2000).

2. Richard Rhodes (1999), who tells the story of the work of criminologist Lonnie Athens, insists that Athens is a maverick among social scientists. But it seems to me that Athens's

are suggesting that violence is our legacy from the great apes, and specifically from the "demonic males" among them who gathered in "small, self-perpetuating, self-aggrandizing bands" for the paradigmatic acts of intragroup violence (Wrangham and Peterson 1996: 248).

These four types of research have much to teach us, but they definitely perpetuate simplifications. They ignore the many forms of violence and the many functions those forms serve, as they ignore the complex interplay of nature and nurture in any given form.[3] Similarly, the research focuses simply on a group, those who have committed violent crimes, especially very violent crimes, especially homicide and rape, and then makes inferences from this construction ("the violent ones") about violence in general or in any specific form. Further, within this focus, research on violent children and delinquent adolescents grew faster than any other kind (not surprising, given the images, so salient in our current national consciousness, of children and adolescents wielding lethal weapons), much as research on people involved in political violence—student rebels, terrorists, revolutionaries—grew apace in the 1960s. And it was even thought, as an FBI report showed, that "the violent ones" among adolescents could be identified—some would use the word "profiled"—before they make it into the criminal justice system. The corollary now in public attention is the literature that purports to describe "the terrorist," a young male who resembles in

work is not at all incompatible with psychoanalytic insights about the intergenerational transmission of trauma and violence, with which both Athens and Rhodes are apparently quite unfamiliar.

3. First, there is the interspecies violence that all animals engage in to feed themselves and the intraspecies violence that they all engage in as part of mating. Then there is the intraspecies violence that only humans and a very few primates engage in, which has been taken for granted through much of human history and been considered abnormal or pathological only recently. (Child abuse, for example, has only recently been considered abuse and not the right of parents and other adult disciplinarians.) There are many degrees of violence and types of violent acts, running from a punch right on up to genocide and the specter of species destruction from weapons of violence capable of eliminating even the perpetrators, an invention of the twentieth century. There are many locations of violence: in the private sphere (domestic violence); in unregulated or extralegal public spheres; in regulated public spaces under the rule of governments, which have their own agencies of violence such as the police and the military. There are many types of criminal violence and some types for which legal exceptions are made, like violence in self-defense or violence by reason of insanity. There is violence in fantasy or in art and violence in action, and there is impulsive violence and premeditated violence. Different kinds of violence are possible at different stages of life. Different kinds of persons and social or cultural groups engage in different kinds of violence. Finally, there are many motives and functions for the violences of these many kinds and appearances.

many respects the delinquent American adolescents who were "the violent ones" before September 11. And terrorism becomes something we have to define in such a way that we can extirpate it, root and branch.

II. CLINICAL VIGNETTES: OBJECT CHOICE FOR VIOLENCE

Let me consider now what psychoanalytic clinical work and theory can offer. To begin negatively, I will suggest that psychoanalytic inquiry ought to avoid conceptualizing violence or violent deeds as the end point of a process, like the leaves of a plant growing from "roots of violence," for this conceptualization blocks questions about whether the violence serves some function other than expression of the designated roots, the completion of the process.

Let me continue by going to my research lab—my consulting room—and considering three patients. None of these three is violent in deeds, but all have persistent and repetitive violent fantasies, all frequently report very violent dreams, and all tell me often how they would like to kill this or that person. Although they are not "the violent ones," I assume that their dreams and fantasies are not very different from those who are less able or willing to keep themselves from acting on their images. However, I think it is noteworthy that my patients have not to any great degree *consciously* connected up their images with images existing in their sociocultural surrounds and thereby received social sanctioning of their prejudices and violence. On the contrary, they are consciously pacifistic, unprejudiced people, firmly defended (often by reaction formation) against associating with violent people or violence. In their conscious minds, they abhor the very prejudices that their images and associated violences resemble, so they consciously inhibit themselves.[4] Their violence is, as it were, private, mental, although their images of their victims resemble those available in common social prejudices.

First a woman, extremely bright, a professional who spends her days assessing and helping children, told me at the beginning of our work that revealing her sexual fantasies would be the hardest part of what she knew she had to do in order to figure out why she gets so depressed, with suicidal thoughts, and why she has to engage in so many obsessional actions, especially ones involving scheduling her time, doing her laundry, and managing her money. Like her dreams, her fantasies, she told me, are violent, full of mutilated bodies, shooting scenes, people getting torn apart by wild animals. Very ashamed, she confessed that all through her adolescence she had attacked her two younger siblings in what she

---

4. The phenomenon of inhibition of violence is of great importance, but I cannot take it up in this essay.

now describes as "a sexual manner." Her current partner has complained that she is sometimes too rough in bed. She bites, and she has said bitingly mean things. Why does she want to do this? She begs me to explain. The only thing harder for her to talk about, she said later, is religion, and that's because, even though she has extricated herself from the fundamentalist milieu in which she grew up, she fears that she still has that harsh, punitive mentality in her, and that it will come out in her relationships, that she will punish with a terrible swift sword someone she loves. Certainly, violence was normal in her house—her father beat her on her bare buttocks with a belt or a yardstick for any infraction, her mother threatened her with God's wrath. Now she is "a pacifist." But then, she tells me, she gets frightened and imagines that everyone is "trying to get a piece" of her—everyone wants her time, her care, her money. So she has to guard herself constantly against being intruded upon and "sucked dry." The image that guides her violent thoughts is "Everyone is a bloodsucker." Ultimately, she finally tells me, she wants anybody who tries to take advantage of her time or her money "to disappear." She wants them cleaned out.

Second, there is a woman, characterologically hysterical, with a great deal of anxiety, who, despite her anxiety, is enormously capable and productive, charming and sensitive. But sometimes too sensitive, she notes, for her own good, and too given to making dramas all the time, getting herself and others into uproars, anxieties. She tells me one day that, once again, she has had one of her torture dreams. A wounded man was brought in on a stretcher by a group of medics. They were going to try to save his life, but then they turned on him, and they were going to torture him with their scalpels, to kill him. She wanted to go down and help the man, but she didn't, because it was too dangerous, the medics were so menacing, and also—this was the part of the dream that filled her with horror—because she really wanted the man to be hurt. She would like to have cut him up herself. Why does she keep having these dreams in which she wants to torture? Can she be so angry with her wonderful, larger-than-life father, a war hero, who was, as she always says, "the love of my life." She had been so angry that he was an alcoholic, that he kept having heart attacks and became a terrible burden for her, that he died and left her alone with her anxious, clinging mother and with a group of crazy half-siblings who were old enough to be her parents. Slowly, over many months, with much resistance, she told me the two fantasies she built up as a child to compensate for her sense of powerlessness to help her beloved father. In the first, she is a great (male) Indian warrior who triumphs over all his enemies, winning tremendous adulation for skill with knives and spears in hand-to-hand combats. In the second, she is a princess who gets to be loved by a king, and who is more able than any other women to win men, to get power over any man who tries to get power over her. In both versions, her enemies are the bad ones; and this projection of her own badness and her father's badness onto them is key to what her violence against them does for her. They are people of the weak white race, to be humiliated, while she gets her father— in an idealized form.

Third is a man who, although he has many obsessional features, is a narcissistic character. Some days, he knows himself to be better than all the people around him—smarter, more talented. Other days, he feels terrible about himself, thinking he has been ruined by his harsh, perfectionist parents. During a recent session, he told me about spending the evening before with a new love interest, a woman who excites him tremendously but also baffles him and hurts him with her remoteness, her coldness. She can be so enchanting, he sighed, but she has "this unavailable quality." Maybe, he speculated, her harshness comes from her relationship with her father, who abused her verbally and physically, who was brutalizing. Our thoughts went to his pattern of choosing women who have been hurt by their critical fathers—as he has been by his mercilessly critical father. Narcissistically, he loves himself in them. After a long pause, he said that he needed to tell me something awful about the evening, something shameful. They were in the kitchen cutting up vegetables for a ratatouille when she turned away from him and suddenly an image flashed before his eyes of himself plunging the knife he was using into her back, deep, between her shoulder blades, blood gushing from the wound. The really awful thing, he said, crying, is that this very image has jumped into his mind with other women, in other kitchens. In fact, with all the women he has dated. "I feel like a murderer just telling you this. I know it's about being with my mother in our kitchen, and how angry I am at her for rejecting me. Or for loving me sometimes and rejecting me. Or whatever it was that she did that made me feel so goddamn weak." His image of the woman he stabs seems to say, "Women—they all betray and abandon." This is the sexism of a man who supports feminism conscientiously and well.

The obsessional woman wants to eliminate from her life all the people who creep in and threaten to steal her time or money and suck her dry. The hysterical woman wants to humiliate all rivals for her father's love and to idealize him, assigning his disappointing qualities to others of another race. The narcissistic man wants to wield phallic control over his girlfriends, whom he experiences as phallic women who have control over him, so he fantasizes cutting the women down, cutting them off.

When I consider these patients—and others—and consider at the same time the psychoanalytic literature on violence, I find one feature common to all kinds and degrees of violence—and this is not a common root or ultimate cause; it is a feature, a mechanism. No matter whether just fantasized or enacted, violence against people (or against people indirectly, representatively, in the medium of violence against institutions or things or nonhuman creatures) seems to me to be always aimed at a target whom the perpetrator feels to be a member of a group previously constructed in the perpetrator's mind. Or, to put the matter another way, the violence expresses a prejudice in the most literal sense of the word, a prejudgment. Even with violence that looks like it could be described with words like "impulsive" or "reactive" or "unpremeditated," the perpetrator is always carrying prefabricated images of hated enemies—of dangerous, hurtful, destructive, or disappointing people, or people who are just different—and the one or ones against whom the perpetrator acts or fantasizes acting is *one of them,* part of that group. Unlike objects of love and of sexual desire, which are, I think developmentally earlier, objects of violence are not individuals; they are "them." We have little motivation to generalize or make group formations out of our experiences of sex and love satisfaction, out of our happiness; our prejudices are formed mostly on the basis of experiences of frustration or rejection, they are negative images, composites, generalizations that anticipate future frustrations that will resemble past frustrations.

Now this claim brings me immediately onto the territory of theory of violence and aggression, not to mention theory of object relations and object choice. I am assuming that as their instinctual drives for connection (affectional or sexual) are frustrated, people—initially, as children, but over their lifetimes—build up images of the source of their frustration in a generalizing manner, arriving at an image of the frustrating group. Over time, for example, my narcissistic patient's neglectful mother became "women, who will not care for me." As expectation of care turns into an expectation of hurt and rejection, these generalizations also attach to or are displaced onto generalizations shared with others, preexisting social and cultural prejudices. In this process, the painful experiences of particular loved ones who were frustrating are covered over, removed from consciousness, while the group image dominates. New group images come into being in evolving social circumstances—as the image of "the violent ones" is doing now, appealing to people who can use such a group image of domestic or foreign terrorists to focus their frustrations.

This conceptualization, which I have sketched so briefly, depends upon an assumption about instinctual drives that I want to make explicit. In Freud's second instinct theory there are two broad types of drives: the life instincts and the death instinct, from which aggression, the energy source of violence, is ultimately derived. For reasons that I am not going to offer here, I do not accept this formulation, but I find it much less abstract and speculative to think of aggression as a frustration reaction to the thwarting of one or both of the two types of instinctual drive Freud compassed in his first, more Darwinian instinct theory, namely, the species reproductive sexual instincts and the self-preservative ego instincts (Sex and Hunger, as Freud named them for short). People's objects of violence, I think, tend to fall into two broad categories, or represent two broad groups: (1) rivals for sexual satisfaction, and (2) those who disappoint ego instinctual or nurturing and caretaking object relations. People attack those whom they have constructed as getting sexual satisfaction (while they themselves do not) and those whom they construct as withholding the nurture and affection they need. The categories or images simultaneously operate as the legitimators and rationalizers of the violence, permitting the perpetrator to say in one way or another that the violence was justified or necessary because this *kind of person* deserves it, asks for it, provokes it, can only be controlled by it, and so forth. The feeling that the victim is a member of a group means that the victim does not have to be viewed or experienced in his or her personhood, as a specific person, or in his or her association with a frustrating person who was or remains close, loved. The literature on prejudice long ago informed us that people are more able to be violent when they do not experience their victims as individuals; but this is as true for a child attacking a familial rival as it is for a soldier attacking enemies who have been dehumanized for him by a propaganda campaign or located out of his sight by virtue of his long-range, technologically sophisticated weapons.

Each individual's central and derived group images are unique to him or her and critically shaped by the object relational experiences of early childhood, the Oedipal period, and early adolescence. But, as I noted, each individual's images will fit in with, meld with, be reinforced by, be displaced onto, existing images available in the social surround, that is, existing prejudices shared by groups. A man who attacks a woman is attacking her as an individual but also her as a member of a category such as "women, those who cut men down" or "women, those who abandon." Violence expresses the way a person has learned to classify people and to interpret relationships among them, how the person's mechanisms of defense have over time been generalized and structured into social mechanisms of defense or prejudices. For example, if a person operates characteristically with the defense mechanism called by Anna Freud and others "identification with the aggressor," that person will also, over time, construct (consciously or unconsciously) a category of aggressive people and operate by identifying with them and attacking their victims.

When people's images of groups are shared and become normative for a social unit—a family, a society, a nation—they legitimate all kinds of actions toward the groups imaged, including violent ones. When violent actions become linked to some ideologically justified image of a group or some cultural system of meaning that pervades the social unit, they are no longer perceived as violent and certainly not as pathological. They become normal. So child abuse was normal—it was called discipline—in many European and American social milieus until the eighteenth century because there was a pervasively held image of children as born bad, born sinful, and in need of chastisement so that they did not hurt those who disciplined them. This idea has hardly disappeared, and there are certainly many who still hold to it among those now who would like to imprison violent children.

III. CHARACTERS AND PREJUDICES

When you think of violence (or violences) in the way I have briefly sketched, it is logical to explore the types of violence through the types of images or prejudices that people construct. And, I want to suggest further, it is logical to consider the types of images or prejudices through the lens of people's character types. Just as people's modes of loving are central to their character types, so are their modes of aggressing.

In Freudian theory, different types of characters are dominated by different types of defense mechanisms against the instincts (or the id), against the superego, and against reality (as experienced by the ego).[5] The three basic character types that Freud proposed, which he called hysterical, obsessional, and narcissistic, each has a typical direction of defense and defense structure. Repression, Freud always emphasized, is key to hysteria and to the hysterical type of character, in which threats from the powers of the instincts, the reservoir of the id, are most salient. Dissociation, too, is common, particularly among hysterical people who have been abused. By contrast, obsessionals are those who are most strongly dominated by or threatened by their own aggressive superegos, their internal commands of conscience, their agency of refusing pleasures. Among obsessionals, the more "intellectual" defenses are typical: rationalization, externalization (or blaming of others), isolation (particularly of intellect from affect), doing and undoing. Narcissistic characters are those most determined by their relationships with external reality. Freud did not study the defenses of narcissistic characters specifically; but from considering the subsequent literature and my own experience, I think that narcissistic characters operate chiefly with forms of denial or disavowal of reality: they deny other people's desires and thoughts and characteristics, even going so far as to deny their existences as separate beings. Certain of the mechanisms of defense—like identification with the aggressor—are common to all character types, but take different forms in each. For example, the narcissist will usually identify with the aggressor's power, inflating his own power thereby; the obsessional will identify with the aggressor's ability to control and set up protections; and the hysteric, with the aggressor's capacity to get sex or love.

As I have argued at length in *The Anatomy of Prejudices,* each person also has typical social mechanisms of defense, by which I mean characteristic ways in which his or her ego uses social categories or social designations—social prejudices—to defend against felt threats from reality or from the dimensions of the psyche that Freud called id and superego. Images of "the other" are used to keep forbidden wishes out of consciousness, to appease the demands of conscience, to shape and mold reality, and so forth. And, as I have suggested, along with the

5. Some of the descriptive material in what follows has been previously published in Young-Bruehl 1996.

characteristic prejudices go characteristic types of violence, which are a way of expressing the prejudices. Violence, imagined or enacted, helps fulfill the purpose of a prejudice. Prejudice is the idea for which violence is a mode of action. Prejudice says what violence does.

To make this case for the relation of character types to types of prejudice and violence, I will begin by sketching in greater detail the three character types (following the order followed in my case illustrations) and the prejudices of each; I will then turn to their correlative violences. I will try to indicate briefly, too, the kinds of social relations in which each of the character types is fostered or promoted. Societies do not have characters—as though they were large individuals, macrocosms of an individual microcosm—but one character type or another always predominates in them (in power or number), and their arrangements reflect those predominances.

I'll begin by considering characterologically obsessional people like the first patient I described, who often have paranoid features and are marked by their rigidity, moralistic conventionality (reflecting either a very severe or a very faulty superego), and tight-fisted focus on money; by their conformity (reflecting their inability to keep from splitting affects off from intellectual operations), and by a kind of cold rationality or hyperrationality. Obsessional people tend to sweep all kinds of out-groups or others into their prejudices because all groups seem connected in a vast conspiratorial system or a plot, usually one controlled by a scheming, wily leadership group, like the Jews. This character type flourishes in families and institutions (especially the military) that promote money discipline, order for order's sake, the Protestant ethic or "Prussian" values, sexual suppression, enviousness and affectless intellectualism.[6]

A second type is characterologically hysterical and most recognizable by the way in which he or she splits up or dissociates into opposing selves: a good, chaste self and a bad, lascivious self; a real self and an impostor self; a conventional self and a renegade. In her fantasy life, the second patient I described was a much more powerful and violent self than she is in her day-to-day self. Such a person's split can allow her or him to be an upstanding citizen by day and to live another life by night; hypocrisy is so much her or his way of life that she or he will dis-

6. This obsessional type appeared in a range of postwar psychoanalytic research projects and descriptive works: Frankfurt School research on "the authoritarian personality"; the sociologist William Whyte's *The Organization Man* (1956); and the work of cultural psychoanalysts such as Erich Fromm, who wrote about the rigidly conformist "marketing character," and Karen Horney, who described "the neurotic character in our time." Many young adults who ended up as research subjects for Frankfurt School–influenced projects had grown up in the 1930s in milieus marked by the fears and austerities of the Depression and then reached adulthood during the war or in the early 1950s, a period in which the prevailing social style was obsessional.

avow or dissociate from the other half's activities, as do people who belong to secret societies, clubs of rebels or outlaws, histrionic gangs, and so forth. Contemporary hysterics often have the bodily symptoms (conversion symptoms) that are typical of the "classic" hysterics known to Freud, especially the disordered eating and preoccupations with food, body image, and health (often involving some form of hypochondria). But many hysterical people (particularly males whose upbringings shape them for projecting their conflicts outward) have their bodily symptoms on the bodies of others—they make others ill, keep them down in sickening conditions, beat them, and focus all kinds of violence (real or symbolic) upon their genitals, from castration to rape.

This type flourishes in milieus where the family life is double tiered, where a family of slaves or domestic servants or colonials is woven into the primary family, so there are two mothers, two fathers, two sibling groups, and the hysterical character can assign one part of himself to each family. In contemporary America, the two-tier family is often a merged or blended family, one in which adults bring children from previous relationships into a new unit, and this was the case in the family of my hysterical patient. The hysterical person's lower and darker self searches for love in the low (class) or dark (race) or new (family tier), while his lighter and higher self idealizes the high, the light, or the original parent or sibling group. Incestuous desires and rivalries can be fantasized or acted out with a parent or sibling who is not the biological parent or sibling. So the prejudices (and violent actions) of such characters are endlessly sexualized. Their victims are imagined as archaic, primitive "natives" of grotesque sexual appetite—the id personified—whose intellectual abilities are inferior.

A third type is characterologically narcissistic and its male members are identifiable by their grandiosity, their complex phallocentrism. They worship both their own phalluses and the phalluses they magically attribute to their female victims; they have little empathy or ability to see things from another's perspective, and they radiate the expectation that they should be privileged, lucky, indulged.[7] At the same time, however, they may—like the third patient I described—have a very low opinion of themselves, a damaged sense of self, and oscillate between the two poles with what the psychoanalyst Annie Reich named "faulty self-esteem regulation."

7. I am going to discuss male sexism here, but female sexism certainly exists in the muted forms that patriarchal social conditions permit. Women do not generally have the expectation that all beings are phallic; rather, they usually imagine all beings are like themselves and their omnipotent mothers. Their disillusionment may lead to penis envy—as Freud assumed, falsely universalizing—but it can have many other outcomes, among them denigration of the phallus and alliance with other women, extended mother-bonding. But the great variability of female developmental lines away from omnipotence seems to me to contrast sharply with the relative invariability of the male story.

I think it is helpful to distinguish body narcissists, who emphasize that everyone has or should have a body like their own, from more developmentally complex mental narcissists, who, having recognized that not all bodies are alike, having registered the fact of sexual difference, insist that the other, the not-me or not-us, is mentally inferior, culturally deficient.[8] But most mental narcissists retain their earlier bodily narcissism, so that their images of the other are layered and contradictory. For them, the other is both the same and different; she is both saintly and whorish, pure and impure, spiritually adept and mindless, beautiful and dangerous, desirable and terrifying, and so forth. The victims of the prejudice called sexism are compelled to battle their own confusion when they are elevated and despised in the same act, the same sentence, the same institutions.

Among psychoanalytically influenced feminists, the sexism of males has usually been attributed to their need to disidentify with their mothers and be taken up into male peer groups. Men disparage the femininity that they must reject in themselves, and this necessity also explains their homophobia, in the sense that they reject all forms of femininity in males. But I think that this prevailing feminist psychoanalytic understanding of sexism is partial because it does not rest on an interpretation of narcissism, and thus it has not investigated what kind of social institutions and societies promote narcissism. The rule of thumb here is, I think, that the smaller and more insulated and intra-generationally eroticized families are (that is, the more they focus on reproduction and prolonging of childhood, and the more nuclear they are), the more elaborate the narcissistic entitlements they support and the more complex, layered, and contradictory their sexism is. The central feature of the complex sexism of nuclear families is male control over every controllable facet of reproduction, which means that men reproduce themselves in every way but the actual bearing and birthing of children. More extended families or clans in more agricultural settings do, of course, repress women, often very violently and in bodily forms like genital mutilation, but the primary reason for this repression is to secure claims of paternity and ownership of the children who are future laborers. The aim is not to become, as much as possible, the reproducers. Awe of female reproductivity gives

8. In terms of their visions of human sexuality, male bodily narcissists imagine that all people have the male genital. Females have an interior or inverted phallus—that is what their genitals consist of. Mental narcissists recognize that there are two different sexes, with different genitalia, but they believe that there is only one kind of mind, the masculine; women are mindless. There are, accordingly, two types of in-group sexism, that which attributes all sexuality and reproduction to male organs—the male sperm is, for example, a little man who is harbored for nine months in the female's inverted phallus—and that which acknowledges female reproductivity and ova but wants that reproductivity under male domination. On these sexual theories see Laqueur 1992.

way in complex industrializing cultures to envy and the characteristic of the envious—that they attack what they cannot be or have.

IV. TYPES OF VIOLENCE

I have described three types of characters and their characteristic prejudices, and now I'd like to sketch their typical victim groups and forms of violence. Each type finds its victim group by paying attention to real qualities in people, but each also constructs or imagines the group, fictionalizes it. The types of violence used against the victims reflect the imaged relationship between victimizer and victim, that is, what the victimizer wants (consciously or unconsciously) to accomplish with his or her prejudice.

Obsessional characters react with particular intensity and violence to groups that they perceive as penetrating the fortresses of defenses they have erected to keep their acquisitive (especially their anal, hoarding) desires in control. Their enemies come in from the outside, as immigrants or refugees, and penetrate—the metaphors are usually of anal rape—right into the commercial bowels that the obsessional considers crucial to the workings of the society. The penetration is usually imagined to be slow and invidious; but when the obsessional is reacting to actual violence (and one can hardly imagine violence more horrible and symbolically laden than the penetration and explosion of a locus of capitalism like the World Trade Center) the obsessional's fantasies concentrate on threats of ever greater violence. The strangers are or become what sociologists call "middleman minorities." By the obsessional's definitions, the strangers are spies, secret agents, infiltrators, and propagandists for a vast network in their place of origin and in the new homes of their relatives and co-conspirators. Animosity against such people simmers among obsessionals, but it turns deadly on a large scale, in social and political terms, under specific conditions. An economic depression or deterioration has wiped out the savings and the security, the sense of future, of classes that have moved upward through huge effort or spent great amounts of prestige on staying in power, or war conditions have destroyed many of the rules and regulations that have checked aggression. Someone must be blamed and eliminated to restore law and order. The blameworthy group is accused of taking over the government, so that obsessional prejudice becomes antistate, ultimately supranationalist. The world becomes supranationally Manichean: East versus West, Muslim versus Christian. Genocide is the logical punishment; it is the purgative "final solution" to a threat that would continue to threaten if it survived as a remnant.

The antistate, antipolitical rhetoric of the obsessional prejudices—so obvious currently in America in the pronouncements against Jews and against homosexuals of the Christian Coalition and its leader the Reverend Pat Robertson—is one of the key features distinguishing the obsessional prejudices from the hysterical. Hysterical characters need victims that they can humiliate, so they do not try to eliminate them from an expansionary supranational movement; they are not "ethnic cleansers." Rather, they appropriate existing political means to split the victim group so that the victims cannot breed normally or gather their resources for rebellion. They rape and impregnate women of the victim group, they beat and castrate the men; they treat both women and men as rivals who need to be bested in every domain, especially any domain that involves intelligence, which the victims are said to lack because they are people of the body and its appetites. Discrimination against these victims and violence grow worse whenever they threaten to move up in the world, out of their place in the hierarchy that the hysterical think is natural. Moving up is most critically represented by marrying up, so miscegenation is the cardinal sin in the sexualized world of the hysterically prejudiced. The apparatus of the state is coveted by the hysterically prejudiced for institutionalizing their prejudices; in political orientation they are not antistate but pro–states' rights—they like their politics very local, very familial, very like *la famiglia*.

In America, racism has been fostered by a long tradition of two-tier families, in the contexts of slavery and then domestic servitude, in the South and in the North, to the point where an entrenched image of the African Americans as a servant group is pervasive across classes. Much of the anti-immigrant fervor that is so widespread in America now is hysterical and modeled on the traditional racism: the point of its legislative forms is to humiliate the victims and break up their families (even to attack the health and safety of their children, as California initiatives against illegal immigrants do). Miscegenation that in any way admits the lower into the higher group is, as always, the central racist focus (Hockenos 1993: 36). Men of color are usually beaten up, in more or less symbolic acts of castration, as we have seen in highly publicized episodes, from the police beating of Rodney King in Los Angeles to the dragging behind a car of James Byrd in Texas. In Europe, where anti-immigrant activity, supported by right-wing political parities, is also very common, there are many episodes of racist violence, but also many episodes of anti-immigrant violence that are more obsessional—that is, aimed ultimately at eliminating rather than humiliating. In Germany, for example, fire-bombings of buildings in which Turkish families live fulfill the obsessional purpose of eliminating a group that in terms of their clan organizations and business success is very "Jewish," a middleman minority group. The attacks upon and detention of men who are associated with "the terrorists" is more obsessional than hysterical: "the terrorists" are wily, intelligent, ruthless agents connected to a network of their Muslim clansmen at home, who are capable of living among "us" undetected, plotting.

The violence that is associated with narcissistic prejudices is often domestic violence or violence in places that are understood as arenas of sexual display. It is aimed at people who are threatening to narcissists because of their sex and gender, their key marks of difference. Narcissistic violence is violence against the marks of difference, either to eliminate them or to appropriate them (as in the violence of the antiabortion movement).

Racism and sexism are obviously very closely linked, in the sense that racism is gendered—it falls differently on its male and female victims, since it takes different forms in its male and female perpetrators. Racism, as Frantz Fanon (1967) wrote, exists "on the genital level." But it seems to me that the sexism that is directed by the men of one group at the women of another, construed as lower, should be called sexist racism (or sexist classism) to distinguish it from that sexism that is directed at women of a sexist's own group. Narcissistic characters, I think, focus first on women of their own group, women whom they model on their own mothers. But "other" women, darker, lower, can become carriers of the images first constructed for in-group women, particularly the bodily narcissistic images of phallic women. Among whites, dark-skinned women are phallicized; even when they are construed as "mammy" figures, hypermothers, they are said to be matriarchal, male-dominating, often castrating, dangerous. Rape is a way to keep them in their place, but also to assign their half-breed children to a lower status. The obsessionally prejudiced, by contrast, forbid all sexual relations with the polluting people they hate.[9]

There are, of course, many people in whom the traits of the various character types mingle, as there are social circumstances that promote more than one kind of prejudice and associated violence. But it does seem to me that most people have a main prejudice, as they have a prevailing trait or characterological pattern. As for the objects of their bias, many groups will be primarily suited to be targets of one type of prejudice, but some groups can serve a plurality of prejudices. Adolescents, homosexuals, and immigrants or foreigners, for example, can be construed as cunning infiltrators like Jews, as primitively sexual like blacks, or as lacking the phallus as (or like) women. They can be blamed and envied, put in their places, or controlled in their reproductive sexuality. The group of "the violent ones" (particularly juveniles) is being constructed in this multipurpose way. The main reason why the study of homophobia is still so preliminary, so

9. One measure of the complexity of the situation that evolved during the 1990s in the former Yugoslavia is that the Muslims, who are "Jews" to their Serbian oppressors (that is, they are construed as an interloper mercantile and culturally conspiratorial group with clan connections across the Middle East), were displaced and sent to concentration camps on the Nazi model, but their women were also subject to programmatic rape, something that is usually a feature of hysterical but not of obsessional prejudices. What may be reflected here is a difference in psychic and sociocultural formation between the rural Serb army soldiers— the rapists—and the more urban and better-educated ideologues who envisioned and engineered the ethnic cleansing campaign against the Muslims, focusing their attention on the cosmopolitan Muslim culture of Sarajevo.

riven with clichés, and so overburdened with the whole history of social scientific bias about prejudice is that homophobia is usually construed as a single prejudice—when we ought to be, at the least, speaking of the homophobias, and not just because prejudices against male and female homosexuals take different forms. Homophobic violence can be directed toward homosexuals construed as infiltrators or underminers of family life (in the Christian Coalition manner); against homosexuals construed as a "lower" type living too close for comfort among the "straights" and representing, thus, a constant temptation or the possibility of another life; or against homosexuals construed as threats to the stability of the gender order, challenges to narcissistically grounded identity, so that they must be violently reduced to being "like us." I think that conversion therapy for homosexuals is a kind of psychic violence reflecting the narcissism of the therapists who practice it and who insist on making homosexuals "like us."

An essay like this one, which surveys wide territories and proposes a multifaceted, speculatively theoretical approach, is bound to raise many questions. I am well aware that I have made assertions at every turn that are arguable, but there is little space here for argument or even for nuance. But after witnessing several months ago (I am writing in January 2002) a stunning act of violence against America—a criminal, terrorist act, not an act of war—and a "war on terrorism" in response (on the territory of Afghanistan and at the cost of many Afghanistan civilian lives and ruined cities), I am more than ever convinced that it is urgent that we try to shift our discussion of violence away from pursuit of "the root of violence" toward more phenomenologically complex descriptions and interpretations. From the perspective that I have outlined here, the enormous danger of our present circumstance is that the attack made against us by an internationally networked terrorist organization is an obsessional nightmare come true, come real, and it thus seems to call for and justify all the classic, characteristic obsessional responses. Overriding constitutional rights for the sake of security, sweeping innocent people of many nations into a vision of conspiracy (all who "harbor" terrorists), and assuming a fortress mentality that rigidly defines what is and is not patriotic—these tendencies have attracted widespread support. Under attack of this sort, the obsessional in everyone is mobilized, and especially the obsessional in obsessionals, who are very numerous in military and governmental bureaucracies. But increasingly we are hearing voices of caution about how we conduct the "war on terrorism" and voices of concern about how we uphold our Constitution and protect the human rights of all, and these critics need a diversity of voices of psychological (especially psychoanalytic) and sociopolitical analysis to draw upon.

8 : RACISM AND IMPURE HEARTS

Racism seems to be, in a fundamental way, a matter of belief. One who possesses what we might call "racist beliefs"—such as that the members of a given racial or ethnic group G are intellectually or morally inferior to members of one's own group, or that G members ought to be prevented from living or intermixing among them—is ipso facto a racist, in common usage, even if these beliefs are never visibly manifested in affect, in construals of events, texts, or situations, or in verbal or other behavior. In particular, not yet acting upon such beliefs does not preclude one from being a "closet" racist (who could, moreover, begin overtly manifesting racism at any time). On the other hand, it is an effective defense to a behavior-based accusation of racism that the person does not hold any racist beliefs and that the suspect behavior is therefore explicable in some other manner. Of course, it can be difficult to adjudicate, in particular cases, whether the offending beliefs in question are in fact nonexistent or whether, instead, there is only self-deception, denial, or other lack of conscious access to them. But the care and effort that go into such adjudications offer significant verification that attributions of racism turn upon the existence or nonexistence of the relevant kind of belief.[1]

Racist beliefs thus strike unreflective common sense as being both necessary and sufficient for an attribution of racism, as that concept is commonly deployed.[2] One's "heart" is either pure on this score, or it is not—in which latter

---

1. By "belief" here I include all manner of cognitive resources, including assumptions and presuppositions, whether embodied in representations that are sentential or imagistic. In this way, the conception in the text extends even to varieties of racism that show up only in habits of behavior not produced by reasoning with beliefs—such as having "visceral" hostile or aversive reactions (as some dogs have been known to display), unthinkingly shifting into patronizing street slang and slouching whenever meeting black men, and perhaps handing out compliments for articulateness only to blacks. Note also that the term "belief" in this chapter is intended to comprehend, on the sentential side, not only sentences that amount to full-fledged beliefs of the cognizer, but also others that are not so attributable yet are nonetheless parts of his standing cognitive endowment and, once activated from memory, can be accepted by him temporarily but unqualifiedly for purposes of reasoning, just as are his beliefs. (These latter are referred to as "nonbeliefs" in Beyer 1999.)

2. Some accounts of racism do not view racist cognitions as being at its source (e.g., Garcia 1996). But the analysis in this chapter applies to all accounts of racism insofar as racist beliefs are conceived as important causal contributors whose eradication would be desirable.

case one is either very racist, slightly racist, or something in between. The deciding factor is one's system of beliefs.

How, then, to purge oneself, or someone else, of racism? The logical course, it would seem, is education: present information that undermines the racist beliefs, whether by explicit credible teachings that contradict them or by experiences from which the racist can glean their falsehood (such as working or playing alongside members of the disfavored group G). Racism's cure involves removal, in one way or another, of all racist beliefs.[3] Only with such cleansing can a person rightly reckon himself untainted by racism, conscious or unconscious.

Or at least such is the standard view. In this essay, I hope to show that this understanding of the nature of racism and its cure is misleadingly, even counterproductively, oversimplified. A more complicated and nuanced view, though one still concentrating on racism's roots in cognition, offers more astute guidance for moral evaluation, more helpful practical recommendations for those seeking to conquer racism, and a more subtle and accurate picture of the nature of racism. To begin, the next section will show that, due to two kinds of obstacles in the way of racist-belief eradication—(i) the ease with which beliefs of this kind can deflect counterevidence; and (ii) the phenomena of belief perseverance and continuing cognitive usage of already-rejected ideas—the standard view holds out little hope that racists can escape their condition. This will be followed, however, by a discussion of ways by which ineradicable racist beliefs can be rendered ineffectual—which achieves the core of what we seek when we endeavor to eliminate someone's racism. In sum, what I aim to show is that racist beliefs are resistant to subjective rejection; that even those that are so rejected are resistant to lasting expulsion from one's belief system; and that those that remain available for use in cognition can shape thought and behavior even in the event that one has recognized their falsehood. Yet if one is intent upon combating the racism within one's mind, one is not without effective weapons, and we will examine some of the available cognitive countermeasures.

I. THE TROUBLE WITH PURIFICATION

Racist beliefs, it will be argued in this section, possess two features that tend to make their eradication from a person's mind quite a daunting, if not flatly impossible, undertaking. The first is that racist beliefs are among the beliefs whose subjective repudiation is particularly difficult to bring about via an encounter

3. In focusing my analysis of racism upon beliefs, I do not intend to suggest that belief change is a purely intellectual matter. I take no position in this essay on whether belief revision processes typically, or ever, involve emotions, desires, or other mental states or events that are not strictly cognitive.

with evidence. The second feature is one that appears to be characteristic of beliefs generally: even if a racist belief does come to be repudiated by its holder, it might well linger in memory, get activated in certain contexts, and thus manifest in verbal or other behavior.[4]

REPUDIATION DOES NOT COME EASILY

Racist beliefs are false—or so I shall assume throughout. (If some of them are actually true, then coming to reject and expunge these from one's mind presents additional challenges over and above those we will be examining.) An important feature they share is that they are often quite deep-seated compared to certain familiar kinds of beliefs, in that in their possessors' eyes they are not logically dependent upon other factual beliefs that are readily susceptible to disconfirmation, and thus they typically are not readily jettisoned in response to the acquisition of additional evidence. To see this, consider the following array of beliefs:

1. The milk on the top shelf of our refrigerator is fresh.
2. The president is being honest about his noninvolvement in the corruption scandal.
3. Increasing U.S. trade with China will increase the likelihood of political democratization there.
4. Asian people are, as a group, generally untrustworthy.
5. Blacks are inferior in intellect and morality to persons of other races.

These beliefs are alike (and like all beliefs) in that, as W. V. O. Quine famously pointed out, they are all in theory potentially immune from convincing refutation: no matter what supposedly contrary evidence is encountered by a believer of any one of them, such evidence can be reinterpreted or explained away in such fashion as to preserve the commitment to the belief. Each of the beliefs can thus be shielded from conclusive disproof: one can never be logically compelled by evidence to grant its falsehood, as long as one is willing to react to the evidence by instead making alterations, however implausible, *elsewhere* in one's belief system.[5]

But for all but those most single-mindedly (or pathologically) committed to

4. Whether this is indeed equally characteristic of all beliefs, or solely or especially affects only certain kinds—such as those having more emotion-laden origins, or those that have been longer in memory or more often used without being consciously rejected by their possessors—is a question meriting further research.

5. See, e.g., Quine 1992: 13–14. The locus classicus for this idea is Quine's "Two Dogmas of Empiricism" (1964: 20–46, esp. 42–44): "Any statement can be held true come what may, if we make drastic enough adjustments elsewhere in the system" (43). One straightforward overview of the Quine-Duhem Thesis, along with further citations to Quine's work on holism, can be found in Klee 1997: 64–65.

the defense of certain beliefs come what may, this in-theory feature common to all beliefs does not, of course, dictate their in-practice subjective susceptibility to counterevidence—a susceptibility that definitely varies across beliefs. Whatever insulation of them from evidence is *possible*, in actual psychological fact we do experience contrary evidence as imposing varying degrees of rational compulsion upon us to revise or abandon our beliefs. In the case of those listed above, we feel such compulsion more for the beliefs toward the top of the list than for those toward the bottom, with racist beliefs tending to be among the kinds of beliefs less open, from their possessors' standpoints, to rational challenge.[6]

So yes, if I taste that milk in the refrigerator, and it clearly seems sour, no logic can bar me from patching up my belief system to preserve my belief '1', that it is fresh. I could add a bit of new speculative theory about how fresh milk can sometimes taste sour, or a new factual conjecture that my taste buds are out of order or that I have been slipped a mind-altering drug. But let's be realistic. In all but the most extraordinary circumstances, as soon as I detect that sourness, I will revise my belief. I will repudiate '1', intending never again to use it seriously in the role of a belief.

In this respect, '2' ('The president is being honest about his non-involvement in the corruption scandal') differs importantly from '1'. If one believes it, one will be more prone than in the case of '1' to react initially to direct counterevidence by discounting that evidence rather than by simply accepting it as showing the falsehood of one's belief. This might be due to one or more of a number of related yet distinguishable factors, including the availability of alternative accounts of the counterevidence's source, the availability of alternative interpretations of the counterevidence itself, and the conceptual connections between such interpretations and the belief in question.

First, that is, the source of counterevidence to '2' (say, press reports or unearthed tapes indicating that the president himself ordered the scandalous acts) will be, by comparison with that for '1', more open to multiple explanations, some

6. Given my focus upon *rational* challenges to beliefs, some will understandably wonder about motivated *nonrational* or *irrational* pressures for racist-belief maintenance or revision—extraordinary, and maybe even routine, pressures exerted upon beliefs by wishes, dislikes, emotional needs, and so forth. I intend to avoid such concededly interesting matters in this chapter, however, because I think that the explanatory power of the model of rational belief formation and revision (including innocent—i.e., unmotivated—irrationality) has not yet been fully explored and is far from being exhausted, thus rendering somewhat premature the resort to motivated mechanisms in order to explain why people believe what they do. (For example, my notion of "perspect," set out below, points toward an innocent explanation for internal inconsistencies within a person's belief system.) Before we adopt the (comforting) view that racists have lost normal rational cognitive control over their belief systems, let's first see how much of racism might be comprehensible as a product of our ordinarily rational cognitive processes.

of which show the counterevidence to be of dubious reliability—the product of disinformation fed to the press, irresponsible journalistic practice, deviously edited tapes, utterances misleadingly taken out of context, or the like. Second, even if the counterevidence to '2' is deemed to be uncorrupted and from a trustworthy source, it would be less likely to demand a repudiating response from the believer due to its greater openness, compared to counterevidence to '1', to multiple plausible readings of its meaning. Sensations of sour taste, or even printed sell-by dates, are relatively unambiguous informational inputs, whereas an (accurate, undoctored, unedited) tape of a conversation involving the president might well be susceptible to varying reasonable interpretations that impute differing verbal acts and states of mind to him. Third, not only are diverse plausible interpretations of counterevidence to '2' available, but some of these allow for a committed believer to maintain '2' without inconsistency, whereas the incompatibility between belief '1' and the meaning of its counterevidence is relatively inescapable—commitment to '1' cannot help one evade the logical pressure brought by the counterevidence. A belief about the freshness of milk in a given container cannot by itself (at least without extraordinary strain) alter one's sense-based perception that some of that milk is in fact sour or otherwise not fresh, and neither can it alter one's understanding of the logical incompatibility between such a perception and one's belief. By contrast, if the president's honesty is treated as a given to which the evidence can acceptably be made to conform, then some of the supposed counterevidence might readily, and not implausibly, be construed so as not to constitute *counter*evidence. (Most simply: might the president have been joking, intentionally deceptive, or tipsy when he issued the incriminating utterance?) More generally, some beliefs are such that not only is their counterevidence open to varied construals, but those of the construals that conflict with the beliefs are more easily discountable because fewer in number and lesser in degree of plausibility. The upshot of all this is that counterevidence to '2' is less likely to seem conclusive than counterevidence to '1', and accordingly less likely to instigate a subjective rejection of the belief.

Nevertheless, the evidence that one faces can be such that one feels inescapably compelled to reject '2' and to regard any reasonably intelligent person who insists upon holding onto it as beset by some irrational, cognition-distorting emotional wish, need, or compulsion. With '3', though ('Increasing U.S. trade with China will increase the likelihood of political democratization there'), we move still further from the clarity of '1' because of the more general, theoretical nature of the cognitive commitment it involves. Thus it is even more likely than '2' to be used in interpreting evidence that bears upon its truth or falsehood and to self-protectively cause such evidence to be construed in belief-upholding ways. But it is still a kind of belief for which evidence might be encountered that, even if open to multiple interpretations, is on all but the most implausible of these so blatantly and unambiguously contrary that a believer cannot, in good conscience and without self-deception, construe it away. Hence the belief, despite its power to color the evidence regarding it, is ultimately still open to revision or elimination to a significant degree.

What about '4' and '5'? These are typical racist beliefs, directed against Asians and blacks, respectively. And it seems that they are more akin to beliefs like '3' than beliefs like '1'. They color the evidence that a believer in them encounters. A significant portion of the available counterevidence is testimony of others that can be dismissed as not supported by objective data and maybe even as tainted by ideology (by multiculturalist or egalitarian political commitments, say). Other evidence, obtained from direct but limited acquaintance with the group G members in question, does not bring with it an unavoidable contra-belief reading, but is readily susceptible to alternate plausible interpretations that confirm, rather than refute, the racist beliefs.[7] Beliefs like these are not completely resistant to change via evidence; but the kind of evidence most difficult to construe or rationalize away—involved acquaintance with a range of G members in settings that allow them to reveal unambiguously their possession of traits opposite to the negative ones imputed by '4' and '5'—is of a kind rarely encountered by racists. In sum, we see in this section how rational processes tend to work against revision or jettisoning of racist beliefs, given the relatively great (though not uniquely great) "distance" of such beliefs from their evidentiary supports. The road to psychological rejection of racist beliefs is thus one that tends not to be traversed by the believers, for reasons that are partly a matter of the dictates of rational belief revision.

A DEEPER OBSTACLE TO PURIFICATION

Not only do holders of racist beliefs tend not to find themselves rationally compelled by the evidence that they encounter to subjectively renounce those beliefs, but they face a still more profound impediment to the purging of them. Even after they are renounced as false, racist beliefs, like other beliefs, often continue to reside within a person's cognitive endowment, where (as with dormant viruses) the right circumstances can cause them to be activated and employed in emotion- and behavior-influencing cognitive processes. Racism thus is akin to a disease that, once contracted, is forever present within the body and capable, when activated, of degrading its health.

Now, this picture does conflict with at least two standard assumptions about the operation of human cognitive systems: (i) that once an idea is rejected as false, it is barred or expelled from a person's belief system; (ii) that an idea

7. Part of the explanation of this phenomenon no doubt resides with the widespread emotional (but rationally warranted) tendency to favor preservation of our existing beliefs over their alteration, a conservatism that provides greater stability of worldview and the accompanying practical and psychic advantages.

thought by someone to be false cannot, in any event, enter into his cognizing—in other words, that when engaging in "serious" or "sincere" (i.e., non-hypothetical, non-suppositional, non-joking, non-acting, etc.) mental operations, people employ only ideas that they hold to be true. But there are weighty reasons to think that it is these assumptions, rather than the picture I am proposing, that is at odds with reality.

Repudiation without Elimination

Even where a cognizer ascertains that a sentence (or other representation) in his endowment is deserving of expulsion, and goes on to will this, it is typically difficult to effectuate such a willing. Call this *belief perseverance*.[8] Judging a sentence false is apparently not as consequential an act as we might be tempted to think: it does not always prevent the sentence's initial entry into a person's cognitive endowment, and neither does it, in general, result in the elimination of the sentence from that endowment once there—or, as will be discussed in the next section, prevent its activation and usage in subsequent cognizing.

This is a well-attested fact about the mind. The psychologist Daniel Wegner writes of "thoughts that we cannot erase from our mind" that "continue to influence our further thinking" (1989: 100). With regard to such a thought, "Suggesting [to oneself] that the thought is wrong or false or silly or mistaken will not make it truly disappear" (113). He writes,

> When we have an idea that . . . just cries out to be wiped off the face of the earth, the most direct attack we can imagine making on it is to say it is false. The fact that disbelieved ideas do not "go away," however, leaves us with this potentially tricky, oscillating idea in our mind. Sometimes we will remember it is false, and we will make decisions accordingly. But at other times we may lose track of our disbelief, or our resolution to disregard this idea, and so make judgments that follow from the belief that the thought is true. (116)

The psychological evidence suggests that "it takes much more than a retraction to produce a lasting and effective suppression." It seems that "the will to disbe-

---

8. This class of phenomena, referred to as "(non)belief perseverance" in Beyer 1999, is more general than what goes by the name "belief perseverance" in the psychological literature, which involves continuing to maintain a belief that one has derived from one's experiences in an experiment even after one has been debriefed by the experimenters about the phoniness of the experimental "evidence" upon which one based one's belief. See, e.g., Harman 1986: 35–38. Wegner participated in an experiment extending this result to cases where *pre*-experiment briefings were used in order to warn subjects, and found that "the majority fell for the false feedback" nonetheless (Wegner 1989: 105). Wegner concludes: "Whether we learn before, during, or after we encounter a piece of information that the information is false, we may subsequently use the information in just the same way" (104).

lieve is not, by itself, sufficient to clear our minds of false thoughts or their unwanted implications" (100, 117).

One reason that belief perseverance gets overlooked at times within philosophy might be that certain kinds of illustrative example tend to influence theoretical reflection in this area. Treating, for example, the old chestnut

It is raining (here and now)

(e.g., Williams 1973: 136) as one's central source of data concerning belief can dis-
tort one's view. A just-formed instance of this prototypical belief sentence might
indeed disappear immediately upon a glance out the window at the weather; this
is one way that ordinary learning of facts occurs. But a belief that, say, one's
father was an honest man might well be more tenacious in the face of acknowl-
edgedly powerful disconfirming information. One might accept the new evidence, recognize that it dispositively entails a lack of honesty on one's father's
part, and still, on numerous subsequent occasions, sincerely declare one's father
to have been honest or engage in reasonings or imaginings that take him to have
been so. The cognitive representations containing the information that one's father was an honest will not have been expunged, and one will have also lost mental
access, temporarily if not permanently, to (i) the counterevidence that one
deemed (and would still deem) a conclusive refutation of one's belief, and likely
also to (ii) one's earlier experience(s) of having rejected the belief based upon
that counterevidence. (The variations in how beliefs resist expulsion despite
acknowledged disconfirmation are, of course, not to be confused with the ear-
lier-discussed variations in how beliefs deflect or discourage subjective acknowledgment of their disconfirmation in the face of counterevidence.)

Despite the general neglect of belief perseverance, some philosophers have
enriched their portrayals of cognition by taking notice of the phenomenon.
Gilbert Harman, for instance, writes, "Of course, there are cases in which one has
to struggle in order to abandon a belief one takes to be discredited. One finds
oneself coming back to thoughts one realizes one should no longer accept" (1986:
38). We can add that, unfortunately, one does not always "find oneself" doing this
when it occurs; one sometimes comes back to supposedly discredited thoughts
unawares. Alvin Goldman, too, has insightful things to say on the topic. He
speaks of the cognitive state that remains even after it has been repudiated (and
even after a corrected state has been added to the cognitive endowment) as a
"credal residue" and recognizes that these "are important to acknowledge because, like a phoenix, they can be reborn—as beliefs" (1986: 223–24).

While there is considerable illumination to be gained simply by bringing this
perseverance phenomenon into contact with issues of racism, it is only with an
explanation of the difficulties of belief eradication that a fully satisfying account
will be attained. A good start in this direction can be made by introducing a

richer, more realistic model of cognition. The commonsense view, influenced by the analogy of the mind to a computer, takes a person's cognizing simply to involve manipulations carried out upon a single set of sentential beliefs; but by adding two sorts of complications that render this view more true to life, it becomes possible to discern in greater detail some of the mechanisms that thwart people's attempts to rid their minds permanently of repudiated beliefs.

Man Does Not Think by Sentences Alone. The first complication is that memory contributes to cognition more than just sententially embodied information—so that even were one to eradicate a given racist belief sentence 'p' from one's memory, one might retain other kinds of parallel mental representations, due to which one might find oneself at a later point again accepting 'p' or reasoning or acting as if one accepts it. To begin with, humans possess an "episodic memory" system that stores memories of past experiences—memories *of* the experiences themselves,[9] rather than memories *about* them: memories of *eating* the apple, or *seeing* that it was green, as opposed to sentential memories *that* one ate the apple or *that* it was green.[10]

One use that is made of episodic memories is the derivation from them of sentences that can then enter into ordinary reasoning and even be added to a person's permanent store of knowledge. Though this ordinarily facilitates effective cognizing—supplying a wealth of otherwise-unavailable information to ongoing thought processes—it can undermine one's intentions to rid oneself lastingly of a racist belief, even supposing that one is able in the first place to expunge the belief from one's store of cognitive assets. In the simplest kind of case, one retains an episodic memory of having thought or argued the racist position in question, and upon recalling this simply accepts that position once more. This can readily occur, because it is not uncommon for one who maintains confidence in one's own thought processes to come newly to accept a sentence 'p' by trusting that the episodic memory of one having *earlier* accepted it provides two assurances: (i) that one did indeed accept 'p' earlier, and (ii) that it is worthy of acceptance once again. Of course, if one also has grounds for suspecting that 'p' is false—maybe grounds also thrown up by episodic memory, such as the recollection of having later come to doubt 'p'—then the new taking up of 'p' might be inhibited. Thus, if one recalls not just having held or articulated the racist belief in question, but also having later repudiated it, one will not be induced to accept it afresh. But if, as seems common enough, the experience leading to repudiation is isolated in a region of memory unconnected with some experiences

9. The memories might not be veridical. They can be distorted by initial expectations, interpretations, misperceptions, and misunderstandings, and perhaps also by analogous processes that occur subsequent to initial storage.

10. See, e.g., Tulving 2002: 1999. Another example of episodic-memory content was the above-mentioned recollected "earlier experience(s) of having rejected the belief" that one's father was honest.

of unhesitatingly using the racist belief, then recollecting the latter could well reinject that belief into one's immediate reasonings and even potentially back into the pool of permanently stored resources available generally for cognizing.

There are also more complex paths by which recollection of episodic memories can lead to the resuscitation of a previously rejected racist belief. Recollecting having thought that q, having thought that r, and having thought that s might induce one to treat those three sentences as legitimate premises for reasoning, whereupon one might infer to one's old racist belief, 'p'. Or one might remember having certain experiences that now, in one's current reflections upon them, cause one to conclude afresh that p. In such ways, one's racist belief can be discredited, subjectively rejected, and (let us suppose) eliminated from one's pool of ready-to-use cognitive resources—yet still be reconstituted from the echoes of past experience.

There is a second kind of nonsentential memory input into cognition that poses a similar problem to the would-be self-purifying racist. It seems clear that we store in memory, for future mental use, not only sentences, such as the racist beliefs to be eradicated, but also *images* (or image sequences) of various sorts:[11] one's own imagined tennis serve; John McEnroe's tennis serve; dream and fantasy sequences; someone holding onto the edge of a roof (an image obtained from film or television); a precedent instance of the interactions at the end of a first date (perhaps simplified or idealized into generic form); what one's niece looked like at age ten; how she greedily tried to grab her younger brother's candy. Like episodic memories, these, if trusted by their possessor to be reliable sources of truth—which is often eminently reasonable, as there is frequently much to be learned about the world from them—can contain the seeds from which extinguished racist beliefs might be regenerated anew. The stored image of an episode of dealing with a merchant who is Jewish and is relentless about not giving up ground in negotiations, even if obtained from reading or viewing fiction, is one from which one might now extract and accept a racist belief about Jews, or by virtue of which one might presuppose such a view in one's reasonings. Thus, true cleansing of one's racist attitude that Jews are stingy and greedy demands not only the elimination of all sentences to that effect (plus other sentences from which such a view might be derived), as well as all episodic memories of personal mental experiencings from which one might take over or reconstruct such an attitude, but also the modification or expunging of all other standing cognitive resources in image form that one might construe (using one's remaining cognitive resources) as accurately portraying Jews as such.

This sort of self-cleansing would appear to be quite a difficult, if not hopeless, task. But the futility of trying to guarantee the nonoccurrence of racist cogni-

11. I am using "image" in an unanalyzed, everyday, nonscientific sense, as a contrast with verbally encoded information.

tions by purging one's mental cupboard of all ingredients from which they might be fabricated is not cause for despair, as there is another, more efficacious course that we will consider in sections 2 and 3 below.

The Cognitive System Is Not Fully Integrated. The second of the two complications neglected by the usual computer-analogized model of mind is that cognition is not a fully integrated process. That is, one's cognitive endowment, the pool of resources stored in memory for utilization in thinking, is *not* a single fund from which any and all assets are available to be activated whenever relevant to the current topic of cognition. Rather than provide in such fashion a single *perspective* upon the world and a single *personality* for engaging with it, one's endowment is compartmentalized in a complex pattern that actually supports many distinct, partial, partly overlapping, situation-triggered (and sometimes mutually inconsistent) *perspects* along with a corresponding set of *personas* (Beyer 1999). The stream of cognizing involves a continual shifting from one perspect (and its corresponding persona) to another. As a result, how one thinks or behaves in one kind of setting is no sure indicator of how one thinks or behaves in a different one. Indeed, one can even sometimes be found reasoning earnestly in perspect P1 with a premise that is *contradictory* to its counterpart that one earnestly employs in P2.

If this is an accurate portrayal—and there is much reason to think so (Beyer 1999)—then it would seem to offer belief perseverance still another advantage in its contest with purification-by-belief-eradication. Suppose that one awakens to the recognition that one's racist belief 'p' is out-and-out false and wrongheaded, and that this realization leads somehow to the internal acts and circumstances that suffice for effecting belief eradication. Given how substantially independent from one another are the thought processes that a person undertakes in differing perspects, would we expect one's anti-'p' realization to result in the expulsion of 'p' from one's entire cognitive endowment—or instead from only a certain kind of perspect, so that, yes, when one is, say, again discussing public policy issues with colleagues or strangers, one will never again be tempted by that racist idea, while in other contexts one might continue to find 'p' being offered up by one's memory as an untainted tool for thinking? Whether this is so is an empirical, and not logical, question, of course; but the latter conjecture seems strongly supported by ordinary experience with mental dividedness and how lessons learned in one context fail to carry over to others. It seems, then, that the snuffing out of a racist belief in one perspect would not be expected to undermine its continuing availability in others. Moreover, such recalcitrance to systemic uprooting might be expected especially for those sentences that are not newly formed but are of long standing and are integrated into numerous perspects—which certainly might often characterize racist beliefs.

And matters are even worse still, of course. For we have simply assumed that one's realization of the racist belief's falsity would bring about its snuffing in the particular perspective activated at that moment. Yet experience also teaches that even a sincere banishment of a belief often turns out to be only a temporary superseding of it limited to the immediate cognitive episode, with no lasting effects even for this very perspective. Especially where the racist belief has long been activated in this kind of perspective, the insight or information that it is false might be quickly forgotten (or confined to episodic memory) once the current thought episode passes, and not only fail to oust 'p' permanently from all of memory, but even fail to bring about its exclusion from the "activation list" for this one perspect. Despite the temporary setback, it lives on within this perspective to fight another day. It is a familiar experience to learn something, but have the lesson not "take," such that in future pragmatic situations of the same type one just reverts to one's old view.

Cognizing with Ideas One Deems to Be False

Even if it were to prove impossible to banish from one's cognitive endowment the subjectively repudiated items from which racist thoughts and acts arise, this would be of little concern as long as those items could be counted on to remain dormant and inert. And such an expectation is not prima facie unreasonable, at least insofar as we are dealing with items (let us again focus upon sentential beliefs) that have been repudiated because they are viewed as being false. How, after all, can one be expected to use, say, racist belief 'p' in one's theoretical or practical reasoning when one rejects 'p' as false?

There is a good deal to be said about the remarkably complicated relation between cognition and truth, but our purposes do not require going into great detail here. Suppose that we grant, for the sake of argument, the plausible psychological principle that one cannot make sincere, serious use in cognition of sentences that one at that time regards to be false. This would still provide little comfort to those seeking to become reformed racists via the route of purification. For there are good reasons to think that the principle would not prevent one from using those racist ideas that continue, despite one's intentions, to reside within one's cognitive endowment.

To begin with, there is the fact of what we might call *epistemic reticence:* cognitive contents do not come labeled in ways that immediately and dependably announce the truth values that their possessors take them to have.[12] We some-

---

12. Indeed, the considerations discussed in this paragraph, combined with the multiple-perspectives account of compartmentalized cognition, suggest that "the truth values that their possessors take them to have" are sometimes not even unitary, determinate values at all. One can make varied assessments of a sentence's truth value, with none of these clearly deserving to be regarded as *the* view, or considered view, that one takes of it.

times unwittingly utilize, in our reasonings, sentences that we would deem upon reflection to be false—or, indeed, even those that we have already in the past so deemed. When these are newly obtained sentences that come from outside information sources or internal inferential processes rather than from memory, this is only to be expected, since we sometimes accept new ideas on trust without testing their epistemic credentials. But even the reused sentences that simply get activated from our standing cognitive endowments do not wear their epistemic statuses on their sleeves. We readily lose track of our past assessments of them (see Harman 1986: 41), and there is in general no immediately introspectible feature that allows us to recapture these (or even the facts about whether we have performed such assessments). Of course, we do in many cases recognize sentences' epistemic statuses while we are employing them in reasoning—not because the sentences automatically announce these, but because we actively institute checks on them during the reasoning process. Introspection informs us that we do this checking only sometimes, however, and this is confirmed by the limitations of our mental machinery: as cognizing is occurring in real time, there is inadequate time and processing power for conducting on-the-spot evaluations of every item about to be utilized in reasoning. (Not to mention the difficulties we would face in trying to muster all the information needed for making such determinations.)

There is other evidence that we sometimes unhesitatingly use sentences in reasoning without scrutinizing them—and thus that racist beliefs might go on influencing cognition if, despite having been repudiated, they linger within our cognitive endowments.[13] But we have established adequately that racism elimination by purification faces imposing obstacles.

13. Some of this evidence is phenomenological: much of our cognitive utilization of sentences, especially that which involves no explicit assent or affirmation, seems to be conducted often in a stance of unskeptical, unconcerned trust. Some evidence is provided by the occasions where someone's challenge to our statement "p" causes us immediately to show, and feel, diffident hesitation, apparently suggesting (in some, though not all, cases) that we did not perform a prior truth assessment. Further support is provided by those who have observed that human cognition commonly occurs in a posture of "unquestioning acceptance" that derives from a natural tendency toward "primitive credulity" (Price 1969: 208–16; see also James 1950; Coady 1992: 121, 123, 46–47; Levi 1991: 71–79; Dancy 1985: 171). Note that even a contemporaneous awareness, or readily available awareness, of the falsehood of a sentence does not interfere with using it in reasoning, as shown by activities like contrary-to-fact supposing, playing devil's advocate, talking off the top of one's head, unknowingly putting on an act, and making believe. (See also Dennett 1978: 308: "Habits of thought tied to [merely] well-turned phrases may persist long after one has denied the relevant assertions.")

II. VIRTUE WITHOUT PURITY

It seems, then, that the prospects are dim for curing a person's racism through a purging of his cognitive system. For the reasons given above, it is likely that he will not be led to subjectively repudiate the racist beliefs that he holds, and that even if he does, they will not be eliminated from his active fund of cognitive tools or they (or similar sentences) will be readily reconstituted out of other, less obviously troublesome ingredients available in his cognitive warehouse. Either way, they will continue to manifest themselves in reasoning and behavior.

This might seem a counsel of despair. But in fact there is an alternative course that combating an individual's racism might take, an ethical goal both more achievable and more constructive than the simplistic picture of the pure heart. Racism can be effectively defeated in the many individual hearts that harbor it, but only by eschewing a sentimental and overly ambitious ideal for an approach that is more adult, sober, pragmatic, and realistic. The aim should be *management* of one's racist ideas, not their absolute elimination. Rather than make futile efforts to simplify one's cognitive system by uprooting the racist ideas, one ought to seek to *complicate* that system in ways that offer control over the offending ideas' influence and manifestations.[14]

This proposal might appear less unfamiliar if compared to our ways of handling unruly *desires*—desires that tormentingly mock our inabilities to satisfy them, or lead us to make choices we regret or to be people we don't respect. Sometimes, of course, we forsake any attempt even to control such desires, but instead accept and cope with their ramifications, perhaps by restructuring our lives so as to minimize their problematic features. (We continue to indulge a weakness for ice cream, but compensate by exercising more vigorously.) When we cannot or will not adopt this approach, then our ideal is to eliminate the burdensome desires altogether by gaining new information or insight that undermines the attraction of their fulfillments (or the aversiveness of their nonfulfillments). The logical link from input to desire-elimination might be immediate, as when we hear credible reports that a restaurant dish we had been eager to try is actually unpleasantly dry and way oversalted; or it might be indirect, as

---

14. Thus it might well be that in certain parts of the world the tide of racism has actually receded somewhat in the past generation—notwithstanding the impediments to racist-belief eradication that we have been examining. The explanation for such a shift, if indeed there has been one, could be that (i) racist-belief eradication *efforts* have increased over time, bringing about a parallel, if far smaller, increase in eradication *success* (if we plausibly assume that *n* percent of such efforts are successful despite the obstacles, and that *n* has not changed in recent decades); and, more important, (ii) the techniques discussed in this section and the next are more commonly practiced nowadays.

when reorienting our lives toward public service, or toward enhanced life opportunities for our newborn, erases our desire to continue living the life of a ski bum. Quite commonly, though, we cannot entirely uproot a troublesome desire, so we make do with taming or limiting it. Think of people's never ending battles against ineradicable desires for alcohol, for certain foods or the activity of consuming them, or for erotic intimacy with those who are off limits; in a different vein, there are lingering desires for activities or other objects that are understood to be worthwhile but that we recognize we must rightly subdue for the sake of, say, our spouses or parents or country.

So how is it that we cope with an ineradicable desire? We might dwell on certain thoughts that cast the desire, or its satisfaction, in a very dim light, and so for now fortify our will to resist its allure. We might prod ourselves to thoughts of unrelated matters, including unrelated desires, and by thus distracting ourselves release the desire's grip for the time being. We might try to commit ourselves to a course of action that makes yielding to the desire impossible—or one that yields to the desire, but in a strictly confined way. In any case, our view of desires is such that we regard them as states that often, maybe typically, must be endured in some manner. Eradication is psychologically out of the question, so the task becomes one of management: managing one's mind, one's life, or the world as it impinges upon one's life, in order to minimize the desires' free rein.

Our standard, textbook view of beliefs is quite different, because the criterion of (apparent) truth exerts so much influence upon whether we retain a belief or not. But as we have seen, this influence is not as great as we might expect (or wish), as it can leave us powerless to the ongoing participation of undesirable ideas in our cognitive processes. We would do well, then, to look for belief-related analogues to the techniques of desire-management.

I cannot purport to provide an exhaustive catalog of the belief-management toolkit, but the overall approach can be glimpsed by considering some of its basic constituents. As is to be expected, these tend to be devices designed not for circumventing the obstacles standing in the way of subjective repudiation of racist beliefs as false,[15] but rather for overcoming our tendencies to retain and continue using belief-like states that we have unambiguously repudiated as epistemically or even merely pragmatically flawed (i.e., as false, or as practically

15. The rationale: if one's thinking tends not to portray certain of one's beliefs as false, one will lack the motivation to devise and employ belief-management strategies regarding them. But there is at least one important exception: the person who sees himself as specially susceptible to certain kinds of false ideas (perhaps of a racist nature, but possibly dealing with, say, religious matters, pseudoscientific ones, hoaxes, UFOs, fortunetellers, etc.). If he views himself as having a weakness for being duped into swallowing false ideas, he might well seek out methods of cognitive self-control that would combat such a weakness by promoting skeptical scrutiny.

troublesome or morally misguided, respectively). The techniques must be routinized if they are to be effective, with some internal triggering mechanisms that are alert to the situations a person faces and that instigate the technique in the appropriate ones. They are not techniques of self-deception—quite the opposite, in fact, in that they are designed to prevent us from welcoming into our reasonings those ideas that we have already determined to be unworthy—but they do bear a kinship to them, for both are used for purposes of avoiding the entry of certain ideas into our thoughts and calculations.

First is a cognition-management strategy for reducing the impact of epistemic reticence: recomputing the truth values of sentences of certain kinds when one is about to use them in any episodes of reasoning that stand to have important consequences for one's actions or feelings. (A corresponding epistemic reevaluation might be instigated for nonsentential, imagistic representations.) The recomputing need not aim for comprehensiveness—that, after all, is quite a tall order—but might confine itself to checking for certain features that warrant epistemic suspicion. So one might, for example, quickly review one's episodic memory for signs that the belief in question has a dubious origin or otherwise checkered past. One might thereby recall having come across weighty counterevidence to 'p' at some earlier time. Or having initially merely *supposed* that p, maybe even contrary to one's conviction at the time, while playing devil's advocate or trying out a new position during an extended discussion on social policy. Or having previously recognized 'p' as tainted by the circumstances in which one acquired it. (One now recalls, for instance, having previously reflected that one originally formed one's particular anti-Asian belief while still only a child, possibly influenced by neighbors or parents, during a period of strained relations with an Asian classmate.) Analogous processes of recomputation can be undertaken to check for signs indicating potential practical or ethical (rather than epistemic) problems with the cognitive assets that one is about to use in possibly consequential reasoning episodes.[16]

Of course, a credential-rechecking arrangement of this kind provides very imperfect protection against the forgetting of a sentence's epistemic or pragmatic status. For one thing, the rechecking is limited by the perspect from which

16. While these procedures are aimed primarily at assisting those persons who have already renounced some of their own racist beliefs as false, immoral, or more trouble than they're worth, they might also be implemented by (and have benign effects upon) some racists who have not yet reached this point. Consider, for instance, the intellectually scrupulous racist who is generally committed to maintaining a rationally defensible belief system and to prudently not acting on ideas that haven't been vetted or that might be corrupted. Or the wavering racist, who finds himself uncertain about the truth (or utility, or morality) of his racist beliefs. For such persons, the credential-checking practices mentioned in the text might serve to bring them toward repudiation of their racist beliefs, rather than to help them deal with already repudiated ones.

it is undertaken, a perspect within which some crucial considerations might be invisible even though they do reside within one's cognitive endowment. Thus, one might give 'p' a go-ahead, but regret this later while cognizing from a different perspect—one that, say, includes evidence that the first one omitted, or affords the recognition that some of the originally considered evidence is unreliable. Second, life occurs in real time: the stream of cognitive tasks thrown one's way does not always permit the luxury of reviewing the credentials of the representations that get mobilized. (Indeed, one often does not even have conscious access to what those representations are.) Even the most rational among us do not maintain clear, ever-updated systems of epistemic and pragmatic classifications for all the representational resources kept on hand.

There is a second process by which one might come to identify the epistemic or pragmatic status of a sentence that one is (considering) employing in reasoning. One might actually possess an explicit belief 'e(p)' specifically about this status, and activate the secondary item whenever using the primary item 'p'. It is not unusual to adopt an activation policy of this nature intentionally, due to regarding 'p' as false or pernicious and worrying that one might nonetheless go ahead and use it unwittingly. To institute such a policy, one inserts into one's perspect-switching system (in whatever mysterious way such things are accomplished) a transition rule that, upon one perceiving that one has accepted 'p' in current cognition (or contemplated accepting it), immediately treats this as a context calling for scrutiny of 'p' and thus brings about a shift to a perspect in which 'e(p)' is accepted. That is, whenever one discovers oneself thinking that p, one immediately activates those cognitive states that indicate that 'p' has no support, or that it is inferior to alternative hypotheses, or that it is imprudent or unethical to accept in one's cognizings. In this way, one "catches oneself" before acceptance of 'p' can do much damage.

This self-monitoring arrangement can apparently come about unintentionally, too, perhaps due to emotional causes. For example, the above-mentioned revelation about the dishonesty of one's father might have such an emotional impact that one cannot think about one's father, or at least about aspects of his character and action that concern truthfulness or rectitude, without immediately recalling that experience of revelation (or perhaps simply the corrective information that it contained).

If such a correction of 'p' happens nearly instantaneously in each instance—and rather than 'e(p)', the activated superseding belief might even be 'not-p', optionally joined by supporting beliefs such as 'e(p)'—then for many practical purposes it is as if one has eliminated 'p' from the set of usable cognitive tools in one's mind, though one actually has not. And perhaps enough of these corrections, or of corrections executed with the right psychological (affective?) accompaniments, actually do succeed in preventing, and not merely correcting, activations of 'p' in these perspects.[17] Of course, if one's corrections are not so thoroughgoing, the sentence might continue being utilized within certain perspects even as it is effectively, functionally eliminated (and perhaps replaced by 'not-p') in others.

The basic process of self-correction is illustrated in the following example:

> Suppose you believe for a long time (as all the books used to show) that brontosauruses had very small heads. Later evidence is unearthed to show that they did not have such small heads after all. What happens when you learn this, is that . . . [p]erhaps you also add a note, or correction, to the old small-headedness node, which says: "No, no, this is wrong." Later, if asked the size of brontosauruses' heads, you might initially retrieve "small head." But then you will retrieve the correction as well. (Goldman 1986: 224)

But a more helpful illustration, one with greater relevance to the control of racist beliefs, can be extracted from one of the most renowned episodes of the long-running *Seinfeld* TV comedy show. Jerry and his buddy George repeatedly think that they are mistakenly being taken to be gay, which exasperates them; but every time they complain about being thought gay, they immediately and automatically follow up with a cautionary "*Not* that there's anything wrong with being gay," or words to that effect. The *Seinfeld* writers may have been aiming to poke fun at the internalized compulsions of "political correctness," but they helpfully portrayed a familiar but underappreciated process of cognitive self-management.

Transposition of such examples to the racism context is straightforward. We can easily imagine someone repeatedly being inclined to invoke a certain group-denigrating belief or assumption, but then correcting himself more or less immediately, perhaps even before the item in question has had a chance to manifest in reasoning, let alone in utterance or other behavior. Indeed, precisely this kind of mental condition would appear to mark the relationship of many people to racist ideas—and to explain some of the difficulty that we have in knowing how to classify people on the "racist"-"nonracist" dichotomy. For do we rightly regard Jeb, who engages in routine auto-correction of his racist inclinations, as racist? He does, after all, possess a racist belief and the repeated initial inclinations, in triggering situations, to use it. Or ought Jeb be characterized as nonracist, given

---

17. On this model, one might never directly cause 'p' to be finally erased; it would just cease to be activated in any perspect, and either remain in a dormant limbo forever or perhaps eventually fade away from disuse. (Goldman [1986: 223] implies that psychologists maintain that "there is never any real *loss* of material" from long-term memory, but his only supporting quotation refers only to whether such material can ever be *deliberately* forgotten.)

that it would seem grossly unfair to him, as well as a distortion of the reality, to assimilate under the same "racist" label both him and his brother Jake, who neither is self-critical or repentant about his inclinations, nor has "wired" his mind to limit their impact?

Much of self-control is effected in this general way, building self-monitoring into one's perspect-switching system, precisely because cognitive resources are epistemically (and pragmatically) reticent, difficult to eradicate, and so liable sometimes to influence one's thought, feeling, or behavior despite one's contrary wishes or hopes (wishes and hopes that, unfortunately, reside only in other of one's perspects). Efforts at such self-control are not always successful, of course. And inebriation, or other physiological impairment, can interfere with the proper activation of self-corrective mechanisms too. But such failures provide no reason to shy away from techniques that have repeatedly proven their worth.

III. IMPLICATIONS FOR PRACTICE

Because it is the actual deployment of racist ideas in cognitive activity that is essential to, and sufficient for, a person being *effectively* racist, and not merely nominally or technically so, we might be wise to redirect some of society's efforts that are aimed at eliminating racism in individuals. Rather than ask people to focus upon the largely fruitless task of recapturing their moral purity by eradicating racist beliefs from their cognitive endowments, we might attend more than we now do to inculcating habitual psychological methods of minimizing the *usage* of such beliefs. What is more important, after all—whether racist beliefs are present somewhere within a person's psyche, or whether such beliefs actually manifest in the person's feelings, construals, reasonings, and behavior? Rather than invest resources exclusively in converting racists into pure-hearted, racist-belief-free nonracists, that is, we might work at turning them into merely "potential racists"—people whose racism is dormant, inert, only potentially causally active. They do remain racist according to our original conception, and not just potentially so, yet the term "potential racist" is warranted both by analogy with "potential energy," which is itself a kind of energy, and by the desire to suggest terminologically that having present yet inactive racist attitudes is more akin to not being a racist than to being one.

The general type of approach being proposed is one of countering racism by addition rather than subtraction: corrective or prophylactic resources are to be added to the cognitive endowment and actively employed whenever old racist representations get activated or new racism-instigating information is encountered. The strategy of cognitive cleansing, by contrast, not only faces the difficulties described earlier but also provides no ongoing protection against racism; even total success can be later undone. Simply eliminating existing racist beliefs, by itself, provides no protection against a reinfection with new ones. For this protection, affirmative cognitive antibodies must be added to the psychic circulatory system. Some of these are not racism-specific, but rather the constituents of good general epistemological hygiene. For instance, there are general concerns that one can "keep in mind" about the influence upon one's cognition of the following: bias, wishful thinking, and self-deception; limited and incorrect evidence; faulty memory, both for facts and for one's own earlier views and experiences; fatigue, illness, and transitory moods; past dreams, previously encountered fictions, early indoctrination, and lingering childhood ideas; and so on. But these varieties of mindfulness, important rational assets though they are, offer less than fully adequate protection against the (re)generation of racism. One might know all these things, and mobilize them when appropriate, yet still adopt racist beliefs—and be reasonable in doing so.

For even if we assume that ideal exposure to all pertinent evidence would lead a person who possesses general rational habits of mind to bar racist ideas from his belief system—in other words, that anyone who adopts a racist belief is someone about whom we can say, "If only he were better informed"—we unfortunately cannot count on people being fully informed about matters bearing upon their attitudes regarding race and ethnicity. There are many folks who are not well educated about these matters; many who have had, at least to their knowledge, little contact in their lives with blacks, or Jews, or Asians, etc.; many who live in communities in which racist views are neither rare nor disdained. Growing up and living under such conditions, people might find themselves reasonably accepting racist beliefs, even if they abide by the set of general rational norms of belief formation and maintenance mentioned above.

To inoculate against racist beliefs, intellectual habits that are more specifically antiracist are needed. One might maintain at the ready a belief about the psychological tendencies of people to see themselves or their own in-groups as superior, one about the falsehood of at least most past racial claims, one about the epistemologically corrupt, politicized roots of racist depictions and doctrines (such as in the *Protocols of the Elders of Zion*), and the like. The central practical solution to racism is thus affirmatively educating people, and helping them train themselves to continually activate such lessons as needed. It is not to seek to bring about in their minds *tabulae rasae* regarding race and ethnicity.

The current dominant understanding, which takes purification as the standard for whether people have transcended their racism, is not only misguided in theory but harmful in practice. Because the standard is so high, it can dishearten, and discourage from further efforts, those whose attempts at full eradication of their racist attitudes do not meet with success, even if their efforts are paying off in increasing control of those attitudes and undermining of their influence upon reasoning and behavior. Treating self-purification as the only happy outcome, in all-or-nothing fashion, also is likely to produce unproductive excesses of self-doubt about possessing an unerasable racist taint, even in those who come to manage their racist attitudes effectively in ways like those described above. (Such self-doubt might be especially insidious for those who worry, despite little supporting evidence, that they possess *unconscious* racist beliefs.) Where such self-doubt crosses over into self-loathing, the direct costs are greater still—and so would appear to be the risks that the feelings will be redirected outward against others, maybe even against the targets of the previously well-reined-in racism.

Do the foregoing recommendations apply only to a minuscule proportion of racists, leaving us no closer to understanding the vast majority or to lifting them out of their racism? No; such a sense of futility is unwarranted. First, it seems likely that quite a substantial proportion of all racists, at least in "Western" societies, doubt the wisdom of maintaining their racist beliefs and might be amenable to utilizing cognitive tools for corralling them. The message that such beliefs are false and harmful, even evil, and that people ought to feel ashamed of possessing them, seems to have been disseminated with quite impressive success in schools and in the mass media, even if racism does still thrive in some subcultures. Second, if, as some commentators maintain, racist beliefs are in fact pervasive albeit predominantly hidden from view, then the processes of cognitive management that we have discussed are relevant to vast numbers of people. In sum, the cognitive mechanisms discussed in this chapter are of central, rather than marginal, relevance to the problem of racism.

In fact, the ideas we have considered extend naturally beyond racism to other ethically undesirable cognition-centered traits. The ideal of a pure heart, unsullied by thoughts that are malicious, selfish, or otherwise unsavory, may be largely unattainable in practice for ordinary human beings who care about being good, its pursuit quite possibly counterproductive. If the mind is a trap from which certain cognitive items cannot be entirely removed, then the appropriate ethical ideal for adults who have already been permanently stained by earlier influences and reasoning cannot be self-purification of their belief systems through the purging of the evil elements. Instead, it must be complicating those belief systems in ways that effectively counterbalance the undesired elements, never allowing them to direct serious thought or action uncontested.

9 : PSYCHOANALYSIS, RACISM, AND ENVY

Some people (like me) see most of what a person does as in one way or another concerned with achieving satisfactory relations with other people and with themselves—with object relations, as psychoanalysts say—both in their outward circumstances and in the inner world of imagination where phantasy counterfeits for agency. Dependence on others, the need for loving attachment, and seeking to be valued and understood by others and by oneself are the most far-reaching features of a human life. Those features tend to be ignored in much contemporary thinking in philosophy and the human sciences, much of which, indeed, seems to be unconsciously animated by a need to deny them. Their influence, however, penetrates even into matters that seem on the surface remote from object-relating activity: vocation, politics, the adoption of philosophical and religious views, the way one shines one's shoes; and their apt appreciation will, naturally, influence one's understanding of what constitutes the chief focus in the investigation of racism: a psychology of racism centered on object-relational concerns occupies the central place in it. By and large, the primary expressions of racism will be viewed as motivated—often unconsciously but nevertheless intentionally[1]—and directed at such object-mediated ends as the sustainment of self-esteem and identity, the suppression of fear and anxiety, the mitigation of guilt and envy, and the fulfillment of wishes for specialness, superiority, and belonging.

I want to explore a number of related themes in the individual psychology of racism. The first concerns motivation in racism. Another is the irrationality of much racism. A third, for the purpose of illustration, concerns the role of envy, a passion that manifests in many expressions of racism. And the fourth is a theme which, though certainly provoked by psychoanalytic thinking about racism, seems largely to be unrecognized in it: the ways in which *racialist* doctrine—doctrines, theories, sets of beliefs according to which humankind divides into ex-

I wish to thank Raimond Gaita and Michael Levine for their very helpful comments on an earlier version of this chapter.

1. I use "motive" very broadly here to designate any psychological element with teleology and motivational force. On unconscious motivation and agency see Pataki 1996, 2000. On the significance of object relations see Pataki 2003.

clusive, racially defined classes (usually, though not necessarily, ranked according to some scale of excellence)—interlocks with individual *motives* to satisfy some of the emotional needs of the racist mind. It is of some importance to distinguish between the ways in which psychological needs are able to *exploit* existing racialist ideology and the ways in which some racist structures and ideologies are *engendered* or *fashioned* by them.

The study of its psychology is, of course, by no means the whole of the study of racism, and the relationships between its psychology and its individual, institutional, social, and political expressions are by no means straightforward. But I think that the psychology is central and, as I indicate below, even the *conceptual* investigation of individual racism cannot be conducted independently of the study of motives to it. Although I argue that there are types of racism where psychoanalytic explanation has limited purchase, in locating most of the phenomena associated with the racist mind in an object-relational context, as motivated or defensive and wish-fulfilling processes, the present approach is, I think, essentially psychoanalytic. There is an attractive historical logic in proceeding from psychoanalysis. It seems to be only quite recently that analytic philosophers have recognized that vicious affective and orectic passions are at the core of individual racism. J.-P. Sartre, it is true, had long ago emphasized that racism (including anti-Semitism) is primarily a passion, not a doctrine, idea, or opinion. But psychoanalysis has from its earliest considerations focused on motive, on racism's affective and orectic (desiderative or wishful) aspects; the doctrinal content it has tended to consider as derivative from racism's individual psychology.

It is common in the public domain today to find almost any enmity in which the parties *can* be distinguished by features loosely conceived to be racial as involving racism: distinctions between race, ethnic and cultural group, religion, nationality, citizenship, and "way of life" pass unnoticed, as do distinctions between racist and indirect racial discrimination, and between the presence or absence of racist intent. Hence the muddled tabloid headlines—"Moslem Youths Rape Australian Girls"—appearing over stories purporting to report racial conflicts or racism. The conflation of the different group concepts occurs for a variety of reasons, including the fact that the conceptions of race, dominant in the West from the mid-eighteenth to the mid-twentieth century, now discredited and eschewed by the disciplines that once fostered them, have become vague and promiscuous ideas in the popular mind. The support for race theory in physical anthropology, history, philology, and genetics has largely evaporated with progressive understanding in these disciplines. The classical conceptions have proved neither coherent nor useful. In that earlier period, however, the race theorists claimed to uncover some very definite conceptions of race, and European public perception seems to have been that racial classification and ranking were hard science.[2] These conceptions, though they varied in important respects, were at one in dividing humankind into something like natural kinds or species (see, e.g., Banton 1998, Gould 1996), and sharply distinguished race from culture, nationality, and the like. The racism of that time, though of course it neither consisted in nor was singly motivated by racialist conceptions, whether scientific, historical, or philological, supervened in several respects on those conceptions.

Contemporary racism—I just mean the loosely related class of phenomena that are popularly described as involving racism—is a much more amorphous affair. It conflates classical racial conceptions with others such as *culture* and *nationality* that were specifically to be excluded by the racial conceptions; it is more accommodating to "selective" exceptions (Blum 2002); and it includes phenomena such as indirect, institutional, social discrimination and exclusion in which the role of individual racism or prejudice is problematic. Although the classical race conceptions have been discredited, it is of some importance not to lose sight of them; their features, and the distinctions they mark between themselves and related group concepts, reflect features and distinctions of considerable psychological significance. The various psychological substructures we shall notice are most clearly visible in the forms of racism that are shaped, in part, by the classical conceptions. Moreover, the contemporary racisms remain in important respects sufficiently like their predecessors to be illuminated by them. The psychological substructures that once found abode under classical race concepts have migrated and fashioned new homes in their own image. They *racialize* other enmities.[3] The process can be discerned in certain features of the recrudescent ethnic, religious, and nationalist conflicts of our time, in classism and sexism, and perhaps even (as Michael Dummett avers in chapter 1) in the rough treatment of smokers. Despite the various affinities between these enmities, it is best to regard them as separate—a conceptual segregation that is in accord with classical racism, and is its sole virtue.

I. SOME FEATURES OF RACISM

First, then, (classical) racists conceive of their objects under some recognizably *racial* conception or invoke some racial theory, even if the conception or

2. A brief history of classical conceptions of race is provided in the introduction to this volume. It doesn't follow from the discrediting of the classical conceptions of race that *all* racial conceptions, such as those currently used by paleoanthropologists and population geneticists, are incoherent.

3. Radicalization may be a complex, often extended sociohistorical process. But it can also occur with remarkable rapidity when psychological projective and dissociative processes are mobilized on a large scale.

theory is very muddled or attenuated. This must be so; otherwise we would have no grounds for classifying certain kinds of group enmities *as racist.* There are enmities directed at many kinds of group—ethnic or national groups, bankers, public servants—but these are not, strictly, racial enmities. The details of the racial conceptions may vary, often confusedly, in the minds of racists and need not correspond in every respect to the paradigms that began to evolve during the seventeenth century, but in order to be recognized *as racial conceptions* they must bear some essential similarity to them. We recognize the relevant conceptions by seeing where the paradigmatic cases cast their shadows.

The main features of these racial conceptions can be summarized roughly as follows. The characteristics assigned as definitive of each race are (i) essential (every member of any race necessarily has certain defining characteristics); (ii) inherited (the defining characteristics of each race are transmitted through passage of genes, blood, soul, germ plasm); (iii) exclusive (if one is a member of a particular race one cannot also be a member of another race); (iv) immutable (the essential characteristics cannot be removed or altered); and (v) consistent with "the doctrine of the countenance"[4] (there is a correlation between specific physical characteristics of each race and its intellectual and moral capabilities). Madison Grant in his racist *The Passing of the Great Race* (1916) sums up much of this in a typical way: "The great lesson of the science of race is the immutability of somatological or bodily characters, with which is closely associated the immutability of psychical predispositions and impulses" (Hannaford 1996: 358).

Biological classification has been important in this understanding of race, but not exclusively. In the messianic racism of the pan-German and pan-Slavic movements of the last two centuries there was little attempt to link "the soul characteristics of races" (Voegelin 1997), supposedly hereditary spiritual traits, to biological constitution. But the central idea that the most fundamental way of classifying humankind remained: the use of inherited, essential, immutable, and exclusive moral and intellectual characteristics, often correlated with salient phenotypical markers. The conception of deep, impermeable divisions within humankind is, as we'll see, of very great psychological significance. Raphael Ezekiel's observation of the terrified young members of the neo-Nazi Death's-Head Strike Group applies generally: for them "race is an absolute category, and the presumed characteristics of a member of a racial group are taken as God-given and unalterable" (Ezekiel 1995: 310). The need to keep things apart, keep things simple, keep them steady, which racism satisfies, was noted by Sartre when he drew attention to the Manichean character of anti-Semitism, though he much

4. The idea that there are correspondences between physical and intellectual and moral characteristics in individuals, if not groups, is of ancient provenance. The Cabala developed an elaborate and influential variation on the idea and gave it this name (Hannaford 1996: 36).

oversimplified its motives. The dread of miscegenation has much to do with this need.[5]

In contrast, ethnic,[6] national, and religious identities are permeable and exchangeable, so that the enmities and prejudices associated with them—ethnic contempt, religious intolerance, and the like—are generally less rigid and more vulnerable to exemptions. By and large, these group conceptions do not entail the unbridgeable differences between groups so important in a variety of ways to the racist mind. They can, however, become racialized, understood *as if they were* racial conceptions; and this is, as was earlier noted, a salient feature of the contemporary scene. The sort of enmity directed against Muslims in various quarters today is in substance, if not in form, racist enmity.

The targets of racism must not only be picked out under conceptions that are recognizably racial, they must be targeted *because they are representatives of that race.* That latter phrase requires some unpacking. The Australian anthropologist W. E. H. Stanner, writing in the days of the White Australia policy, argued that race issues emerged in Australia after the middle of the nineteenth century as a result of the importation and migration of cheap labor from the Pacific and China. He said that "we are usually prejudiced about race because of other things. . . . It was the cheap labour threat to wage employment and social standards that really mattered" (Stanner 1971: 10, 11). His suggestion seems to be that the original conflict was primarily economic (and perhaps that, at bottom, it always remains economic) and that, at worst, racism supervened on that conflict. Well, if that were *all* that was going on to begin with, then the hatreds and bloody confrontations that were generated by the perceived economic threat would not, originally, have involved *racist* conflict and hatred. Why not? Because even

5. Although classical race theorists have usually operated with four or five racial categories (see Gould 1996), most racists rarely show interest in more than two or three, the third one often being connected to the second with some neat but crazy device—for example, as the Jew is to the black in some contemporary American racisms: "the black is just an instrument of the Jew" or "the black man is only the Jew turned inside out." It should be noted that although commitment to racial conceptions (concerning natural human types, lineage, hierarchies) may not, generally, be *sufficient* grounds for the ascription of racism, some degree of commitment is necessary. It may not be sufficient because the mere making of racial distinctions and evaluations—a practice that, following others, I call "racialist"—is consistent with unqualified positive attitudes to the distinguished races; and it seems that racism, on the common understanding, always involves a degree of enmity or adverse discrimination, even though in some cases this may be disguised.

6. The use of "ethnic" to contrast with "racial" is not universally accepted but common. Thus Gordon Allport writes: "Racial and ethnic. . . . The former term of course, refers to the hereditary ties, the latter to social and cultural ties" (1954: 107). Similarly Philip Kitcher: "The core view that there are ethnic groups is that distinct sets of cultural items . . . are transmitted across the generations by a process akin to biological inheritance" (1999: 107).

though the contending groups could be identified under the race concepts people then employed, the animosities didn't originally take race as defining their target: the Chinese weren't targeted *qua* representatives of a supposed race, but *qua* economic competitors, and so the animosities weren't racially motivated. And this, of course, reinforces the first feature of racism we noted: without some minimal conception of race, one cannot target someone as a representative of a race.

Now, how do people come to be targeted *because of their race*? Racist animosity targets a group because its members are believed to have specific properties (usually believed to be inherited, essential, exclusive, and immutable) which are, in one word, contemned. Color could be one such property, though animus against color per se is very rare. That is something more like a phobia than racism: conflicts over identity and self-boundaries are sometimes expressed through or in the skin; and children develop color phobias that may persist in various forms (Young-Bruehl 1996: 261–69, 365 n. 18). But, obviously, color is usually not the problem for the racist; it is the "folk theory" or lore that the racist has about the person who has the color that is the problem. The same applies for the other major phenotypical markers. Generally, racism targets imputed intellectual and moral characteristics such as laziness, cunning, lasciviousness, or avarice, of which conspicuous phenotypic differences are supposed to be markers. Of course, the contemned characteristics rarely if ever inhere in their objects; it is enough that they are believed to inhere in them; and frequently, we know, they are disavowed features of the racist's own self-image. In the main, *these* characteristics—not the phenotypic markers—animate racist enmity, envy, devaluation, and fear. They are also the "switches" that enable the transformation of one prejudice into another, or their displacement from one target to another. For example, by characterizing Middle Eastern asylum seekers and refugees as pushy "queue jumpers" who have "amassed large sums of money" which they use to buy their "devious" passage to Australia's shores and penetrate her borders, the Australian government has recently succeeded in converting a considerable amount of latent anti-Semitic and related sentiment into derogation of asylum seekers.

Racism universalizes under conceptions of racial identity. For example, enmities or prejudices limited to Hungarian Jews or Italian waiters do not constitute racism unless the racist conceives of such groups as forming something like the (natural) kinds that have been classically employed by racists. Only if the hatred in the Australian goldfields would in principle have generalized and targeted all members of the (supposed) racial group, *all* Chinese (which it certainly eventually did)—in the way, for example, that young neo-Nazis in America hate, or think they hate, all blacks and all Jews no matter where they are—can it strictly be considered a candidate for racism. Racists can be selective and make exceptions of individuals, for various reasons, often because they think they discern overriding virtues in the exceptions; but that doesn't qualify the operative conception of racism; it qualifies the racist's consistency.

It follows from its universalizing character together with the fact that we live inescapably in collectivities of various sorts that racism creates distinct, exclusive groups, *them* and *us*. The racist's emphasis may oscillate between hatred or derogation of the *them* and idealization or exaltation of the *us*. Belonging to a group—feeling or imagining that one belongs to a group whose worthy qualities and achievements are identified with or magically appropriated (in phantasy)—can be as important for the racist as despising or persecuting another. The idea of race supremacy does not, it seems, logically entail hatred or ill will, or perhaps even disrespect, for the alien groups. But contingently, of course, the idea of race supremacy and hatred mostly go hand in hand.

II. IRRATIONALITY AND RACISM

The final feature of individual racism to be mentioned requires a more extended discussion. I contend that although it is not analytically true of racism that it is irrational, *most* racism is contingently irrational: a person can be a racist without being irrational, though most racists are (in their racism) irrational.[7] The contention implies that *some* racism is rational. Although I have no conclusive argument for this proposition, a number of considerations suggest that it corresponds most closely to the common understanding of racism.

David Hume's aspersive commentary on Negroes in 1766 would certainly seem on the face of it to be the expression of racist beliefs.[8] Was Hume thereby a racist, and if so, could he have been rational in holding such beliefs? It seems to me that Hume *was* a racist, if for no other reason than because of his racist beliefs, but that he *may* have held these beliefs rationally—that is, as a rational racist. Several objections could be directed against this contention. Disarming the objections supports, though of course it does not prove, the contention.

It could be objected that although Hume's beliefs may have been racist, *he*

7. They can be irrational in different ways: in belief, emotion, or action. D. T. Goldberg (1999) argues that racism is not "inherently" irrational. To establish that conclusion he tries to demonstrate that aspects of racist thinking—stereotyping, overgeneralizing, etc.—are not *necessarily* irrational. It seems to me that at key stages of his argument Goldberg equivocates between "racism is irrational" and "racism is necessarily (logically) irrational." In any case, my proposal is only that *most* racism turns out to be contingently irrational. Moreover, Goldberg focuses on the rationality of racist beliefs and their modes of acquisition: "Whether racism can be rational in any circumstances turns on the rationality of the racist *beliefs*, ascriptions, and acts at issue" (371). His arguments leave racist emotions, desires, and some of the acts which spring from them untouched.

8. I quote Hume's 1766 commentary in the introduction to this volume.

wasn't. It has been suggested, for example, that "racist beliefs don't make one a real racist . . . beliefs are racist only in a derivative sense" (Garcia 1996: 44). On this account beliefs are racist only if they spring from, give expression to, or are rationalizations of vicious affective or volitional attitudes. This account has attractions: it can exculpate children and some ignorant or ingenuous people who unreflectively accept racist propositions but bear no real animosity or ill will toward their targets, even if their declarations do.

A second argument pointing to the same conclusion goes as follows. All racism is prejudice, and prejudice understood properly, in its primary sense, is *always* irrational. The term "prejudice" has several different meanings. It is sometimes used to denote *any* derogatory or intolerant view held in relation to individuals or groups, without explicit implications for the view's rationality. Such is the case with certain ethnocentric, "homophobic," or sexist beliefs. More commonly, prejudice is taken to involve prejudgment or other cognitive error: faulty generalization, inattention to relevant evidence, conclusions based on inadequate evidence, and so forth. But, most commonly, we seem to regard only a subclass of such cognitive mishaps as leading to or involving prejudice: those cases where emotional factors, bias, or wishes have intruded and distorted the cognitive process. These provide the *primary* instances of prejudice. The remainder of the cognitive mishaps are just that—cognitive mishaps. Now, some conditions can defuse the charge of irrationality: ignorance or childlike innocence, for example.[9] If Hume was ignorant (or "innocent" in the way of children) and therefore not prejudiced in the primary sense, then it may be contended that he was not a racist.

But, third, it could be argued, as Michael Dummett does in chapter 1, that although Hume was a racist all right, he wasn't, in this instance, rational: racism is *always* irrational.

> No one can rationally think that the great majority of members of any racial group are intellectually or artistically inferior to the great majority of members of some other group. . . . It would need a remarkable ignorance to put forward such a proposition; but then, some people, though rational, are remarkably ignorant. Can a rational belief be based on ignorance? Not if the ignorant individual palpably knows too little to form a judgment on the matter. An ignorant but rational person can be no more than agnostic about questions that require a moderate degree of knowledge to answer.

9. Children often do, simply, learn disparaging beliefs about different groups that do not *in them* spring from racist sentiment; these learned beliefs persist with little conflict and play no significant role in the economy of desire, emotion, and object-relational pursuits. They are sometimes just part of the social entrance exams that Elisabeth Young-Bruehl (1996) calls "ethnocentric prejudices." To a child these false demeaning beliefs—prejudices in a weaker sense—appear normal: "It is normal to them because it is their norm" (72). In some social fabrics racism appears rational.

In sum, the arguments against Hume being a *rational racist* are these. First, he may not have been a *racist* because his holding racist beliefs doesn't entail that *he* was racist; or he may not have been a racist because he wasn't prejudiced in the primary sense—because he wasn't irrational. Second, he *was* a racist, but he wasn't *rational.*

These considerations are cogent and worth rehearsing. But once clearly stated they seem to underscore the friction between them and the grain of common understanding. Racists, we do say, *can* be ignorant, innocent, and rational in the ways we have touched on. None of these conditions preclude the charge. To take only the most conspicuous instance, in most circumstances persons expressing racist beliefs, even in conditions of ignorance, are still judged as being racist: common understanding would have us withhold, not the judgment that they are racist, but the opprobrium that would usually attach to the charge. Consider the young neo-Nazis and Klansmen of whom Ralph Ezekiel writes: "There is no way to overestimate the amount of ignorance in the racist movement. Many of the players are working with only the scrappiest of educations. What they do know is jumbled chaotically in their heads. They have put together information from sources in unorganised fashion; they really don't have any structured conceptions of reality, any organised body of knowledge that would allow them to recognise absurdity. Anything is possible in their worlds" (1995: 312–13). Their worldviews and perceptions of their targets are distorted and diminished, and they are ignorant. But they are racists. And they may be rational.

In relation to Dummett's argument that all racism is irrational, it may be accepted as true that a rational and informed Hume would not have resolved an opinion. But ignorance is a boundless country, and rarely do we realize how ignorant we are. If Hume was ignorant (in the relevant respects), and ignorant also of his ignorance, then he was not necessarily irrational; and therefore not necessarily prejudiced in the primary sense, and therefore not a racist. Dummett is clearly right in those instances where the ignorant person knows that they are ignorant or has reasonable grounds for suspecting that they are; for then, if they were rational, they would remain agnostic. However, it remains open that Hume, though ignorant, was rational, and may therefore have been an instance of rational racism.

It must be conceded that uncertainty surrounds the putative instances of rational racist belief. There is, however, no uncertainty in the class of cases where belief is engendered by or in the service of racist orectic and affective dispositions. Though it is possible that Hume held his beliefs rationally, and without malevolence or condescension, it seems much more likely that his beliefs had a place in structures of desire and emotional disposition that are racist. Beliefs can become so situated in at least two different ways. People often arrive at beliefs, not for probative reasons, but because they are congenial to them and provide satisfactions. Sartre argued that anti-Semites do not hate because they hold beliefs that provide grounds for their enmity; rather, they believe because they are predisposed to hate. This observation can be generalized: desire and emotion can cause belief (though they may need to take detours such as manufacturing bogus evidence in phantasy; Pataki 1996, 2000). But even if not engendered by desire or emotion, beliefs can be satisfying adventitiously. Racist beliefs or opinions are tremendously attractive to the psychic economy because beliefs such as that one is special or better than others are very pleasurable to us. They are especially attractive where racist structures of desire and emotional disposition are already in place.

This suggests that the irrationality of emotion and desire may be more significant for racism than irrationality of belief or doctrine. The significance of affective, orectic, and related states in defining racism has been recognized, but not the real significance of their irrationality. For example, J. L. A. Garcia writes: "We conceive of racism as fundamentally a vicious kind of racially based disregard for the welfare of certain people. In its central and most vicious forms it is hatred, ill will directed against a person or persons on account of their assigned race. . . . Racism, then, is something that involves not our beliefs and their rationality or irrationality, but our wants, intentions, likes and dislikes and their distance from the moral virtues" (1996: 6).

I think that this emphasis on volitional and affective states is pointed in the right direction, though I have already suggested that there is a cool racism of belief or doctrine unconnected with such states, and that at least some of its instances are not immoral. But there is a more consequential problem with this kind of account. Sometimes hatred, ill will, and disrespect are normatively appropriate responses to their putative objects and, so, rational. The odious Martian race has unjustly inflicted terrible wrongs on us and we hate them. Hatred of Martians in such a case would not necessarily be regarded as racism, any more than, mutatis mutandis, the reaction of Holocaust survivors to Germans, conceived as a race, and as culpable in their entirety, would be regarded as racism. You might reply that Martian hatred *could* be racist because there is a false generalization from the perpetrators to the entire group which renders it irrational, and that this fact lames the example. But suppose that there are only six Martians constituting the race and all are responsible! Then there would be no irrationality resting on a false numerical generalization and perhaps no irrationality at all; and though there would be hatred of a race, there would be no racism. This example introduces the obvious but important point that before it can be determined whether racially based ill will, disregard, and so forth *is* racist, we need to know the reasons, motives, or grounds for those attitudes and passions. But when we inquire for these we find that, usually, there is *no reason that makes sense*. Rationalizations and pretexts abound, but, by and large, there are no reasons that can render racist passions rational, as appropriate to their putative objects. The irrationality of (most) racism consists not (only) in evidently false generalizations over a large group, or in the manufacturing of factitious racial groups, but in the inappropriateness of affective or volitional states to putative objects.

It seems that Garcia's account is deficient in failing to notice that most racism is irrationally motivated and that an account of the causes or motives of racial enmity is essential to an account of racism. In one word, it overlooks the fact that most racism is prejudice in its primary meaning.[10] We cannot determine whether an instance of enmity is *racist* enmity unless we know enough about its causes or motives to determine whether the enmity is rational or not. And that often means we need to know quite a lot. This issue arises in an interesting fashion in Garcia's brief consideration of psychoanalytic claims that (as he expresses it) link sexual insecurity and racism:

> Even if this claim about the psychological causes of racism is true, it leaves unaffected our claim about what racism consists in. It is implausible to think such insecurity essential to (a necessary condition for) racism, even for white racism, because if we came across someone who hated black people, thought us inherently inferior . . . and so on, but came to all this for reasons other than sexual insecurity, we would and should still classify her attitude as racism. . . . "Psychocultural explanation" is unlikely to reveal (logically) necessary truths about the nature of racism. (1996: 29)

To begin with, why should we think that explanation of the nature of racism should reveal logically necessary truths about it? If we are interested in the nature of gasses on Jupiter we will carry out empirical investigations, and it will be a contingent fact if the gasses turn out to be so many percent nitrogen, hydrogen, and so on. If there is a link between fear of black sexuality and a certain kind of racism, that will be a contingent fact, but nonetheless revelatory of the nature of that kind of racism. But secondly, it may be that empirical investigation yields strong correlations between certain kinds of racism and certain psychological substructures; between, say, antiblack racism and sexual insecurity, between anti-Semitism and unconscious guilt, or between the more fine-grained correlates discussed below. In that case we would have *discovered* something of the causal or motivational constitution of racist minds, and therefore something of what racism consists in. Confronted with deviations from these general causal constitutions, we might very well revise descriptions of specific instances. Descriptions and evaluations of actions and emotions are constantly revised in the light of newly discovered motives. What appears to be an instance of love reveals itself to be envy or idealizing hatred; kindness turns out to be an expression of

10. To be sure, Garcia does give an account of the *kind* of ill will that racism consists in— for instance, in terms of the virtues it offends and the kind of vices it instantiates. But consider: imagine that all moral categories just dropped out of the world. Could there still not be racism?

guilt, and so on. It would merely be a special case of such revision were we to withdraw a description of an instance of ill will as racist if the ill will were found justified or rational.

In *The Origins of Totalitarianism* Hannah Arendt noted that the eighteenth-century racial thinkers were never "seriously concerned with discrimination against other peoples as lower races." "There is a world of difference," she averred, "between the men of brilliant and facile conceptions and men of brutal deeds and active bestiality" (1979: 182, 183). Racialist or racist beliefs and doctrines alone rarely drive people to deep enmity and atrocity. Even where racist beliefs play a part in the regulation of the psychic economy, in irrationally sustaining self-esteem or a sense of belonging, racism can remain a relatively cool affair. But there are the defining extremes Arendt and others have vividly described: the rigid convictions, mad discriminations, enmities, segregations, and extermina-tions of the racisms of the last two centuries. Here passion, not opinion, holds sway and is wildly incommensurate to the circumstances; conviction subtends from flimsy evidence and considerations and persists tenaciously in the teeth of contrary evidence; fantastic groups, mythologies, and historical scenarios are conjured up, and baseless ideas of supremacy reign. These "paradigms" of racism, of the racist mind, are deeply irrational in desire, emotion, or belief; and, typi-cally, irrationality of belief is engendered by or serves orectic or affective dispo-sitions. No account that fails to accommodate them can be considered adequate.

III. RACISM WITHOUT MOTIVE

Before attempting to sketch an accommodation of these central cases of racism, it is instructive to consider a family of views that seem to be altogether different from, or on one side of, the sort of spectrum of racism I am outlining here. On these views racism is fundamentally neither a matter of doctrines or beliefs, nor of emotion or volition. Racism arises from incapacity or inability to make appropriate kinds of discriminations, recognitions, or conceptualizations. Perhaps Hannah Arendt's extraordinary account of the Boer's inability to see the African as fully human belongs here.[11] Bernard Boxill's development of the idea that (some) racism arises from a kind of failure of imaginative identification which results in an inability to pity or empathize with others—either because they are so different physically or culturally or because our own identities are so important to us that we "cannot or will not exchange them, even in imagina-tion"—also belongs in this group (see chapter 10). They have this striking fea-ture in common. Although it is recognized in them that the kinds of cognitive or imaginative failures or errors on which, in their different ways, they construct

11. See note 18 below.

racism can advantage their subjects—it can be very much to one's advantage *not* to experience the other as human—they neglect or underplay the extent to which these failures are not just exploited but also motivated by the orectic or affective dispositions that gain satisfaction through them.

Raimond Gaita's *A Common Humanity* contains a detailed and careful example of the kind of view traced above, and its provenance in the Australian context makes it exceptionally interesting. Gaita's focus is on the kind of racism that is "directed against people whose skin and whose facial features are significantly different" from those of whites. Though what he says about this must also be applicable in reverse, it is evident that his account cannot apply where racist and victim are physically very similar. The essence of racism according to Gaita is "the denial of the full humanity of its victims." This denial is not of a piece with verbal claims that blacks belong to a different, lesser species. Nor is it denial in the psychoanalytic sense, which presupposes an unconscious acknowledgment of that which is denied. The denial is neither a biological claim nor a psychological process. It is the expression of a kind of incapacity or inability: racists simply find it unintelligible that their victims could have "an inner life of any depth and complexity," such as their own, in which the ordinary attributions of suffering, grief, and joy can find purchase. At the center, or rather the origin, of racism, is not a set of beliefs, nor a vicious animus or other motivation. Racism *befalls* its subjects. James Isdell, Protector of Aborigines in Western Australia at the beginning of the twentieth century, was sincere when he said that he "would not hesitate for one moment to separate any half-caste from its Aboriginal mother, no matter how frantic her momentary grief might be at the time. They soon forget their offspring" (Gaita 2000: 57). The racist's "incredulity at the suggestion that one could wrong 'them' as we can wrong one another is genuine. James Isdell would have been sincerely incredulous at the suggestion that an Aboriginal mother's soul could be lacerated by the loss of her child" (63).

Maybe. But then how does the racist come by this incapacity to recognize full humanity in the human? Gaita seems to think that it is a matter of brute perception:

> The "Black and White Minstrel Show" face was a caricature which revealed how many whites saw Afro-American faces. As reflected in the caricature, those faces did not appear to white racists as only accidentally incapable of expressing anything deep, as the face of a white person who was terribly disfigured in an accident would. The racist's thought is "that is how they look" essentially, and the fact that they look like that to him is fundamental to what makes them "them" and to why he finds it inconceivable that they should be treated as "one of us." (Gaita 2000: 61)

It seems to me that the assertion that "the 'Black and White Minstrel Show' face was a caricature which revealed how many whites saw Afro-American faces" is just false. Caricature is willful distortion. That minstrel show face is not reve-latory of what was seen; it was an instrument of racist denigration, as was, prob-ably, the institution of the minstrel show. But not much follows from flat contradiction. In the first place, Gaita might reply, the minstrel show face as a re-vealing caricature is only one, dispensable, illustration of a particular perceptual discrimination; and even without that illustration, it could still be insisted that the minstrel show face was how racists saw black faces. In the second place, it could be argued that the discernment of racist motivation in these caricatures is just one more example of that psychologistic wrong-headedness which mistak-enly discerns motivation in racism. There's little profit in arguing about moti-vation in caricature when its role in the larger issue is under challenge.

Letting caricature be as it may, is there *any* plausibility to the claim that the racist actually sees the black face as if it was a minstrel show face, or as some-thing similar that occludes the appreciation of full humanity? I think that what-ever plausibility the claim possesses is borrowed from this proposition:

> 1. There are people whose faces are such that some other people can-not see in them the lineaments of full humanity.

This is true, but it is not the proposition for which Gaita contends, which is:

> 2. There are entire races of people whose faces are such that other people—all or most white antiblack racists—cannot see in them the lineaments of full humanity.

Gaita thinks that from (2) the core phenomena of racism follow. This is a re-markable incapacity in the racist. How is it to be explained? Could the racist's (mis)perceptions or (mis)apprehensions be motivated (by hatred or guilt, for example)? That is a complex question, but I think it would be agreed that moti-vated misperception of the sort relevant to this discussion would involve some deeper engagement with the victim's inner life and an attempt to misconstrue the true character of that engagement. Gaita, however, insists that in the case of antiblack racism "one should not assume . . . that racists must really know in their hearts that their victims are fully human" (2000: 72). So it seems that this account dispenses with the possibility of motivated misperception and the deeper human engagement that it presupposes. It follows either that there is no misperception involved or that there is, but it is brute and unmotivated. The racist is the passive victim of his (mis)perceptions and just cannot attach the rel-evant human characteristics to his victims.

I suppose that something like that *can* happen. But it seems to be a marginal phenomenon, affecting only some people and, indeed, a fluctuating constitu-ency. To make the view plausible an explanation is required of why these perceptual limitations afflict only some people, and only at some stages of their lives. Children, for example, don't seem to have the problem. In any case, as a general explanation of racism it faces an insurmountable difficulty, even where there really are significant physical differences between the parties. It is this. There is no direct path from a failure to perceive the full humanity of a person to the enmities and actions that are the hallmarks of racism. Racists sometimes do atrocious things: mass murder, systematic humiliation, lynchings, mutilations. On Gaita's account these things are not essentially connected to racism as particular expressions of it. Instead, racism is conceived of as a kind of *permissive* cause that allows these acts to proceed. Instead of being part of the explanation of what motivates the racist to bear ill will, exact deference, perform atrocities, racism is understood as *external* to that motivation. But that understanding fails to capture a fundamental relationship between racism and the acts in which it is manifested. This objection is, I think, fatal to this kind of account, if it claims more than marginal relevance.

IV. THE RACIST MIND

I return to the question of motivation in racism. I suggested above that *most* individual racism is irrational: that there are no prima facie conditions for most racist beliefs, affective and orectic states that can render them normatively appropriate to their putative objects. I now want to add that a major reason for irrationality in the racist mind—not, of course, the only reason—is unconscious motivation; and I need to show, at least in outline, how unconscious wishes, phantasies, and dispositions can motivate racism.

The idea that racism is unconsciously motivated is hardly novel. Under the impress of psychoanalysis a spate of psychodynamic theories of racism have emerged over the last century. These theories usually have one master idea: racists are authoritarian personalities obsessively at war with their instinctual impulses and rigid superegos; racists are people driven to displace aggression onto scapegoats; racists are hysterics, projecting their libidinal impulses onto blacks or their superegos onto Jews. Some researchers stress the ubiquity of the racist search for self-esteem by exacting deference from victims; others stress the similarities between racism and psychotic conditions.[12] I think that there is much to be said for these theories, but they are inadequate in a number of general ways that are worth noting. They tend to exaggerate their scope, providing more or less unitary psychodynamic explanations for a very diverse range of racist phenomena. In fact, while each illuminates some form of racism, or some aspect of a form of racism,

12. For a survey of the neurotica, see the exposition in Young-Bruehl 1996, parts 1 and 2. On racism as related to psychotic process, see Rustin 1991 and chapter 6 of this volume.

none explains all; we should be prepared to find that there are multifarious defensive, wish-fulfilling processes and strategies underlying much racism.

Moreover, in focusing more or less exclusively on psychodynamic processes they tend to neglect the role of culturally given racist discourse, ideology, or lore. Some racist lore immanent in a culture is assimilated without significant psychodynamic consequences. It is important at least notionally to distinguish this situation from two others: the situation where such lore acquires unconscious significance for the racist and plays a significant part in the psychic economy, and the situation where the constitutive beliefs are (largely) manufactured, reinforced, or augmented by individual unconscious activity and dispositions. So, for example, considering the conspicuous Manichean structure of some racism, its idealization of the *us* and devaluation of the *them,* psychodynamic thinkers are apt to conclude that unconscious processes such as projection and splitting of the object world are involved and that these Manichean structures are individual psychological constructions. But many racists do not need to *actively* split their object world or to project their bad self-conceptions onto their targets. The object world may already be satisfactorily split for them once they assimilate racist lore,[13] and their targets may already be marked *in the discourse* by some of the very characteristics (greed, unacceptable sexual phantasies, etc.) they wish to disavow.

(It would be a serious mistake, however, to underestimate the extent to which unconscious processes influence vicissitudes such as the historical evolution of racist lore, the degree to which it will be embraced, which features of it will be most attractive, the degree of gratification it provides, the kinds of actions that will flow from its acceptance, and the extent to which it engenders further wish-fulfilling or defensive phantasies and actions. Also, it is evident that some racists almost abandon the discourse altogether and lapse into a kind of racial insanity.[14] Reality testing evaporates and racist delusions with only tenuous attachments to reality fill the void.)

A third deficiency in some of these accounts is their failure to attend to the actual features of the victims and to the historical circumstances which in part precipitate expressions of racism. Psychodynamic processes, like projection, for example, do not occur willy-nilly or in a vacuum. Not *any* object is suitable for incorporation into the psychic economy. That is why simple scapegoat theories in which the victims are viewed as fungible bystanders generally fail. It is evident that a complete account is going to be very complex. Such an account would have to consider the correspondences between "real" features of victims (e.g., dark skin), racist ideology (e.g., the association of dark skin with filth or sexuality),

13. Though it may not be psychodynamically split. There may be no attendant ego-splitting.

14. See the essay by Neil Altman and Johanna Tiemann in this volume.

the unconscious phantasies or constructions placed on these things (e.g., the association of dark skin and sexuality with anal or phallic significance), and the social circumstances in which the various connections are mobilized (e.g., a depressed economy). To my knowledge only Elisabeth Young-Bruehl, influenced by both Hannah Arendt and psychoanalysis, has developed an account of the prejudices that is sensitive to all these considerations.[15]

These strictures notwithstanding, psychodynamic theories offer illumination at many of those important junctions where most philosophical, sociological, and historical accounts give out. In *I'm Not a Racist, But ...*, for example, Lawrence Blum notices "the continuing vitality of the idea of race" and of racism despite the increasingly inhospitable climate of mainstream culture (2002: 106). Why this persistence? Blum suggests that it is partly because these ideas and attitudes have remained "outside the domain of reflectively endorsed ideas" and because of "the weight of racialized history and the current legacy of racial depredations" (106, 146). In particular, Blum remarks on the persistence of inherentist thinking about race, albeit in uncommitted or unreflective forms. "People," Blum says, "have soaked up inherentist ways of thinking about racial groups and may not be entirely aware of having done so" (136). So on this view the persistence of race thinking and racism supervenes on a kind of inertia or failure to arraign racist conceptions before the tribunal of reflection. But why the inertia? And how do such ideas about reflective failure (or the various learning theories of sociologists and cognitive psychologists, for that matter) sit with the *atrocious* acts, the defining extremes, that are still motivated by racism? Isn't the real rea-

---

15. The introduction to this volume summarizes some main contentions in *The Anatomy of Prejudices*. One major problem in that work is the failure to distinguish between symptom and character trait and therefore between prejudice and pathology. Character, in this work, is principally determined by the preponderance of favored defense mechanisms, and is therefore not different dynamically from neurotic structure. Prejudices are regarded as, in part, surface expressions of *active* unconscious wishes and defenses. Freud (1959, 1961a) distinguished character trait and symptom when he emphasized that character traits are more or less normal, the results of sublimation or reaction formation, and no longer symbolic of their instinctual causes or sources (or, in another language, do not discharge libido). He was right to observe this distinction. There are important differences between circumstances in which actions (like segregating a people perceived as polluting infiltrators) are caused in part by an unconscious obsessional need to cleanse oneself of internal persecutors, and circumstances in which such actions do *not* have that unconscious significance (or contemporary causation) but are merely part of the (delibidinized) habitual repertoire, the general tendencies, of the obsessional *character*. Young-Bruehl insists that prejudice is not pathology, but it is unclear how she can do so. The way she deploys the notion of character obscures this kind of distinction, and therefore the distinctions between prejudice and pathology. If my line of reasoning were followed through, we should have to recognize at least two subclasses of orectic prejudice, the pathological and the characterological.

son why racial thinking and racism have remained so durable, why racism can be so desperate and destructive, why ethnic, religious, and class conflicts become so rapidly racialized, that they satisfy a host of powerful, often unconscious psychological needs?

There is usually only one point at which many philosophers and historians recognize the incidence of such needs: the claim that racist ideology emerged as the *rationalization* of slavery. This genetic explanation of racism is partial. Race ideology and racism have a far more complex history than their association with slavery. But it is at least on the right track. Rationalizations—strategies of excuse, disguise, palliation—are usually motivated by adverse judgments on one's own behavior or character and so involve the intrapsychic or reflexive attitudes we have to ourselves. Racist ideology and racism *were* convenient in the ways philosophers and historians have recognized, as rationalizing economic domination, exploitation, and privilege. But that explanation doesn't carry far: historically, ruling classes have rarely bothered to go to the trouble of rationalizing such things, even in fundamentally egalitarian dispensations: think of contemporary United States where labor practices and forms of discrimination not much better than slavery continue apace without overt attempts to palliate them with silly biological doctrines. The deeper discernment is that much racism springs reflexively from motives and aspects of character more sensitive and peremptory. Racism is primarily a device for regulating the internal affective and orectic economy: for denying guilt, defending against disavowed instinctual wishes, coping with ineluctable passions like envy, sustaining self-esteem, creating illusions of belonging. These kinds of human needs, wishes, and projects—usually unconscious, very powerful, quick to forge disguise, to dissemble ("Did anybody seriously confess to envy?" Melville asked)—have over the centuries contributed to shaping race thinking and motivating racism as well as finding satisfaction in them.

How, then, do unconscious structures motivate (some forms of) racism? I will first give a very general characterization and then discuss in some detail a specific instance. I employ without supporting argument some basic premises of psychoanalytic theory. The general answer goes like this. In the defining, irrational racisms, unconscious desires, representations of archaic (i.e., early parental) objects, phantasies, and emotions manage to intrude into the active economy of mind. The circumstances and mechanisms are very varied; some of them will be discussed below.[16] When it happens, people, groups, events, and institutions take on unconscious meanings, usually of a multivalent character, which sub-

---

16. Young-Bruehl 1996 is the outstanding discussion of how unconscious wishes and the like enter into the active economy of mind and of how racism and prejudice in general operate as defense mechanisms. A further important, closely related issue concerns the means whereby unconscious wishes find satisfaction in racism. That issue touches on the machinery of Freudian wish fulfillment described in detail in Pataki 1996, 2000.

tend from matters of intense strife in the individual's childhood. Some things are exigent for every child: staying attached to mother, securing or manufacturing the illusion of her love, surviving the loss of objects and of oneself in rage or despair, integrating the bad in experience with the good, and coping with ambivalence and painful feelings of deprivation, abandonment, and envy. These vicissitudes have their correspondences later in life. They reverberate in the experiences of economic depression, social deracination, and deprivation. For example, the "perception" that one's nation is being "swamped" by foreigners or "cheap labor" tends to create in vulnerable classes insecurity and fear of impending loss. Conviction that the unemployed are parasites, or that tax-funded Aboriginal organizations are, as an Australian deputy prime minister put it, blood-sucking leeches, may cause resentment and envy. The belief that there are diseased, pushy queue jumpers—as the Australian government currently characterizes Middle Eastern refugees—trying to enter "your" country, who may compete for welfare or jobs or, worse, receive "special treatment," is likely to mobilize insecurity and envious rivalry. These "perceptions" and beliefs are, of course, already colored and distorted by the lens of earlier experiences, unconscious dispositions, and other sources of bias, and the reactions to them are invariably incommensurate to the actual impositions. But the situation assumes an altogether more desperate complexion when groups of "outsiders" unconsciously take on still deeper infantile significance: for example, that of greedy siblings or parasites who, in the infant and regressed mind, threaten literally to starve it, or stir up early envious rivalry too painful to bear. It is not just that the heat goes up a notch; certain typical patterns of response emerge that are now radically and problematically or, in my catholic use of the term, irrationally connected to the circumstances. The current circumstances get wildly misinterpreted and provoke primitive reactions: angry avoidance (turning away), envious despoliation, segregation, dehumanization (de-animation or fetishization), aggressive incorporation, annihilation.

V. ENVY AND RACISM IN AUSTRALIA

Let's consider in some detail the role of envy in some forms of racism. I do not propose, of course, that envy underlies all forms of racism, but it seems to be very significant in many of them, and may play some part in all.[17] The asso-

17. It seems to me that those constellations which Young-Bruehl 1996 describes as antipaternal and antisibling forms of hysterical prejudice (e.g., 365–77, 407–11) could be further illuminated by a consideration of the role of envy: in the first case, of the paternal penis; in the second, of other siblings. See Young-Bruehl 1996: 270–74, where "envy" could be substituted for "sibling rivalry" without distortion. Young-Bruehl notes that Arendt treated the anti-Semitism of the pan-Germanic movement as essentially an anti-Semitism of envy (360).

ciation has long been recognized, to a degree. The "truism," for example, that anti-Semitism is just a form of envy is almost as old as anti-Semitism itself. In general, however, there seems now to be less conscious awareness of the potency and pervasiveness of envy than in earlier times. That may be because envy is one the great engines of consumerist capitalism, and familiarity, in the great republic of accumulation and accountancy, has made us blind to it. It was not always so. Christianity made envy one of the seven deadly sins, and according to Chaucer it is the worst of them: "for all other sins are sins against only one virtue, whereas envy is against all virtue and all goodness" (Klein 1975: 189). For Herodotus *phthonis*—the envy of the gods provoked by the success of mortals—determined the pattern of history. Deity, he says, is always "jealous and interfering."

E. R. Dodds said that in the archaic world "men knew that it was dangerous to be happy" (1951: 31). Why *dangerous*? Because envy, divine and mortal, is not merely pained at another's possession of what one covets, it often seeks to spoil or destroy that thing and its possessor. Shortly before the collapse of communism a cartoon appeared linking, stereotypically, some national types to stages of envy. A genie appears and is prepared to grant wishes. The English woman says, "Genie, Catherine has such a beautiful cottage; I want one just like it." A French woman says, "Genie, Magali has such a huge chalet, I want one twice as big." A Russian says, "Genie, Boris has a pig and I don't; kill Boris's pig." The latter kind of spoiling or destructive envy was first investigated in detail by Melanie Klein. On the Kleinian view envy is an expression of destructive instinctual drives and operates from birth. Part of what that means is that envy is not just an emotional reaction, the way in which anger or fear are, for example; it is an innate drive that searches out its objects. Shakespeare may have had something like that in mind:

> But jealous souls will not be answer'd so;
> They are not ever jealous for the cause,
> But jealous for they are jealous; 'tis a monster
> Begot upon itself, born on itself. (*Othello* 3.4)

Whether or not envy is begotten upon itself, we understand how deprivation, frustration, and loss stimulate envy, and very few escape those vicissitudes. Even when they have been rendered unconscious or split off, the central personality remains subject to their influence and intrusions. The intrusion of unconscious envy into adult consciousness may be particularly threatening and painful, and there are many defenses against conscious experience of it. One defense is to *spoil* or eliminate the envied objects. If the object is ruined or destroyed, envy is preempted. Another defense is to *identify with the object*, for then it seems that one has what the object has. Something like this is often at the heart of some kinds of nationalism and other group identity formations in which the "little man" preens himself with borrowed glory. In *devaluation* the value of the envied object or its possessor is denied or disparaged. Envy is a motive to *split the object world* in a way that is well accommodated in, and reinforces, the racist diremption of the human world. The object may not only be devalued, it may be excluded altogether from the world of human bonds and consideration: dehumanized. The object is no longer in the domain of the enviable. The dehumanization of the sort that is at the center of Gaita's account and others is, I think, one such strategy.[18]

It won't convert the skeptics, but a commonplace example of unconscious envy at work may be helpful at this point. Some people drive their convertibles with roof retracted even in the height of Melbourne's summer. The traffic is bad, the sun scorching, the roads pungent and choking with fumes. Why do they do it? Well, some may be on their way to Monte Carlo and some, having bought a car that can do tricks, want it to perform. But we know that much of this is "showing off." But what's that? Attention is welcome, wherever it comes from, but there seems to be more to it than that. Their intention, which we implicitly

---

18. Arendt writes on South Africa:

[Racism's] . . . basis, and its excuse, were still experience itself, a horrifying experience of something alien beyond imagination or comprehension; it was tempting indeed simply to declare that these were not human beings. Since, however, despite all ideological explanations the black man stubbornly insisted on retaining their human features, the "white men" could not but reconsider their own humanity and decided that they themselves were more than human and obviously chosen by God to be the gods of the black men. This conclusion was logical and unavoidable *if one wanted to deny radically all common bonds with the savages.* (1979: 195; italics added)

But now why this denial and recoil? Arendt says it was caused by fear and pride.

The Boers were never able to forget their first horrible fright before a species of men *whom human pride and the sense of human dignity could not allow them to accept as fellow-men. This fright of something like oneself that still under no circumstances ought to be like oneself remained at the basis for a race society*. . . . [The Africans] were, as it were, "natural" human beings who lacked the specifically human character, the specifically human reality, so that when European men massacred them they somehow were not aware that they had committed murder. (192; italics added)

None of this rings true. Neither pride nor dignity is motive to recoil from fellow men or to expunge their humanity. Arendt appears to lean almost exclusively on Conrad's descriptions of racial encounter in *The Heart of Darkness*. In fact, Conrad saw more deeply. Only a spinsterish reading could overlook the charge of sexual attraction, admiration, and envy that Conrad and Marlow clearly shared: "They shouted, sang; their bodies streamed with perspiration; they had faces like grotesque masks—these chaps; but they had bone, muscle, a wild vitality, an intense energy of movement, that was as natural and true as the surf along their coast. They wanted no excuse for being there. They were a great comfort to look at" (Conrad 1982: 20; see also 23–25, 51–52, 59–60, 73, 87).

understand, is to provoke envy in others. But now why do *that*? At this point I think we need to pass slightly beyond folk psychology to psychoanalysis. One common reason is this: the driver has the convertible but hasn't got what he or she wants much more (and unconsciously thinks that other people have: *freedom from envy;* and, being envious, the driver wants to spoil that. We can glimpse this dynamic, almost pre-theoretically, though much of it is transacted unconsciously.

Some things are envied more than others. Melanie Klein said that creativity is the most envied thing of all because its psychogenetic roots can be traced back to the life-giving breast. Some other conditions hugely envied are freedom from envy, greed, and frenzy, which brings serenity; being loved and in confident possession of mother; beauty, of course; and childlike playfulness, vitality, spontaneity, and what is imagined to be a carefree life. Siblings are envied, either because they appear more magnificent and gifted or because they attract more parental love. Finally, sexual vigor and license and absence of inhibition. Enviable objects don't actually have to possess the coveted characteristics, of course; it is necessary only that they be thought or phantasized to possess them.

Anyone familiar with the psychosocial literature on American antiblack racism, with the fiction of James Baldwin or Ralph Ellison, or the work of Frantz Fanon, will be familiar with the idea that envy of more or less phantastically constructed black sexuality underlies much of that racism. This is a cogent conception, but I want to attempt a less familiar theme that I think is more relevant to contemporary racism in Australia. I want to consider some reasons for thinking that envious hatred of children, including the "child within oneself"[19] and, in particular, envy in sibling rivalry, play a very significant part in some of our contemporary racism.

To begin with, it really is remarkable how frequently and tendentiously the people whom Europeans until quite recently regarded as subject races, most especially Africans, have been derogated as children. Here are a few samples from the huge literature of "scientific" racism and colonialism.[20] The distinguished anatomist Carl Vogt wrote in 1864: "By its rounded apex and less developed posterior lobe the Negro brain resembles that of our children, and by the protuberance of the parietal lobe, that of our females. . . . The grown-up Negro partakes, as regards his intellectual faculties, of the nature of the child, the female, and the senile white" (Gould 1996: 135). Vogt offered advice to slaveholders: "the general rule . . . is that Negro slaves must be treated like neglected and badly brought up children" (Banton 1998: 76).

These passages from Vogt are representative of one of the most fanciful scientific distortions of the nineteenth century, the extension of the theory of re-

19. The child that one *is* in certain personations (Pataki 2003).
20. See Gould 1996, Banton 1998, and Reynolds 1989 for many examples.

capitulationism (ontogeny recapitulates phylogeny), itself poorly founded, to fashion an absurd doctrine according to which racial variation and cultural development recapitulate ontogeny. A contributor to the *Anthropological Review* of 1866 explains: "As the type of the Negro is foetal, so that of the Mongol is infantile. And in strict accordance with this, we find that their government, literature and art are infantile also. They are beardless children whose life is a task and whose chief virtue consists in unquestioning obedience" (Hobsbawm 1995: 267).

This kind of view was enormously popular with the learned, and the spirit of it remained popular with the unlearned long after the spurious observations and biology it was based on had been discarded.

Here is S. Burt, attorney general of Western Australia, addressing the parliament in 1892:

> I have come to the conclusion myself, and have done so for years, that the only way of effectually dealing with all these coloured races, whether blackfellows, or Indians, or Chinamen, is to treat them like children. I have proved it—in my own small experience. You can only deal with them effectually, like you deal with naughty children—whip them. It is the only argument they recognise, brute force. It is no use talking to these blackfellows, and be kind to them, and expect them to take any notice; not the slightest use. . . . But give a blackfellow a little stick—if he deserves it, mind: I draw attention to that, for if you give it to them when they don't deserve it, it only makes them infinitely worse; but give them a little stick when they really deserve it, and it does them a power of good—far more good than any other punishment. If they deserve it they never forget it. They rather delight in it, in fact; they will tell you so afterwards, and thank you for it. (Reynolds 1989: 142)

What is at the back of these persistent beliefs that not only *inferiorize* but also *infantilize* the racially designated groups? Many things. There is the influence of absurd but gratifying racialist theories—themselves fashioned to a large degree under the impress of racism—that tell the European he is a superior breed: the adult among races! These theories and associated popular beliefs and prejudices conveniently palliate colonial domination and exploitation as something like parental obligation. Not far in the background is the effort to mitigate the guilt of wronging others by denying them the maturity and capacity to feel injustice. (The present Australian government, which belittles Aboriginal claims for respect by its condescending rhetoric of "practical reconciliation" and the satisfaction of "basic needs," provides a particularly obnoxious example of this.) The pleasures of contempt and sadism can effectively disguise themselves in the punishment of juveniles. But underlying these things there is a significant but less conspicuous influence: the unconscious envy of groups who are imagined to possess characteristics, generally though imperceptively imputed to children, which are desired but also hated and devalued.

I've already mentioned a few of these characteristics. Some others are: the capacity for spontaneous and effortless enjoyment, the serenity that comes from feeling loved unconditionally, closeness to the Earth (which is mother's body), and ease with one's own body. Some of these characteristics, and their transformations, are attributions of racist lore that whites have constructed about indigenous peoples in many parts of the world. But the lore itself has been influenced by unconscious constructions and is also selectively perceived through them. Moreover, we know that in many people the characteristics they perceive are really projections of their own condemned and hated impulses and self-representations. The latter become condemned and hated because, roughly speaking, they are associated with childish wants, instinctual desires, and self-conceptions that are unacceptable to the adult world. In the language of classical psychoanalysis they are id-like features projected under superego pressure. So the projections can be viewed as defensive measures against self-hatred and associated depression. The projections, as it were, empty one of intolerable urges and self-conceptions. In fact, these things get hated twice over: first as aspects of oneself, of the despised and disowned "child within"; and then as projected features of the racist's victims. But these childlike aspects of oneself are not only repudiated and hated, they are also greatly desired. They are at the core of one's being and condition pleasures that cannot easily be renounced. So they are, as well, greatly envied in those in whom they are imagined to have free play and must, therefore, by the logic of spoiling envy, be debased or devalued. The eye of envy is the eye of the child, and the racist's preoccupation with these envied features testifies to their attractive power.

But rationality too has its claims, and the features are rationalized and in the process transformed: freedom from the frenzy of envy and greed becomes laziness and ineffectuality; guiltless sexuality becomes depravity; childlike spontaneity and vigor become irresponsibility and parasitism, and so on. Envy turned to hatred may lead to attempts to segregate, disparage, punish, or destroy the people who are unconsciously imagined to embody the envied characteristics. So, for example, the punitive, persecutory attitude of the Australian government in 2003—and of the many bigots who support it—toward Aborigines, asylum seekers, the unemployed, the young, and drug addicts is, paradoxical though it may seem, in part a reflection of an underlying envious hatred of these groups, apprehended under their identification with the bigot's own despised and repudiated childish impulses and self-conceptions. These bigots can tolerate neither the dependency nor the vitality of the child. They reflect the misery and unconscious self-hatred of an infantilized social dispensation, of people who, despite lives constructed around its denial, feel fundamentally deprived and envious.

A cluster of themes associated with deprivation and envy transparently linked to sibling rivalry have recently acquired prominence in Australian political consciousness. The ground had been prepared by Prime Minister Howard, but they were precipitated on the nation by an inexperienced, populist politician, Pauline Hanson. They can be summed up in a few plaints: "Someone is getting more," "Someone is getting something for nothing," "They must be kept in their place."[21] In her parliamentary maiden speech Hanson complained that "Aboriginals received more benefits than non-Aboriginals" and bemoaned "the privileges Aboriginals enjoy over other Australians." "Reconciliation" between Aboriginals and whites, she says, "is everyone recognizing and treating each other as equals." Now, by and large, Australian Aborigines have among the worst living conditions and prospects of any dispossessed indigenous peoples. They weren't, however, Hanson's only targets. Australia was also being "swamped" by Asian immigrants whose loyalty to the state was equivocal and who drew lavishly on welfare, while "ordinary Australians got nothing." And then there were the arrivals of mainly Middle Eastern and Afghan asylum seekers. Hanson succeeded in stirring up a good deal of racist and related sentiment, and Howard has since adroitly exploited it.

The unconscious meaning of the Hansonite perspective seems to be something like this. The nation is perceived as mother unfairly apportioning milk to her infants. People whose social and individual identities are fragile are prone unconsciously to apprehend large, receptive bodies such as races or nations as *mother,* and to seek narcissistic identification with them. The underlying anxiety and insecurity of *not really belonging* mobilizes this need for identification and merger into a larger whole. Such merger may also be motivated as a defense against envy by magical or phantastic appropriation of the race's or nation's possessions and achievements, as well as against the primordial envy of mother. Unconsciously, they may identify with the group while at the same time idealizing and endeavoring to maintain a special relationship of identity or ownership with it: one "owns" one's mother. The "special relationship" may emerge as a kind of vaunted and exaggerated patriotism. As Hobsbawm (1987) and others have pointed out, since the emergence of nation states patriotism has often been employed to compensate for social inferiority. But in these cases the patriotism is shallow and the animus for these patriots is not love of their country but the desperate illusion that they own it.

Now, Hanson was worried that the mother nation (with which she seemed overtly to identify in accepting the appellation "mother of the nation," i.e., mother of the children of the nation) could be torn apart by the unmastered diversity of her demanding children. Her unsettling plea "To survive in peace and harmony, united and strong, we must have one people, one nation, one flag" (i.e.,

---

21. The theme of "getting something for nothing" has been vigorously exploited against welfare recipients, especially in the introduction of the popular "work for the dole scheme." What was once a universal entitlement has been transformed into an impost of charity against which the taxpayer has been encouraged to vent his indignation.

one fair mother, no sibling rivalry) appeared to pass over the heads of an Australian public untroubled by its sinister resonance. The younger siblings—the childlike Aborigines, Asians, and especially the new arrivals—were *getting too much*. And they had *done nothing* to deserve the assistance they got; they were just there, on the doorstep, like some runaway, homeless child. They should be kept out of the house altogether or, at least, kept in their inferior place. The older child has learned to fear usurpation: "I'm the king of the castle and you're the dirty rascal." And of course Hanson is the privileged, older child, the one who was in the house first, with proprietary rights: "If I can invite who I like into my home, then I should have the right to have a say in who comes into my country." (Later, Prime Minister Howard's most successful election slogan was "*We* will decide who comes into our country!") The infantile pathos and currents of envious sibling rivalry in these plaints are barely concealed by the political veils they partly manufacture, partly borrow.

The currents have engulfed the nation's attitudes to asylum seekers, with pernicious consequences. The psychological impact of strange new arrivals has, of course, multiple determinants. Different individuals will be affected in different ways, and the same individuals differently in varied circumstances and at different times. There can be little doubt that a significant part of the hostility to outsiders, especially from people of vulnerable socioeconomic status, arises from the perception that the new arrivals are potential competitors for work or welfare. That, though important, cannot be the whole of the explanation, as is evident from the fact that these perceptions are nearly always distorted, and in ways that are discernibly motivated. The kinds of fears and apprehensions that fall under the rubric of xenophobia are also very important. So, too, is the peculiar *downward envy* that Francis Bacon noticed: "Men of noble birth are noted to be envious towards new men when they rise. For the distance is altered, and it is like a deceit of the eye, that when others come on they think themselves go back" (Schoeck 1969: 197). People don't like upcomers and newcomers, especially if there is a suspicion that the arrivals may "overtake" them.

There are several specific reasons why blacks and other groups considered to be dark, primitive, or merely outsiders or newcomers come to be apprehended as younger siblings and objects of envy. Certain infantile equations such as blackness and shittyness, darkness and sexuality, no doubt play a part in some cases. As well, the child has an understanding of his inferior station and ineffectuality and associates childishness with weakness and the latter with motherlessness and homelessness. The refugee has no hearth and therefore is motherless, weak, and childish. The connection in the child's mind between new babies in the household and strangers, new arrivals, is also a potent association. And there are the individual developmental vicissitudes that impress on each personal template specific objects of fear, avoidance, and so forth: in particular, the child notices selective disparagement in the conversation of adults.

Coming from the waters often signifies birth, and it is notable that in the dreams of some racists boats regularly figure as mother and siblings as blacks (Young-Bruehl 1996: 269–74). It is possible, then, that the asylum seekers who come to Australia in boats—who, because of their vulnerability and hardships, have a particular claim upon hospitality and respect—may for these and related reasons become exceptionally threatening. Their very neediness and destitution may mobilize in some people the unconscious apprehension of hungry or sick siblings that there seems to be a primordial need to repel (Tustin 1992: 18). These needy but envied siblings may be experienced unconsciously as trying to invade mother and as getting from her—"getting more," "getting something for nothing"—what we could not. In people who already feel harrowed and deprived, and perhaps actually are so, it doesn't take much to stir these deeper sources of deprivation and envy and to defend themselves against it by the kind of exclusion, dehumanization, and hard-heartedness that the asylum seekers met in Australia. (It needs to be understood that Australia's "asylum-seeker problem" is in fact minuscule, a question of a few thousand souls.)

The Australian government's policy in dealing with asylum seekers is named the Pacific Solution. It consists in preventing asylum seekers from landing on the mainland, dispersing them into concentration camps in neighboring Pacific Islands, preventing media access so as to make them faceless, depriving them of amenities to the limits of international law (to deter others, it is said), and publicly vilifying them. It is a psychologically brilliant but wicked strategy. It resonates with much of the public's mood and, indeed, functions in the public's collective understanding to legitimize it. Its success is largely underwritten by widespread racialized enmity. Ignorance, racism, and moral stupor have conspired to occlude the sick ironies in its name.

III

RACISM, MORALITY, POLITICS

10 : WHY WE SHOULD NOT THINK OF OURSELVES AS DIVIDED BY RACE

The title of Ashley Montagu's (1974) great book against the race idea, *Man's Most Dangerous Myth: The Fallacy of Race,* suggests that this idea is both false and dangerous. These two suggestions are not necessarily connected; ideas do not have to be false to be dangerous. Unaccountably, however, most philosophers who appreciate the evil consequences of the race idea focus their energies on trying to show that it is false.[1] Presumably they would defend this strategy on the ground that the race idea can have evil consequences only if it is believed, and that it will not be believed if it is shown to be false. But this reasoning is unsound; people often continue to believe in things that have been shown to be false. Further, philosophers are probably not in the best position to prove that there are no races. Full-time biologists seem to be in a better position, given that by "race" we mean here *biological* race, namely a group of individuals defined biologically, like a breed or a subspecies.[2] Some philosophers who deny that there are races appear to accept this, and try to settle the issue in their favor by claiming that "no reputable biologist believes in race." But, of course, in order to know who is a reputable biologist may require a greater familiarity with biology than most philosophers have. In any case this appeal to authority fails. Stephen Jay Gould and Jared Diamond are among the biologists most often cited by philosophers who deny the existence of race, and they seem to think that Ernst Mayr is a reputable biologist. Gould refers to him as the "the world's greatest living evolutionary biologist," and Jared Diamond describes him as "one of the greatest biologists of our own day." But Mayr claims bluntly that those who subscribe to the opinion that "there are no human races" are "obviously ignorant of modern biology."[3]

1. Among the most insistent are Kwame Appiah (1985) and Naomi Zack (1998).

2. Recently, "race" has sometimes come to have a different meaning, as referring to a social construct. The existence of race as a social construct is not controversial and I do not discuss it in this chapter.

3. The comments by Gould and Diamond appear on the dust jacket of Mayr 2001. Mayr's comment appears in Mayr 2002: 89.

The issue is controversial, and most philosophers simply do not know enough about it to be really convincing one way or another. Accordingly in this chapter I take up the second suggestion in Montagu's title, and I try to show just how and why the race idea is dangerous. If I am successful, we will be in a better position to deal with it. Perhaps we will decide that the best strategy is the one already being tried, namely, to show that there are no races; but as we shall see there are other possibilities.

In the following sections, I offer samples of how some philosophers argue that there are no races, then rebut some false but popular accounts of why the idea of race is dangerous, and finally propose a theory of why the idea of race is dangerous.

I

One of the most popular arguments philosophers use to show that there are no races centers on the fact that biologists have never found racial essences (see, for example, Zack 1998: 3). Apparently there are a few genes that only Europeans or American Indians have, but these are not racial essences because they do not account for the physical and alleged intellectual differences between the races (Lewontin 1984: 126). But the inference that there are no races is invalid because it may be possible to classify people into races without assuming that they have essences. Thus, Mayr notes that while Darwin made "essentialist" thinking obsolete in biology, he did not thereby make classification obsolete. Classification proceeds in biology, but it is now based on "population thinking." As Mayr puts it, population thinking "stresses the uniqueness of everything in the organic world." Classification can proceed in "population thinking" but only, in Mayr's words, "in statistical terms." "If the average difference between two groups of individuals is sufficiently great to be recognizable on sight, we refer to these groups of individuals as different races." Mayr claims that race, understood thus, is "a universal phenomenon of nature occurring not only in a man but in two thirds of all species of animals and plants" (Mayr 1997: 162, 165).

The standard response of the no-race theorists, that many people are difficult to classify into races, fails completely because the claim that there are biological races does not imply that people are easy to classify into races or even that everyone is a member of a biological race. Perhaps it would be a problem if all or most people were difficult to classify. But all or most people are not difficult to classify. As Jared Diamond (1992: 11) notes, "Simply by looking at a person, even laymen can often tell what part of the world that person comes from. . . . For example, given one person each from Sweden, Nigeria and Japan, none of us would have any trouble deciding at a glance which person was from which country." Further, even if many people are difficult to classify, it still does not follow that there are no races. Should we conclude that there are no breeds of dogs simply because many dogs are mongrels and difficult to classify as this or that breed?

Although Jared Diamond allows that it is usually easy to classify people into Europeans, Africans, and Asians on the basis of their physical characteristics, at another place he claims that "there are many different, equally valid procedures for defining races, and those different procedures yield very different classifications." For example, one such procedure would group "Italians and Greeks with most African blacks. . . . Another equally valid procedure would place Swedes with Fulani (a Nigerian 'black' group) and not with Italians, who would again be grouped with most other African blacks," and so on (Diamond 1994: 84). This is also a favorite argument among philosophers, but it too fails. I doubt very much that any race theorist ever said that the only "valid" way to classify people was to classify them into races. There may be "valid" reasons to classify greyhounds with Great Danes—both are very tall—but it does not follow that there are no greyhounds and Great Danes.

The most popular argument among philosophers for the nonexistence of races is taken from the famous geneticist Richard Lewontin. Allowing that many people can be classified as Europeans, Africans, and Asians, Lewontin observes that racists take the "evident differences" between the groups in question, and "claim that they demonstrate major genetic separation between 'races'" (1984: 121). But, he counters, there is no major genetic separation between the "races," and on that basis he concludes that Europeans, Africans, and Asians are not races (126). But Lewontin's argument depends on foisting a definition of race on the people who believe in biological races. They never said that there must be a "major" genetic separation between the races. It was Lewontin who said that. They only said that there are genetic differences between the races that determine other important differences. This commits them to the claim that there are major genetic differences between the races only if slight genetic differences between the races cannot determine important differences between the races. But Lewontin has told us nothing that would rule out that possibility. On the contrary, other biologists tell us that slight genetic differences between species may possibly determine important intellectual differences between them. According to Diamond, "98.4 percent of our DNA is just normal chimp DNA. . . . Our important visible distinctions from the other chimps—our upright posture, large brains, ability to speak, sparse body hair, and peculiar sexual lives—must be concentrated in a mere 1.6 percent of our genetic program" (1992: 23). But if the slight genetic differences between ourselves and chimps are compatible with the enormous differences between humans and chimps, why can't the slight genetic differences between the "races" be compatible with important differences between them? I do not myself believe for a moment that there are such differences, but I also cannot say that Lewontin's argument has put me in a position to say that I *know* this. Yet many philosophers seem to think that the argument is decisive.

Let us leave the question of the existence or nonexistence of the races.

II

Many people seem to think that the idea of race is obviously dangerous—and false—because it was invented and designed to justify Europe's enslavement of Africans and its subjugation of the non-European world. Indeed, it is common to find the idea dismissed contemptuously on this very ground. People seem to think that it shows that the idea of race is not only false but also dangerous. Presumably the argument would go as follows: since the idea of race was invented and designed to justify Europe's enslavement of Africans and its subjugation of the non-European world, people who believe in it will probably be inclined to believe that Europe was justified in enslaving Africans and subjugating the non-European world. But any idea that inclines people to believe that Europe was justified in enslaving and subjugating the non-European world must be a dangerous idea. This justifiable enslavement is a dangerous thing for people to believe. Hence the idea of race is dangerous. But the major premise of this argument is false. It is simply not true that the idea of race was invented and designed to justify Europe's enslavement of Africans and its subjugation of the non-European world.

In his informative essay "Who Invented the Concept of Race?" Robert Bernasconi (2001) has given excellent reasons for crediting Kant with the invention of the race idea, and I will assume that he is right. But why did Kant invent the idea of race? To some people the fact that he despised black people answers the question; he must have invented the idea of race to justify enslaving black people. But this inference is unwarranted. The fact that Kant had a certain attitude does not mean that he did everything he did because he had that attitude. We could not validly infer that he invented his race idea to support slavery even if he did support slavery. Bernasconi is perfectly consistent in claiming both that Kant invented the race idea to defend monogenesis and also that Kant possibly supported slavery.

If we read Kant's essays on race without preconceived ideas about what he was up to, and if we do not assume that these essays have to be "decoded" (to use the current jargon), their plain intent seems to be to explain human variety. There is absolutely nothing surprising about this. Ever since Europeans had expanded into Asia, Africa, and America they had been struck by the physical variety of human beings, and inevitably their scientists tried to explain the differences. As the historian David Brion Davis put it, observers "searched for categories with which to explain the astounding fact that creatures could be so obviously human and yet so different" (1966: 466). Many published speculations on the topic, Johann Friedrich Blumenbach notably entitling his book on the subject *On the Natural Variety of Mankind* (1865). Without definite evidence to the contrary, there is every reason to suppose that Kant was engaged in the same endeavor in his essays on race. It may be objected, however, that his argument rested on essentialist assumptions, and essentialism was by then already well known to be bad, outmoded science (Zack 2001: 44). If this is correct, we might reasonably suspect that when Kant invented his idea of race he was doing something less respectable than trying to explain human physical variety, and instead cooking up a rationalization for slavery. But essentialist thinking was not outmoded when Kant was using it in his race idea. Darwin wrote almost a century after Kant, and according to Mayr it was Darwin who made essentialist thinking obsolete in biology. Further, essentialist thinking was notably fruitful in chemistry (Sober 1980: 350–83). Chemists postulated that the elements had essences and searched for and discovered these essences. In particular they discovered that all elements had atomic numbers, that all samples of the same element have the same atomic number, and that the atomic numbers of the various elements played a major role in explaining their chemical properties. As a result they were able to invent the periodic table of elements and to predict the existence and properties of elements that had not even yet been discovered. Since the idea of essences was proving to be so fruitful in chemistry, it would have been natural for thinkers like Kant to suppose that it would be equally fruitful in biology. In particular, environmental explanations for human physical variety—for example, that the hot sun of the tropics burned Africans black—had failed: certain American Indians endemic to the tropics were not black, and Africans remained black even when they moved to Europe, while Europeans who had moved to the tropics and become tanned lost the tan when they moved back to Europe.[4] Evidently there was something permanent in blacks and whites that explained why they looked so different. Yet how was this possible if they were descended from a common stock? Kant proposed that human beings, who originated in Europe, possessed "seeds" that provided them with a built-in capacity to develop characteristics enabling them to survive in the various climates in the world, though such adaptations were permanent once they occurred. Although this turned out to be mistaken, it allowed Kant to maintain that human beings were descended from a common stock and shared a common essence, and yet could be classified into races that were permanently different from one another. In sum, Kant's essentialist assumptions give us no reason to "decode" his essays or to discern a "subtext" in them. They were mistaken, but they seem to have been made in good faith, and on what, at the time, appeared to be reasonable scientific assumptions.

We would still have reason to suspect Kant and his invention if Europeans had been in need of a rationalization for enslaving Africans, and the idea he invented fitted the bill too well for this not to be intentional. But it is not clear that Europeans needed an idea of race to rationalize slavery. Apparently Locke was rationalizing slavery without the idea of race. According to Peter Laslett (1967: 302), Locke (1967: 302; chap. 4, sec. 23) justified the enslavement of Africans on the ground that they waged unjust wars and consequently forfeited their natural rights to liberty, and he provided the basis for a similar argument to justify en-

4. We can see Kant working through these problems in Kant 1997: 38–49.

slaving Native Americans. These arguments do not, of course, justify the practice of enslaving the slaves' children, but slaveholders did not have to invent the idea of race to get around this difficulty. A genuine enemy of slavery had inadvertently showed them how. According to Rousseau, Aristotle had mistaken the effect for the cause when he claimed that some men were natural slaves. "Slaves lose everything in their chains," Rousseau declared, "even the desire to escape from them: they love their servitude" (1950: 6; bk. 1, chap. 2). Jefferson for one used this kind of argument to claim that the children of slaves should be kept in slavery for their own good (Jefferson 1999: 494).

But it may be objected that Europeans needed a rationalization for slavery that would justify enslaving Africans specifically, and that the idea of race supplied them with the basis for constructing such a rationalization. It would go as follows: If there are races, and races have special moral and intellectual qualities, and Africans are a race, then Africans could be a race of natural slaves. This argument certainly shows that the idea of race could be used to construct a rationalization of slavery. But it does not follow that it was invented for that purpose. Most inventions are used to do things their inventors never dreamed of. Kant's invention suffered that fate. Soon after Kant laid down his race idea various Europeans and Americans saw that they could use it to justify slavery and other evils. Stephen Jay Gould (1996) presents us with a rogues' gallery of these characters. But it is a blunder to infer that Kant must have invented the idea of race for similar reasons. This blunder is especially egregious since the apologists for slavery had to modify Kant's idea before they could use it for their purposes. They said that Africans were natural slaves, but Kant never said that. Kant believed that blacks and American Indians were the least intelligent human beings, but it does not follow that he believed that they were natural slaves. No one in his right mind could have thought that it did. Jefferson (1999: 492) was only appealing to common sense when he wrote in a letter to Henri Grégoire, "Because Sir Isaac Newton was superior to others in learning, he was not therefore lord of the person or property of others." It is also a marked theme of Kant's moral philosophy that people of very ordinary talents have the intellectual capacity to be moral agents, and consequently possess a dignity that is incompatible with being natural slaves. For example, in *The Metaphysics of Morals,* Kant (1991: 159) insisted that Europeans were permitted to settle in the lands of the Hottentots and American Indians "only by contract, and indeed by a contract that does not take advantage of the ignorance of those inhabitants."[5] Since only moral agents can make contracts, Kant must have believed that the Hottentots and American Indians were moral agents and consequently were not natural slaves.[6]

5. For further discussion see Hill and Boxill 2001: 448–71.
6. See, for example, his condemnation of the European domination of blacks (Kant 1970: 106, 107).

That Kant's idea of race assumed monogenesis is especially significant. If Kant had invented his idea of race to justify slavery, it would have been easy for him to invent an idea that favored polygenesis, for the evidence available at the time was ambiguous enough to enable many authorities at the time to favor it, and polygenesis is more easily compatible with slavery than monogenesis. I am not disputing Bernasconi's claim that Kant favored monogenesis because the Bible favored it. I am suggesting that Kant was adept enough to make polygenesis compatible with the Bible if he had wanted to invent an idea of race to justify slavery. Of course, Georg Forster, in his debate against Kant on the merits of monogenesis, denied that it was a problem for the supporters of slavery. "Let me ask," Forster wrote, "whether the thought that blacks are our brothers has ever anywhere even once meant that the raised whip of the slavedriver was put away?" (Bernasconi 2001: 21). This is good rhetoric, but worthless as argument since Forster did not undertake to prove that slave drivers did think of blacks as their brothers. Further, many supporters of slavery, like Edward Long in his notorious *History of Jamaica* (1774), defended polygenesis precisely because they saw that it was more congenial to slavery than monogenesis.

I conclude that the popular view that the race idea was invented to rationalize slavery is false, and consequently that it cannot provide the ground for the dangerousness of that idea. But Isaiah Berlin has made some suggestive general claims about the potency of certain ideas that may be more helpful in this respect. According to Berlin (1996: 234), ideas "at times develop lives and powers of their own" and are like "seeds" that in "propitious soil" may grow into plants that bear flowers their sower never imagined, and can sometimes even "turn into their opposites." This suggests a new way in which the idea of race could be dangerous. If it is like one of Berlin's "seeds," then perhaps it is dangerous because it develops a life of its own and bears "flowers" like polygenetic theory or the theory that Africans are a race of natural slaves. But Berlin's illustration of his thesis, Kant's "impeccably enlightened rationalism" turning into its opposite, the "pathological forms" of nationalism, obscures its truth. At one point he simply changes two crucial assumptions in Kant's enlightened rationalism, which, thus mutilated, arguably leads to pathological nationalism. But this maneuver only shows that people, the "propitious soil" into which ideas may fall, can change such ideas. It does not show that ideas ever develop "lives and powers of their own."

At another point Berlin observes that there is an "anti-Enlightenment" pietist strain in Kant's system of thought in addition to his enlightenment faith in reason, and he then derives various conclusions from the mix. But even if pathological nationalism is among these conclusions, it is highly misleading to declare that we have a case of enlightenment rationalism turning into its opposite. The totality of a person's ideas, even a great philosopher's, are hardly ever altogether consistent, so it should be no surprise that some of Kant's thoughts can be used to derive conclusions at odds with the views he is best known for, or would insist on if the inconsistency in his thoughts were put forcibly and clearly before him. For example, students of Buffon's thought have often noted that despite his emphatic and repeated arguments for monogenesis, his writings contain assertions that later polygenesists like Lord Kames used to argue for polygenesis (Sloan 1973: 309–10). But this is not a case of monogenesis turning into its opposite, but a case of a man holding views that clash with his most considered view.

Although Berlin fails to illustrate his thesis that certain ideas "may develop lives and powers of their own," there is a sense in which it is profoundly true. Properly understood, the thesis explains the dangerousness of the race idea. As I argue in the next section, the race idea does develop a power of its own. It is dangerous because of this power. It tends to corrupt the people who believe in it; and having corrupted them it bears, from the soil that it has thus created, evil flowers that its inventors never imagined.

III

Although the race idea was not invented to rationalize slavery, its association with morally horrendous practices is no accident. For some reason people seem to have a decided tendency to use it to rationalize some very awful crimes. This is somewhat puzzling since the rationalizations they thus offer are often full of obvious and gross logical blunders. As I have already noted, one does not have to be a rocket scientist to see that people are not justifiably enslaved or abused or exploited just because they are not as smart as other people.

Part of the solution to the puzzle is that the race idea is usually embedded in a complex system of factual, moral, and philosophical assumptions when it is used to rationalize horrendous crimes. For example, Jefferson's proposal to deport the slaves after freeing them did not depend only on his race idea. It also depended on a complex teleological view that we should leave the "gradations" in the "department of man as distinct as nature has formed them." It can also be demonstrated that certain of Kant's mistaken teleological views supported his racist contempt for nonwhite peoples.[7] But this solution to the puzzle does not get us very far. It does not show that anything morally horrendous *follows* from the race idea if it is embedded in an acceptable moral theory and factual assumptions. It only shows that certain teleological views lead to morally horrendous conclusions when combined with the race idea. So the question remains, why is the race idea so dangerous? Should we conclude that it is dangerous in the way that guns are dangerous, that is, that it is dangerous because wicked and foolish people tend to misuse it? Or is there reason to believe that it dangerous in a further sense?

7. I have made an attempt in Boxill 2003.

I believe there is. It is not simply that wicked people tend to misuse the race idea. The race idea tends to make people wicked. This is its power. The general idea is not so farfetched. The tools we use change us. We may acquire guns because we have certain personality traits, but having and using guns may cause us to develop further traits. Something similar goes on with the words and concepts we use, in particular the race idea. Once we begin to believe an idea and take it seriously, certain things start to happen to us. This is the true meaning of Berlin's claim that certain ideas may develop "powers of their own." One of the more striking powers of the race idea is to make those who believe in it gullible. Consider the teleological views that support horrendous practices when they are combined with the race idea. Some of these views are incredibly obtuse. For example, Jefferson's teleological argument for deporting the slaves (1999: 477), namely, that we should leave the "gradations" in the "department of man as distinct as nature has formed them," is, as he himself put it in rudely dismissing the poetry of Phillis Wheatley, "below the dignity of criticism."[8] There has to be some special reason why a man of Jefferson's genius countenanced that argument for a second. I believe that the race idea besotted him, and I will presently try to suggest how. Kant's more complicated views on teleology, which helped supported his contempt for nonwhites, also strain credulity, and I think that the race idea is also partly responsible for his believing them.

My argument is inspired by Rousseau. Rousseau taught that human beings develop a variety of characteristics, differing from age to age and from place to place, as a result of the inventions they make. The moderns are not only more knowledgeable than the ancients; because of the way that reason affects the passions, the needs, sentiments, virtues, and vices of the moderns differ from those of the ancients. Rousseau thought that certain inventions were pivotal. For example, the invention of language helped to make us social; the invention of metallurgy, agriculture, and the state civilized us; and the invention of property began our moral corruption. I propose that we add the invention of race to that fateful list. Its inventors may have designed it for legitimate scientific reasons, but it had terrible and unforeseen effects. First, those who believed it tended to become hardhearted to people they perceived as racially different, and this considerably reduced European compassion for the slaves. A further effect was perhaps more serious. If the reason affects the passions, the passions also affect the reason. Compassion, in particular, helps us to notice important facts about the nature, plight, and predicament of others less fortunate than ourselves. Conversely, the lack of compassion blinds us to these facts, and as Rousseau noted in his Second Discourse, we are "monsters" when we do not have pity to support our reason (1950: 161). Consequently, as Europe lost compassion for the slaves because

8. As if to add insult to insult Jefferson misspelled her name "Whately." Her first name is sometimes spelled "Phyllis."

of its invention of the race idea, it also blinded itself to the humanity and talents of the slaves, and to their suffering, and this enabled it to construct and to believe the tendentious and contrived theories it fabricated to justify enslaving them. And the process continued. These theories made Europeans even more hardhearted and even more blind, and being more blind, they began to concoct and to believe racial theories that were really preposterous. The race idea is not logically connected to the racist theories described in Gould's book, but by the process I have just described, it helped to make people gullible enough to take these stupid theories seriously. Consider too how slavery, which, of course, was not originally restricted to black people, tended to become so after the invention of the race idea. Bernasconi (2001: 11) says that the invention of idea of race "lent an air of apparent legitimacy" to the enslavement of Africans. I agree, though not for the reasons he would give. The race idea lent an air of apparent legitimacy to slavery, first by blinding people to its enormity, and then by making them gullible enough to believe the incredibly stupid rationalizations they gave for it.

David Brion Davis (1966: ix), the eminent historian of slavery, notes that slavery had "always been a source of social and psychological tension." Nevertheless it was only in the eighteenth century that a powerful *moral* opposition to slavery in the Americas developed in Europe. How were the ancients able to handle the social and psychological tensions of slavery for so long, and to practice their crime with such apparent equanimity? Davis's book is an attempt to answer this question. In it, he says, he tries to "explain the significance of a profound transformation in moral perception, a transformation that led a growing number of Europeans and Americans to see the full horror of a social evil to which mankind had been blind for centuries" (1966: 111).

One might suppose that Davis found his explanation in the Enlightenment, when, as he says, "reason unveiled the truths of nature, vindicated the rights of man, and pointed the way to human perfectibility and happiness." But he immediately and properly rejects this explanation on the ground that it was in the "age of Enlightenment that the African slave trade and the West Indian plantation enjoyed their golden years" (Davis 1966: 391). The popular response to this view is that although Europeans believed that human beings had natural rights, they denied that Africans and Native Americans were full-fledged human beings. But this response fails, for the Enlightenment philosophers who justified slavery did so, not on the ground that the slaves lacked natural rights, but on the ground that slavery was compatible with natural rights. Further, although Europeans were amazed at the appearance of Africans, it does not follow that they denied their humanity. I have already quoted Davis's observation that Europeans found non-Europeans to be "obviously human" though they were puzzled by the fact that they were so "different" (466).

For Davis (1966: 348) antislavery thought arose and grew because of the emergence of a new ethic of benevolence. This ethic had many sources in the seventeenth century, but Davis points to Francis Hutcheson as its philosopher. According to Davis (1966: 375, 378), Hutcheson's teaching that the essence of morality lay in "man's instinctive and unpremeditated compassion for his fellow creatures," not in his reason, became a "vital part of the antislavery creed" because it encouraged people to respect their compassion for the slave—a compassion that a rationalistic ethics had taught them to set aside as a sentimental distraction from the moral truths that reason laid down. But a rationalistic ethics cannot be entirely to blame for the equanimity with which, historians tell us, people practiced slavery. Slavery is necessarily cruel, and therefore always causes suffering.[9] If we were naturally disposed to pity the suffering of others, the slaveholders could not have gone about their bloody business with equanimity. It was not as if they felt compassion for their slaves and set it aside; they seemed to feel no compassion. I try to account for this by developing an important qualification Rousseau placed on the disposition to pity others. According to Rousseau (1986: 132), we have a natural repugnance, which he called pity, to seeing any being like ourselves perish or suffer. This implies that slaveholding people would have felt little pity for their slaves' suffering, and accordingly would have practiced their crime with equanimity, if they thought their slaves were not like them.

Rousseau thought that pitying others depends on seeing them to be "like ourselves" because pitying others involves "transporting ourselves outside of ourselves and identifying with the suffering animal, by leaving, as it were, our own being to take on its being" (Rousseau 1979: 224). Notice that on this account, feeling pity for someone's suffering requires more than putting oneself in his place; it also requires that one take on his "being" in imagination. This seems reasonable. Houdini will not feel the panic the claustrophobic feels in a confined space if he only puts himself imaginatively in such a place. He will feel what he would feel in a confined place, perhaps a mixture of confidence and exhilaration, and consequently will not understand how the claustrophobic suffers or feel pity for him. To feel pity for the claustrophobic he must understand how the claustrophobic suffers, and to do that he must imagine that he has the claustrophobic's frailties and then leave his own being and, in imagination, take up that of the claustrophobic.

But why must we think that others are "like" us in order to take on their being in imagination? To answer this crucial question we must answer the logically prior question of what it means to think that others are "like" us. It is obviously not necessary that we think they resemble us in every respect, nor, on the other hand, would it be sufficient that we think that they resemble us in a few superficial respects. To get a feel for the issues, consider, for example, Mary. Mary had a strict Catholic upbringing and believes that it has affected her profoundly,

9. Frederick Douglass made this point repeatedly. See for example, Douglass 1950: 154–65. The historian Kenneth Stampp (1956: 171–91) also makes the point.

making her for better or worse the person she is. On meeting others with a similar upbringing, she assumes that they were similarly affected by it. She consequently believes that while they do not resemble her in every respect, they are like her in some deep and important sense. Mary could reasonably make a similar assumption about people brought up in her own country, ethnicity, culture, language, and economic and social class, and also those of her own sex. She need not suppose that they are the passive products of the country they grew up in or that they resemble her in every way. They make different choices, and consequently make different persons of themselves. But the first and most fundamental circumstances in which we make our choices, which we generally do not choose, divide us into large classes of people who are like each other in certain respects. The French are like each other in certain respects, and so are the rich, the poor, those of the same gender, and those reared as Catholics or as Methodists.

The properties we develop because of the choices we make may be more significant morally that those we acquire because of the unchosen circumstances we grow up in, but in a certain sense, the latter go deeper. For example, it is hard to imagine Jefferson's national, regional, and cultural characteristics to be other than what they were. These seem to be fixed aspects of his identity, and a Yankee Jefferson or an English Jefferson is almost a contradiction in terms. The qualities he developed in virtue of the choices he made seem less fixed, and consequently easier to imagine being other than what they were. It is difficult to imagine the person Jefferson would have become had he released his slaves, but it is surely much more difficult than imagining him as a Yankee.

When people share the same nationality, ethnicity, and culture, each will be able to imagine herself one of the others without having to imagine away any of the most fixed aspects of her identity. Probably Jefferson could fairly easily have imagined himself Madison because they were both Virginians, male, and Southern. He would have had a much harder time imagining himself someone of a different nationality, ethnicity, gender, and culture, for this would have required that he imagine away several relatively fixed aspects of their own identity. It does not follow that we must see others as sharing these characteristics if we are to take on their being in imagination. These characteristics are not even unalterable, despite their depth and relative fixity. Immigrants become Americanized, social climbers sometimes make themselves indistinguishable from the hereditary elite, and in general people do become acculturated, sometimes very thoroughly. Supposing that what can be done in fact can also be done in imagination, it follows that people must be able to take on in imagination the being of those whose nationality, culture, and ethnicity differ from their own, and consequently may be able to pity such people.

But they do not do so very readily. National, cultural, and ethnic differences seem to provide standard excuses for people to be cruel to each other, and even more tellingly, to be so with composure. Think, for example, of the wars between highly patriotic nations, and ethnic wars everywhere. Sometimes cultural differences substitute for ethnic and national differences as barriers to pity. In the American Civil War, for example, Northerners and Southerners may not have been ethnically very different, but they were culturally different, and if this difference made it difficult for them to imagine themselves the other, neither would have felt much pity for the suffering of the other. Apparently people become so attached to their ethnic, cultural, and national characteristics that they cannot or will not exchange them, even in imagination, for different ethnic and national characteristics. This is due in part to a reluctance to part with one's own identity, even in imagination, but it may also be due to an ignorance of the nationality, ethnicity, and culture of the other, because, of course, one cannot imagine being what one does not know. If this is correct, the equanimity with which the ancients practiced slavery should occasion no surprise, given Davis's (1966: 47, 53) observation that ancient societies thought of slavery as a "degrading and contemptible condition suitable only for aliens and enemies."

It may be objected, however, that the ancients did not only enslave aliens, for the Greeks enslaved other Greeks, and more generally people are often very cruel to those of their own ethnicity, culture, and nationality. The short answer to this objection is that I never said that we cannot be cruel to those we pity. We can, if we think the gains from cruelty are high enough. My point was simply that pity makes cruelty harder. But the objection may be that people enslave and are cruel to those of their own ethnicity and nationality, and feel no more pity for them than for the aliens they enslave and abuse. Again, however, I never said that national, cultural, and ethnic differences are the only things that limit our capacity to pity others. Aesthetic differences can do so as well. For example, the fact that European culture associated blackness with evil and ugliness may explain why Martin Delany (1999: 98) could complain in 1850 that African Americans' complexion distanced them from their oppressors' sympathy although they had merged in habits with them. It may also explain why the English treated Africans more cruelly than they treated Native Americans. Nationally, culturally, and ethnically, Africans and Native Americans were both alien to the English. But the English were repulsed by the physical appearance, especially the color, of Africans, and we naturally resist imagining ourselves to be what we are repelled by.

Pity may also be limited by revulsion from what we take to be despicable moral qualities. Heroes scorn cowards because they find cowardice so repulsive that they cannot take it on even in imagination. Frederick Douglass (1987: 151) stated famously that "a man without force, is without the essential dignity of humanity. Human nature is so constituted that it cannot honor a helpless man, although it can pity him; and even this it cannot do long if the signs of power do not arise." Douglass is right if force or power is necessary for dignity, for then we must be revolted by the idea of a man without force. We consequently cannot easily imagine ourselves to be such a man, and consequently cannot pity him. Ignorance of others may be the most obvious limit on our capacity to pity them. Rousseau asked, "Why are the rich so hard toward the poor?" and answering his own question replied, "It is because they have no fear of being poor" (Rousseau 1979: 224). But here he seems to assume that the crucial condition for pitying another in distress is that one put oneself in the other's place, whereas, as I argued earlier, on his own account, the crucial condition is that one take on the other's being in imagination. If that account is correct, the rich may be without pity for the poor not only because they have no fear of being poor, but also because they are revolted by the thought of being poor. This would probably be reinforced by their ignorance of the poor, for one cannot imagine being what one does not understand. Finally, we should not forget Davis's suggestion that the ancients sometimes relied on "simulated" ethnic barriers to distance themselves from their slaves. This indicates that the ancients were not unaware of how to render themselves hardhearted, and to enslave their own people with equanimity.

If these considerations are sound, we are not disposed to pity others uniformly or according to the extent that they suffer, as the ethic of benevolence may suggest. We are disposed to pity others to the extent that we see them as having properties and characteristics we can easily imagine ourselves having. Normally these are limited to those of our own nation, ethnicity, and culture. But we need not pity the sufferings of even such people. If they have qualities we find it difficult to imagine ourselves having, whether because we do not understand these qualities or because we find them repulsive, morally or aesthetically, we may manage to enslave or abuse them with composure. It may even be the case, as Douglass suggests, that cruelty that is at first inflicted with pity can become cruelty that is inflicted without pity, if the victims do not resist their tormentors. If we find such compliance so repulsive that we cannot imagine ourselves similarly submissive, we will cease to pity them, and may even come to despise them.

Let us now see how the invention of the race idea erected yet another barrier to compassion. When Kant invented the idea of race and made whites the superior race, Europeans made their membership in that race central to their identities. This was not simply because they enjoyed thinking of themselves as superior. It is because membership in a superior group gave them an unconditional ground for their self-esteem, and self-esteem is necessary for fulfillment and happiness. It may be objected that the proper ground for self-esteem is personal achievement and that only people who are failures substitute membership in a superior group for it. But people bolster their self-esteem by membership in a superior group whether or not this is the "proper" way to do it. Whites are proud because they are white although they can take absolutely no personal credit for being white, and abject failures feel good about themselves because they are related to aristocrats. Further, it is not true that only failures cherish their membership in a superior group as a way to bolster their self-esteem. All of us develop an unrelenting desire for self-esteem because we feel so disillusioned when it is undermined, and although we may at first seek to ground it on personal achievement, learning how uncertain this is, we are all drawn to the unconditional ground of membership in a biologically superior group.

If I am right about this, then given the strength of our desire for self-esteem, membership in a race alleged to be superior will be treasured as a pearl of great price, and those lucky enough to possess it will think of it as the thing that makes them who they are essentially, and as among the deepest and most fixed aspects of their identity. Once this happens they will find it difficult to feel compassion for the people of the other races. There are two main reasons for this. First, as I argued earlier, when people are strongly attached to certain of their characteristics, they naturally shrink from imagining these characteristics away. But the members of a superior race will necessarily be strongly attached to their membership in that race, because only if they are so attached will they have an unconditional basis for their self-esteem. Consequently they will shrink from even imagining themselves to be the members of another inferior race, and will feel no compassion for them. Second, as I also argued earlier, all of us shrink from supposing, even in imagination, that we have characteristics we despise. But those who think of themselves as members of a superior race will naturally despise the characteristics of races they consider inferior, and for this reason too they will not usually imagine themselves to be the members of the inferior races, or consequently feel any pity for them.

The ideas of other collectivities like the nation, ethnic group, and tribe are dangerous too, and for some of the same reasons as the race idea. But the idea of race is more objectionable. National feeling encourages trust, cooperation, and altruism among the citizens of a state, and these help the state to establish domestic justice and welfare. Similarly, although the plurality of ethnicities presents the modern state with serious challenges, it has good consequences as well, providing the society with a variety of viewpoints that is both stimulating and helpful to finding and appreciating the truth. Moreover, people normally are drawn to their ethnic groups and to their nations because of a desire to belong. This desire need not be a desire for a ground for self-esteem, but simply a desire to be among like-minded people and in circumstances that one knows, understands, and finds congenial. As W. E. B. Du Bois noted, belonging gives one "a social world and mental peace." The desire for membership in a race is not a desire to belong in this sense. It is not a desire to be among like-minded people who share circumstances they understand and find congenial. It is a desire to have an unconditional ground for self-esteem, and since only membership in a superior race will provide such a ground, it necessarily constrains compassion. Finally, the race idea is more dangerously exclusive than the national idea. Immigrants can become members of a nation (and not merely of a state) even if they share no ancestors with the natives. But a definitive feature of a race is that its members share ancestors. A person cannot be European if any of his ancestors come from Africa. If one's ancestors help make one the person one is, this means that a European can imagine himself to be African only if he can perform the difficult task of imagining that his ancestors are entirely different from what he knows them to be.

Philosophers have been trying strenuously, but not I think very convincingly, to prove that there are no such things as races. Their object is not to disabuse the public of a harmless falsehood, but to relieve it of a dangerous belief. Strangely, however, they have not tried to show how and why the idea of race is dangerous. Perhaps they assume that it must be dangerous because of its association with horrendous crimes, or because they mistakenly believe that it was invented for evil purposes. In any case, on the ground that we must understand the disease before we can prescribe a cure, I have attempted in this chapter to explain why the idea of race is dangerous. I have suggested that it is dangerous because it limits our compassion or sympathy for those of other races, thereby facilitating the fabrication of vicious and preposterous theories about such people, and making us gullible enough to believe these theories. I think I have given some reasons for taking the first part of this claim seriously, namely, that the idea of race limits our capacity for compassion. Unfortunately, I have not had the space to argue for the second part.[10] I can therefore only make some cursory remarks about how we should deal with the race idea. The standard strategy now is evidently to try to persuade people not to believe in it. But if I am right that the race idea is dangerous because it makes us gullible, and inclined to believe foolish rationalizations, another strategy might be to be take such rationalizations more seriously; the race idea may make us gullible, but it cannot make us invincibly credulous. I hope, however, that I have said enough to persuade philosophers to spend less time arguing that there are no races, and more time exploring the dangerousness of the race idea.

10. I have tried to show how fear affects our perceptions and theorizing in Boxill 1993: 713–44.

11 : UPSIDE-DOWN EQUALITY
A RESPONSE TO KANTIAN THOUGHT

My belief is not just that all social and political arrangements so far devised are unsatisfactory. . . . But there is a deeper problem—not merely practical, but theoretical: We do not yet possess an acceptable political ideal . . .
     —*Thomas Nagel,* Equality and Impartiality
Where, then, is it most appropriate to locate the cut-off point between a moral and an immoral life?
     —*Kurt Baier,* The Moral and Social Order

A Story from South Africa. Benjamin is a white South African. He was born, raised, and educated in South Africa. LT met Benjamin around 1994 while Benjamin was on a postdoctoral fellowship in the United States. Upon finishing the fellowship, Benjamin went on to do some teaching at an American college. But he longed for his homeland. LT certainly had no trouble understanding this, though he grasped, however vaguely, that things could be difficult for a white in South Africa. Benjamin secured a position at one of South Africa's flagship universities; and LT had the pleasure of visiting him in 1997 as the Kovler Lecturer for one of South Africa's medical schools.

Naturally enough, Benjamin invited LT to give a lecture to his philosophy class. As LT walked into the class, he was caught completely off guard. For this philosophy class was unlike any other that LT had ever taught at a major university: Of the two hundred or so students, only a handful were white. So very many thoughts went through LT's mind as he found his way to a seat, but one of them was "So this is what Benjamin wanted to come back to!" He wanted to come back to South Africa and teach students the vast majority of whom would be black—or at least not white.

I am grateful to Michael Levine and Lawrence Blum for initial comments on this essay, and Tamas Pataki for helping me to fine-tune points. A special word of thanks goes to Howard McGary, who not only commented upon this essay but has encouraged me throughout my career to pursue the relationship between meta-ethics and race. My biggest debt of gratitude, however, goes to Sébastien Baron, a Parisian café waiter, who was the sounding board for a number of arguments presented herein as I endeavored to be mindful in my arguments about non-American cultures. The example of eating dog flesh was inspired by him in our discussion of foods that the French consume and the ways of labeling them.

LT was not naïve about the racial composition of the country of South Africa. LT was well aware both of the fact that the vast majority of its citizens are black and of the fact that apartheid had ended. Still, it never entered LT's head that the overwhelming majority of the students would be black. No doubt Benjamin deserves some credit for this. He never articulated his desire to return to South Africa in terms of some redemptive mission, or a wish to make up for past wrongs done by whites to blacks. Nor did he ever hint at concerns about adjusting to the new South Africa, one in which he is governed by blacks: upside-down equality (as I shall refer to it). Benjamin wanted to go home, and he articulated that desire as any person from a thriving and stable first-tier country (Germany or Japan, for instance) might have done. In any case, the one thought that immediately struck LT as both obvious and sublime is that Benjamin has a more profound sense of equality than he (LT) has.

I. THE PARAMETERS OF THE ARGUMENT

At the outset, two preliminary remarks are in order regarding the story from South Africa. First, I shall take Benjamin to be representative of the attitude of many whites who voluntarily chose to remain in South Africa knowing that predominantly black rule would be established, where their reason for staying is that South Africa is their home. I am thinking here of whites who could have gone elsewhere, owing to their having the means, skills, or contacts to do so, but who refrained. Hence, I do not have in mind whites who begrudgingly stayed because, in terms of resources, they were too ill-prepared to leave.

On the other hand, I shall take LT's experience to be representative of a person born, raised, and educated in a society that is governed by whites. LT has the sensibilities of a typical American, in this instance, who believes in racial equality, which, crudely put, can be characterized as follows. Skin color or ethnic identity is morally irrelevant per se and, in any case, no race has a lock on intellectual talent or moral wherewithal; accordingly, insofar as there are differences along these lines that track this or that racial or ethnic group, these differences admit either of some social explanation or an explanation of personal choice (or some combination thereof). In fact, from an evolutionary point of view the very idea of race is intellectually bankrupt. It is human beings that have endowed skin color, and other physical features, with the deep social significances that they now have.

One might think that LT was simply not being logical enough in working through the information available to him regarding South Africa and Benjamin's teaching. After all, whom would Benjamin be teaching if not mostly blacks, a conclusion that simple syllogistic reasoning yields, since apartheid had ended and the vast majority of South Africa's citizens are black? However, there are various reasons for why we do not think through things; and sometimes these reasons are a comment not so much on our inferential powers or lack thereof as on the background assumptions that have a hold upon our lives. The way we routinely experience the world does not just yield a probabilistic set of expectations, it also yields at the very minimum a view about what is normal under the circumstances in question; and sometimes it yields a view about what is both normal and good.

Thus, many people think that it is only "natural" that a man should be president of the United States—and not just that it is statistically likely that a man will be president. Many people think this although some of the most impressive leaders in recent history have been women: Golda Meir of Israel and Margaret Thatcher of England. A major university with mostly black students simply does not exist in either Europe or North America. This truth could be merely a statistical point: most major universities have had mostly white students; therefore, it is highly probable and reasonable to suppose that this major university will have mostly white students. Or it could represent a deep visceral association, however unintended, between whiteness, major universities, and intellectual talent. For LT it is the latter, which may reflect something shameful about him. I would hold that the same goes for most people born and raised in either Europe or North America. For LT, equality comes with a certain configuration: equality in a society governed by whites. And this, I submit, is how most people similarly raised and acculturated think of equality.

The locution "a society governed by such and such Ethnic People" is to be understood here as purely descriptive and in the broad sense that these Ethnic People are the primary holders of most of the basic positions in all the basic institutions in society, including fiduciary ones. The exception would be familial and religious institutions. I shall simplify things by talking in terms of whites and blacks. But, of course, this is not the only color or ethnic divide over which issues of racism arise.

The second preliminary remark is this. I hold that in an unjust social context (and only an unjust one), a society governed by a given Ethnic People (EP) creates a visceral emotional resonance regarding the Good that favors the governing EP, where the Good ranges over numerous things including intelligence, strength of character, emotional stability, and so forth. So if in society S, the EP who govern are Xs, then a visceral emotional resonance between X-ness and goodness, which favors Xs, is inculcated in the lives of those born and raised in S, whether those born and raised in S are Xs or not. And where a visceral emotional resonance exists, then so do expectations about suitability for holding a position. Thus, where a visceral emotional resonance exists a default mode is created in terms of suitability and expectations. So if Xs are the governing people, then certain behavior on the part of Xs will be seen as reasonable or reflecting becoming social posture simply because they are Xs, and the same behavior on the part of non-Xs will be seen as unreasonable or reflecting unbecoming social posture simply because they are non-Xs. For example, it was certainly true in the past that a certain amount of aggressive behavior on the part of high-powered men was taken as not only the norm but appropriate, whereas like behavior on the part of women equally positioned was seen as unbecoming. A no-nonsense man was strong; a no-nonsense woman was bitchy. Of course, in a society ruled by Xs, there can always be a Y who not only governs but who gains the admiration of Xs generally. As is well known, however, exceptions of this sort prove the rule.

Importantly, visceral emotional resonances may so define our default line and our conception of what should be (that is, what we take to be normal) that alternatives simply do not occur to us. An interesting example in this regard is that of waiters in Paris. Although the population of Paris is extremely ethnically diverse, the vast majority of servers (garçons) in the immensely popular Parisian cafés are white males ranging in age from their early twenties to at least their middle fifties. I do not know the explanation for this; and I do not think racism is the explanation. I have never heard anyone complain about the matter. At any rate, with regard to the point at hand, what is most striking is that many Parisians who are extremely open-minded with respect to matters of race have failed to notice this; and are quite surprised when I bring it to their attention—initially thinking that I must be mistaken only to concur upon reflection. There are no malicious sentiments at play here, and so nothing that might be called unconscious racism. In fact, it was not until approximately three years ago that I had this realization. As a default expectation, this social phenomenon seems to be as pervasive as the expectation that one drives on this or that side of the road. (As an aside, the problem of a visceral emotional resonance favoring an EP is compounded mightily if the governing EP over many societies is the same group or can be readily seen as such from a certain vantage point.)

I shall not defend these remarks about visceral emotional resonance (VER).[1] They strike me as obvious. Indeed, the idea of visceral emotional resonance favoring the EP who govern is based upon the innocuous assumption that moral and social sensibilities are shaped by the cultural environment in which we live. VERs, taken in and of themselves, are neither morally good nor bad. Most human beings have a VER with respect to their parents, and that, generally speaking, is a good thing. Some people have a VER with respect to Jews and money, holding that Jews some how have an innate talent for getting money out of non-Jews; and that is a bad thing. This VER can, in fact, masquerade as a false positive: Jews are really good at handling money. But, as it happens, one holds that

---

1. This terminology, especially a false positive VER, was inspired by Lawrence Blum's wonderful book *I'm Not a Racist, But . . . : The Moral Quandary of Race*. See Blum 2002, esp. chap. 7.

this is so only because they have an innately corrupt character. Or, to take a different group, someone could hold that no one can sing like blacks. But, then again, the person holds that singing is just about all that they can do well. Asians have been stereotyped as being good in mathematics, but in a way that all but invites one to turn a deaf ear to the Asian poet.

Returning to the experiences of Benjamin and LT: My view is that their respective experiences present a problem for Kantian thought. For if I am right that Benjamin has a more profound sense of equality than LT does, then precisely the problem is that Kantian thought cannot explain how this can be so. The reason for this is that when it comes to equality, subjective experiences are more important than Kantian thought seems to allow. What is more, the idea of equality is much richer than is generally allowed. Or so I shall argue in both cases.

Benjamin is a person of admirable moral character, with a firm commitment to racial equality; and LT would certainly like to think that the same holds for him. The relevant fundamental difference between Benjamin and LT regarding racial sensibilities is that Benjamin is living the experience of being governed by blacks. Of course, all morally decent whites throughout the world believe in racial equality.[2] But with the exception of those whites who chose to remain in South Africa after the end of apartheid, most whites do not have the experience of being governed by blacks. More important, most whites do not even entertain this state of affairs when they think of racial equality. Nor, quite significantly, do most blacks who were born and raised, and who have remained, in a society governed mostly by whites. Take the United States, where there are lots of public and private institutions of higher education. When a black or white American thinks of a flagship university, she thinks of a predominantly white university, where most of the students, faculty, and administration are white. And a white or black

2. As Monique Canto-Sperber (2003: 89) remarked: "On observe, au sein de nos cultures occidentales, une très grande unanimité sur un petit noyau de principes moraux. Ces principes forment le cadre stable par rapport auquel il est possible de répondre à des questions normatives. Ils ont trait, en gros, au respect dû à la personne humaine, au refus de profiter de la faiblesse d'autrui, à l'obligation de traiter également les personnes, quels que soient leur race, leur religion, leur nationalité ou leur sexe." [There exists, as a part of the very fabric of Western cultures, considerable unanimity surrounding a small nexus of moral principles, which form a stable framework for answering normative questions. By and large, these moral principles are concerned with basic respect for human beings such as the impropriety of taking advantage of the weaknesses of others and the obligation to treat others equally regardless of their race, religion, nationality, or sex.] She goes on to add that while we can endlessly debate the basis for the justification of these principles, it remains true nonetheless that "ils soient considérés par l'immense majorité d'entre nous comme *des points fixes, intangibles, qui ne vacillent pas*" [they are considered by the vast of majority of individuals among us as fixed and intangible points that do not change] (89; emphasis added).

in pursuit of academic success will want to be at a predominantly white university.

So Benjamin knows by way of experience something that LT does not know about racial equality, namely, that he, Benjamin, believes in and personally (as opposed to just intellectually) accepts upside-down equality. As I have said, this presents a problem for Kantian thought; and I shall use Barbara Herman's marvelous essay "Integrity and Impartiality" to illustrate this difficulty (1993).[3] This essay has struck me as particularly relevant because Herman introduces an important piece of technical apparatus to facilitate Kantian thought, one that is very much in keeping with what I have called visceral emotional resonance. In introducing this technical apparatus, one of Herman's aims was to make subjective experiences more relevant to Kantian thought than many would suppose is allowed. Most arguments against Kant in this regard have revolved around personal relationships. Her technical apparatus takes us beyond that. Still, the point that I wish to make is that at times more subjectivity is needed than even her argument allows, though her very aim has been to introduce subjectivity without compromising the Categorical Imperative procedure. There is a difference between moral knowledge in the ideal world—the Kingdom of Ends, if you will—and moral knowledge in the nonideal world; and Kantian scholarship has not attended sufficiently to this truth, and so to matters of moral correction in the nonideal world. In fact, moral philosophy in general has not. Everyone seems to be arguing about what we should do, without much thought to why it happens that we live in a world wherein so many fail to do what they should do. Thomas Nagel (1991) seems to be at least mindful of this tension, likewise for Kurt Baier (1993) and Annette Baier (1995). Alasdair MacIntyre (1999) is also doing very interesting work in this regard.[4]

The argument of this essay has an obvious kinship with the views of Bernard Williams (1981), Michael Stocker (1976), and Lawrence Blum (1980). Just so, I do not know whether any of these authors would be happy with the particular line of thought that I develop here. These individuals have argued that the affective is an ineliminable part of the moral life, even when it comes to explaining the proper motivational structure of moral behavior. Essentially, I am interested in

---

3. In this essay Herman defends Kant against the view that emotions can have no place in moral behavior. I wish to point out that in her Tanner Lectures (Herman 1998), Herman extends her theory of Kant's moral philosophy by introducing the idea of a "new moral fact." Her aim, however, is not to revise the concept of Rules of Moral Salience as she uses it in the essay under discussion. In fact, the concept is not at the center of her Tanner Lectures. Though I have reason to believe that she has some sympathy with the criticisms I raise regarding rules of moral salience, I cannot say how she would revise the concept were that her project.

4. In Nagel 1991 see especially chapter 3; in Baier 1995, her essays on trust.

the role of the affective as it pertains to experiencing the other as having equal moral worth,[5] and not what is constitutive of the proper motivational structure of moral behavior. Herman's essay, which no doubt was intended to deflect some of the criticisms of the three authors just mentioned, also provides a remarkable framework for the concern that I wish to raise.

II. MORAL SALIENCE

Herman introduces the extraordinarily fecund idea of Rules of Moral Salience (RMS), as a way of explicating the employment of the Categorical Imperative. On her account, RMS are not, themselves, part of the Categorical Imperative. She explicitly remarks that "the C[atgegorical] I[imperative] procedure can function without RMS" (Herman 1993: 78). What is more, she insists that RMS do not have moral weight, although they let "the agent see where moral judgment is necessary" (78). The Rules of Moral Salience "enable [the agent] to pick out those elements of his circumstances or of his proposed actions that require moral attention" (77). Our moral sensitivity, she tells us, is anchored by RMS. The Rules of Moral Salience represent the background sensibilities that individuals bring to moral situations. I would say that RMS are intimately tied to VERs, in that the former are the cognitive basis for the latter. RMS, then, seem to bring much-needed subjectivity to Kantian thought. Persons are not merely making a priori judgments using the CI-procedure, but judgments richly informed by her or his subjective experiences as delivered by Rules of Moral Salience, as delivered by the moral education and socialization of the person's culture. Though I am doubtful that RMS can be as shorn of moral weight as Herman suggests, I shall allow this point for the sake of argument.[6]

Let me illustrate her thesis about RMS with an example. Take the moral imperative to tell the truth that the CI procedure is traditionally thought to require. As we all know, however, there are many ways to tell the truth. Indeed, one can be quite vindictive in one's truth telling. At any rate, telling the truth to a young adolescent dripping with insecurities is one thing, whereas telling the truth to a seasoned and successful middle-aged adult is quite another. The proper way to

5. I have drawn attention to this in two other essays: Thomas 2001a and Thomas 2001b.

6. I have challenged Herman's claim in Thomas 2003. In that essay I have distinguished between constitutive wrongs and phenomenological wrongs. Even if all wrongs are delivered to us by the Categorical Imperative, it does not follow from this consideration alone that we thereby understand the nature of all wrongs. Some things, and not just some wrongs, seem to require experience for their comprehension. Imagine someone claiming to understand fully the sex act owing to having read much that has been written on the subject. The person would strike us as woefully naïve.

go about telling the truth in each case along with our sensibilities here are delivered by the RMS society, although in each case the CI procedure yields the conclusion that we should tell the truth.

On Herman's view, it seems that we should think of RMS as a means to the end of acting in accordance with the CI procedure. Hence, it is not so much that they give us moral knowledge as it is that they help to implement the moral knowledge that the CI procedure delivers to us. Thus, recall her remark, to which I drew attention earlier, that the Categorical Imperative can function without Rules of Moral Salience. For Herman, then, what is significant about RMS is that they allow us to employ our subjective experiences as delivered by socialization without corrupting, as it were, the source of our moral knowledge, namely, the Categorical Imperative. Thus, a place is made for the affective in the Kantian scheme.

If RMS allow a link between our moral knowledge and the affective, without corrupting the former, then a certain kind of ongoing criticism of Kantian ethics, namely, that it does not allow for the affective, is at least diffused, if not met entirely. The affective is an ineliminable part of our moral education, and therefore so too is our grasp of what should be of moral concern to us, though, strictly speaking, the affective has no place in the actual application of the Categorical Imperative. That is, although acts of right and wrong are not determined by the affective, the affective rightly informs our behavior.

This is a philosophically beautiful move. One could debate whether RMS give sufficient weight to the affective, or whether they allow for the affective at the right moral juncture. And so on. But that would be another essay. I need to introduce one more aspect of Herman's account. She tells us that Rules of Moral Salience may be erroneous in two ways: they may be reasonable and innocent, or they may be erroneous in ways that are neither reasonable nor innocent (1993: 89–91); hence, we have culpability. She offers Nazi society as an example of the latter: "It is not as if individual Nazis were in no position to see (because of impoverishment of culture or upbringing, say) who was and who wasn't a person or didn't know . . . what kinds of things it was morally permissible to do to persons" (91). Herman does not offer an example of RMS that are reasonable and innocent, but here is one. Contrast the view that many of us now have regarding dolphins—namely, they are quite intelligent mammals—with the view that the ancient Greeks, including the master taxonomist Aristotle himself, must have had regarding dolphins—namely, they are simply large fish. The ancient Greeks were in error, yet their error was reasonable and innocent. Given the best scientific evidence of the time, the conclusion that dolphins were mammals of some intelligence was highly unwarranted. The difference between these two views also entails a difference in moral attitudes, as we think that it is wrong to kill dolphins (as opposed to mere fish) merely for food consumption.

Additionally, Herman holds that in different societies the RMS may be nonidentical, although the rules from each society may overlap in their content. In

1940, for example, the RMS of Nazi Germany were not completely identical to the RMS of either Canadian or American societies (the prevalence of anti-Semitism in these societies notwithstanding), since the society of Nazi Germany, unlike the latter two, was committed to exterminating the Jews. All the same, these three societies held similar moral views concerning marriage and child rearing. If so, then there would be overlap in the content of the RMS of these societies.

Together, the considerations in the preceding two paragraph entail that (1) RMS may vary across societies and (2) in any given society, RMS may be (a) erroneous but reasonable and innocent or (b) erroneous without being reasonable and innocent. In the case of (2a), Herman holds that while agents who come to the Categorical Imperative with such RMS are guilty of moral failure, they are not guilty of moral fault. Such individuals miss the moral mark, though through no fault of their own. She tells us that "not all ways of failing to act as morality requires (in a strict sense) are morally equivalent" (1993: 89). And perhaps this is as it should be; for omniscience is not a condition of moral agency, as Herman notes (1993: 89).

III. MORAL AND PERSONAL SOCIAL EQUALITY

As Herman observed, the Nazis could have hardly excused their behavior on the grounds that they did not grasp that Jews were human beings. Indeed, this point seems to hold with respect to any two human beings. As I noted in *Vessels of Evil* (Thomas 1993), no one has ever in an eye-to-eye encounter supposed that she or he was interacting with a person when, in fact, the being in question was an animal (or conversely).

Now, of course, the wrongs that the Nazis committed presupposed no other knowledge than that the Jews were human beings. The Nazis could not help but experience the Jews as persons. More precisely, the subjective experiences of Nazis made it unquestionably clear that the Jews were persons. This truth, though, does not entail another truth, namely, that the Nazis could not help but experience the Jews as thoroughgoing equals. The logic of personhood is not such that inescapably experiencing a person as a person thereby entails experiencing that person as a thoroughgoing equal. Experiencing another as a thoroughgoing equal entails experiencing the other both as having equal moral worth and as a personal social index (PSI) equal. Minimally, person Alpha regards person Beta as a PSI-equal if Alpha regards Beta as worthy qua individual of the quality of life that she, Alpha, lives or even a higher quality of life; and Alpha regards individuals *qua* members of a group as PSI equals if Alpha would think this way regarding individuals of the group randomly chosen, where nothing is known about the randomly chosen individual save that she or he is a member of the group in question. Hence, we can distinguish between individual

PSI-equality (this or that person is my PSI-equal) and group PSI-equality (these belonging to that group are my PSI-equal). Ideally, one wants PSI-equality across racial and ethnic racial groups. Just so, there is no formal incompatibility at all in thinking of a group of people as having equal moral worth (vis-à-vis oneself), in the strict Kantian sense of that term, but not as one's social equal, just as there is no formal incompatibility in thinking of two people as having equal moral worth but as being neither intellectual equals nor physical equals. Thus, and this gets to the heart of the matter, it is possible to condemn egregious moral wrongs committed against a people without at all having the sense that these very same individuals are, or should be, one's PSI-equals. Presently, I shall say more about this in reference to Kant's own thought.

As I am understanding it, PSI-equality refers not so much to moral behavior as to lifestyle, accomplishments, and the viscerally desirous (the images, experiences, and hopes that resonate with one in a very positive way). The person one dreams of marrying or the career one dreams of having constitutes a part of the viscerally desirous. Thus, a person could be indignant over the murder of individuals who belong to a certain group, though the thought of marrying someone from this group simply cannot obtain a purchase upon his life. Nor does he believe that persons from this group are, on the whole, as capable as those from his group of socially and intellectually admirable pursuits. No one has ever interpreted Kantian moral theory as requiring that we be open to marrying someone regardless of the group to which the person belongs, or as requiring that we be open to seeing members of another group as equally talented. Kantian arguments show, perhaps with great clarity and force, that we must not wrong others and that we must come to their aid, regardless of their physical features or religious convictions. But this is, in fact, a long way from requiring that we want them to be a part of our lives personally or from requiring that we regard them as our intellectual or social equals. Indeed, there is a sense in which one shows greater Kantian rectitude, if you will, in the moral treatment of precisely those individuals whom one would never put on the same PSI-plane as oneself. After all, there is a fraternity that operates between equals that does not operate between unequals.

This brings us to upside-down equality. One might have thought that a person who is committed to equality would be indifferent to the racial composition of those governing, just so long as they do their jobs competently. It is easy to deceive ourselves into thinking that we are indifferent because there is always the exceptional black, for instance—and most would not mind if that person ruled or if others blacks ruled just so long as they were sufficiently like this exceptional black. Unfortunately, this is just the point. In modern times, whites have governed in all first-tier societies; and lots of these whites—the vast majority, in fact—have been ever so ordinary, exhibiting poor reasoning and behaving in quite indefensible ways.

Most people, white or black, are not exceptional. There are the Winston Churchills, the Colin Powells, the Golda Meirs, the Margaret Thatchers, the Theodore Roosevelts, and the Nelson Mandelas. And most people, whether black or white, are not the equal of any of these in abilities realized. All the same, whites do not fix upon the exceptional white, and then intone that it is all right for whites to govern just so long as the other governing whites are like this exceptionally good one. To be committed to upside-down equality in the case of blacks and whites is to be committed to ordinary blacks, with all their foibles, governing. It is simply disingenuous to point to Mandela, say, as proof that one has no trouble with blacks governing, just as it is disingenuous to point to Albert Einstein as proof that one has no trouble with people not finishing high school.

In particular, it should be observed that a commitment to treating people as having equal moral worth does not entail a commitment to upside-down equality, because it does not entail a commitment to PSI-equality. In terms of PSI-equality, upside-down equality essentially speaks to the conviction that we judge blacks to be worthy of being in charge of things, both tangible and intangible, that bear upon our lives in both foreseeable and unforeseeable ways. Well, just as a person who would never murder blacks, and who would abhor anyone who did, need not want them to be a part of her or his life, most people who would not murder blacks would be uncomfortable living in a social context of upside-down equality, where for the most part blacks are in charge of things that bear upon their lives. One can read what has just been written as a claim about whites. This, though, would be a mistake. That is the point of the LT story: It is also true of most blacks raised in Western societies that they do not envision upside-down equality when they talk about equality.

I have just a made claim regarding Kantian thought that many will regard as most counterintuitive—so much so that many will think that there is a "not" where one is not supposed to be. Not so, however. It is my view that in the non-ideal world equal moral worth in the strict Kantian sense of that term does not entail a commitment to upside-down equality. Herman is quite right in noting that we do not need experience as such in order to grasp that it is wrong to lie or steal or kill another. But, alas, the judgment that someone is fit to govern our lives or fit to marry makes no sense independent of experience. So the judgment that we should not wrong another does not carry in its wake the judgment that we should accept being governed by that person or accept that person as our spouse. This cannot be the case by the very argument that Kantian scholars have advanced, namely, that moral behavior must be such that it could be a universal maxim (see, e.g., O'Neil 1975, Darwall 1983). This test was intended to show that the fundamental moral precepts flow from the very nature of our humanity.

Kant most certainly did not think it followed from the nature of our humanity that all persons were equally fit to govern or to marry one another or to form other ties with one another. Nor did he think himself committed to such a view on account of his argument about the moral worth of all persons. In his essay "Observations on the Feelings of the Beautiful and the Sublime," Kant makes it clear that he takes blacks to be intellectually inferior: "So fundamental is the difference between [the Negro and White] races of man, and it appears to be as great in regard to mental capacities as in color . . ." I am not at all interested in whether Kant's remarks should be an embarrassment or whether they admit of an exculpatory explanation. The only point I wish to make is that these remarks are consistent with his general moral theory. For presumably, intellectually deprived individuals should be treated as having equal moral worth. It is just as wrong to steal from or lie to the intellectually bereft as it is to steal from or lie to anyone else. Surely, then, Kant himself could not have thought that treating all persons as having equal moral worth entailed a commitment to upside-down equality, since upside-down equality entails a judgment about who is fit to govern. Accordingly, Kant scholars are right to observe that Kant's moral theory is hardly felled by the remark quoted above. Nonetheless, they are wrong in failing to notice the poignant implication of this remark, when taken seriously: namely, that equal moral worth à la Kant does not entail PSI-equality; hence, it does not entail upside-down equality.[7] You may have Kantian respect for me without, on any number of fronts, thinking that I am your equal.

IV. EQUALITY AND RULES OF MORAL SALIENCE

It will be recalled that according to Barbara Herman, RMS fine-tune our moral sensibilities and give us insight into how to implement our moral obligations. This sounds innocuous enough. We all need insight into how to live our lives and to do what is morally right. And it is quite obvious that so much of that insight comes from the lessons that were part of the fabric of our upbringing— not so much what we went to school to learn, but what we attribute to commonsense. Recall, also, that she holds that RMS can be erroneous in two ways. We have an innocent RMS mistake when, owing to no fault of our own, we simply got the facts wrong and both our behavior and sensibilities reflect this. We have a culpable RMS mistake, by contrast, when we have practices that ignore important moral considerations. What I want to draw attention to is the idea that when it comes to equality RMS may be erroneous by being substantially un-

---

7. Fortunately, Blum 2002 does not ignore Kant here, nor does Goldberg 1993. See also Mills 1997. Kant's theory is not felled by his remarks quoted above. Yet, if I am right, then there are serious limitations to the "rational pull" about which Christine Korsgaard writes (1996). As a white, I may loathe the idea of killing a black man even as I loathe the highly educated, well-off black man who wishes to marry my daughter. There is no noose of formal inconsistency here to hang around my neck.

derinformed—not because one failed to be attentive to the relevant considerations, but because it would not have been possible to be attentive to the relevant considerations in the just the right way in the absence of being in the appropriate context.

Being underinformed is a factor in many areas of life. For example, everyone knows that rape is wrong.[8] But it is women who understandably have a special sensibility to rape. It is not so much that there are more facts to which men should attend or better attend, though this is undoubtedly true in some instances. Rather, it is that being a man generally precludes one from being in the relevant context. Both women and men may fear for their lives while walking down the street at night. However, with rare exception, it is only women who are warranted in having the additional fear of being sexually violated. No amount of empathy or sympathy will warrant this latter fear on the part of men. Being a woman is a defining feature of the context. Accordingly, there are sensibilities that women have regarding male behavior that men do not have.

So in the case of understanding the wrong of rape, there is a subjective element that is not captured by the rules of moral salience as Herman has envisaged them. This is why in the matter of rape men generally owe women what I have elsewhere (Thomas 1998) called moral deference. Without listening to women, most men simply could not grasp the angst of rape that concerns women. This would be so even if most men dressed like women and walked the streets alone at night. For even if that deception were convincing, there is the act of rape itself; and the deception would be exposed soon enough by the biological facts; and this revelation would extinguish the desire to rape the man dressed as a woman, even if other forms of violence were occasioned by the deception.

Though sexual violence may be the most intuitive example of a subjective element not captured by RMS, because these rules are under informed. However, it is not the only one. Another example is the devastation that often comes with a single instance of marital infidelity. The offending party did no physical harm to the spouse; and it often turns out that there was no emotional attachment to the person with whom the offense was committed—it was an instance of the proverbial one-night stand. Yet, a few hours of adultery can entirely unravel a marriage, causing pain that only someone who has experienced the same kind of betrayal can fully fathom.

Now, equality would seem to be quite unlike any of the above examples. This is because ineliminable differences are ineliminably relevant in each of these

8. Though males can be raped, the discussion of rape that follows focuses upon the rape of females. In a heterosexually oriented society, female victims of rape have a particularly poignant problem with normalizing sexual relations again. I am grateful to Marcia Baron and Thomas Wartenberg for insisting that I mention this. The sexual violation of children is a different matter entirely. See Thomas 1996: 144–67.

cases. With equality, on the other hand, precisely what we hold to be true is that race and ethnicity are irrelevant—or at least not relevant in the way that they are now. What is more, in the ideal world, this would be the case. But none of us has ever lived in that world. And in the real world, blackness and whiteness are not just color options. Rather, they are imbued with all sorts of significance ranging across all aspects of life: from a look of innocence to the appearance of physical attractiveness; from default assumptions regarding intelligence to our willingness to give the other a vote of confidence; and, in particular, from assumptions regarding moral wherewithal to assumptions regarding worthiness of one's subordination.

Following Herman's account, we can say that skin color came to have these unsavory significances shaping our moral sensibilities, owing to erroneous and non-innocent Rules of Moral Salience being in place. The problem is that the nonideal world in which skin color is so profoundly imbued with unsavory meanings has ill prepared us for the ideal one in which skin color is shorn of these meanings. For one thing, these unsavory meanings have an emotional imprimatur upon our lives in ways that are often imperceptible. For another, these unsavory meanings often define the norm and so do not, in the first place, strike us as a bias that needs to be addressed.

In other words, as a result of the erroneous RMS, there is a set of visceral emotional resonances well in place. One consequence of these VERs is that often enough blacks are not "felt" to measure up to whites in terms of PSI-equality, even as the ideal of equality is embraced. There is no ideological commitment in place to holding that blacks actually are inferior. And one holds in principle that they are not. Rather, it is that one's subjective sense of them is such that one rarely experiences a black as one's equal. And in the name of wanting to do the right thing regarding blacks, what often happens is the following: one feels a reason to be cautious, to scrutinize further, all the while being completely open to the possibility that this black shall be the right one; yet, no black in fact ever turns out to be the right one; hence, the status quo is maintained. The surprise, if that is the word for it, is that judgments here often reveal a bias.

As I have allowed, Kantian thought shows clearly and forcefully that one must acknowledge, at some level or the other, the humanity of other persons. This, of course, certainly seems to require some experience with human beings. A human being who never interacted with another human being, having been raised entirely by Martians (say), would not be very good at being responsive to the weal and woe of human beings. This seems to vindicate Herman's concern to give Kantian thought a very human face, as opposed to fixing upon the human self as a rational creature. And once this move is allowed, then certainly the details of society are relevant, which gets us to Herman's Rules of Moral Salience, in particular.

The problem, however, comes with correcting for the moral damage caused by erroneous RMS and the visceral emotional resonances to which they have given rise. As I have indicated, it is a striking feature of Kantian scholarship that it pays next to no attention to the problem of correcting moral and social injustices. It is characteristic of Kantian scholarship to craft an example and then to argue that Kantian theory requires that we behave in a certain way. So far so good. But the painfully obvious truth is that many people do not behave as they morally ought to behave. It is a truth that cries out for an explanation. Regarding the matter of equality, this essay proffers at least a partial explanation.

The inappropriate VERs that result from morally bankrupt RMS do not just dissipate; nor can one simply will into place the correct VERs. On other hand, I do hold that one can take steps that over time will result in the inappropriate VERs being replaced by more appropriate ones. And this is the subjective aspect to which Kantian theory, including Herman's novel idea, seems not to have given sufficient room.

It might be instructive here to offer a quite unrelated example. The Chinese consume dog meat; most people in European and North American countries do not consume the flesh of dogs, although they consume the flesh of lots of other animals. There is no defensible principle that would warrant the consumption of pig flesh (for example) but not dog flesh; for as far as animals go, pigs are held to be quite intelligent animals. Yet, for most European and North American denizens, consuming dog flesh goes way beyond being an option not to be exercised: it is downright repulsive. There are deep, deep VERs in place here tied to certain RMS about dogs—so much so that most people would be reluctant to eat off plates on which dog flesh had been served. Nonetheless, a denizen of any of these countries could change. Undoubtedly, she would have to live in China for awhile, see dog and pig side by side, and perhaps witness "respectable" others consume such flesh. As a further step, she might request that on some occasion a dish with such meat be served to her unannounced, and then that she be informed of this at a suitably later time. With concrete experiences, she could over time eliminate her old VERs toward the consumption of dog flesh. But it would certainly take concrete experiences, and not ratiocination alone. Specifically, there are not facts about either dog or pig that make the difference.

The point of the analogy is obvious. Why would anyone think erroneous attitudes regarding race can simply be willed away by acts of ratiocination? From an experiential standpoint, eating pig is to eating dog as one ethnic groups is to another ethnic group in an unjust world in which one group governs the other. And if overcoming deep VERs differentiating pig and dog requires concrete experiences, then surely the same holds for overcoming deep VERs differentiating two ethnic groups. That is, if for the former case experience is ineliminably necessary for the change, then so it is for the latter.

On Herman's view, experience is relevant merely because it fills in the necessary bits of information that are needed. However, that is not true in either case at hand: eating the flesh of dog or upside-down equality. That is, although experience is decidedly relevant, this is not because it merely fills in the necessary bits of information needed. In fact, from the standpoint of information it is not clear that anything needed is added. This is because the problem of changing is not one of information at all. It is, instead, exclusively one of visceral emotional resonances delivered by the experiences of our culture. In either case, without resulting in new information as such, experience yields a knowledge about the other that no amount of ratiocination can possibly yield.

Now, the Categorical Imperative does not speak to the issue of which animals we should consume for food. Although it does unmistakably require that we recognize the ultimate moral worth of all persons, the problem is that equal moral worth in the Kantian sense does not entail thoroughgoing equality, which on my view involves both equal moral worth and PSI-equality. So, although we do not need to experience one another in order to know that others are equal in moral worth to us, we do need to experience one another in order to know that others are our PSI-equals. In the Kingdom of Ends, by contrast, group PSI-equality would be a given.[9] For there would be no deep moral distortions of ethnic or racial groups to overcome with regard to judging them as worthy of governing. There would be no distorted VER default lines that needed to be removed; and PSI-equality would not track race or ethnic identity. In the nonideal world, however, all these things are precisely the case.

It is for this reason that in the nonideal world experiencing other racial and ethnic groups is transforming—not so much because we learn some new set of facts about ourselves or others, though that sometimes happens, but because such experiences turn our in-principle commitments into an experiential reality: one is engaged by the other and the other is engaged by one. A mere in-principle commitment to equality can no more substitute for this experiential engagement than can watching and listening to a DVD recording of a live concert substitute for being in the audience. The person who attended the concert and the person who saw the concert on DVD both have the same knowledge regarding what happened. They both hear the same music, see the same movements, and so forth. All the same, one was there when it happened, and witnessed things as they unfolded in real time; and nothing can take the place of that.

In the nonideal world, the belief—the sincere and genuine belief—that peo-

9. The Kingdom of Ends is a marvelous heuristic device. And while it seems to me clear that racism of all kinds would have no place in the Kingdom of Ends, there is no reason to think that all significant differences between human beings would disappear. What is more, people need not be indifferent to whom their spouses or friends might be just because all persons are equally moral. If so, then it seems that there might be room even in the Kingdom of Ends for some instances of individual PSI-*inequality*. Ex hypothesi, though, these PSI-inequalities would not track race or ethnicity.

ple of a certain race or ethnic kind are as trustworthy or as intelligent or as morally profound as "we" are is not the same as trusting that person, marveling at her or his intelligence, and being guided by the individual's intellectual and moral wisdom. These experiences make the person who belongs to that race or ethnic group a part of life and our personal history. And this yields knowledge about ourselves and the other that we could not otherwise have. The in-principle belief alone leaves us barren in this regard. After all, no matter how committed I am to the equality of Xs, it is only in experiencing an X in the ways just mentioned can my life serve as a testimony to that equality.

V. CONCLUSION: THE IDEAL OF EQUALITY

The ideal of equality is easy enough to state; and in a fleeting moment, Martin Luther King captured that ideal most eloquently when he spoke of living in a nation where people "will not be judged by the color of their skin but by the content of their character." When this ideal is realized, then (a) in a society with many ethnic groups there will not be one ethnic group whose members are the primary holders of governing positions in the basic institutions of that society, and (b) the skin color and other markers of ethnicity of those who govern will be utterly irrelevant to those who are governed. The suggestion with (a) is not that the percentage of those belonging to any one ethnic group who hold governing positions in the basic institutions of society will be isomorphic to the percentage of this ethnic group in the population at large. That would be very contrived and artificial. Rather, it is that there will not be any VERs favoring any ethnic group in terms of its members holding such roles. Together, (a) and (b) are compatible with the ethnic groups in power changing over time and the population-at-large attaching no significance to this, precisely because there is no significance at all attached to the fact that this or that ethnic group happens to be in power. Suppose, for instance, that 75 percent of the people in a room turned out to be left-handed. This would be quite a coincidence. But that is exactly what it would be—a coincidence and nothing more. Any attempt to attach any significance to this outcome should turn out to be ludicrous.

As an aside, I should mention why I have focused upon governing roles in the basic institutions of society. The idea is not that other aspects of life are irrelevant. Rather, it is that we are able to appreciate the cultural contributions (from example) from afar; whereas being governed directly touches our lives. In terms of PSI-equality, we do not have to believe that someone is our PSI-equal in order to believe that she or he sings or dances well. We may yet be uncomfortable with such a person marrying our children. By contrast, we do have to believe that someone is our PSI-equal in order to believe that this person is fit to govern us. Or, at any rate, we are more like to believe this regarding those whom we think fit to govern us. Moreover, we are much more likely to see this person as someone whom we would be pleased to have our children marry. It will be remembered that the basic institutions of society are wide-ranging. So if we have complete equality there, it is most likely that we will have it in other aspects of society.

Though most people (whether black or white) who live in a society governed by whites pay lip service to the ideal of equality as I have just articulated it, and so express indifference to upside-down equality, few (whether black or white) are prepared for upside-down equality. Or so it is if I am right about VERs and PSI-equality. All the same, the very circumstances of life fuel the delusion on the part of most that they are actually prepared for upside-down equality. Why? Because most people who live in a society governed by whites have no reason whatsoever to think that in their lifetime their very own society shall be governed by blacks—such an eventuality, they assume, is highly improbable. Hence their moral bluff is never called, even as their expressions of public commitment to this ideal massages the ego. This is rather like promising to do something where the promise is made conditional upon the promisee also doing something, where one knows all too well that the promisee does not have the wherewithal so to behave. One gets a bit of moral credit for committing oneself to so acting, although one is disingenuous from the start.

This brings us back to the experiences of Benjamin and LT. What Benjamin knows about himself is that he is actually accepting of upside-down equality. For this is the world in which he lives. Indeed, this is the world in which he freely chose to live, fully aware that he was choosing this world. And this is the world in which he continues to live as a matter of his own choosing. Insofar as self-knowledge is possible, Benjamin knows that he is accepting of upside-down equality. This, however, is precisely the knowledge about himself that LT does not have. Thus, Benjamin has a most profound piece of moral knowledge about himself that LT does not have about himself. And Benjamin's moral knowledge is generated not so much by new information about blacks (which LT does not possess) as it is by experiencing blacks in an entirely different way, one completely foreign to LT's experiences. In the nonideal world, this makes the subjective experience more important to a fundamental aspect of our moral knowledge than Herman's argument, and Kantian thought as represented by her, would seem to allow.

In the nonideal world, moral knowledge about ourselves comes with a price, paid in the coin of experience. When it comes to equality, most of us living in Western societies continue to right write checks. Or so it is if I am right that most of us are open to the idea of upside-down equality, because, after all, we know that we will never have to live it, let alone have to choose to live it.

CYNTHIA WILLETT

12 : THE SOCIAL ELEMENT
A PHENOMENOLOGY OF
RACIALIZED SPACE AND
THE LIMITS OF LIBERALISM

In the novel *Moo,* Jane Smiley depicts various characters adjusting to life at a large state university in the Midwest. A new student named Keri, described as a "one of those pretty but vapid girls," rents a small room in a house that suits her very well, and perhaps even a little too well. "She could . . . look around this tiny, empty room and recognize it perfectly as the mold of the person she was going to become," the narrator explains (Smiley 1998: 403). An African-American student named Mary is more troubled by her surroundings: "When she thought of the campus or her classes or even her room, she was absent. . . . No amount of friendliness on the part of her roommates (white) or approval on the part of her professors (white) or partisanship on the part of her friends (black) . . . got at the root of her problem—the longer she stayed here, and here was the whitest place she had ever been . . . the less she seemed to exist" (402).

What is the space that we inhabit as social creatures? How might we capture the effect of this space on our sense of individuality and freedom? It is not easy to identify the features of the social landscape. We respond to the climate of the workplace, the home, or the college campus as we walk down pathways and around physical barriers, largely without direct awareness. While Maurice Merleau-Ponty did not elaborate upon the social meanings of space, his study of embodiment sheds light on the relationship between social space and our sense of self. Most significantly, he argued that the oriented response of the body to its environment calls into question the persistent Cartesianism of social theory and philosophy. Under the influence of this Cartesianism, theorists and philosophers model space as a flat, empty, and preexistent place, and view the subject as first of all cognitive and only secondarily embodied.[1] This model of space and sub-

I am especially grateful to Duane Davis, Alia Al-Saji, David Carr, Dalia Judovitz, Michael Levine, an anonymous reviewer, and the audience at the International Merleau-Ponty Circle (University of North Carolina at Asheville, September 2001) for helpful responses to this essay.

1. While I will focus on Merleau-Ponty's critique of Cartesian rationalism in this essay, it

jectivity does not allow for the fact that our posture, gestures, and physical movements respond without conscious intervention to the world around us. Moreover, the objects that we perceive respond to us. We compose dimensions of space by the way in which we move through it.

Not only are features of the social and physical landscape rarely the focus of our attention, much of what we respond to may not be available for conscious or discursive analysis at all. Typically we respond to the surroundings through our peripheral vision. There is, however, one highly visible feature of the social landscape, and this is the dimension of color. Social observers have puzzled over the fact that long after the end of legal apartheid in the United States, blacks and whites do not live in the same neighborhoods or join the same churches, private clubs, or civic organizations. It is difficult to understand why this segregation continues long after the demise of publicly sanctioned racist ideologies and when the concept of race has lost all claim to scientific validity. Are we choosing voluntarily to separate from one another by race when we do not even think that race exists?

Liberal traditions of social and political theory focus on individual or institutional racism as well as individual choice as the primary factors for segregation, and I think that each of these factors accounts for much of the persistence of racial division. African Americans who choose to avoid certain neighborhoods or schools do so, in part, in response to specific racist incidents or persistent practices of exclusion or discrimination. The student Mary described in Smiley's novel, however, is not bothered primarily by racist events or practices at her university. Her sense that something is wrong is more vague and more pervasive, and yet, as the narrator tells us, "Mary herself knew just what it was. It was that she could not imagine herself here. . . . [H]ere was the whitest place she had ever been" (Smiley 1998: 402).

Neither the traditional liberal view of the individual as an autonomous agent nor the contemporary model of social space as a set of institutional practices provides us sufficient tools for explaining the malaise that Mary experiences. As a black student at a liberal white university, Mary experiences a sense of not belonging that has less to do with the racist events and practices that she experiences than the whiteness of the space that she inhabits. Liberal theory lacks the conceptual resources to account for the impact of racism on the space in which we encounter one another. Following Merleau-Ponty, I will argue that this failure of liberal theory traces back to its implicit Cartesianism. Liberalism views the subject of political rights as disembodied, and the space the subject inhabits as a set of positions in a void. I will then explain the perpetuation of Cartesianism

---

is important to understand that Merleau-Ponty was equally concerned with the limitations of empiricism. The empiricist's focus on causality is just as reductive as the Cartesian's focus on the geometry of space, both abstracting from the nondiscursive meanings that are embedded in space.

in the dialectical philosophy of Hegel and Marx. Merleau-Ponty's unfinished ontological study of space (developed late in his life) helps us to see past the lingering Cartesianism of contemporary liberal and leftist theory, while opening for philosophical reflection the space that can nourish or destroy us as embodied social subjects.

In his struggle to capture the elusive nature of this space, Merleau-Ponty borrows images and themes from Greek mythology. Merleau-Ponty, however, neither elaborates upon the significance of these borrowed images and themes nor reflects upon their meaning in the Greek context. The final section of my essay examines the political function of Greek mythology in ancient Greek democracy. The Greeks named the crimes that damage social space as acts of hubris, and they used the theater as well as the assembly to warn the elites of the consequences of hubris for the social milieu. Western democracy theory today needs to reacquaint itself with ancient legal and moral tools against social domination.

I. TOWARD A NEW HUMANISM

Merleau-Ponty's political views are never fully developed. He appears to shift from Marxism toward liberalism between the writing of *Humanism and Terror* in the 1940s and of *Adventures of the Dialectic* in the 1950s. But while he clearly grows more suspicious of the undemocratic politics of the Soviet Union and Marxist ideology, he remains wary of liberalism's blindness to the impact of class on democratic politics. As Merleau-Ponty argues, Marxist critique teaches us something important about the situatedness of the individual in a social and economic structure, which liberalism fails to fully grasp. In the epilogue of *Adventures of the Dialectic*, he calls at once for a new liberalism and a noncommunist left. In his shifting and sometimes ambiguous political positions, I view Merleau-Ponty as seeking a humanism that would acknowledge the concerns of liberals and their Marxist critics, while not yielding to the excesses of either side. Merleau-Ponty gives us a clue as to where this new humanism lies in his brief but persistent allusions to ancient Greek mythology and culture.

Merleau-Ponty draws upon Greek themes both in his Marxist critique of liberalism in *Humanism and Terror* as well as in his later critique of Marxism. In *Humanism and Terror* (1969: xxi), he defends Marxism as exposing the blind arrogance, or, as he writes, the tragic "*hybris,*" of liberalism's formal conception of human rights. These formal, bourgeois rights fail to protect the social, cultural, and economic rights of individuals and repressed groups against the excesses of capitalism. Marxist regimes also have their excesses. Once again alluding to Greek themes, Merleau-Ponty explains (1973: esp. 207, 226) that the liberals are right to point out the need for "limits" on state power, and to insist on the importance of political "contestation" (or, as the Greeks would write, *agon*).

While Merleau-Ponty never elaborates on the political significance of his poetics of space, or the Greek mythos upon which this poetics draws in his later
work, he clearly believes that he could find in this poetics the basis for a broader
social humanism. Today, in our second decade after the end of the Cold War, we
may believe that Marxist ideology is dead and that liberalism has won the twentieth-century war of ideologies. But the Marxist interest in class consciousness
has returned and multiplied through the guise of American-style identity politics, anti-globalization movements, and the mounting critique of U.S. arrogance
voiced by oppressed peoples. These diverse movements suggest the need to moderate the excesses of liberal capitalism, but they fail in their differences to articulate a vision for a common humanity. Merleau-Ponty's poetics of space allows
us to attend to some of the tears in the social fabric that these movements critique while giving us a sense of the interconnections that we need to sustain for
a global humanism.

Before we tease out a political vision from Merleau-Ponty's poetics of space,
we need to examine the specific critique of liberalism that his method yields. In
Humanism and Terror, Merleau-Ponty critiques liberalism on the basis of insights from his early work on the phenomenology of perception. The problem
with liberalism, he argues, is that it works only in theory. While liberalism aims
to protect the individual against many forms of coercion, it fails to protect the
individual against exploitative labor practices. The contemporary liberal theorist John Rawls intends to correct for the injustices of these economic policies
through a strong commitment to redistributive justice. In various respects, however, Rawlsian liberalism fails to meet the challenges that Merleau-Ponty poses.
Along with other liberal theorists, Rawls defends as the central moral claim of
liberalism the principle that we should treat each individual as an "end in himself," or as a "pure consciousness" (Kymlicka 1990: 103). In *A Theory of Justice,*
Rawls (1971: 12) argues that the ability of the rational ego to think uninfluenced
by social status, class position, and the like is critical for entering what he terms
the "original position" and constructing principles of justice. More generally, liberal theory presupposes the moral capacity to judge another apart from morally
irrelevant categories such as status, class, and race. Without this capacity for abstraction, according to liberal theory, we would lack the capacity to treat each
other as moral equals (12).

But if the rational mind is inextricably linked with a body-in-space, as Merleau-Ponty's early phenomenology suggests, then it is impossible in principle to
treat the other person from a perspective that abstracts altogether from our social position. Liberalism's important goal of moral equality requires a more realistic foundation. Merleau-Ponty's early phenomenological studies of the
embodied subject demonstrate that we do not encounter "naked" subjects, but
only persons with specific roles or positions in socioeconomic systems. This does
not mean that we do not see their individuality, as Merleau-Ponty suggests in his

discussion of some of our more authentic personal roles and relationships: "As in love, in affection, or in friendship, we do not encounter face to face 'consciousnesses' whose absolute individuality we could respect at every moment, but [unique!] beings qualified as 'my son', 'my wife', 'my friend'" (1969: 110). The fact that we do not experience ourselves as bare individuals but as individuals-in-relationships throws into question liberalism's focus on autonomy as the ultimate measure of freedom: "If one loves, one finds one's freedom precisely in the act of loving, and not in a vain autonomy," he adds (1964: 154). There does not exist a "plurality of subjects [as liberalism presupposes], but an intersubjectivity, and that is why there exists a common measure of the evil inflicted upon certain people and of the good gotten out of it by others" (Merleau-Ponty 1969: 110).[2]

The liberal conception of basic freedoms is designed to guarantee individuals a private space to carve out their own identity as they choose. Freedom for the liberal means first of all noninterference. A larger perspective reveals the role that well-intentioned individuals occupy in a socioeconomic system, and this system, as the Marxists argue, exploits workers and creates patterns of domination through status. Abstracting liberal theory from social realities is the essential error, in fact, the "tragic blindness," of liberal traditions of philosophy. To "understand and judge a society, one has to penetrate . . . to the human bond upon which it is built; this undoubtedly depends upon legal relations, but also upon forms of labor, ways of loving, living, and dying" (Merleau-Ponty 1969: xiv). The liberal, or existential, "ideology of choice" is blind to the way in which "my tasks are presented to me, not as objects or ends, but as reliefs and configurations, that is to say, in the landscape of praxis" (Merleau-Ponty 1973: 198–99). We need to acknowledge, Merleau-Ponty concludes, that there is more to the world than "men and things," as liberal theory presupposes. As individuals, we mediate our relationships through symbols, and these symbols, I would add, can secure or destroy the social milieu. Our actions cannot be judged by their intentions or causal consequences alone; they must be judged as well through "the effect that they will have as a meaningful gesture." "Truly all action is symbolic" (200, 201).

Contemporary critics of liberalism (including communitarians, Marxists, and many feminists) join with Merleau-Ponty to accuse liberals of over-valorizing the role of choice. These critics agree that liberal theorists fail to acknowledge the full significance of social, historical, or cultural dimensions of the

2. Among interesting discussions of an ethics that might emerge from Merleau-Ponty's work, see Davis 1991: 31–46; Oliver 2001. For discussions of the relevance of Merleau-Ponty's phenomenology for social theory, see Young 1990b: 141–59; Sullivan 2001b: 65–87; Alcoff 2000a: 235–62. For interesting studies of race that draw upon Merleau-Ponty's phenomenology of perception, see Sullivan 2001b and Fielding forthcoming.

individual. I think these critics are, in part, right. Rawlsian theory maintains that access to civil liberties, equal opportunities, and basic material goods suffices to secure individuals a meaningful experience of freedom. Freedom is conceived narrowly in terms of the ability to choose one's own lifestyle apart from external coercion. Of course, the liberal does not deny the importance of social relationships, cultural traditions, or historical embeddedness, but liberalism's primary aim is to protect the autonomy of the individual and the moral neutrality (or relative neutrality) of the state. If freedom for the liberal means noninterference, then the individual does not expect the state or other civic authority to foster forms of interdependence and social relatedness. If, as Merleau-Ponty argues, we encounter individuals always already in relation with one another, then the view of space as an arena for autonomous decision making and self-chosen relationships does not cohere with lived experience.

As the critics point out, the liberal conception of civil society models the individual as an atom in the void, and as a consequence overlooks the importance of the social fabric for weaving together the relationships that sustain us. For these critics, individual choices operate best when they occur within the relationships that make these choices meaningful. The state should not take as its primary aim the need to protect individual choice, although this remains a concern. More important, the state or community needs to protect the relationships that make choices meaningful.

While liberals recognize that human beings are by nature social creatures in need of meaningful human relationships, I do not think that even the most socially minded liberal theory has plumbed the depth of meaning that underlies our social life. Rawls (1971: 440) handles the social question in large part by adding the "social bases of self-respect" to the list of primary goods (including basic liberties, opportunities, and wealth) that are to be protected by the state. Certainly, consideration of the "social bases of self-respect" is an important tool for correcting social inequalities. As Will Kymlicka explains, "the US Supreme Court struck down segregated education for blacks, even where the facilities were funded equally, because it was perceived as a badge of inferiority, damaging black children's motivation and self-respect" (1990: 153). Whether liberals today argue for the integration of public schools or favor equal funding for community-based schools, they typically base their arguments on the need for self-respect as a primary good.

The inclusion of self-respect as a primary social good marks an advance in liberal theory. While Rawls theorizes the individual as a rational, self-interested ego, and not first of all as a social being, he acknowledges the impact of social forces on one's ownmost sense of self (Rawls 1971: 148). As Kymlicka rightly points out, Rawlsian liberalism "demands that each person start life with an equal share of society's resources, which is a striking attack on the entrenched divisions of class, race, and gender in our society" (1990: 86). The problem with liberalism's focus on self-respect is that it reduces our immersion in social space to a psychological dimension of the individual, in fact, one more dimension alongside rational capacities and physical needs. The African-American girl that Jane Smiley describes in her novel does not suffer from diminished self-esteem, but she does suffer from a sense of malaise while attending the white university.[3] The focus on the personality of the individual does not come to terms with the fact that sociality is not only a dimension of the individual; it is the air that we breathe, the element of our lives.

If liberalism fails to capture the element of our social lives, Marxism does not fare much better. Like liberalism, Marxism may sound good in theory, but it does not work in practice. While the traditional liberal perceives space through the abstract constructions of Cartesian geometry, the Marxist ideologue reduces the social landscape to a materialist operation defined by cause and effect. As a consequence, much of Marxism (and too much of leftist identity politics, I would add) sees individuals in terms of their social positions and then authorizes the abuse of those who do not occupy the positions that are politically correct. Merleau-Ponty observes that the doctrinaire Marxist is forced to abandon the possibility of a universal ethics and to think instead in terms of the violence of class politics. The Marxist then tries to regain some moral legitimacy by distinguishing progressive and regressive forms of violence. As Merleau-Ponty explains, this legitimacy relies solely upon granting the perspective of one social group, the proletariat, universal moral relevance. On the Marxist view, the unmediated aims of a single class carries the world toward a greater humanism.

One of the immediate problems with the Marxist view is that the proletariat is not in fact the "pure" class that doctrinaire Marxists (and the younger Merleau-Ponty) seek. This proletariat is divided by ethnic and religious differences and, most crucially perhaps in the American setting, by race. The support among U.S. workers of NAFTA as a preventive measure against Mexican immigration, of an expanded prison system, and of ending welfare is based not on shared interests but on white racism. The liberal or leftist aim of "build[ing] coalitions 'no longer bedeviled by race' perfectly illustrates the tendency to remove the 'workers' from the considerations of 'white workers,'" historian David Roediger writes (1988: 55). The political appeal to a pure class of dispossessed workers fails to take into account the way in which whiteness functions in the United States as a source of capital (or, as one historian writes, "property").[4]

Color, as the most prominent indicator of race, is not the only factor dividing workers. What legal theorist Kimberle Crenshaw lays out as an intersectional

3. See McGary 1998: 259–75.
4. See Lipsitz 1998: 36 for discussion of Cheryl Harris's term.

analysis of the position of women of color reveals that multiple and often conflicting factors affect status and power.[5] This analysis rules out any hypothesis of a "pure" class (or race or gender) identity.

The ideological claim that some class or culture (for example, liberal capitalism) stands totally outside of power, and represents the universal, reflects a dialectical logic that sharply opposes two (or more) perspectives. Social theorist Patricia Hill Collins (1988: 5) uses the term "outsider within" in place of the Marxist concept of the pure proletariat in order to clarify the more ambiguous situation of the black workers in the U.S. economy. The black service worker does not stand outside of the socioeconomic system with nothing to lose but her chains. She is tied to the system through her need to support her family, friends, and community as well as through the limited status and power that she acquires through her work. Society is not radically divided between two (or more) classes or perspectives, but stratified in such a way that individuals have varying degrees of status and power. The all-or-nothing ontology of dialectic, no less than the formalism of liberalism, abstracts from the diverse forces that impact individual lives in the stratified social sphere. The question posed by an intersectional analysis is how to acknowledge the multiple perspectives and social positions of American identity politics, and yet locate what holds together a common humanity.

Perhaps the most exciting contribution of Merleau-Ponty to a theory of social justice is not his political philosophy or even his early studies of perception. His most exciting contribution to justice theory comes from his late, unfinished studies on the space in which perceiving subjects and perceived objects are immersed.[6] In these studies Merleau-Ponty argued that philosophers following Descartes, including Hegel and Marx, have tried to map space through a multidimensional determination of a set of positions. The Cartesian-Hegelian (or Marxist) model empties space of texture and meaning. Merleau-Ponty offers in its place a poetics that respects the tacit resonances and curved lines of space; he develops this poetics from his study of depth and color in visual art. From this study, he describes space as an interconnecting tissue of sensitivities, and he names this tissue "flesh."

Space as an experience of depth and color, or of an interconnecting "tissue" of sensitivities, offers a way of understanding the persistence of racial segregation. Merleau-Ponty, focusing for most of his life on the problems of perception, did not give much attention to the politics of space. In his poetics, he describes space as of a piece, without tears in its fine fabric or dissonance in the play of its oblique meanings. What if we were to bring his ontology of space to the political arena? Could his appreciation for depth and color help us to discern the in-

5. See Crenshaw 1995: 357–83.
6. See Johnson 1993: 121–49. Also see Merleau-Ponty 1968: 130–55.

visible barriers of the social landscape? Could this political landscape bring us beyond the contemporary polemics of liberals and their critics to a new humanism?

II. THE POETICS OF SPACE

In the essay "Eye and Mind," Merleau-Ponty notes that "the 'problems' of painting that structure its history are often solved obliquely, not in the course of inquiries instigated to solve them but, on the contrary, at some point when painters, having reached an impasse, apparently forget those problems and allow themselves to be attracted by other things. Then suddenly, their attention elsewhere, they happen upon the old problems and surmount the obstacle" (Merleau-Ponty 1993: 149). Perhaps too some problems of our political life are best confronted not directly but, as Merleau-Ponty suggests, through circuitous paths. For this reason, I will swerve away from major social issues, and take a detour through Merleau-Ponty's remarks on color and depth in painting.

In his late essays, including "Eye and Mind" and "The Intertwining—the Chiasm," Merleau-Ponty takes a step back from his earlier focus on the perceiving subject and the visible object to consider the "thereness" of space. Space is not itself visible, and yet it is in space that subjects and objects appear. We might first think of space as akin to an empty box or to a grid point on a plane. Beginning with these intuitions, Descartes, and Hegel after him, explained space in terms of intersecting planes based on three dimensions.[7] Merleau-Ponty points out that this Cartesian-Hegelian conception of space reflects the technical advances of Renaissance painting. While medieval and classical artists drew figures as though they were ornaments on a flat surface, Renaissance painters were able to convey depth on the flat canvas by constructing lines of perspective. Merleau-Ponty questions whether the techno-scientific constructivism of the Renaissance artists marks genuine progress in our ability to represent space. Nonfigurative paintings from the twentieth century such as Paul Klee's 1938 *Park near Lucerne* and Cézanne's late watercolors provide a clue as to what the artists of the Renaissance neglect. In Cézanne's watercolor of Mont Sainte-Victoire (1900) "space . . . radiates around planes that cannot be assigned any place at all" (Merleau-Ponty 1993: 141). Merleau-Ponty contrasts the "flowing movement" of the watercolor with the mechanical line of Renaissance perspective painting. As Galen Johnson (1993: 39, 41) explains, Renaissance painting belongs to a "world of scientific and technological domination" that "imposes a fixed, univocal perspective of godlike survey." But Merleau-Ponty does not see in modern painting the simple fragmentation of multiple perspectives. He sees planes bent around a

7. See Fóti 1993: 293–308.

space in which these multiple perspectives are submerged. Nonfigurative art is not about multiple subjects and objects but about the space that we inhabit together. This space is not composed of a series of straight lines that define either single or multiple perspectives. Space curves around meanings that linger in the air through which we move. Modern twentieth-century art does not oppose Renaissance univocality with its own perspectivalism. Modern art evokes the space in which perspectival subjects and visible objects are submerged.

The nondiscursive meanings that nonfigurative art evokes give space its depth. Describing the voluminousness of space as less a dimension than a medium, Edward Casey writes that "depth is something that we first of all feel." "Like an aura or atmosphere . . . it is neither a substance nor a relation, but subtends both" (Casey 1991: 134). This space is neither homogenous nor static. Merleau-Ponty describes it as a density with ebbs and flows, and even turbulence, like water (1993: 123). "When through the water's thickness I see the tiled bottom of the pool, I do not see it despite the water. . . . I see it through [that medium] and because [of it]" (142). While the thickness of space resists measurement, it has its distinct expressive unity and coherence, or style. Characteristic rhythms, colors, tone, and textures distinguish one part of space from another, giving space its directionality and asymmetry (cf. Casey 1991: 134). Johnson identifies "the inner animation" of space as a "source of the self" (1993: 46). This is a source of the self that is experienced but not known, or as Merleau-Ponty remarks in a note (1968: 257), this space of origin "exists . . . kinesthetically" but not conceptually, withdrawing ever to the fringes of our perception.

"To designate [this space]," Merleau-Ponty continues (1968: 139), "we should need the old term 'element,' in the sense it was used to speak of water, air, earth, and fire. . . . a sort of incarnate principle that brings a style of being wherever there is a fragment of being." The thickness that he describes in terms of a classic element from Greek mythology he also names as flesh. What we see in the visible world, Merleau-Ponty writes, are "things we could not dream of seeing 'all naked' because the gaze itself envelops them, clothes them with its own flesh." "Tissue that lines [the visibles], sustains them, [and] nourishes them . . . is not a thing, but . . . a flesh of things" (131, 132–33).

The flesh of space is no more transparent than is the flesh of our body, and like our flesh, space is known through the dimension of color. While modern philosophers and engravers may dismiss color as a "secondary quality," "the return to color has the virtue of getting somewhat nearer to 'the heart of things'" (Merleau-Ponty 1993: 141, quoting Paul Klee). "Cézanne . . . went directly to the solid, to space—and came to find that inside this space—this box or container too large for them—[that] the things began to move, color against color. . . . The problem [for the painter] . . . is no longer solely that of distance, line and form; it is also, and equally, the problem of color" (140–41).

This is because any particular instance of a color receives its meaning "only by connecting up from its place . . . with other colors it dominates or that dominate it, that it attracts or . . . repels" (Merleau-Ponty 1968: 132). The precise red used by a painter or found in our surroundings takes on a rhythm, texture, and feel from an invisible fabric of meanings that gives this red its particular force. These meanings may not be discursive, but they are not lacking in historical, political, or social references. As Merleau-Ponty writes, a particular red "is a punctuation in the field of red things, which includes the tiles of roof tops, the flags of gatekeepers and of the Revolution" (132). The colors that we encounter have specific cultural and political meanings. Some of these meanings may call for war, social unrest, or revolutionary violence.

"Philosophy paints without colors in black and white, like copperplate engravings," Merleau-Ponty remarks (quoted in Fóti 1993: 293). For "colors," as Véronique Fóti (1993: 293) explains, "are suspected by philosophy. . . . [T]he light of reason, supposedly, is achromatic." It is also true that the perceiver ordinarily does not see color, or at least not consciously. Along with lighting, shadows, and reflections, color "exists at the threshold of profane vision"; it is "not ordinarily seen," Merleau-Ponty writes (1993: 128). But if the perceiver, unlike the artist, does not observe color, she nonetheless responds to it. As Merleau-Ponty explains (1993: 125), "my body is . . . caught in the fabric of the world. . . . Things are an annex or prolongation of [my body]; they are incrusted in its flesh." I do not find these things in a space that is flat, empty, and preexistent—these things are wrapped in my own flesh.

III. RACIALIZATION OF SPACE

In a front-page article in a Pulitzer Prize–winning series on race for the *New York Times,* a journalist interviews school age children in Maplewood, New Jersey. This "is the kind of place where people—black and white—talk a lot about the virtues of diversity and worry about white flight, where hundreds will turn out to discuss the book 'Why Are All the Black Kids Sitting Together in the Cafeteria?'. . . . But even here, as if pulled by internal magnets, black and white children begin to separate at sixth grade. These are children who walked to school together, learned to read together, slept over at each other's houses. But despite all the personal history, all the community good will, race divides them as they grow up" (Lewin 2000: 14).

The issue of self-segregation in primary and secondary schools in America may appear to be relatively benign; this issue is connected, however, to a more pressing one in a society that claims to base rewards on merit and not color. On every major measure of academic achievement, white children perform better than black children, and this gap remains even after controlling for educational and class background of the children's families (Lewin 2000: 15). Moreover, this issue does not disappear in higher education. In *The Agony of Education* (Feagin, Vera, and Imani 1996), several sociologists interview black college students at white colleges and universities, seeking answers to the question of poor black advancement in higher education. These social scientists come to the same conclusion as the report on the public schools: the integration of the American educational system is not working.

Some of the causes for the failure of schools are well documented. There is no doubt that the educational achievement of whites owes much to institutional discrimination against nonwhite children in school (including the differential tracking of students), prejudices of white teachers against children of color, and larger patterns of discrimination against black families (housing, loans, jobs, etc.). Prisons, in America, expand faster than do schools, and these prisons are full of disadvantaged populations who too often are presumed but not proven guilty. Many of the more sensitive adolescents respond to these hypocrisies by turning their back on the system and identifying with prison culture (gansta rap, butt breeches, and crack cocaine). Liberal political leaders, including the former Atlanta mayor Andrew Young (2001), point out the urgent need to overcome disparities between whites and blacks in access to capital, and they are right to do so. But if the gap between white and black performance in schools remains after controlling for the economic and educational backgrounds of families, then something besides access to capital is perpetuating segregation among our children.

This more subtle factor may be impossible to conceptualize, but black families know that it is there. These families tell of how black honor students reject admission to prestigious white institutions because of the vague sense that something "felt bad" or because they felt "out of place" despite the honor student's clear merit (Feagin, Vera, and Imani 1996: 5). They perceive these institutions as reeking of "whiteness," and one parent explains that this is just "a thing you can feel . . . nothing [no racial incident] happened. It's just an atmosphere" (73).

The sociologists explain that black students attending white schools are "forced to adapt to white views, norms, and practices. Predominantly white colleges and universities . . . are more than demographically white; typically, they are white in their basic cultures and climates" (Feagin, Vera, and Imani 1996: xi). In fact, these schools never did aim in their policies to change basic norms and climates to welcome black students; on the contrary, integrative policies function to "assimilate young black people in a unidirectional manner to the dominant white . . . culture" (12). The research into white space directly challenges what these social scientists refer to as the "passive container" model of space. "Most human beings," they argue, "view space expressively and symbolically" (49). When black students report of schools that reek of whiteness, they are "speaking of the overall character and tone of that campus space" (16). "For these African Americans, as for most other Americans, the basic unity of human reality is not the individual human being but rather a cluster of social ties and relations that extend across space and time. The experiential reality of *space* is at the heart of interpersonal ties and is a critical element of U.S. racial relations," these sociologists explain (16).

White students and teachers often enough express their dismay that black students choose to self-segregate, and it is true that segregation in the schools is largely initiated by blacks. I have discussed with other faculty at Emory the curious fact that while our university boasts a very high proportion of black students relative to other historically white universities, black students are much more likely to miss classes than are other students; these black students are also more likely to miss not just a few classes but a sizable amount of the semester; and black students are much more likely to drop out of Emory before graduation. The sociological study points out that with or without awareness, white students and teachers have in fact marked what they perceive to be neutral public or quasi-public spaces as their own. They mark these spaces through gestures, classroom practices, and other embodied styles of expression. These signs send messages that blacks are anomalous, if not intruders onto white space. This tacit racialization of space through style explains why the occasional black student in the classroom at a predominantly white university, no less than the black philosopher at the American Philosophical Society, stands out as highly visible. This space has been marked as white turf by body gestures and styles of movement that work below the threshold of consciousness. This is not simply an issue of whether the percentage of blacks in a particular institution reflects the percentage of blacks in the larger society. Liberal white students and teachers may or may not affirm the principle of integration, but they continue to act white. In order to reclaim a space of their own, black students develop styles that mark their distinct identity and challenge white domination. One of the consequences may appear in standard measures of merit. If whites own the tests, the honors classes, and even the schools, then performing well by allegedly neutral academic standards is equivalent to "acting white" (Lewin 2000: 15).

In his major essays on space, "The Intertwining—the Chiasm" and "Eye and Mind," Merleau-Ponty does not discuss the political ramifications of his phenomenology. He elaborates upon the prediscursive meanings of space through images drawn primarily from Greek mythology, while excising these images from the political context that was their home. He describes space as an element like water, and he depicts the perceiving subject through the mythic figure of Narcissus. "The seer is caught up in what he sees, and it is still himself he sees: there is a fundamental narcissism of all vision," he writes (Merleau-Ponty 1968: 139). Through this poetics, he envisions the stylization of space as an experience that is originally (although not finally) as solitary as the work of the modern painter. The sociologists (Feagin, Vera, and Imani 1996) approach the poetics of space not through modern art but through racial politics, and their metaphors center around turf marking, visibility, and recognition. Other writers approach this space differently again. Toni Morrison (1998: 10) describes the desire for belonging through images of home, acknowledgment, and a paying-out of homage due.

When Merleau-Ponty expands his focus in these essays beyond the solitary individual to the social realm, he does not describe the middle distance of the turf war or the haunted intimacy of a homecoming. He describes the "synergy" that exists between "different organisms." He believes that "this synergy derives in part from the fact that we share the same sense of a particular color" (1968: 142). "I recognize in my green his green," he writes (142). For those who are sensitive to the role of color in the social and political landscape, this statement appears naive. Space is charged with divisive political meanings, and in the United States these meanings are racially coded. The black children in Maplewood, New Jersey, no less than writers like Morrison, aim to create new meanings for color, performing through their elaboration of a style what Merleau-Ponty calls the "labor of vision" (1993: 129). For the hip-hop generation, this labor of vision appears in reappropriating white space through "black noise" (both mainstream and underground rap music), break dancing, and graffiti art. For Morrison, the broken lyrical style of her narratives pays homage to lives denied by white history. However much they differ, these authors and artists agree that space is not a vacuum, and that we are submerged in a depth that is larger than ourselves. They also agree that this space is indexed by color. But then what are the political implications of this space?

IV. THE POLITICS OF SPACE

Merleau-Ponty's remarks on the ontology of space point beyond the liberal model of space as empty place as well as the leftist demarcation of space as a set of social positions. These models focus on the perspective of rational egos or social groups, while neglecting the space in which we are all immersed. Both views of space draw implicitly upon the Cartesianism that Merleau-Ponty critiques most fully in his study of painting. There he explains that the Cartesian model of space reduces the individual's experience of depth to a matter of perspective, and he urges us to "eschew . . . thinking by planes and perspectives" (1968: 138). We are not spectators on life representing a point of view, but individuals with embodied styles of responding to what we see around us. The presence of style makes it difficult to determine the boundaries between the individual and the world. Just as the things that we encounter are "incrusted" upon our flesh, so we inscribe our style upon our surroundings. The social sphere contains the meanings that we inscribe with our bodies and communicates these meanings to others. Without the mapping of my style into the social realm, and the encounter there of limits imposed on what we can do through the gestures of others, "there would be no humanity" (Merleau-Ponty 1993: 125). As neither pure subjects nor pure objects, neither ends nor means, our distinct individuality takes shape through the styles that we embody in the social milieu. Before we adopt the liberal procedures of an abstract self-consciousness or the positional consciousness of identity theory, we develop a sense of ourselves through our style of comportment in our surroundings.

Like the Renaissance engraver, the liberal theorist abstracts the individual from the space in which he is immersed and imposes "a fixed, univocal perspective of godlike survey" (Merleau-Ponty 1993: 141).[8] The liberal constructs principles of justice on the basis of unconditional respect for the other despite the fact that the other-in-a-situation is never encountered stripped bare of his or her habits, or of what Merleau-Ponty terms style. The style of expression testifies to the class, race, and gender affiliations of an individual. But these social markings do not determine the choices or perspective of an individual, and they do not limit her perspective to her social position. These markings do introduce meanings to which the individual consciously or unconsciously responds.

Leftist social theory makes it seem almost impossible to understand how we can transcend the perspective of our class or other social position. According to the Marxist, the capitalist sees the worker as nothing more than an instrument of labor. Marxism "had understood that it is inevitable that our understanding of history should be partial since every consciousness is historically situated" (Merleau-Ponty 1969: 19). Certainly the capitalist does treat the worker as nothing more than an instrument of labor, but Merleau-Ponty's model of the space as flesh helps us to understand how it is also possible for the capitalist to stand close enough to the worker so as to "hear his breath and feel his effervescence and his fatigue" (Merleau-Ponty 1968: 144). It is possible for the capitalist to know the worker not only as an instrument but also as an individual character with a style of his or her own.

Neither the liberal nor the Marxist has the theoretical tools to explore the space that binds the capitalist and worker together or the element of style that gives each a sense of his or her own individuality. Space is neither a void nor a set of possible positions on a Cartesian plane. Space is weighted, dense with equivalences, curved by forces of repulsion and attraction, animated by specters from the past, and revitalized through nonsubjective sources of value and pleasure. Through its curved lines, space takes us beyond ourselves and our "posi-

8. Merleau-Ponty traces the abstract thinking of the liberal to Calvinism: "Summoned to break the vital alliance that we have with time, with others, and with the world, the Calvinist pushes to its limits a demystification that is also a depoetization. . . . The . . . church [and even] human friendships . . . are rejected as magic" (1973: 14–15). It is this classic liberalism that disturbs him throughout his life.

tions" to feel in our own way with, or against, others. This space is an extension of the individual who possesses a rational ego and a class position, but who is more essentially defined through his or her style of comportment. Neither the liberal concept of autonomy nor the Marxist concept of social position provide us with moral norms for the embodied subject. Merleau-Ponty gives us a clue as to where to find these norms in his constant reference to images and themes from classical Greek culture.

V. JUSTICE IN THE SOCIAL ELEMENT

In *Humanism and Terror,* Merleau-Ponty suggests that we might discover the moral meaning of human life in classical tragedy. The tragedy of human life, he offers, is that while our individual worth should be measured by inner motives, our worth will in fact be measured by actions whose meaning we will never know (1969: 62). For "man can neither suppress his nature as freedom . . . nor question . . . [the] tribunal" of history which sets his tragic fate (64). Classical tragedy may in fact teach us much about the meaning of modern life. But while the conflict between public and private spheres defines a prominent theme for the middle class in the nineteenth and twentieth centuries, this conflict does not capture the moral forces articulated in ancient law and literature. For the ancient Greek people, man was in essence, as Aristotle wrote, the social animal. The moral turmoil of classical tragedy did not focus on threats to the inner worth of the private man or his moral right to autonomy. In classical drama, moral turmoil centers on the violation of social bonds (or *philia*). Merleau-Ponty is right to turn to Greek theater for a place where art, culture, and politics would meet, but ancient theater reveals categories of justice beyond the liberalism of the modern middle class.

Oedipus Rex signals this alternative focus at the opening of the play, where Sophocles portrays a city beset with plague. The general malaise of the city points beyond the physical ailments of the inhabitants and the infertility of the land to the social pollution of the community itself. The priest speaks of his city as a ship that "pitches wildly, [and] cannot lift her head from the depths, the red waves of death." The audience learns a terrible crime has left the city a "wasteland . . . stripped of men alive within it, living all as one" (Sophocles 1984, lines 30, 67). The crime that defines the plot of ancient tragic drama does not harm only the victim. The consequences of the crime boomerang to bring down the perpetrator and befoul a whole community. But what was the nature of this crime?

Contemporary scholars emphasize the importance of understanding Greek plays in the context of performance rather than simply through a formal analysis of their meaning or structure, and Merleau-Ponty would surely have to agree. One of the most revealing features of these plays is the composition of choruses. These choruses were composed of ordinary citizens, primarily the poor craftsmen and farmers, who were drafted in lieu of military service.[9] The participation of the ordinary citizen in theater may have played at least as important a role in maintaining Athenian democracy as the assembly. One scholar (Ober 1989: 208–12) argues persuasively that the masses, or *demos,* turned to the theater in order to communicate political concerns to the elite, and they communicated these concerns through the music, gesture, and dance of the chorus in tragic plays. While some scholars emphasize that citizens who performed in the chorus represented the largely working poor population of Athens, another group of scholars observes that "in their dramatic persona, they represent, remarkably often, a socially marginal segment of society—women, old men, foreigners, underlings, or even slaves. They are thus far from being an embodiment of the Athenian polis . . . in the abstract" (Blondell et al. 1999: 39).

While the democratic choruses of Greek tragedies represent diverse social positions, these choruses sing in a unified voice. "Hubris breeds the tyrant," the chorus of *Oedipus* rings out to the audience (line 964). Through their songs, the choruses warn the elite of the moral crime of hubris, and of the consequences of arrogance for the well-being of the city. The hubris of the elites does not just harm individuals and the relationships between them; hubris weakens the fabric that holds a community together. In ancient Athenian democracy, the *demos* had the legal right to charge the elite with arrogance and bring these individuals before the courts. These charges focus not just on the substance of the hubristic act but on the immoderate manner (or style) in which the agent acts. Laws and social codes against hubris served to protect individuals of lower status against the excesses of those of higher status. While modern liberalism articulates principles of justice in abstraction from the stratification of society, Marxism conceives of strata in starkly economic terms. Both liberalism and Marxism lack the category of hubris and, as a consequence, fail to acknowledge specters of domination and violence that haunt the highly stratified public domain.

Liberalism dreams that it can "exorcize these specters, . . . brush them to one side of an unequivocal world," Merleau-Ponty writes (1993: 130). The liberal ideal of a color-blind society is one such dream, for it assumes capacities that we do not have. We may transform the meaning of color, but we cannot abstract from color or other signs of status and view each other entirely outside of our social positions. In the name of an impossible ideal, liberals attack nonliberal regimes for failing to recognize the individual as an end in itself, and for contaminating the public sphere with religious ideology or other moral values. This is our hubris. The normative American citizen inscribes whiteness wherever he or she goes. We may not see the whiteness that is inscribed; color and other nondiscursive qualities in our space hover at the periphery of our ordinary consciousness. Only the racist focuses directly on color and judges an individual

9. See the introduction in Blondell et al. 1999: 39.

accordingly. But the liberal is wrong to think that we can construct formal principles of fairness in abstraction from social realities.[10] We do not live and work in a void but in a space that establishes our status and power, in part, through color. We need to construct our principles of moral equality from an awareness of the stratification of society and not in abstraction from it. This is liberalism's mistake.

When the African-American character in Jane Smiley's novel reflects upon campus life at her liberal white university she experiences a general malaise. The white professors and students are friendly, she has her black friends, and yet "when she thought of the campus . . . she was absent. There wasn't even a space where a black person should be. Embarrassed as she would have been to admit it, this seemed to be the ultimate effect of THAT TIME in the commons," the narrator explains (Smiley 1998: 402). "THAT TIME" refers to a relatively minor incident in the school cafeteria when a white boy had called her the "N word." This single, isolated event might be harmless by itself but, in the racial climate of the United States, the event touches off associations and resonates with past harms. These harms did not begin in the United States; they began hundreds of years ago in Africa, and they continue to haunt our social space. It is common to report, as the *New York Times* journalist does, on the sensitivity of blacks to "slights from friends of a different race" (Lewin 2000: 15). It is less common to understand why this sensitivity occurs. The *Times* article links themes of sensitivity and insult with style and space, the central themes of Merleau-Ponty's phenomenology. And like Merleau-Ponty, the article alludes to central themes of ancient Greek culture. It describes the schoolchildren of Maplewood, New Jersey, as "like a Greek chorus" and warns that these children's experiences warn us to expect "tricky currents ahead" for interracial friendships in their schools and communities (14). The choruses of classic tragedy understood slights among those who should be friends as acts of hubris, and they communicated through rhythm and tone the turbulence these assaults bring, not only to individuals but also to the moral climate for generations to come. Hubris was understood to be the cause of war, social unrest, and revolutionary violence. For this reason, the Greeks constructed moral codes and laws against it. In modern middle-class democracies, we understand arrogance as an individual moral failing, but this is not enough. We need as well to understand hubris as a category in our law and literature and in our theories of national and international justice.[11]

10. This is what Rawls (1971: 12) describes as the original position.
11. For more on this topic, see Willett 2001.

13 : IF YOU SAY SO
FEMINIST PHILOSOPHY
AND ANTIRACISM

Reflection on the relationship between sexist and racist forms of oppression can generate insights into the structure and experience of both oppressions. In recent years, white feminist philosophers have been criticized for elements of racism in their work by, for example, bell hooks (1987), Elizabeth Spelman (1988), and Melissa Lucashenko (1994). In particular, the use of analogies between sexism and racism has been strongly criticized. The idea of constructing analogies between sexism and racism has started to function within feminist discourse rather like the notion of essentialism—as a term of accusation with little possibility of reply.[1] The most powerful critiques have shown that some feminists, in their attempts to demonstrate that sexism is more fundamental than racism, have made the experience of black women and men invisible and have disregarded the specificity of oppressions and the problem of understanding simultaneous oppressions.[2]

A serious problem with some feminist comparisons of sex and sexism is that they involve the attempt to establish a conceptual priority of sex and sexism over race and racism. Elizabeth Spelman, in *Inessential Woman* (1988) criticizes feminists such as Kate Millett in *Sexual Politics* (1969), Shulamith Firestone in *The Dialectic of Sex* (1970), and Mary Daly in *Beyond God the Father* (1973) for arguing that sexism is in some sense more fundamental than racism.[3] The view that sexism is more fundamental than racism, or at least the view that sex is more

I would like to thank Michael Levine for talking over the issues with me; Frances Gray, Sally Haslanger, and an anonymous reader for their written feedback; Damian Cox for his insightful comments; and colleagues at the Women in Philosophy Conference, Hobart 2001, and at the University of Queensland for helping me to develop my ideas.

1. Naomi Schor analyzes the "intellectual terrorism" in accusations of essentialism (1995: 46).

2. Drawing parallels between sexism and racism can make black women's experience invisible because black women experience both oppressions simultaneously. See, for example, Carby 1982.

3. Millett (1969), for example, argues that sexism is more fundamental than racism in three senses: it is "sturdier" than racism so harder to eradicate; it has a more "pervasive ideology" than racism, and it provides the most basic concept of power.

fundamental than race, can also be found in the work of contemporary feminist philosophers.[4] Spelman argues that feminist theory has contributed to what Adrienne Rich calls "white solipsism" (1988: 116). White solipsism involves taking white experience as the paradigm through which to understand the world.

Spelman demonstrates the problems with theories that concentrate on the question of whether sexism or racism is more fundamental. She argues that "If sexism and racism must be seen as interlocking, and not as piled upon each other, serious problems arise for the claim that one of them is more fundamental than the other" (1988: 123). Spelman exposes the problems with what she calls the "additive" notion of oppression, the neglect of the relationship between oppressions, the way some feminist work has reflected and perpetuated racism, and the way racist oppression inflects our understanding of sexist oppression. By the "additive" notion (what she also calls "the ampersand problem") she means the idea that black women, for example, suffer from two distinct forms of oppression, sexist oppression and racist oppression, which are added to each other, rather than experiencing a different kind of oppression from both white women and black men. She says that an additive analysis fails to take into account the way that racist oppression and class oppression imply that sexist oppression will take very different forms—different stereotypes and expectations of black women and different sources of resistance. For example, the image of women as frail and dependent is taken only to apply to white women; and in Spelman's view the family has been a source of resistance of blacks, but a site of oppression for white women (1988: 123). The lesson that can be drawn from Spelman's discussion is that we should be vigilant in relation to discussions of racism versus sexism and not assume that one is more fundamental than the other. Nevertheless, I argue that we can learn a great deal from examining the way in which racism and sexism have been analogized.

However, even those feminist philosophers who have most forcefully presented those criticisms have then suggested a number of significant analogies between racism and sexism. Spelman, for example, in criticizing the notion that there are no positive features of a black identity, notes that blackness is not only about pain and suffering and that one can identify as a black woman in ways that are not racist, just as one can identify as a woman in ways that are not sexist (1988: 125). The problems with comparisons between racism and sexism arise if the analogy is constructed asymmetrically—for example, if the theory of racism is modeled on an understanding of sexism. A more promising approach is to use

4. Some contemporary feminist philosophers also argue that sex is more fundamental than other distinctions between human beings. For example, Luce Irigaray claims that sex is more fundamental because it is ontological (1985a: 145), whereas other sorts of differences are empirical differences, and Elizabeth Grosz in *Volatile Bodies* argues that sex is more fundamental because it is pre-ontological (1994: 209).

an explanatory analogy, where two things are compared in order to shed light on both. Such a comparison might lead to helpful arguments by analogy—for example, if racism and sexism are thought to be similar in certain ways, then it can be argued that the way that we must overcome them will be similar also. If both racism and sexism are used as points of comparison with each other, if their relation is analytically reciprocal, we gain insights into the general structure and the experience of oppression.

When antiracist feminist philosophy takes into consideration the problems that arise in constructing analogies between racism and sexism, it can present an account sensitive to the specificity of race and sex and gender and the interaction between them. In my view, a consistent feminism is antiracist as well. As Linda Martín Alcoff expresses it, "The problem of racial difference and racism operates increasingly as a crucial condition of adequacy for acceptable feminist theory" (1998: 477). Furthermore, as Michèle Le Doeuff observes, "It is not a pure coincidence that many feminists are also active in anti-racist movements" (1991: 281). The connection is both conceptual and empirical, in that the particular ideas and issues feminists consider, and the ways they reflect on sexism, are linked with an intellectual and practical concern with racism.

My argument is that while the two forms of oppression are distinctive, they share a general structure which emerges in personal experiences of oppression, in institutionalized racism and sexism, and in approaches to overcoming oppression. First I will briefly sketch the central analogies between analyses of racism and sexism in feminist philosophical work. This sketch provides a background for a critical reassessment of the usefulness of the analogy, one that takes into account Spelman's articulation of the risks involved. I find Simone de Beauvoir's work useful in assessing the structure and experience of racist and sexist oppressions, their interaction, and strategies of resistance.

I. ANALOGIES AND DISANALOGIES BETWEEN RACISM AND SEXISM

Some of the analogies between racism and sexism emerge at the level of analysis. By this I mean that it is the theorizing *about* racism and sexism that is similar, rather than (necessarily) racism and sexism themselves. There are parallels in the status attributed to race and sex. It has been noted in numerous discussions of racism that the idea of race as biologically based is a fiction, even if race is important socially (Frye 1983, Zack 1998, Haslanger 2000). Marilyn Frye, in *The Politics of Reality*, argues that the criteria that are supposed to distinguish one race from another are chimerical (1983: 113–18). They have no serious biological basis, and commonplace attempts to use them to characterize races are completely inadequate. For example, skin color does not distinguish whiteness from blackness, as people with white skin may be counted as black, Mexican, Puerto Rican, or Native American, and some people who are dark-skinned are counted as white, such as people of Indian and Pakistani background (Frye is describing the U.S. context). It is sometimes thought to follow from the point that race isn't biologically based and the fact that racist oppression involves racially based categorization that the concept of race cannot be part of a nonracist future (Zack 1998), although Frye herself does not hold this view. The parallel argument with regard to gender goes like this: gender is a fiction, and the idea of gender has been used to oppress women, so we should abandon gender categories in favor of androgyny (Jaggar 1979, Okin 1989). What this would mean in practice is that there is no public recognition of differences between men and women, although there might be private recognition of sex differences.

Judith Butler takes things one step further by arguing that "sex" is also a political construction or fiction rather than a biological base on which or in relation to which gender is constructed (Butler 1990: 147). She argues that the category of sex is itself gendered, and so cannot act as the basis on which gender is constructed or performed (Butler 1993: xi). On this view, we are socially and politically categorized as sexed, as either "male" or "female," subjected to the norms of heterosexuality, and we perform gendered identities as "man" or "woman," which makes it appear that there is a basis or substance behind these performances. Butler concludes that we should give up the norms of sex and gender to allow gender to proliferate and thus undermine the limitations and restrictions of current gender identities.[5]

Another interesting similarity between theories about racism and sexism is the idea that race and sex both involve two explanatory levels: one level that is cultural or socially constructed, and the other that is more basic, natural, harder to change, and perhaps more valuable. First, many feminists are committed to the view that sex can be distinguished from gender, a distinction that is understood in a variety of different ways. Second, the cultural and social aspects of race and racism are distinguished from deeper and more personal experience of race. One example of the different explanatory levels is Adrienne Rich's distinction between institution and embodiment, which she uses to explain how although

5. It should be noted that these arguments concerning the biology of sex are different from arguments pertaining to the biology of race, because the arguments about race do not depend on breaking down a two-part distinction. Cases of indeterminate sex are thought to be more problematic for the sex distinction than they are for race. However, while these historical changes show that people have had different ideas about sex, they do not imply that we should reject the concept of sex, although they could suggest that we should reject the view that there are only two sexes or that every human being is one of two sexes. As in the case of race, it is argued that because the idea of sex has been used in an oppressive way, it should be abandoned or deconstructed. Judith Butler (1990) and Nancy Fraser (1997) hold this view, although for slightly different reasons.

motherhood as an institution is composed of damaging myths, it may be a freely chosen experience (1976: 273–80). Spelman uses this idea to distinguish between the devastating effects of racism and the importance of pride in one's race (1988: 129). Again, the concept of whiteness, used to refer to a racist construction of white identity that whites can challenge, has the cultural and social characteristics gender is thought to have. Frye argues that "whiteness" is the socially constructed idea of the entitlement and superiority of whites (1983: 114–18). In a more recent paper, she introduces the terms "whitely" and "whiteliness" "as terms whose grammar is analogous to that of 'masculine' and 'masculinity'" (2001: 87).

Sally Haslanger provides a complex set of parallels to sex and gender. She regards "color" as parallel to sex, and ethnicity as parallel to gender (as a generic category). "Color" indicates those physical characteristics that are taken to differentiate social categories (2000: 53).[6] She believes that hierarchical gender and race divisions need to be eliminated, as opposed to sex, nonhierarchical genders and nonhierarchical ethnicity: "I'm suggesting that we should work to undermine the forces that make being a man, a woman, or a member of a racialized group possible; we should refuse to be gendered man or woman, refuse to be raced." "I believe it is part of the project of feminism to bring about a day when there are no more women (though, of course, we should not aim to do away with females!)" (48, 46). However, she concludes that it can be left open whether feminists should aim to develop new nonhierarchical genders or aim to eliminate gender and all ethno-racial groupings (50). In a more recent essay, Haslanger argues that "in the short run, it would be a mistake not to recognize the ways in which race and sex oppression divide us into hierarchical classes" (2002: 2). She takes it that race and gender are important to subjectivity and that we need the *concept* of race to overcome oppression. The implication, however, is that in the longer run, or when we have equitable social conditions, these concepts will be discarded because they will no longer be necessary. Or at most there will be nonhierarchical ethno-racial groupings. A significant distinction within feminist antiracist theorists, therefore, is not just whether they take race and sex or gender to be valuable concepts for analyzing current circumstances, but whether these concepts will be valuable in circumstances where there is no racist and sexist oppression.

The final analogy between racism and sexism, which I will discuss in the next section, involves the false choice we are given between "equality feminism" and "difference feminism," and between what we can call equality antiracism and difference antiracism. In both cases we are often presented with a stark choice between a "difference" position, supposedly based on essentialist views of race and

6. Haslanger also distinguishes three other dimensions of analysis: specific social categories, normative characteristics, and psychological characteristics.

sex, and an "equality" position, purportedly based on social constructionist views. There is a range of difference positions, but all share the view that race and sex are significant features of our identity that should be recognized even when there is no racist and sexist oppression.[7] There is also a range of equality views, some of which take race and sex to be significant features of identity but also presuppose, as a near or ultimate goal, a society with no public recognition of race and sex. (See Fuss 1989 on essentialism and constructionism.) One of the benefits of examining the analogies between racism and sexism is finding a view that refuses that choice, as I will discuss next. The strategies of difference and equality are both flawed, I argue, because they do not take into account either the complexity of our experience of identity or the complexity of racism and sexism.

II. ACCEPTING RACE AND SEX

The complexity of experience and of the forms of oppression can only be understood through an acceptance of the role race and sex play in that experience. A number of feminist philosophers, such as Beauvoir (1983), hooks (1987), and Young (1990a), have articulated the importance of race and sex to our subjectivity. There are two different senses in which this more complex position could be interpreted. One could be called a metaphysical sense, in which there is an attempt to give a coherent account of what it is to belong to a group. This is an interesting project; however, I will focus on the political sense of group identity. It is relevant to the current social and political construction of "race" that generally whites are the ones who decide who is white—which means that whites control membership in that privileged group (Frye 1983: 115). One response to this fact has been to celebrate black identity or black consciousness. Similarly, in the case of sex, it is predominantly men who are able to decide when sex matters—when women should be thought of as specifically women and when sex is irrelevant. There is a parallel response in the case of sexism in the assertion of the value of the feminine, by such disparate feminists as Gilligan (1982), Irigaray (1985b), and Greer (1999).[8] These approaches have been criticized for affirming

7. There are also commonly parallels between the analyses that are given of race and those given of sex or gender, as distinct from class. Nancy Fraser, who highlights the distinctions between different forms of oppression, sees race and sex as forms of identity that we may wish to claim something from, even if we were no longer oppressed, but sees class as something that has to disappear with oppression, or as she says "the logic of the remedy is to put the group out of business as a group" (1997: 19). Race and sex are theorized as relevant to our sense of self, or at least more salient than class.

8. In her book on Beauvoir, Moi argues that "in *The Second Sex*, there is no mention of the purely negative need for an 'anti-sexist sexism'" (Moi 1994: 210).

stereotypes or essentializing women. While there is value in these approaches, they may not have analyzed the problem with sufficient subtlety, because it is too complex to be solved by an exclusive focus on celebrating racial or gender identity.

One approach that takes into account the insights of both the equality and difference positions within feminism as well as within antiracism, and that can also overcome the limitations of both positions, is Beauvoir's in *The Second Sex*. Here Beauvoir shows an awareness of the pitfalls of both an approach that rejects membership in a group (such as race or class) and one that essentializes its members—views that she calls nominalism (or constructionism) and conceptualism (or essentialism) respectively.[9] In discussing the relevance of racist oppression to the oppression of women, she argues that there are "deep similarities between the situation of woman and that of the Negro. Both are being emancipated today from a like paternalism, and the former master class wishes to 'keep them in their place'—that is, the place chosen for them" (1983: 23).[10] Beauvoir's dissection of the sources of women's oppression was influenced by contemporary analyses of racism. Margaret Simons describes the influence on Beauvoir of Richard Wright's descriptions of the way that oppression affects psychological development, his emphasis on the lived experience of racism, and his belief in the necessity of race consciousness (Simons 1999).[11] In her search for a solution to oppression, Beauvoir does not take the path of rejecting the concepts of race or sex, and I argue that is because she foresaw the problems that would arise from this approach. Her solution is to contend that a woman should assert herself as *both* human and female: "She refuses to confine herself to her role as female, because she will not accept mutilation; but it would also be a mutilation to repudiate her sex. . . . To renounce her femininity is to renounce a part of her humanity" (1983: 691–92).[12] Both denying one's sex and denying one's humanity is a form of mutilation.

Beauvoir believes that we should reject the myth of the "eternal feminine," but

9. Moi notes that "after reading Beauvoir's account of America in 1947, contemporary postmodern nominalism in America starts to look like the discredited humanist nominalism of the postwar period" (1999: 187).

10. Elizabeth Young-Bruehl criticizes Beauvoir for trying to argue both that there is an analogy between racism and sexism *and* that sexism is unique (1996: 119–20). This is a coherent position provided that one does not take unique to mean "shares no features with other forms of oppression." Racism and sexism can have some similar features and occur simultaneously while each remains unique.

11. He was in turn influenced by W. E. B. Du Bois's idea of double-consciousness, or seeing oneself through the eyes of others (Du Bois 1986).

12. Beauvoir is often claimed to hold the view that women must reject femininity. For example, Naomi Schor (1995: 52) argues that Beauvoir risks "saming": the view that women must be the same as men.

at the same time she argues that it would be bad faith to deny one's race or sex. In her essay "What Is a Woman?" Toril Moi highlights this aspect of Beauvoir's work and elucidates the complexity of her account. Taking a position between the two extremes of nominalism and conceptualism enables her to describe how race and sex are of varying salience. While race and sex are features of our embodiment, they are not *always* the most important ways we think about ourselves, nor can they be used to justify oppressive treatment by others. Beauvoir's project is to give a complex phenomenological description of women's lives. As she writes in the introduction to the second volume of *The Second Sex:* "The point here is not to proclaim eternal truths, but rather to describe the common background from which every particular female existence stands out" (1983: 31; Moi's translation [1999: 198]). Moi's interpretation of this statement is that one's body is a potential source of meaning, and "it follows from Beauvoir's analysis that in some situations the fact of sex will be less important than the fact of class or race; in other situations it will not" (1999: 201).[13] Moi points out that sometimes there will be a hierarchy of these features of our identity and sometimes they will be equally salient. This is the most plausible interpretation of Beauvoir's views, as she says unequivocally that many women experience race or class as more important to their sense of self than sex. This view makes sense; our experience depends on our particular situation. For Jewish women living in Nazi Germany, for example, their Jewishness was likely to be experienced as more central to their identity than their sex.

One of the most fascinating sections in Moi's discussion is her reading of an anecdote that Beauvoir tells about herself. I find this anecdote particularly useful for explaining her position regarding sexism and for developing and extending its insights into the nature of the experience of oppression in general. "In the midst of an abstract discussion," Beauvoir relates, "it is vexing to hear a man say: 'You think thus and so because you are a woman'" and she points out the difficulty of responding to such a remark (1983: 15). It appears that her only defense is to say, "No, I think it because it is true"; but doing so removes her embodied subjectivity from the argument. Beauvoir says it would be out of the question to say, "And you think what you do because you are a man," for it is understood that the fact of being a man is no peculiarity" (1983: 15). Such a reply is out of the question, Moi believes, because it just would not be understood or would be seen as a sign of abandoning the abstract discussion. Furthermore, in such a case of *ad feminam* attack, as Moi calls it, there is little point in stooping to the same level. The moral of this story is that Beauvoir is being forced to a choice that is oppressive: between accepting that her views are determined by her sex or removing her embodied self from the context.

An alternative response Moi suggests is using a defiant silence (distinct from

13. This point poses a challenge to Spelman's claim that Beauvoir prioritizes sex over race.

the silence that is being forced on Beauvoir)—turning on one's heels and walking away. However, this strategy can only work if it is clear that this silence is different from the silence that is being imposed by the man's remark. Although Moi does not recommend that Beauvoir should say, "Yes, I do think that because I am a woman," many of Moi's students claim they would. Yet this response is also problematic, because again there is unlikely to be any "uptake" of such a response. It is unlikely to be understood or taken seriously by the male interlocutor. Moi's students provide different contexts, where it might be held as a claim to expertise: "I think this because of my special insight as a woman." Moi notes that when Beauvoir asserts the truth of her views, she is not denying that her being a woman may be relevant. Moi's point is that if one tries to separate one's sex from one's thought, one will not have access to all of one's own experiences. What are the experiences that we have *just as human beings*? Such experiences could not be distinguished from those we have as raced and sexed beings. None of the possible responses seem to affirm both one's humanity and one's sex.

Moi draws a valuable conclusion from her discussion of Beauvoir's example. She says that women's oppression is "the compulsory foregrounding of the female body at all times" and that it "prevent[s] women from foregrounding the female body when they want it to be significant" (1999: 202).[14] The example Moi gives from Beauvoir is a personal one that expresses the point of view of the oppressed. The insight highlighted in the anecdote can be usefully developed by reflecting on what it demonstrates about the nature of racism and sexism, and I will show how it is relevant more broadly in legal frameworks and the sociopolitical context. Examples of the compulsory foregrounding of women's sex are discrimination and sexual harassment, laws against the employment of women, and the insistence that women change their names on marriage. Examples of attempts to background women's sex are reaction against affirmative action, derogation of women's groups, and denial of maternity leave. In both sets of cases, others decide whether women's sex is relevant or not.

Moi argues that the same logic works in racism. On the one hand, people are made conscious of their race when they would prefer to be forgetful of it. As Frantz Fanon says in *Black Skin, White Masks*, "All I wanted was to be a man among other men" (1967: 112–13). On the other hand, there could be reasons for highlighting one's group membership—even if one believes that race is a fiction. If Beauvoir's example is read in terms of race, readers may not feel that she gives the best possible interpretation of this situation. Perhaps if someone was accused of holding a particular view because of their race they might be able to say proudly, "Of course I think that because of my race." Alcoff describes the experience of an Asian lecturer teaching introductory philosophy to a primarily white

14. Le Doeuff (1991: 28–29) argues that a feminist view is one that acknowledges that sometimes sex is irrelevant and sometimes it is very important.

class in upstate New York. The students were comfortable with him as a teacher until he started to discuss cognitive aspects of racism. Then some of the students refused to look at or speak to him (Bernasconi 2001: 280). In this instance, the lecturer is claiming that race is relevant to the philosophy course, and some students could not accept that.

What is central to the structure of racism is the power to decide when race is relevant. Furthermore, what is most frustrating about racist attitudes is that they involve holding two views simultaneously: race is said to be both irrelevant and omnipresent. In the national inquiry known as the Bringing Them Home Report, an Aboriginal woman observes that Aboriginal children were taken from their families to be brought up as whites, but at the same time they were expected to defer to whites: "They tried to make us act like white kids but at the same time we had to give up our seat for a whitefella because an Aboriginal never sits down when a white person is present" (Human Rights Commission 1997, submission 640). Aboriginal identity was taken to be of no cultural relevance in a positive sense but to be a marker of lesser privilege. Aboriginal people had no say in whether or when their aboriginality mattered.

The poor thinking and irrationalism conveyed in both racism and sexism involve this particular exercise of power. This aspect of racism, which is often commented on, results from the commitment to racism and its fundamentally irrational basis. One day, race does not matter at all; the next day it is of the greatest importance.[15] Jean-Paul Sartre shows the sloppiness and bad faith of anti-Semitic thinking, where the same vice or virtue is interpreted differently, depending on whether one is discussing a Jewish person or a Christian (1995: 56). In the case of sexism, Le Doeuff demonstrates how male philosophers, in particular, do not live up to their own standards of reasoning when they write about women (1991: 70).

Ideology and institutional structures mirror views about whether one's "particularity" must be foregrounded or not. These structures can create racist actions and attitudes, as well as reflecting them. In the Bringing Them Home Report the documents testify to the way successive governments denied Aboriginal humanity by claiming that Aboriginal mothers soon forgot their children. A protector in Western Australia boasted, "I would not hesitate for one moment to separate any half-caste from its aboriginal mother, no matter how frantic her momentary grief might be at the time. They soon forget their offspring" (Human Rights Commission 1997, submission 385). Of course, the subtext here is

---

15 This characterization of racism itself may seem to need explaining—for example, by arguing that racists hold the views they do in order to gain a sense of self-worth. Although this is a significant consideration, I will leave it aside here to focus on the structure of the thinking.

that the feelings of Aboriginal mothers toward their children are inferior to white mothers'. At the same time, white government officials denied the importance of aboriginality by claiming that Aboriginal children would be perfectly happy with a white family. In the Australian context, the view that race is irrelevant can be seen in the demand for sameness of treatment of white and indigenous Australians, and in the failure to recognize unique historical and cultural circumstances and their implications for the present. Some contemporary political currents such as Hansonism in Australia involve the desire to reduce difference. The claim that indigenous people are gaining "special treatment" is based on the idea that we are all the same and no one should be treated differently.[16] In the general refusal to countenance reserved seats in parliament for indigenous people, their unique position is not recognized; in the government's refusal to apologize for past injustices, the unique history is not recognized; and in the attacks on *Mabo* and *Wik* (court judgments acknowledging Aboriginal land rights), Aboriginal people's unique connection to the land is ignored. However, in racist claims about crime, for example, aboriginality is often treated as most salient. Claims by whites to be Aboriginal involve taking the power of self-definition away from Aboriginal people.

One caveat to this analysis is that probably the most extreme forms of racism and sexism involve the highlighting of one's race or sex at all times. Current Australian immigration policy involves highlighting the differences of refugees by describing them as the sort of people who would throw their children into the water, for example. The cases I have given may suggest that what is really involved in racism and sexism is the foregrounding or not foregrounding of race and sex to the detriment of the oppressed. If this were the correct interpretation of my account, then the highlighting of race or race to a person's benefit or advantage would be a sign of antiracism or sexism. One example is the idea that people would like to have women bosses or women colleagues. Yet this example is also a sign of assuming the power to determine when sex is relevant and in what way, and it creates oppressive situations through expectations of a certain style or character. Women should be accepted in workplaces without such limiting conditions.

Beauvoir's notion of lived experience is a valuable one for thinking about the intersection or race and sex, because it is the way the body is lived that is important to one's sense of identity and consequently to how others should respond to oppressed groups. It can allow that indigenous women, for example, may sometimes find that being Aboriginal is more important for them than be-

16. Pauline Hanson was the leader of the One Nation Party in Australia, a populist party that trades on the idea that it is not racist because it just wants equal (the same) treatment for everyone.

ing women, or that the two aspects of identity interact in such a complex way that they are inseparable.[17] Beauvoir's analysis shows that antiracist and feminist thought needs to be aware that both extremes—of denying one's membership in a group and highlighting it at all times—contribute to the oppressiveness of racism and sexism. A more complex account is one that recognizes that the significance of race and sex will differ according to context.

My view is that we need the concepts of race, sex, and gender for the foreseeable future and even in a just political future because they are central to people's identity and will remain so even if they are not oppressed. Although there are damaging racist ways to think about race, the idea of race per se is not the problem, and there are reasons for having the elimination of race as a project. A better response is to avoid using these concepts in ways that accept racist identifications and descriptions. Instead, all kinds of differences should be responded to in ways that accept the specificity and autonomy of the other.[18] The concept of race needs to be interrogated and reworked rather than rejected.

Both the concept of ethnicity and the concept of race will be necessary in a just society, because the concept of ethnicity does not do the same work in language as the idea of race. We continue to need the concept of race because there has been so much cultural loss for some groups that "ethnicity" does not suggest their exceptional historical situation. For example, in the Australian context, ethnicity connotes cultural variation, a notion that does not do justice to the unique situation of indigenous people living in this country. Ethnicity relies on particular aspects of culture, such as the idea of a shared language or religion, whereas the idea of race, used in a positive sense, can suggest other connections. Indigenous people may not have a shared language, but they do have a particular set of relations to history and the land. Ethnicity does not convey the sense of acceptable group differences any more than race does, since groups may be oppressed on the basis of religion or culture, as in the former Yugoslavia. There seems to be more variation in the form of that oppression, as shifting waves of immigration have shown. We may not always need the idea of race; it is possible that it will be abandoned in a utopian future "after the revolution." But that future is further off than is sometimes imagined, and our ways of thinking about these questions has to take into account the contemporary situation of oppressed groups.

Of course, there is plenty of room for disagreement about when sex and race should be recognized and when not. A feminist antiracism should be committed to allowing oppressed people to determine this. One criticism of this approach is that it suggests that oppressed people can determine the relevance of their group membership in an arbitrary and inconsistent way. This does not ap-

17. Alcoff takes up the idea of lived experience to argue that race is an aspect of lived reality, so we cannot give up on it as a concept (Bernasconi 2001).

18. The concept of wonder captures this response well. See La Caze 2002.

pear to be a problem because so much thought has already been put into working out a consistent way of thinking about these issues. The criticism itself expresses the racist and sexist view that oppressed people are incapable of thinking through these matters seriously. Oppressed people should be able to make their views heard and taken into account. The connection I see between the phenomenology of oppressed people's experience and issues of justice is that justice must involve respect for oppressed people's experience and sense of identity. This can be contrasted with a view of justice that either denies oppressed people their sense of being members of a group or involves recognition of group membership in all contexts.

So far I have concentrated on the similarities in the general structure of racist and sexist oppression. It should be noted that Beauvoir also claims that there are important disanalogies between racist and sexist oppression. She argues that the othering of women is different from that of other oppressed groups because women internalize the view that others take. Although African Americans feel they are othered, she argues, "the Negroes submit with a feeling of revolt, no privileges compensating for their hard lot, whereas woman is offered inducements to complicity" (1983: 325).[19] However, this particular disanalogy is problematic because those oppressed by racism also internalize the view that the oppressor takes of them, at least to a certain extent, as is made clear by the notion of "double consciousness." Although this notion can be understood as either a negation of black consciousness or as a conflict between black and white ideals, it implies that blacks find it difficult not to be seen through white eyes or, to put it another way, not to be affected by white's perceptions (Allen 1997: 50), just as women are affected by men's perceptions. There can be no real reciprocity between the racist and one who has to live with racism, at least not the kind of reciprocity one finds between people who regard each other as equals. There are "inducements to complicity" for racially oppressed groups as well as women.

Antiracist theorists argue, however, that in the case of racist oppression it is possible to escape double consciousness in a way that one cannot in sexist oppression. As Ernest Allen says, "it was not necessary to the healthy psychological edification of the black individual that African-American self-recognition be tied absolutely to recognition by whites; for there was always the *mutual recognition* which black folk bestowed on one another, an acknowledgement which, under prevailing conditions, served as a bulwark against the possibility of absolute black self-deprecation" (1997: 54; italics in original). It is precisely this mutual recognition that Beauvoir is arguing does not exist between women. Women do not provide each other with that kind of support. However, this claim needs qualification. Oppression is a matter of degree, and as women begin to escape

19. It should be noted that Beauvoir does not use the term "Negroes" in her original text. Rather she uses the expression "les noirs d'Amérique" (Beauvoir 1949, 2:47).

from oppression, women are able to recognize each other in that way, as women and human beings.

Another related disanalogy Beauvoir raises is the lack of solidarity among women compared to other oppressed groups. She argues that women form a group, just as Jewish people and black people do, but do not have the solidarity of those groups because women's lives are bound up with the lives of individual oppressors. Women lack the means to be independent, and some women are "very well pleased with her role as the other" (1983: 21). Another sign of the lack of solidarity among women is the racism some white women express toward black women (Simons 1999: 180; Beauvoir 1998: 231). Elisabeth Young-Bruehl also argues that sexism cannot be modeled directly on racism because women do not form a group separate to men in the way whites ("in-group") separate from blacks ("out-group"). She writes: "Prejudice against women was too close, too intimate, too intrafamilial to be seen in its uniqueness—especially by the predominantly male community of social scientists, where the prejudice was far from absent" (1996: 111).[20] This claim echoes J. S. Mill's statement that women's oppression is peculiar in that women's closeness to particular men is always greater than their closeness to other women (1970: 136). Women's oppressors are fathers, sons, brothers, and husbands. However, in some forms of ethnic hatred, such as in the Rwandan genocide, the members of the different groups can be closely related through marriage and be partners, cousins, aunts, uncles, grand-parents, and grandchildren. The extent of intimacy between oppressed groups and oppressors or warring groups will vary. My point here is not that there are no disanalogies between sexism and other forms of oppression, but they are more fine-grained than these kinds of sweeping suggestions concerning inter-nalization, complicity, and intimacy.

Although there are similar structures involved in racism and sexism, indige-nous women, nonindigenous women, poor women, and women of different re-ligions and ethnicities experience sexism in very different contexts, so different

20. According to Young-Bruehl, sexism is more totalizing than racism; she says that "sex-ism flows through every facet of a sexist's existence, leaving, as it were, no place to stand to see it" (1996: 546). The other difference she believes exists between sexism and both racism and anti-Semitism is that there are more levels or layers to its manifestations (130). It might appear that Young-Bruehl is arguing for what Spelman believes is a racist view—a view which says that sexism is more fundamental than racism—but that is not necessarily the case. Her view suggests that sexism will appear differently because of the contexts it occurs in, such as "cosmological visions." Young-Bruehl argues that sexism is a form of narcissism, and differs from other "-isms" because it is not directed at an Other that it wishes to elimi-nate. She believes that sexism is a "prejudice which denies differences, that fundamentally, under layers of difference marking, wants no others" (1996: 134). By "wants no others" she means that men do not want women to be "marked" as a different group, whereas other prej-udices depend on such "othering."

women may need to explore different forms of liberation. Racism and sexism interact, but they also function independently in some contexts. For example, some aspects of racism may disappear sooner than sexism; sexism becomes more obvious than racial discrimination in salaries and positions; and some aspects of sexism may disappear faster than racism, as when equal rights legislation affects middle-class white women first. The forms of liberation of oppressed races of both sexes may come into conflict with the forms of liberation of some women. My examination of Beauvoir's view of the oppression of women shows that there are insights to be gained from comparing and contrasting racism and sexism.

III. OVERCOMING RACISM

Beauvoir's analysis further suggests why some antiracist strategies are more problematic than others. Even Spelman, who is so critical of the analogy, demonstrates in her work that there are fruitful comparisons to be made between racism and sexism, provided that they are nonreductive and explore both analogies and disanalogies. A mistake in feminist theory like the rejection of the body, she points out, could lead to a mistake in antiracism, and vice versa (Spelman 1988: 127).[21] A failed or successful feminist political strategy may suggest ways to rethink antiracist strategies, and vice versa.

The structure of oppression also affects the structure of responses to it. One sort of response, the desire that one's race or sex be recognized, is at the basis of identity politics. On the one hand, Moi argues that it is not only sexism that tries to trap women in femininity—some feminist thought and practice also attempts to do so. She believes that identity politics goes too far in thinking that race or sex should always be salient. (Not all identity politics goes that far, however; in Young's view [1990a], for example, difference will be irrelevant in many circumstances.) On the other hand, Moi is also critical of women who (in her view) deny their sex by saying, "I am a writer, not a woman writer" or (one can add) "I am a writer, not a black writer." This particular example is problematic because the question here is not simply one of denying one's race or sex. Comments about

21. Some feminists have taken the implications of Spelman's work (and that of others) to be that one cannot make any generalizations at all about women's experiences. Susan Bordo (1990) points out the problems with this approach and the need for generalizations in feminist theory. A more realistic conclusion is that feminist and antiracist philosophers need to take greater care in making generalizations—in describing stereotypes, roles, and experiences and in characterizing oppression. For example, Jan Pettman argues that Aboriginal women find family a place of comfort and validation (1992: 67); so attacks on the family by white feminists are a problem when Aboriginal families are already being attacked by a racist state. This problem is particularly acute in the case of the stolen generations.

women writers and black writers often involve a value judgment about their work, often expressed explicitly in comments such as "She is one of the best women writers in the country." In this context there is an implicit devaluation of women writers, painters, and intellectuals and of black writers, painters, and intellectuals as contrasted with the group or groups they are being compared with. It suggests that someone is good as a woman writer but not as good as most men writers, or good as an indigenous writer but not compared to white writers. A black woman writer is then compared both to nonblack writers of either sex and to male black writers. Moi claims that because people accept the foregrounding of women's sex in such contexts, "the phrase 'an intellectual man' sounds quite odd whereas 'an intellectual woman' sounds quite normal" (1999: 205), although arguably both sound odd. Nevertheless, her point that men are never accused of denying their masculinity when they call themselves writers or philosophers is an important one. To be forced to choose between denying one's race or sex and affirming it at all times is oppressive. Moi sees the debate between equality feminism and difference feminism as a reflection of this oppressive structure, and she considers Beauvoir's project an attempt to think beyond that forced choice, beyond essentialism and nominalism or constructionism.[22] The debate between "equality antiracism" and "difference antiracism" also reflects this oppressive structure.

Beauvoir's position, between essentialism and nominalism or constructionism, shows why some approaches to antiracism are problematic. We have to accept both humanity and difference; but many antiracists believe we must either reject commonalities between human beings (what Moi calls "the universal") or reject the idea of identity, whether it is black identity or whiteness, for example. In general, approaches that only focus on either affirming difference or denying difference will lead to difficulties. An increasingly popular approach (in the United States) is the notion of the "white traitor," a strategy that illustrates in a more complex way the risks in denying group membership. Both Alison Bailey (1998) and Marilyn Frye (1983) argue that it is possible to disaffiliate from the group of whites. Frye argues that white women should reject the attachment to white men, because equality with white men means a share in racial domination. Feminism can seem treacherous to the white race if it involves white men relinquishing control over reproduction. Examples of limited forms of white treachery are protests against the benefits of being white, or Frye's idea that we should not promote "whiteliness" which she sees as the display of certain characteristics, such as assuming authority in relation to people of color.

22. Diana Fuss's characterization of Beauvoir (1989: 3) simply as an anti-essentialist misunderstands her view. See La Caze 1994, where I discuss Beauvoir's understanding of female bodies and sexuality in the light of issues concerning essentialism and constructionism.

Alcoff discusses some of the problems with the notions of white treachery that involve a rejection of white identity. White treachery can be as simple as denying one's whiteness to shopkeepers, or moving to predominantly black neighborhoods. In one series of incidents in Indiana, the behavior of so-called white traitors who dressed in styles judged "black" by other whites made life dangerous for themselves and very dangerous for their African-American neighbors, who had not been consulted (Alcoff 2000: 271–72). Alcoff is critical of these types of actions because, outside the clear-cut political context of strikes, boycotts, and protests such as those of the civil rights movement, their meaning is unpredictable and potentially dangerous. Furthermore, even white traitors benefit from being white. She argues that whites need to develop a "double consciousness" that accepts both a connection of responsibility to the racist past and present and recognizes the ways in which whites have challenged racism. This is yet another use of the notion of double consciousness. It is quite a positive sense, one that accepts different aspects of the past. One could see it as an acceptance of facticity or identity combined with a realization that it is possible to change, to become antiracist.

Alcoff's reasoning is a good example of dealing with racism without acting in bad faith, which is how Beauvoir would understand the thinking behind white treachery. It is parallel to the avoidance of bad faith by members of oppressed groups who, while not denying their identity as members of the group, deny that they are determined to live in a particular way. Some forms of white treachery are examples of bad faith because they involve the denial of one's identity. Although being white might not be the most salient feature of a person at every moment, a political strategy based on the denial of one's own culture and history is likely to be disempowering and risky for oppressed groups and antiracist activists.

Although there are risks in complacently accepting analogies between racism and sexism, the relationship between the two is worthy of reexamination. An interrogation of Beauvoir's work concerning the nature of the oppression of women demonstrates that insights are to be gained from comparing racism and sexism. The structure that Beauvoir identifies in individual experiences is relevant to analyzing sociopolitical issues and policy formation. What emerges is that racism arises, not from paying attention to race, but from paying attention to it in the wrong way at the wrong time in the wrong context. And the same is true of sexism.

It follows from this understanding that color blindness and sex blindness are flawed strategies for dealing with oppression. Color blindness institutes the values of the dominant group, fails to allow self-definition of oppressed peoples of different races, and overlooks the reality of day-to-day discrimination. The strategy of sex blindness cannot be successful because it too imposes the dominant values and fails to recognize the value in being a woman.[23] Strategies that involve highlighting a person's race and sex in all circumstances are also flawed, because they too refuse to allow oppressed people's self-definition and impose demanding and constricting expectations. Racism is constituted by the assumption of the power to determine when oppressed people's race is relevant and when not, a structure similarly constitutive of sexism. A fruitful antiracist feminist philosophy is one that takes into account this basic similarity of structure between racism and sexism while remaining sensitive to the differences and interactions between specific oppressions.

23. A number of antiracists and feminists have argued against the ideals of color blindness and sex blindness (Spelman 1988, Young 1990a).

REFERENCES

Alcoff, Linda Martín. 1998. "Racism." In *A Companion to Feminist Philosophy*, edited by Alison M. Jaggar and Iris Marion Young. Oxford: Blackwell.

——. 2000a. "On Judging Epistemic Credibility." In *Women of Color and Philosophy*, edited by Naomi Zack. Oxford: Blackwell.

——. 2000b. "What Should White People Do?" In *Decentering the Center: Philosophy for a Multicultural, Postcolonial, and Feminist World*, edited by Uma Narayan and Sandra Harding. Bloomington: Indiana University Press.

Allen, Ernest. 1997. "On the Reading of Riddles: Rethinking Du Boisian 'Double Consciousness.'" In *Existence in Black: An Anthology of Black Existential Philosophy*, edited by Lewis Gordon. London: Routledge.

Allport, Gordon. 1954. *The Nature of Prejudice.* Reading, Mass.: Addison Wesley.

Anderson, Elizabeth. 1993. *Value in Ethics and Economics.* Cambridge: Harvard University Press.

——. 1999a. "Reply." In *Brown Electronic Article Review Service*, edited by Jamie Dreier and David Estlund. http://www.brown.edu/Departments/Philosophy/bears/homepage.html [August 2002].

——. 1999b. "What Is the Point of Equality?" *Ethics* 109, no. 2:287–337.

——. 2002. "Should Feminists Reject Rational Choice Theory?" In *A Mind of One's Own*, 2d ed., edited by Louise Antony and Charlotte Witt. Boulder, Colo.: Westview.

Appiah, Kwame Anthony. 1990. "Racisms." In *Anatomy of Racism*, edited by David Theo Goldberg. Minneapolis: University of Minnesota Press.

——. 1992. *In My Father's House.* New York: Oxford University Press.

——. 1999. "Why There Are No Races." In *Racism*, edited by Leonard Harris. New York: Humanity Books.

——. 2002. "Racism: History of Hatred: A Review of George Frederickson's *Racism: A Short History.*" *New York Times*, 4 August, Book Review section, pp. 11–12.

Arendt, Hannah. 1979. *The Origins of Totalitarianism.* Florida: Harcourt, Brace.

——. 1994. *Eichmann in Jerusalem.* New York: Penguin.

Babbitt, Susan E., and Sue Campbell, eds. 1999. *Racism and Philosophy.* Ithaca, N.Y.: Cornell University Press.

Baier, Annette. 1995. *Moral Prejudices.* Cambridge: Harvard University Press.

Baier, Kurt. 1993. *The Moral and Social Order.* Chicago: Open Court.

Bailey, Alison. 1998. "Locating Traitorous Identities: Toward a View of Privilege-Cognizant White Character." *Hypatia: A Journal of Feminist Philosophy* 13, no. 3:27–43.

Baldwin, James. 1967. *The Fire Next Time.* London: Hutchinson.

———. 1995. *Going to Meet the Man.* New York: Vintage Books.

Banton, Michael. 1998. *Racial Theories.* 2d ed. Cambridge: Cambridge University Press.

Barndt, Joseph. 1991. *Dismantling Racism: The Continuing Challenge to White America.* Minneapolis: Augsburg Fortress.

Baron-Cohen, Simon. 1995. *Mindblindness: An Essay on Autism and Theory of Mind.* Cambridge: MIT Press.

Baumann, Zygmunt. 1997. *Postmodernity and Its Discontents.* Oxford: Polity.

Beauvoir, Simone de. 1949. *Le deuxième sexe.* 2 vols. Paris: Gallimard.

———. 1964. *Force of Circumstance.* Translated by Richard Howard. Harmondsworth, England: Penguin.

———. 1983. *The Second Sex.* Translated by H. M. Parshley. London: Penguin.

———. 1998. *America Day by Day.* Translated by Carol Cosman. London: Victor Gollancz.

Benedict, Ruth. 1999. "Racism: The *ism* of the Modern World," and "Why the Race Prejudice?" 1940. Reprinted in *Racism,* edited by Leonard Harris. New York: Humanity Books.

Berlin, Isaiah. 1996. "Kant as an Unfamiliar Source of Nationalism." In *The Sense of Reality,* by Isaiah Berlin. London: Chatto and Windus.

Bernasconi, Robert. 2001. *Race.* Oxford: Blackwell.

Beyer, Lawrence A. 1999. "The Disintegration of Belief." Ph.D. diss., Stanford University.

Bion, W. 1961. *Experiences in Groups.* New York: Basic Books.

Blondell, Ruby, et al. 1999. *Women on the Edge: Four Plays by Euripides.* New York: Routledge.

Blum, Lawrence. 1980. *Friendship, Altruism, and Morality.* Boston: Routledge.

———. 1999. "Moral Asymmetries in Racism." In *Racism and Philosophy,* edited by Susan E. Babbitt and Sue Campbell. Ithaca, N.Y.: Cornell University Press.

———. 2002. *I'm Not a Racist, But . . . : The Moral Quandary of Race.* Ithaca, N.Y.: Cornell University Press.

Blythe, Will. 2000. "The Guru of White Hate." *Rolling Stone,* 8 June, pp. 98–106.

Bordo, Susan. 1990. "Feminism, Postmodernism, and Gender-Scepticism." In *Feminism/Postmodernism,* edited by Linda J. Nicholson. New York: Routledge.

Bowie, Malcolm. 1993. *Psychoanalysis and the Future of Theory.* Oxford: Blackwell.

Boxill, Bernard. 1993. "Fear and Shame as Forms of Moral Suasion in the Thought of Frederick Douglass." *In Transactions of the Charles Peirce Society* 35, no. 4: 713–744.

———. 2003. "Kant and Rousseau on Progress and Teleology." Department of Philosophy, University of North Carolina at Chapel Hill. Photocopy.

———, ed. 2001. *Race and Racism.* Oxford: Oxford University Press.

Bragg, Rick. 2001. "On the Eve of His Execution, McVeigh's Legacy Remains Death and Pain." *New York Times,* 10 June, p. 26.

Butler, Judith. 1990. *Gender Trouble: Feminism and the Subversion of Identity.* London: Routledge.

———. 1993. *Bodies That Matter: On the Discursive Limits of "Sex."* London: Routledge.

Calhoun, Cheshire. 1989. "Responsibility and Reproach." *Ethics* 99, no. 2:389–406.

Canto-Sperber, Monique. 2003. *L'inquiétude morale et la vie humaine*. Paris: Presses Universitaires de France.

Carby, Hazel. 1982. "White Woman Listen! Black Feminism and the Boundaries of Sisterhood." In *The Empire Strikes Back: Race and Racism in 70s Britain*. London: Hutchinson.

Carmichael, Stokeley, and Charles Hamilton. 1968. *Black Power: The Politics of Liberation in America*. Harmondsworth, England: Penguin.

Casey, Edward S. 1991. "'The Element of Voluminousness': Depth and Place Reexamined." In *Merleau-Ponty Vivant*, edited by M. C. Dillon. Albany: State University of New York Press.

Char, René. *Hypnos Waking: Poems and Prose*. Selected and translated by Jackson Matthews, with the collaboration of William Carlos Williams. New York: Random House. 1956.

Coady, C. A. J. 1992. *Testimony: A Philosophical Study*. Oxford: Clarendon.

Cohen, G. A. 1997. "Where the Action Is: On the Site of Distributive Justice." *Philosophy and Public Affairs* 26, no. 1:3–30.

———. 2000. "Justice, Incentives, and Selfishness." In *If You're an Egalitarian, How Come You're So Rich?* Cambridge: Harvard University Press.

Cole, Mike. 1997. "Race and Racism." In *A Dictionary of Cultural and Critical Theory*, edited by Michael Payne. Oxford: Blackwell.

Collins, Patricia Hill. 1998. *Fighting Words: Black Women and the Search for Justice*. Minneapolis: University of Minnesota Press.

Conrad, Joseph. 1982. *The Heart of Darkness*. 1902. Reprint, Harmondsworth, England: Penguin.

Corlett, J. Angelo. 1998. "Analyzing Racism." *Public Affairs Quarterly* 12:23–50.

Crenshaw, Kimberle Williams. 1995. "Mapping the Margins: Intersectionality, Identity Politics, and Violence against Women of Color." In *Critical Race Theory*, edited by Kimberle Crenshaw et al. New York: The New Press.

Cutting-Gray, Joanne. 1996. "Hannah Arendt, Feminism and the Politics of Alterity: 'What Will We Lose If We Win.'" In *Hypatia's Daughters: Fifteen Hundred Years of Women Philosophers*, edited by Linda Lopez McAlister. Bloomington: Indiana University Press.

Dalton, Harlan. 1996. *Racial Healing*. New York: Anchor.

Daly, Mary. 1973. *Beyond God the Father: Toward a Philosophy of Women's Liberation*. Boston: Beacon.

Dancy, Jonathan. 1985. *An Introduction to Contemporary Epistemology*. Oxford: Blackwell.

Darwall, Stephen. 1983. *Impartial Reason*. Ithaca, N.Y.: Cornell University Press.

Davis, David Brion. 1966. *The Problem of Slavery in Western Culture*. Oxford: Oxford University Press.

Davis, Duane. 1991. "Reversible Subjectivity." In *Merleau-Ponty Vivant*, edited by M. C. Dillon. Albany: State University of New York Press.

Davis, Jefferson. 1860. "Jefferson Davis's Reply in the Senate to William H. Seward." www.jeffersondavis.rice.edu/resources.cfm?doc id+1502 [July 2003].

Delany, Martin. 1999. "The Condition, Elevation, Emigration, and Destiny of the Colored People of the United States." In *African American Social and Political Thought, 1850–1920,* edited by Howard Brotz. New Brunswick: Transactions Publishers.

Dennett, Daniel C. 1978. *Brainstorms: Philosophical Essays on Mind and Psychology.* Cambridge, Mass.: MIT Press.

Derman-Sparks, Louise, and Carol Brunson Phillips. 1997. *Teaching/Learning Anti-Racism: A Developmental Approach.* New York: Teachers College Press.

Diamond, Jared. 1992. *The Third Chimpanzee.* New York: HarperCollins.

———. 1994. "Race without Color." *Discover* 15, no. 11 (November):82–89.

Dodds, E. R. 1951. *The Greeks and the Irrational.* Berkeley: University of California Press.

Douglass, Frederick. 1950. "An Appeal to the British People." In *The Life and Writings of Frederick Douglass,* vol. 1, edited by Philip S. Foner. New York: International Publishers.

———. 1987. *My Bondage and My Freedom.* Urbana: University of Illinois Press.

D'Souza, Dinesh. 1995. *The End of Racism: Principles for a Multi-Racial Society.* New York: Free Press.

Du Bois, W. E. B. 1986. *W. E. B. Du Bois: Writings.* New York: The Library of America.

Dummett, Ann. 1973. *A Portrait of English Racism.* London: Penguin.

Dummett, Michael. 2001. *On Immigration and Refugees.* London: Routledge.

Ehrenreich, Barbara. 2001. *Nickel and Dimed: On Not Getting By in America.* New York: Henry Holt.

Erikson, Erik H. 1974. *Identity: Youth and Crisis.* London: Faber and Faber.

Eze, Emmanuel 2001. *Achieving Our Humanity: The Idea of the Postracial Future.* London: Routledge.

———, ed. 1997. *Race and the Enlightenment: A Reader.* Cambridge, Mass.: Blackwell.

Ezekiel, Ralph S. 1995. *The Racist Mind.* New York: Penguin.

Ezorsky, Gertrude. 1991. *Racism and Justice: The Case for Affirmative Action.* Ithaca, N.Y.: Cornell University Press.

Fanon, Frantz. 1967. *Black Skin, White Masks.* New York: Grove.

Feagin, Joe R., Hernan Vera, and Pinar Batur. 2001. *White Racism,* 2d ed. New York: Routledge.

Feagin, Joe R., Hernan Vera, and Nikitah Imani. 1996. *The Agony of Education: Black Students at White Colleges and Universities.* New York: Routledge.

Fielding, Helen. Forthcoming. "White Logic and the Constancy of Colour." In *Feminist Interpretations of Merleau-Ponty,* edited by Dorthea Olkowski and Gail Weiss. State College: Pennsylvania State University Press.

Firestone, Shulamith. 1970. *The Dialectic of Sex: The Case for a Feminist Revolution.* London: Paladin.

Fischer, John Martin, and Mark Ravizza, eds. 1993. *Perspectives on Moral Responsibility.* Ithaca, N.Y.: Cornell University Press.

Fonagy, Peter, and Mary Target. 1998. "Mentalization and the Changing Aims of Psychoanalysis." *Psychoanalytic Dialogues* 8, no. 1:87–114.

Fóti, Véronique M. 1993. "The Dimension of Color." In *The Merleau-Ponty Aesthetics*

Reader: Philosophy and Painting, edited by Galen Johnson. Evanston, Ill.: Northwestern
    University Press.

Foucault, Michel. 1978. *The History of Sexuality,* vol. 1, *An Introduction.* Translated by
    Robert Hurley. New York: Random House.

Fraser, Nancy. 1989a. "Foucault on Modern Power: Empirical Insights and Normative
    Confusions." In *Unruly Practices: Power Discourse and Gender in Contemporary Social
    Theory.* Minneapolis: University of Minnesota Press.

——. 1989b. *Unruly Practices: Power Discourse and Gender in Contemporary Social Theory.*
    Minneapolis: University of Minnesota Press.

——. 1997. *Justice Interruptus: Critical Reflections on the "Postsocialist" Condition.* London:
    Routledge.

Frederickson, George. 1999. "Reflections on the Comparative History and Sociology of
    Racism." In *Racism,* edited by Leonard Harris. New York: Humanity Books.

——. 2000. "Understanding Racism: Reflections of a Comparative Historian." In *The
    Comparative Imagination: On the History of Racism, Nationalism, and Social
    Movements.* Berkeley: University of California Press.

——. 2002. *Racism: A Short History.* Princeton: Princeton University Press.

Freud, Sigmund. 1953. *On Dreams.* In *Standard Edition of the Complete Psychological Works
    of Sigmund Freud,* vol. 5. London: Hogarth.

——. 1955. "Beyond the Pleasure Principle." In *Standard Edition of the Complete
    Psychological Works of Sigmund Freud,* vol. 18. London: Hogarth.

——. 1959. "Character and Anal Erotism." In *Standard Edition of the Complete
    Psychological Works of Sigmund Freud,* vol. 9. London: Hogarth.

——. 1961a. *Civilization and Its Discontents.* In *Standard Edition of the Complete
    Psychological Works of Sigmund Freud,* vol. 21. London: Hogarth.

——. 1961b. "Libidinal Types." In *Standard Edition of the Complete Psychological Works of
    Sigmund Freud,* vol. 21. London: Hogarth.

Frye, Marilyn. 1983. *The Politics of Reality: Essays in Feminist Theory.* Freedom: Crossing.

——. 2001. "White Woman Feminist 1983–1992." In *Race and Racism,* edited by Bernard
    Boxill. Oxford: Oxford University Press.

Fuss, Diana. 1989. *Essentially Speaking: Feminism, Nature and Difference.* New York:
    Routledge.

Gaita, Raimond. 2000. *A Common Humanity.* London: Routledge.

Garcia, J. L. A. 1996. "The Heart of Racism." *Journal of Social Philosophy* 27:5–45.

——. 1997a. "Current Conceptions of Racism: A Critical Examination of Some Recent
    Social Philosophy." *Journal of Social Philosophy* 28, no. 2:5–42.

——. 1997b. "Racism as a Model for Understanding Sexism." In *Race/Sex: Their Sameness,
    Difference and Interplay,* edited by Naomi Zack. New York: Routledge.

——. 1999. "Philosophical Analysis and the Moral Concept of Racism." *Philosophy and
    Social Criticism* 25:1–32.

——. 2001a. "The Racial Contract Hypothesis." *Philosophia Africana* 4:27–42.

——. 2001b. "Racism and Racial Discourse." *Philosophical Forum* 32:125–45.

Gates, Henry Louis, Jr. 1986. "Talkin' That Talk." In *Race, Writing, and Difference,* edited by H. L. Gates, Jr. Chicago: University of Chicago Press.

Gilligan, Carol. 1982. *In a Different Voice: Psychological Theory and Women's Development.* Cambridge: Harvard University Press.

Goldberg, David Theo. 1993. *Racist Culture: Philosophy and the Politics of Meaning.* Oxford: Blackwell Publishers.

———. 1999. "Racism and Rationality: The Need for a New Critique." In *Racism,* edited by Leonard Harris. New York: Humanity Books.

———, ed. 1990. *Anatomy of Racism.* Minneapolis: University of Minnesota Press.

Goldman, Alvin I. 1986. *Epistemology and Cognition.* Cambridge: Harvard University Press.

Gould, Stephen J. 1996. *The Mismeasure of Man.* Rev. ed. Harmondsworth, England: Penguin.

Greer, Germaine. 1999. *The Whole Woman.* London: Doubleday.

Grosz, Elizabeth. 1994. *Volatile Bodies: Toward a Corporeal Feminism.* Sydney: Allen and Unwin.

Hannaford, Ivan. 1996. *Race: The History of an Idea in the West.* Washington, D.C.: Woodrow Wilson Center Press.

Harman, G. 1986. *Change in View.* Cambridge: MIT Press.

Harris, Leonard, ed. 1999. *Racism.* New York: Humanity Books

Haslanger, Sally. 2000. "Gender and Race: (What) Are They? (What) Do We Want Them To Be?" *Noûs* 34, no. 1:31–55.

———. Forthcoming. "You Mixed? Racial Identity without Racial Biology." In *Kith and Kin: Philosophical and Feminist Issues in Adoption,* edited by Charlotte Witt and Sally Haslanger. Ithaca, N.Y.: Cornell University Press.

Herman, Barbara. 1993. *The Practice of Moral Judgment.* Cambridge: Harvard University Press.

———. 1998. "Moral Literacy." In *The Tanner Lectures on Human Values,* vol. 19, edited by Grethe B. Peterson. Salt Lake City: University of Utah Press.

Herodotus. 1992. *The Histories,* edited by Walter Blanco. New York: Norton.

Herrnstein, Richard J., and Charles Murray. 1994. *The Bell Curve: The Reshaping of American Life by Difference in Intelligence.* New York: Free Press.

Hill, Thomas E., Jr., and Bernard Boxill. 2001. "Kant and Race." In *Race and Racism,* edited by Bernard Boxill. Oxford: Oxford University Press.

Hobsbawm, Eric. 1987. *The Age of Empire.* London: Weidenfeld and Nicolson.

———. 1995. *The Age of Capital.* London: Weidenfeld and Nicolson.

Hockenos, Paul. 1993. *Free to Hate: The Rise of the Right in Post-Communist Eastern Europe.* New York: Routledge.

Holy See. 2001. *Intervention by the Head of the Holy See Delegation at the Durban World Conference against Racism, Racial Discrimination, Xenophobia and Related Intolerance.* 3 September. www.vatican.va.

hooks, bell. 1987. "Feminism: A Movement to End Sexist Oppression." In *Feminism and Equality,* edited by Anne Phillips. Oxford: Blackwell.

Human Rights and Equal Opportunity Commission. 1997. *National Inquiry into the Separation of Aboriginal and Torres Strait Islander Children from Their Families.* Canberra.

Hume, David. 1985. *Essays, Moral, Political and Literary.* 1777. Reprint, Indianapolis: Liberty Fund.

Irigaray, Luce. 1985a. *Speculum of the Other Woman.* Translated by Gillian C. Gill. Ithaca, N.Y.: Cornell University Press.

———. 1985b. *This Sex Which Is Not One.* Translated by Catherine Porter with Carolyn Burke. Ithaca, N.Y.: Cornell University Press.

Jaggar, Alison. 1979. "On Sexual Equality." In *Philosophy and Women,* edited by Sharon Bishop and Marjorie Weinzweig. Belmont, Calif.: Wadsworth.

Jahoda, Gustav. 1999. *Images of Savages.* London: Routledge.

James, William. 1950. *The Principles of Psychology.* 2 vols. 1950. Reprint, New York: Dover.

Jaspers, Karl. *The Question of German Guilt.* Translated by E. B. Ashton, with a new introduction by Joseph W. Koterski. New York: Fordham University Press.

Jefferson, Thomas. 1982. "Laws," Query XIV. In *Notes on the State of Virginia,* edited by William Peden. Chapel Hill: University of North Carolina Press.

———. 1999. "To Henri Grégoire." In *Political Writings / Thomas Jefferson,* edited by Joyce Appleby and Terrence Ball. Cambridge: Cambridge University Press.

Johnson, Galen, ed. 1993. *The Merleau-Ponty Aesthetics Reader: Philosophy and Painting.* Evanston, Ill.: Northwestern University Press.

Kant, Immanuel. 1970. "Perpetual Peace." In *Kant's Political Writings,* edited by Hans Reiss. New York: Cambridge University Press.

———. 1991. *The Metaphysics of Morals.* Translated by Mary Gregor. Cambridge: Cambridge University Press.

———. 1997. "On the Different Races of Man." In *Race and the Enlightenment: A Reader,* edited by Emmanuel Eze. Cambridge, Mass.: Blackwell.

Karr-Morse, Robin, and Meredith Wiley. 1997. *Ghosts from the Nursery: Tracing the Roots of Violence.* New York: Atlantic Monthly Press.

Katznelson, Ira. 1996. *Liberalism's Crooked Circle: Letters to Adam Michnik.* Princeton: Princeton University Press.

Kitcher, Philip. 1999 "Race, Ethnicity, Biology, Culture." In *Racism,* edited by Leonard Harris. New York: Humanity Books.

Klee, Robert. 1997. *Introduction to the Philosophy of Science: Cutting Nature at Its Seams.* New York: Oxford University Press.

Klein, Melanie. 1975. "Envy and Gratitude." 1957. Reprinted in *Envy and Gratitude and Other Works.* London: Hogarth.

———. 1976. "Some Theoretical Conclusions Regarding the Emotional Life of the Infant." 1952. Reprinted in *Envy and Gratitude and Other Works.* New York: Delacort.

Korsgaard, Christine. 1996. *The Source of Normativity.* New York: Cambridge University Press.

Kovel, Joel. 2000. "Reflections on White Racism." *Psychoanalytic Dialogues* 10, no. 4:579–87.

Kripke, Saul. 1980. *Naming and Necessity*. Cambridge, Mass.: Harvard University Press.

Kupers, T. 1999. *Prison Madness*. San Francisco: Jossey-Bass.

Kymlicka, Will. 1990. *Contemporary Political Philosophy: An Introduction*. Oxford: Oxford University Press.

La Caze, Marguerite. 1994. "Simone de Beauvoir and Female Bodies." *Australian Feminist Studies* 20:91–105.

——. 2002. "The Encounter between Generosity and Wonder." *Hypatia: A Journal of Feminist Philosophy* 17, no. 3:1–19.

Lane, Christopher, ed. 1998. *The Psychoanalysis of Race*. New York: Columbia University Press.

Laqueur, Thomas. 1992. *Making Sex*. Cambridge: Harvard University Press.

Laslett, Peter, ed. 1967. *Two Treatises of Civil Government*. 2d ed. Cambridge: Cambridge University Press.

Le Doeuff, Michèle. 1991. *Hipparchia's Choice: An Essay concerning Women, Philosophy, etc.* Translated by Trista Selous. Oxford: Blackwell.

Levi, Isaac. 1991. *The Fixation of Belief and Its Undoing: Changing Beliefs through Inquiry*. Cambridge: Cambridge University Press.

Levin, Michael. 1997. *Why Race Matters*. Westport: Praeger.

Levine, Michael P., ed. 2000. *The Analytic Freud*. New York: Routledge.

Lewin, Tamar. 2000. "Growing Up, Growing Apart: Fast Friends Try to Resist the Pressure to Divide by Race." *New York Times*, 25 June.

Lewontin, Richard. 1984. *Not in Our Genes*. New York: Pantheon Books.

Lieberman, Robert C. 1995. "Social Construction (Continued)." *American Political Science Review* 89, no. 2:437–41.

——. 1998. *Shifting the Color Line: Race and the American Welfare State*. Cambridge: Harvard University Press.

Lipsitz, George. 1998. *The Possessive Investment in Whiteness*. Philadelphia: Temple University Press.

Locke, John. 1967. "The Second Treatise of Civil Government." In *Two Treatises of Civil Government,* 2d ed., edited by Peter Laslett. Cambridge: Cambridge University Press.

Loury, Glenn C. 2002. *The Anatomy of Racial Inequality*. Cambridge: Harvard University Press.

Lubiano, Wahneema, ed. 1998. *The House That Race Built*. New York: Vintage.

Lucashenko, Melissa. 1994. "No Other Truth: Aboriginal Women and Australian Feminism." *Social Alternatives* 12, no. 4:21–24.

Lugones, Maria. 1987. "Playfulness, 'World'-Traveling, and Loving Perception." *Hypatia: A Journal of Feminist Philosophy* 2, no. 2:3–21.

Macdonald, Andrew [William Pierce]. 1996. *The Turner Diaries*. New York: Barricade Books.

MacIntyre, Alasdair. 1999. *Dependent Rational Animals: Why Human Beings Need the Virtues*. Chicago: Open Court.

MacKinnon, Catharine. 1989. *Toward a Feminist Theory of the State.* Cambridge: Harvard University Press.

Marshall, Graeme. 2000. "How Far Down Does the Will Go ?" In *The Analytic Freud,* edited by Michael Levine. London: Routledge.

Maxwell, William. 1961. *The Château.* New York: Knopf.

Mayr, Ernst. 1997. "Typological versus Population Thinking." In *Evolution,* edited by Mark Ridley. Oxford: Oxford University Press.

———. 2001. *What Evolution Is.* New York: Basic Books.

———. 2002. "The Biology of Race and the Concept of Equality." In *Daedalus,* winter, 89–94.

McCarthy, Thomas. 1990. "The Critique of Impure Reason: Foucault and the Frankfurt School." *Political Theory* 18, no. 3:437–69.

McGary, Howard. 1998. "Alienation and the African American Experience." In *Theorizing Multiculturalism,* edited by Cynthia Willett. Oxford: Blackwell.

Memmi, Albert. 2000. *Racism.* Translated by Steve Martinot. Minneapolis: University of Minneapolis Press.

Merleau-Ponty, Maurice. 1964. "The Child's Relations with Others." In *The Primacy of Perception,* edited by James M. Edie. Evanston, Ill.: Northwestern University Press.

———. 1968. *The Visible and the Invisible.* Evanston, Ill.: Northwestern University Press.

———. 1969. *Humanism and Terror.* Translated by John O'Neill. Boston: Beacon.

———. 1973. *Adventures of the Dialectic.* Translated by Joseph Bien. Evanston, Ill.: Northwestern University Press.

———. 1993. "Eye and Mind." In *The Merleau-Ponty Aesthetics Reader: Philosophy and Painting,* edited by Galen Johnson. Evanston, Ill.: Northwestern University Press.

Mill, J. S. 1970. "The Subjection of Women." In *Essays on Sex Equality,* edited by Alice Rossi. Chicago: Chicago University Press.

Millett, Kate. 1969. *Sexual Politics.* London: Rupert Hart-Davis.

Mills, Charles W. 1997. *The Racial Contract.* Ithaca, N.Y.: Cornell University Press.

———. 1998. *Blackness Visible.* Ithaca, N.Y.: Cornell University Press.

———. 2002. "The 'Racial Contract' as Methodology (Not Hypothesis): Reply to Jorge Garcia." *Philosophia Africana* 5, no. 1.

Moi, Toril. 1994. *Simone de Beauvoir: The Making of an Intellectual Woman.* Oxford: Blackwell.

———. 1999. *What Is a Woman? and Other Essays.* Oxford: Oxford University Press.

Montagu, Ashley. 1974. *Man's Most Dangerous Myth: The Fallacy of Race.* 5th ed. Oxford: Oxford University Press.

Morrison, Toni. 1993. *Playing in the Dark: Whiteness and the Literary Imagination.* New York: Vintage.

———. 1998. "Home." In *The House That Race Built,* edited by Wahneema Lubiano. New York: Vintage.

Mosley, Albert G. 1999. "Negritude, Nationalism and Racism: Racists or Racialists." In *Racism,* edited by Leonard Harris. New York: Humanity Books.

Moss, D. 2001. "Racism, Homophobia, Misogyny." *Journal of the American Psychoanalytic Association* 49, no. 4:1315–34.

Murphy, Liam. 1999. "Institutions and the Demands of Justice." *Philosophy and Public Affairs* 27, no. 4:251–91.

Nagel, Thomas. 1991. *Equality and Impartiality*. New York: Oxford University Press.

Oakes, Jeannie. 1985. *Keeping Track: How Schools Structure Inequality*. New Haven: Yale University Press.

Oakley, Justin. 1993. *Morality and the Emotions*. London: Routledge.

Ober, Josiah. 1989. *Mass and Elite in Democratic Athens*. Princeton, N.J.: Princeton University Press.

Ogden, Thomas. 1986. *The Matrix of the Mind*. Northvale, N.J.: Jason Aronson.

Okin, Susan. 1989. *Justice, Gender, and the Family*. New York: Basic Books.

Oliver, Kelly. 2001. *Beyond Recognition*. Minneapolis: University of Minnesota Press.

O'Neil, Onora. 1975. *Acting on Principle*. New York: Columbia University Press.

Outhwaite, William, and Tom Bottomore, eds. 1994. *The Blackwell Dictionary of Twentieth Century Social Thought*. Oxford: Blackwell.

Outlaw, Lucius T. 1996. *On Race and Philosophy*. New York: Routledge.

Pataki, Tamas. 1996. "Intention in Wish-fulfilment." *Australasian Journal of Philosophy* 74, no. 1:20–37.

——. 2000 "Freudian Wishfulfilment and Subintentional Explanation." In *The Analytic Freud*, edited by Michael Levine. New York: Routledge.

——. 2003 "Freud, Object-relations, Agency and the Self." In *Psychoanalytic Knowledge and the Nature of Mind*, edited by Man Cheung Chung and Colin Feltham. London: Palgrave.

Pettman, Jan. 1992. *Living in the Margins: Racism, Sexism and Feminism in Australia*. Sydney: Allen and Unwin.

Piper, Adrian. 1990. "Higher-Order Discrimination." In *Identity, Character and Morality*, edited by Amelie O. Rorty and Owen Flanagan. Cambridge: MIT Press.

——. 1993. "Two Kinds of Discrimination." *Yale Journal of Criticism* 6, no. 1:25–74.

Price, H. H. 1969. *Belief*. London: George Allen and Unwin.

Putnam, Hilary. 1975. "Meaning of 'Meaning.'" In *Philosophical Papers*, vol. 2. Cambridge: Cambridge University Press.

Quine, Willard Van Orman. 1964. *From a Logical Point of View*. 2d ed. Cambridge: Harvard University Press.

——. 1992. *Pursuit of Truth*. 2d ed. Cambridge: Harvard University Press.

Racker, Heinrich. 1968. *Transference and Countertransference*. New York: International Universities Press.

Rankin, H. D. 1964. *Plato and the Individual*. London: Methuen.

Rawls, John. 1971. *A Theory of Justice*. Oxford: Oxford University Press.

Reynolds, Henry. 1989. *Dispossession*. St. Leonards: Allen and Unwin.

Rhodes, Richard. 1999. *Why They Kill*. New York: Knopf.

Rich, Adrienne. 1976. *Of Woman Born: Motherhood as Experience and Institution.* London: Virago.

——. 1999. *Midnight Salvage: Poems 1995–1998.* New York: W. W. Norton.

Richards, Graham. 1997. *"Race," Racism and Psychology.* London: Routledge.

Roberts, Dorothy. 2002. *Shattered Bonds: The Color of Child Welfare.* New York: Basic Books.

Roediger, David. 1998. "White Workers, New Democrats, and Affirmative Action." In *The House That Race Built,* edited by Wahneema Lubiano. New York: Vintage.

Rosati, Connie S. 1994. "A Study of Internal Punishment." *Wisconsin Law Review,* no. 1:123–70.

Rousseau, Jean-Jacques. 1950. *The Social Contract and Discourses.* Edited and translated by G. D. H. Cole. New York: Dutton.

——. 1967. "The Discourse on Inequality." In *The Social Contract and Discourse on Inequality,* edited by Lester Crocker. New York: Washington Square.

——. 1979. *Emile, or On Education,* edited by Allan Bloom. New York: Basic Books.

——. 1986. "Preface to the Second Discourse," in *The First and Second Discourses together with Essay on the Origin of Languages,* edited and translated by Victor Gourevitch. New York: Harper and Row.

Ruddick, Sara. 1989. *Maternal Thinking: Toward a Politics of Peace.* Boston: Beacon.

Rustin, Michael. 1991. *The Good Society and the Inner World.* London: Verso.

Samuel, Maurice. 1940. *The Great Hatred.* New York: Knopf.

Sartre, Jean-Paul. 1972. "Portrait of the Antisemite." In *Existentialism,* edited by W. Kaufman. New York: Meridian.

——. 1999. *Anti-Semite and Jew.* Translated by George J. Becker. New York: Schocken Books.

Schlossberger, Eugene. 1986. "Why We Are Responsible for Our Emotions." *Mind* 95:37–56.

——. 1992. *Moral Responsibility and Persons.* Philadelphia: Temple University Press.

Schmid, W. Thomas. 1996 "The Definition of Racism." *Journal of Applied Philosophy* 13:31–40.

Schneider, Anne, and Helen Ingram. 1993. "Social Construction of Target Populations: Implications for Politics and Policy." *American Political Science Review* 87, no. 2:334–47.

——. 1995. "Response." *American Political Science Review* 89, no. 2:441–47.

Schoeck, Helmut. 1969. *Envy: A Theory of Social Behaviour.* Indianapolis: Liberty Fund.

Schor, Naomi. 1995. *Bad Objects: Essays Popular and Unpopular.* Durham: Duke University Press.

Schuman, Howard, et al. 1997. *Racial Attitudes in America.* Rev. ed. Chicago: University of Chicago Press.

Sedgwick, Peter. 1999. "Race/Racism." In *Key Concepts in Cultural Theory,* edited by A. Edgar and P. Sedgwick. London: Routledge.

Shelby, Tommie. 2002. "Is Racism in the Heart?" *Journal of Social Philosophy* 33:411–20.

Simons, Margaret. 1999. *Beauvoir and* The Second Sex: *Feminism, Race, and the Origins of Existentialism.* Lanham, Md.: Rowman and Littlefield.

Sloan, Phillip R. 1973. "The Idea of Racial Degeneracy in Buffon's Histoire Naturelle." In *Racism in the Eighteenth Century: Studies in Eighteenth Century Culture,* edited by Harold E. Pagliaro. Cleveland: Case Western Reserve University Press.

Small, Stephen. 1994. *Racialised Barriers: The Black Experience in the United States and England in the 1980's.* London: Routledge.

Smiley, Jane. 1998. *Moo.* New York: Ivy Books.

Sober, Elliott. 1980. "Evolution, Population Thinking, and Essentialism." *Philosophy of Science* 47:350–83.

Sophocles. 1984. *The Three Theban Plays.* Translated by Robert Fagles. New York: Penguin.

Spelman, Elizabeth. 1988. *Inessential Woman: Problems of Exclusion in Feminist Thought.* Boston: Beacon.

———. 1991. "Simone de Beauvoir and Women: Just Who Does She Think 'We' Is?" In *Feminist Interpretations and Political Theory,* edited by Mary Lyndon Shanley and Carole Pateman. Cambridge: Polity.

Stampp, Kenneth. 1956. *The Peculiar Institution: Slavery in the Ante-Bellum South.* New York: Knopf.

Stanner, W. E. H. "Introduction: Australia and Racialism." In *Racism: The Australian Experience,* edited by F. S. Stevens. Artarman NSW: Australia and New-Zealand Book Company.

Stern, Daniel. 1985. *The Interpersonal World of the Infant.* New York: Basic Books.

Stocker, Michael. 1976. "The Schizophrenia of Modern Ethical Theories." *Journal of Philosophy* 73:453–66.

Sullivan, Harry S. 1953. *The Interpersonal Theory of Psychiatry.* New York: Norton.

Sullivan, Shannon. 2001a. *Living across and through Skins.* Bloomington: Indiana University Press.

———. 2001b. "The Racialization of Space: Toward a Phenomenological Account of Raced and Antiracist Spatiality." In *The Problems of Resistance,* edited by Steve Martinot and Joy James. Amherst, N.Y.: Humanity Books.

Tatum, Beverly. 1997. *"Why Are All the Black Kids Sitting Together in the Cafeteria?" and Other Conversations about Race.* New York: Basic Books.

Taylor, Charles. 1989. *Sources of the Self: The Making of Modern Identity.* Cambridge: Harvard University Press.

Thernstrom, Stephan, and Abigail Thernstrom. 1997. *American in Black and White.* New York: Simon and Schuster.

Thomas, Laurence. 1992. "The Evolution of Antisemitism." *Transition* 57:94–108.

———. 1993. *Vessels of Evil.* Philadelphia: Temple University Press.

———. 1996. "The Grip of Immorality: Child Abuse and Moral Failure." In *Reason, Ethics, and Society: Themes from Kurt Baier,* edited by J. B. Schneewind. Chicago: Open Court.

———. 1998. "Moral Deference." In *Theorizing Multiculturalism,* edited by Cynthia Willett. Malden, Mass.: Blackwell Publishers.

———. 2001a. "The Moral Self in the Face of Injustice." In *Liberal Thought,* edited by James Sterba. London: Routledge.

———. 2001b. "Morality, Consistency, and the Self: A Lesson from Rectification." *Journal of Social Philosophy* 32:374–81.

———. 2001c. "Sexism and Racism: Some Conceptual Differences." In *Race and Racism,* edited by Bernard Boxill. Oxford: Oxford University Press.

———. 2003. "Moral Weight and Rules of Moral Salience." Department of Philosophy, University of Syracuse. Unpublished manuscript.

Thucydides. 1972. *History of the Peloponnesian Wars.* Translated by Rex Warner. London: Penguin Books.

Todorov, Tzvetan. 1986. "Race, Writing, and Culture." In *Race, Writing, and Difference,* edited by H. L. Gates, Jr. Chicago: University of Chicago Press.

Tully, James. 1993. *An Approach to Political Philosophy: Locke in Contexts.* Cambridge: Cambridge University Press.

Tulving, Endel. 1999. "Episodic vs. Semantic Memory." In *The MIT Encyclopedia of the Cognitive Sciences,* edited by Robert A. Wilson and Frank C. Keil. Cambridge: MIT Press.

———. 2002. "Episodic Memory: From Mind to Brain." *Annual Review of Psychology.* http://www.findarticles.com/cf_0/m0961/2002_Annual/83789638/print.jhtml [February 2003].

Ture, Kwame [Stokeley Carmichael], and Charles Hamilton. 1992. *Black Power: The Politics of Liberation.* New York: Vintage Books.

Tustin, Frances. 1992. *Autistic States in Children.* Rev. ed. London: Tavistock/Routledge.

Van den Berghe, Pierre L. 2001. "Does Race Matter?" In *Race and Racism,* edited by Bernard Boxill. Oxford: Oxford University Press.

Voegelin, Eric. 1997. *Race and State.* 1933. Reprint, Baton Rouge: Louisiana State University Press.

Walker, David. 2000. "An Appeal to the Colored Citizens of the World." 1829. Reprinted in *Against Slavery: An Abolitionist Reader,* edited by Mason Lowance. New York: Penguin.

Warren, Mary Anne. 1977. "Secondary Sexism and Quota Hiring." *Philosophy and Public Affairs* 6:240–61.

Wegner, D. M. 1989. *White Bears and Other Unwanted Thoughts: Suppression, Obsession, and the Psychology of Mental Control.* New York: Viking Penguin.

West, Cornel. 1982. *Prophesy Deliverance: An Afro-American Revolutionary Christianity.* Philadelphia: Westminster.

White, Alan. 1985. *Grounds of Liability.* Oxford: Oxford University Press.

Whyte, William. 1956. *The Organization Man.* New York: Simon and Schuster.

Willett, Cynthia. 2001. *The Soul of Justice: Social Bonds and Racial Hubris.* Ithaca, N.Y.: Cornell University Press.

Williams, Bernard. 1973. *Problems of the Self.* New York: Cambridge University Press.

———. 1981. "Persons, Character, and Morality." In *Moral Luck.* New York: Cambridge University Press.

Williams, Eric. 1944. *Capitalism and Slavery.* Chapel Hill: University of North Carolina Press.

Williams, Vernon J., Jr. 1996. *Rethinking Race.* Lexington: University of Kentucky Press.

Wise, Tim. 2000. "Everyday Racism, White Liberals, and the Limits of Tolerance." *LiP Magazine.* http://www.lipmagazine.org/articles/featwise_11_p.htm.

Wolpoff, Milford, and Rachel Caspari. 1997. *Race and Human Evolution.* New York: Simon and Schuster.

Wrangham, Richard, and Dale Peterson. 1996. *Demonic Males: Apes and the Origin of Human Violence.* Boston: Houghton Mifflin.

Young, Andrew. 2001. "Why Young People Embrace Prison Culture." *Atlanta Journal-Constitution,* 1 July, sec. D, p. 1.

Young, Iris. 1980. "Socialist Feminism and the Limits of Dual Systems Theory." *Socialist Review* 50/51:169–88.

———. 1990a. *Justice and the Politics of Difference.* Princeton: Princeton University Press.

———. 1990b. *Throwing like a Girl and Other Essays in Feminist Philosophy and Social Theory.* Bloomington: Indiana University Press.

Young-Bruehl, Elisabeth. 1996. *The Anatomy of Prejudices.* Cambridge: Harvard University Press.

Zack, Naomi. 1998. *Thinking about Race.* Belmont, Calif.: Wadsworth.

———. 2001. "Race and Philosophic Meaning." In *Race and Racism,* edited by Bernard Boxill. Oxford: Oxford University Press.

Zagzebski, Linda. 1996. *Virtues of the Mind.* Cambridge: Cambridge University Press.

CONTRIBUTORS

Neil Altman is Associate Clinical Professor in the Postdoctoral Program in Psychotherapy and Psychoanalysis, New York University. He is the editor of *Psychoanalytic Dialogues: A Journal of Relational Perspectives* and the author of *The Analyst in the Inner City: Race, Class, and Culture through a Psychoanalytic Lens.* He has written numerous articles, including "Psychoanalysis and the Urban Poor" and "Black and White Thinking: A Psychoanalyst Reconsiders Race."

Lawrence Blum is Professor of Philosophy and Distinguished Professor of Liberal Arts and Education at the University of Massachusetts, Boston. He is the author of *Friendship, Altruism, and Morality; Moral Perception and Particularity;* and *"I'm Not a Racist, But . . .": The Moral Quandary of Race.*

Bernard Boxill is Professor of Philosophy at the University of North Carolina at Chapel Hill. He is the author of *Blacks and Social Justice* and the editor of *Race and Racism.* He has also published numerous articles on race, reparations, affirmative action, and other topics in leading philosophical journals.

Michael Dummett is Emeritus Professor of Logic at Oxford University. His many distinguished books on the philosophy of language, mathematics, metaphysics, and social philosophy include *Frege: Philosophy of Language; Origins of Analytical Philosophy; The Seas of Language;* and *On Immigration and Refugees.* He was a member of the executive committee of the Campaign against Racial Discrimination and cofounder of the Joint Council for the Welfare of Immigrants. He was knighted in 1999.

J. L. A. Garcia is Professor of Philosophy at Boston College. In addition to his numerous articles in theoretical and applied ethics, philosophy of mind and action, religious morals, and social theory, his publications include "Heart of Racism," *Journal of Social Philosophy* 27 (1996); "Current Conceptions of Racism," *Journal of Social Philosophy* 28 (1997); and "Racism as a Model for Understanding Sexism," in *Race/Sex: Their Sameness, Difference and Interplay,* edited by Naomi Zack.

Sally Haslanger is Associate Professor in the Department of Linguistics and Philosophy and a faculty affiliate in the Women's Studies Program at the Massachusetts Institute of Technology. Her publications have addressed topics in metaphysics, epistemology, and feminist theory. They include "On Being Objective and Being Objectified," in *A Mind of One's Own,* edited by Louise Antony and Charlotte Witt; and "Gender and Race: (What) Are They? (What) Do We Want Them To Be?" *Noûs* 34 (2000).

Marguerite La Caze is Australian Research Fellow at the University of Queensland. Her publications include *The Analytic Imaginary* and *Integrity and the Fragile Self* (coauthored with Damian Cox and Michael Levine). Her current research concerns the ethics and politics of difference.

Lawrence A. Lengbeyer teaches ethics and philosophy at the United States Naval Academy. His current research concerns the mechanisms and consequences of mental compartmentalization, the cognitive basis of emotion, the appreciation of fictions and of make-believe, the moral rights of artists, language and the Chinese Room argument, the moral psychology of selflessness, and the psychic injuries of racism.

Michael P. Levine is Professor of Philosophy at the University of Western Australia and, in 2004, visiting professor at the University of Colorado's Center for Humanities and Arts. He is a coauthor of *Integrity and the Fragile Self,* the editor of *The Analytic Freud,* the coeditor of a special issue of *Philosophical Forum* on architecture and ethics, and the author of articles on moral psychology, philosophy of religion, history of philosophy, metaphysics, and film. He is currently writing on race, religion, violence, and terror.

Tamas Pataki is Honorary Senior Fellow in the Department of Philosophy, University of Melbourne, where he also lectures, and Honorary Fellow at Deakin University. He has published principally on the philosophy of mind, psychoanalysis, and moral philosophy. His forthcoming book is *The Tyranny of Desire.*

Laurence Thomas teaches philosophy and political science at Syracuse University. He is the author of many articles and several books. His lecture "Happiness and Moral Powers" was presented before Queen Beatrix of Orange in 2000, at the annual Verstichting Conference in Holland.

Johanna Tiemann is an analytic candidate at the New York University Postdoctoral Program in Psychotherapy and Psychoanalysis. She has a private practice in Manhattan.

Cynthia Willett is Associate Professor of Philosophy at Emory University. She is currently writing a book on comedy and freedom. Her previous publications include *The Soul of Justice; Maternal Ethics and Other Slave Moralities;* and *Theorizing Multiculturalism.*

Elisabeth Young-Bruehl is a psychoanalyst practicing in New York City and teaching at the Columbia Center for Psychoanalytic Training and Research. She is the author of many books, including *Creative Characters, Freud on Women, The Anatomy of Prejudices, Cherishment,* biographies of Hannah Arendt and Anna Freud, and three collections of essays including *Where Do We Fall When We Fall In Love?*

NAME INDEX

Vera, Hernan, 71, 254–255
Vogt, Carl, 200

Walker, David, 56–57
Warren, Mary Anne, 111
Wegner, Daniel, 164
West, Cornel, 88–89
Wheatley, Phillis, 217
Whyte, William, 151
Wiley, Meredith, 143
Willett, Cynthia, 21
Williams, Bernard, 165, 230

Winant, Howard, 66
Wise, Tim, 122
Wolpoff, Milford, 7
Wrangham, Richard, 144

Young, Iris, 108, 109–110, 114, 247, 266, 275, 278
Young-Bruehl, Elisabeth, 10, 11, 17–18, 78, 80–93, 184, 186, 193, 195–197, 205, 267, 274

Zack, Naomi, 209–210, 212, 263–264
Zagzebski, Linda, 41

SUBJECT INDEX

Cognitive: accounts of racism, 11; aspects of racism, 195, 270; assets, 173; cleansing, 176; endowment, 163–164, 168–170, 176; error, 186; failure, 190; processes, 163–164; psychologists, 195; representations, 165; resources, 167; self-control, 172 n15, 176; subject, 243

Color blindness and sex blindness, 277–278

Color-blind society, 259

Compassion, 217–219, 223–224; absence of, 139

Conscience, 32, 150

Consequences (moral, social, political), 20, 22–23, 37–38

Consequentialism, 10, 12, 73, 84

Contempt, 15–16, 32, 38, 42–43, 54 n28, 87, 97, 102

Counterevidence, 161–165, 173,190

Cultural: achievement, 4; bias, 97; category, 42 n5; character, 11; differences, 115; imperialism, 109; insensitivity, 57; milieu, 81, 85; networks, 85; norms, 103, 109 n17; practices, 101; prejudice, 148; representations, 112; resources, 106; system of meaning, 149; theory, 37–40; traditions, 248; understanding, 83

Darwinian instinct theory, 148

Death instinct, 127, 148

Democracy, 80–81

Democratic Party, 92, 142

Depressive position, 128, 132–134, 139

Destructive instinctual drives, 198

Developmental accounts, 17

Discrimination, 8–9, 13–14, 91; concepts of, 8; institutional and structural, 13–14, 98–123; primary and secondary, 111, 118; reverse, 92; social and political, 2, 11, 13

Disenfranchisement, 101, 112

Dispositions (volitional, affective, orectic), 12, 190–191

Dissociation, 150, 181 n3

"Doctrine of the countenance," 6, 182

Double consciousness, 273, 277

Doxastic: accounts of racism, 11; structures, 20, 38, 40, 87

Dreams, 78, 96, 177, 145, 205

Economic: anxiety, 30; background, 254; conditions, 2, 15; conflict, 183; depression, 154; forces, 108 n14; justice, 104–105; policy, 92; structures, 245

Educational system, 21, 61, 72–73, 102–103, 106, 225–226, 229–230, 243, 248, 253–255

Ego psychology, 18, 83

Enmity, 1–3, 7–9, 11, 20, 22, 33, 71, 180–183, 187, 189–190, 193, 205

Enslavement, 130, 134, 138, 212–221. See also Slavery

Envy, 18, 20, 89, 95, 154, 156, 179, 189, 196–205; destructive, 198–199; and racism in Australia, 197–205

Epistemic reticence, 169–170

Equality: ideal of, 42 n5, 241–242; moral, 246, 260; pseudo-, 91; racial, 229–230, 238; upside-down, 225–242

Ethnic cleansing, 130, 155–156

Euro-Americans, 130, 134

Europeans, 11, 15, 30, 57, 130, 134, 200–201, 210–212, 222, 224

Evil, 12, 55, 68, 100, 178, 209, 216, 218, 221, 224

Evolution, 6, 136–137, 226

Evolutionary psychologists, 143

False beliefs, 16, 31, 34, 42 n5, 71–72, 79–80, 83, 158–178

Families, 152–157

Family resemblance, 19

Fantasies, 151, 154; violent, 145–148. See also Phantasy

Feminism: difference versus equality, 265–266, 276; and racism, 261–278

Feminist political strategy, 275

Frankfurt School, 151 n6

Freedom, 4, 84, 114, 134, 247–248, 258

Freudianism, 17, 150, 196

Frustration, 93, 148–149

Genetics, 6, 8, 64, 129, 143, 181 n2, 210–211

Genocide, 81 n3, 137, 154

Germans, 6, 30–31, 69, 96 n18. See also Pan-Germanic movement

Germany, 155; Nazi, 268

Greeks. See Ancient Greeks

Groups, 7, 21, 33, 36–38, 41, 59, 61, 71–72, 76, 80–86, 154, 159, 177, 180–185, 195–196, 211, 226, 234, 239–241, 249, 256, 267; belonging to, 266; characteristics of, 18, 68; denigrating, 175; designated, 9, 13, 16, 28–31, 33; domination by, 36–37, 97, 106; group image, 148–149; idea of, 110–111; identifying with, 110; identity, 1–3, 266; inherentist ways of thinking about, 195; membership in, 109, 117, 121, 133, 147, 222–223, 272, 276;

oppression by, 98–123, 272; peer, 153; racial, 64, 68, 182, 189, 265; socially powerless, 64, 146; structural oppression of, 111–119; superior, 222–223; victim, 154

Guilt, 15, 93, 131–135, 138, 140, 179, 189, 192, 196

Gypsies, 33

Ham's transgression, 5
Hate crimes, 68, 108 n16
Hispanics, 3, 60
History, 5–7, 14–15, 56–58, 196
Holocaust, 138, 188
Homophobia, 2, 17, 71, 78, 135, 153, 156–157, 186
Hostility to outsiders, 204
Hubris, 245–260
Humanism, 245–251
Human rights, 79, 157
Hysteria, 84, 150–153, 155, 193

Identification: with aggressor, 150; projective, 17, 128–134
Identity, 3, 22, 32, 42, 220, 223, 271–273; experience of, 266; fixed aspects of, 220; gender, 264: politics, 275; religious, 2
Ignorance and false consciousness, 83, 187
Imagination: failure of, 190; need for, 219–223
Immigration, 28–29, 204–205, 249, 271
Immigration Act (1971), 27
Immorality, 21, 42 n5, 53–54, 74, 79–96, 102
Indians, 4, 29–30
Infantilizing, 200–202
Inferiority, 12, 15, 40, 56, 70–71, 88, 137, 201, 236; biological, 59–60, 65; mental, 153; moral and intellectual, 4, 6, 29; of races, 15, 28–30, 211, 223. *See also* Beliefs: inferiorizing
Injustice. *See* Justice
Innate ability, 4–5
Instinctual drives, 148, 198
Institutional racism, 8, 11, 13–14, 39–40, 61, 79, 92, 98–123
Intelligence, 9, 60, 130
Interracial friendships, 260
Intersectionality, 109
Irrationality, 10–11, 16, 20, 28–29, 33, 87, 185–190, 270
Israeli-Palestinian conflict, 96 n18

Jealousy, 68–69, 95, 198
Jews, 3, 17, 33, 69, 82, 88, 93, 96, 136–139, 141, 151, 154–156, 167, 233, 268, 270, 274
Jobs, 30–31, 74, 101
Justice/injustice, 12, 20, 32, 55, 61–63, 66, 71–

75, 81, 97–123, 135, 201, 239, 246, 250, 258–260, 272–273; principles of, 246, 257, 259

Kantianism, 21–22, 86, 229–232, 234–235, 238–239, 242; moral theory, 225–242; on race, 212–216
Kingdom of Ends, 240
Kleinianism, 129, 131, 133, 135, 138

Latina/os, 72–73, 97
Law, 4, 104–105, 109, 118 n22, 130–131, 154, 260, 269
Laws (Plato), 4 n2
Liberalism, 21, 107, 132–133, 138, 243–260
Life instinct, 127, 148
Literacy tests, 101

Malevolence, 66–69, 128
Management of racist ideas, 171–176
Manic defense, 19, 127–141
Marxism, 245–250, 257–259
Memory, 166–169
Mental states, 90–91
Mexican Americans, 58, 62, 108
Mexicans, 3, 249
Middle Easterners, 7–8
Miscegenation, 131, 139, 155, 183
Misogyny, 71, 95
Moral: agency, 233; agents, 214; appraisal, 10, 12; attitudes, 23, 54, 232; behavior, 231; capabilities, 6, 182; codes, 260; concern, 61–63; condemnation, 57–58, 65, 67–69, 72, 76; consciousness, 60; damage, 238; deference, 237; distortions, 240; equals, 246; exhortation, 34, 91; failings, 102, 106, 260; knowledge, 232, 242; life, 54, 230; neutrality, 248; plurality, 67; principles, 79, 229; psychology, 94 n17; reasons, 70; reform, 105–106; salience, 231–241; sensitivity, 231; significance, 58, 82; terminology, 56–57, 76; theory, 100–101; truths, 219; valence, 67; value, 259; virtues, 41–43, 188; worth, 21, 233–236, 240. *See also* Racism: morality of; Vice
Morally horrendous practices, 216–217
Muslims, 155–156
Myth of the eternal feminine, 267–268

Narcissism, 17–18, 84, 93, 95, 147–157, 203, 255, 274 n20
National Alliance, 19, 135–138, 140–141
National Conference for Community and Justice, 47

Social construction of race, 129nn2, 4, 263–266

Social science, 11, 13–14, 16, 30, 58–59, 83, 85, 98, 142–143, 157

Social scientists, 9–10, 57, 254

Sociology, 13, 143, 255

South Africa, 32, 92, 199, 225–226, 229

Space: poetics of, 251–253; politics of, 256–258; racialization of, 253–256, 260; social aspects of, 243–251; and subjectivity, 243–244

Species, 3, 5, 181

Split object world, 194, 199

Stereotypes/stereotyping, 61, 97, 101, 115, 129–132, 136n8, 139, 229, 267, 275n21

Structural: domination, 74, 88; inequities, 65; oppression, 14, 39, 98–103

Structural racism. *See* Institutional racism

Sublimation, 195n15

Superegos, 150, 193, 202

Superiority, 15, 59–60, 96n19, 179, 201, 222, 265

Teleological views, 216–217

Terrorism/terrorists, 55, 100, 142–145, 155, 157

Turks, 30, 33, 155

Turner Diaries, The, 135–141

Tutsis, 81

Unconscious, the, 15–18, 20, 133, 159, 179, 189, 194

Unconscious: desires, 196; envy, 198–205; identification, 131; meanings, 196, 203; motivation and agency, 179n1, 193; racism, 20, 228; structures, 196; wishes and defenses, 195n15

United States, 21, 27, 32–33, 56, 62, 69, 92, 94–97, 112–114, 130–131, 133–135, 142–143, 155, 157, 196, 244, 256, 276; arrogance, 246; identity politics in, 250

Upside-down equality, 21–22, 225–242

U.S. Civil War, 221, 254

U.S. Congress, 132

U.S. Constitution, 157

U.S. Supreme Court, 101, 130, 248

Value judgments, 35, 40–41, 54

Vice, 10, 13, 40, 65–68, 189n10, 217; intellectual, 41; moral, 41, 67–72, 94–95

Victims: denial of humanity of, 191–193; types of violence against, 154–157

Violence, 64, 142–157, 259; of class politics, 249; rationalization of, 149; revolutionary, 260; roots of, 143–145, 157; systematic, 109; types of, 143–144, 150, 154–157

Virtue, 4, 10, 12, 41–43, 66, 72–73, 94–95, 185, 189n10, 217

Visceral emotional resonance (VER), 227–230, 238–240

Voting, 101

Washington, D.C., 131, 142

White: acting, 255; experience, 262; flight, 62; history, 256; identity, 277; male oppression, 114, 117n21; solipsism, 262; supremacy, 97, 135–140; treachery, 276–277

White Australia policy, 183

"Whiteliness," 265, 276

Whiteness, 137, 249, 254, 259, 265, 277

Whites, 48–49, 53, 97, 114, 119, 122, 139, 225–230, 235, 242, 244–245, 260

Wishes: 15, instinctual, 196; unconscious, 193, 196

Wishful thinking, 177

Wish-fulfillment, 96n19, 179–180, 194, 196n16

World Trade Center, 154

Xenophobia, 71, 204